Approaches to Teaching the Works of Tim O'Brien

Approaches to Teaching World Literature

For a complete listing of titles,
see the last pages of this book.

Approaches to Teaching the Works of Tim O'Brien

Edited by

Alex Vernon
and
Catherine Calloway

The Modern Language Association of America
New York   2010

MLA and the MODERN LANGUAGE ASSOCIATION are trademarks
owned by the Modern Language Association of America.
For information about obtaining permission to reprint material from
MLA book publications, send your request by mail (see address below),
e-mail (permissions@mla.org), or fax (646 458-0030).

Library of Congress Cataloging-in-Publication Data

Approaches to teaching the works of Tim O'Brien /
edited by Alex Vernon and Catherine Calloway.
p. cm. — (Approaches to teaching world literature, ISSN 1059-1133 ; 114)
Includes bibliographical references and index.
ISBN 978-1-60329-075-3 (hardcover : alk. paper)
ISBN 978-1-60329-076-0 (pbk. : alk. paper)
1. O'Brien, Tim, 1946– —Study and teaching. 2. Vietnam War, 1961–1975—
Literature and the war—Study and teaching. 3. War stories, American—
Study and teaching.   I. Vernon, Alex, 1967–   II. Calloway, Catherine, 1952–
PS3565.B75Z55 2010
813' .54—dc22   2010035536

Approaches to Teaching World Literature 114
ISSN 1059-1133

Cover illustration of the paperback edition: *Collateral Damage—Polychrome with Boot
Print*, by Ken Hruby, 2002. Used by permission of the artist

Printed on recycled paper

Published by The Modern Language Association of America
26 Broadway, New York, New York 10004-1789
www.mla.org

CONTENTS

Interpretive Contexts

Classroom Contexts

Introduction

This seems an opportune time to publish a volume on teaching Tim O'Brien. The teachers and scholars from the generation that lived through the Vietnam War era—some of whom served in the military—can be found in leadership positions in English departments throughout the United States. They are professors, department chairs, and deans. But they are beginning to retire, and their classroom wisdom and their experience in teaching the literature of the war need to be captured and passed along.

Moreover, incoming high school and college students have parents who came of age after the war and thus have less understanding of and less investment in the war and the era. They have acquired much of their knowledge of the conflict from films, some of which came out years before they were born. As one reviewer has observed, "American history is strewn with 'forgotten wars': last year's fiftieth anniversary of the start of the Korean conflict serves as a poignant reminder. Even Vietnam seems to be fading into this category of dimly remembered conflicts" (Cooper). Literature, of course, is one of the primary methods of combating cultural forgetfulness, of passing one generation's experiences along to the next.

As of this writing, the United States has been engaged for several years in the war in Iraq and Afghanistan, which many commentators have linked with the Vietnam War. Having an understanding of the Vietnam War seems a necessary educational requirement for today's students, some of whom (or some of whose loved ones) may have served in the Iraq war. If the Vietnam War became a defining event for Tim O'Brien and his generation, Operation Enduring Freedom will doubtless play a similar role for today's students. Studying narratives of the previous war can help us process, intellectually and emotionally, the narratives of the current war. Indeed, the presenting of the 2007 National Book Award to *Tree of Smoke*, Denis Johnson's novel of the Vietnam War, suggests the continuing place of that war in the national psyche.

The works of Tim O'Brien are among the most significant recent contributions to a lengthy canon of war literature that begins with Homer's *Iliad* and extends through such notable works as Stephen Crane's *The Red Badge of Courage*, the poems of Wilfred Owen, E. E. Cummings's *The Enormous Room*, Erich Maria Remarque's *All Quiet on the Western Front*, Ernest Hemingway's *A Farewell to Arms*, Joseph Heller's *Catch-22*, Norman Mailer's *The Naked and the Dead*, James Jones's *The Thin Red Line*, and Larry Heinemann's *Paco's Story*. Of the hundreds of writers who have produced novels and personal narratives about the Vietnam War, O'Brien is one of only a few who have gone beyond a first work to write a second—much less a third or a fourth. He has produced a prolific body of literature that spans more than three decades; that is recognized and praised by contemporary historians and literary critics alike; and that is regularly taught in high school, college, and university classrooms.

The writing of Tim O'Brien serves as an ideal point of entry for discussions of war and its human impact. However, while O'Brien's three major texts, *The Things They Carried*, *Going After Cacciato*, and *In the Lake of the Woods*, are Vietnam War texts, they aren't simply that—they aren't just books for Vietnam War and war literature courses. O'Brien's novels are frequently taught in courses on postmodernism and contemporary American literature; his blurring of fact and fiction and his metafictional writing make him very much an heir to authors like Kurt Vonnegut, Jr., and John Barth. And though Vietnam appears in *The Nuclear Age*, his third novel, the war becomes subsumed under the larger cold war that dominated the second half of the twentieth century. In interviews, O'Brien has resisted the label *war writer*. His concerns are broader ones, for which war serves as a handy metaphor: "The problems and dilemmas presented in a war setting are essentially the problems and dilemmas of living itself" (McNerney, "Responsibly Inventing" 24).

O'Brien's writing transcends the topic of war to encompass such subjects as love, death, courage, fear, truth, memory, imagination, freedom, peace, secrecy, gender, social commitment, and the meaning of existence. His mastery of narrative technique has led scholars to identify in his works a skillful blend of numerous genres, including magic realism, metafiction, fantasy, picaresque adventure, and autobiography. In publications and conference presentations, O'Brien has been compared with Ernest Hemingway, Gabriel García Márquez, Stephen Crane, Ambrose Bierce, Bobbie Ann Mason, and Don DeLillo, among others. The title chapter of *The Things They Carried* is one of the most frequently anthologized selections, appearing in a wide range of literary anthologies, from collections of short fiction and contemporary prose to surveys of American literature, including *The Best American Short Stories of the Century*, edited by John Updike and Katrina Kenison. O'Brien is the author of eight books and over sixty short stories, and he has written nonfiction essays and book reviews. He received the 1979 National Book Award for *Going After Cacciato* and the 1990 Chicago Tribune Heartland Award for *The Things They Carried*. The title story's brilliant conceit has become such a staple allusion in war writing—for example, in the title of Chris Jones's "The Things That Carried Him," an article that follows the body of a United States soldier killed in Iraq to his hometown, and in the opening description of what mules carry for the military in Afghanistan in Susan Orlean's article "Riding High"—that it is fast on its way to becoming a cliché.

O'Brien is the recipient of awards from the Guggenheim Foundation, the Massachusetts Arts and Humanities Foundation, and the National Endowment for the Arts. In 2010 he received the prestigious Katherine Anne Porter Award from the American Academy of Arts and Letters.

In response to an *MLA Newsletter* announcement and a mailing about this project and our intention to write this book, our own general solicitations on two e-mail discussion lists (U.Penn—English and U.Penn—American Studies), and our direct solicitation of colleagues, we received fifty-two completed questionnaires and thirty proposals for essays.

The questionnaires and essay proposals confirmed our initial supposition that the works of Tim O'Brien are taught widely, at all levels of secondary school and undergraduate curricula and in a variety of classroom contexts. The fifty-two questionnaires revealed that O'Brien's works are taught in more than 115 courses. These include:

> *General Courses*: Introduction to Fiction; Introduction to Literature; Introduction to the Short Story; American Literature; Introduction to Literary Analysis; Critical Theory; American Studies
>
> *Period Courses*: Twentieth-Century Literature; American Literature since 1945; Postmodern Literature; Aesthetics of Modernism and Postmodernism
>
> *War Courses*: Vietnam War Narratives; American War Literature; Reading War; War and Civilization; Warring Masculinities
>
> *Genre Studies*: Twentieth-Century American Novel; Historical Novel; Contemporary Novel; Storytelling in United States Fiction
>
> *Writing Courses*: First-Year Composition; Intermediate Composition; Exposition and Argument; Creative Nonfiction
>
> *Autobiography Studies*: Rhetoric of Autobiography; American Lives; Literature, Memory, Trauma; Travel and the Sense of Self
>
> *Cultural Studies*: Cold War Culture; America in the Sixties; American Road Narratives
>
> *Special Courses*: Hemingway and O'Brien; The Works of Tim O'Brien; Metaphor and Creativity; First-Year Seminar

This wide selection of courses confirms that O'Brien's texts are rich with classroom possibilities.

We hope that part 1, "Materials," will benefit not only teachers new to O'Brien but also those already familiar with him. In addition to providing a biography of O'Brien and an overview of his works, and of secondary sources relating to them, we have compiled a survey of material about the historical and literary contexts of O'Brien's writings, such as histories of the Vietnam War and audiovisual resources for classroom use; artistic expressions concerning the Vietnam War, including works created by non-Americans and by civilians; critical texts on the literature and the films of both the Vietnam War and other American military conflicts; and general discussions of O'Brien's literary inheritance and circumstances.

For part 2, "Approaches," we have selected twenty-three essays. There is an introductory essay that frames the others in such a way as to amount to a twenty-fourth essay. The essays are grouped as follows: Historical and Cultural Contexts, Literary Contexts, Interpretive Contexts, and Classroom Contexts. The essays offer insightful explorations of O'Brien's works, and the categories provide viable ways of organizing a wide range of pedagogical approaches.

We are confident that the essays contain essential and useful information and sources for teachers preparing their courses, that they offer imaginative and solid classroom practices, and that they will inspire teachers to experiment with approaches of their own invention. We are pleased with the variety of creative approaches and with the pool of contributors—both emerging teacher-scholars and well-established authorities in the field. Several essays describe classroom conversations about O'Brien in the more contemporary context of the war on terror, especially as waged in Iraq and Afghanistan.

We would like to express our deep gratitude to all our colleagues who contributed to this volume and also to our students, who challenge us daily to better ourselves as teachers, scholars, and mentors.

AV and CC

Part One

MATERIALS

Biography

The eldest of three children, William Timothy O'Brien, Jr., was born in Austin, Minnesota, on 1 October 1946. When he was ten, his family moved to Worthington, Minnesota, an all-American midwestern town known as the Turkey Capital of the World. There he spent the rest of his formative years, growing up in a middle-class family, playing Little League baseball, learning magic tricks, listening to war stories from his father and other veterans, and developing the love of reading and writing that has served him well in his career as an author. After graduation from high school in 1964, he entered Macalaster College in Saint Paul, Minnesota, where he majored in political science and was student body president. He campaigned for Senator Eugene McCarthy's 1968 presidential bid and planned to undertake postgraduate work in government at Harvard University. However, the Vietnam War intervened, and he was drafted into the United States Army within days of graduating summa cum laude and Phi Beta Kappa from Macalaster.

While he was in college, O'Brien opposed the war, but once drafted, he went to Vietnam. "It was an intellectual and physical standoff," which he "did not have the energy" to oppose completely. "I did not want to be a soldier," he writes,

> not even an observer to war. But neither did I want to upset a peculiar balance between the order I knew, the people I knew, and my own private world. It was not just that I valued that order. I also feared its opposite—inevitable chaos, censure, embarrassment, the end of everything that had happened in my life, the end of it all. (*If I Die* 22)[1]

This moral schism is reflected in many of O'Brien's works. In *If I Die in a Combat Zone, Box Me Up and Ship Me Home*, O'Brien reveals that he seriously considered deserting to Canada; in *Going After Cacciato*, Paul Berlin finally rejects his fantasized desertion; in *The Nuclear Age*, William Cowling runs from the military and joins an underground activist group that turns out to be just as militant and demanding; in "On the Rainy River," the Tim O'Brien character faces "a moral freeze" (*Things* 57) and must choose between going to war and going to Canada; and in "Winnipeg," Billy McMann, unlike the rest of these characters, actually crosses the Canadian border and officially deserts.

In August 1968, O'Brien was inducted into the United States Army. He received his basic training at Fort Lewis, Washington, and in 1969–70 was stationed in Quang Ngai Province, Vietnam, in the United States Army's Americal Division. He earned the rank of sergeant and served first as a foot soldier in an area nicknamed "Pinkville," a site near the My Lai massacre of 1968, an event he fictionalizes in his novel *In the Lake of the Woods*. He later served as a clerk.

While O'Brien has never been overly forthcoming about his military accomplishments, his service in Vietnam included such official recognition as a Purple Heart, the Combat Infantry Badge, and a Bronze Star for Valor. Vietnam also saw the beginning of his writing career, with the publication of short sketches in newspapers and other forums that later became sections of *If I Die in a Combat Zone*.

After leaving the military in 1970, O'Brien enrolled in the graduate program in government at Harvard University and worked briefly as a national affairs reporter for the *Washington Post*, but he decided to embark on a career as a writer rather than finish his dissertation.

In 1999, O'Brien left his longtime home of Cambridge, Massachusetts, when he was named to the Roy F. and Joann Mitte Chair at Texas State University, where he teaches creative writing. He currently resides outside Austin, Texas, with his wife and two sons.

No book-length biography of O'Brien exists at this time, though most book-length studies of his work contain biographical chapters or sections. The most significant biographical chapters can be found in two studies by Tobey Herzog: *Tim O'Brien* and *Writing Vietnam, Writing Life: Caputo, Heinemann, O'Brien, Butler*. Each work contains a chronology that lists major events in the author's life, from his birth in 1946 to the time of the work's publication. In addition, the first chapter of *Tim O'Brien* ("Angles of Life and Art: Son, Soldier, and Author") devotes twenty-two pages to his life, and the third chapter of *Writing Vietnam, Writing Life* ("Conversation with Tim O'Brien") offers a forty-five-page interview that interweaves biographical detail with information about his writing.

Mark Heberle in *A Trauma Artist: Tim O'Brien and the Fiction of Vietnam* includes biographical material, especially in the first two chapters, which focus on O'Brien's most autobiographical works: "The Vietnam in Me" and *If I Die in a Combat Zone*. Patrick Smith in *Tim O'Brien: A Critical Companion*, Alex Vernon in *Soldiers Once and Still: Ernest Hemingway, James Salter, and Tim O'Brien*, and Steven Kaplan in *Understanding Tim O'Brien* all include brief biographical sketches of O'Brien's life or career. Each of these scholars notes the significance of O'Brien's life to his writing. As Heberle remarks, O'Brien is skillful at interweaving fact with fiction:

> The blurring of literature and personal experience, fiction and fact, has seldom been so deliberate, so successful, or so productive as it is in the work of this trauma writer. . . . This is writing that refabricates personal experience in order to transcend it through or re-create it as fiction, an art of trauma of which O'Brien is a supreme practitioner.   (33)

The many interviews mentioned below are also worthwhile sources of biographical information, especially Herzog's 2008 work, which is the most recent and which touches on O'Brien's life through 2007. In addition, the pertinent sections in the *Dictionary of Literary Biography*—Thomas Myers's "Tim O'Brien" in *American Novelists since World War II* and "Tim O'Brien" in *American Writers of the Vietnam War*—and Roger Smith's "Tim O'Brien" in *Notable American Novelists* are noteworthy. Instructors can obtain other biographical details from O'Brien's own autobiographical works, noted below, and from the many scholarly essays that have been published on his work. In 2007, O'Brien's archives were acquired by the Harry Ransom Center of the University of Texas, Austin, opening the door to a plethora of additional biographical information.

Primary Works

O'Brien's literary career generally consists of three periods: the early, or apprentice, years of the 1970s, when O'Brien published the memoir *If I Die in a Combat Zone, Box Me Up and Ship Me Home* as well as the novel *Northern Lights*; the critically acclaimed era, between 1978 and 1994, when he published *Going After Cacciato*, *The Nuclear Age*, *The Things They Carried*, and *In the Lake of the Woods*; and the post-1998 period, which thus far has seen the publication of *Tomcat in Love* and *July, July*.

Fiction

Book-Length Works

O'Brien's first novel (and second book), *Northern Lights*, which is set in the fictitious town of Sawmill Landing in northern Minnesota, is probably the least well known of his novels, having been out of print for many years before its 1999 reissue by Broadway Books, and it is most likely taught only in seminars that focus exclusively on O'Brien's work. Generally considered by scholars, as well as by O'Brien himself, an apprentice work blatantly derivative of Hemingway, *Northern Lights* is the story of two brothers, Paul Perry, a farm extension agent, and Harvey Perry, a Vietnam veteran. They must come to terms with their father, an authoritative and domineering Lutheran preacher obsessed with the threat of a nuclear apocalypse. When they undertake a cross-country skiing trip in the Minnesota wilderness, Harvey almost dies and Paul must go for help. Central to the novel is the relationship between the two brothers, one who participated in war and one who feels guilt because he did not and whose courage is now being tested. Also significant is the relationship between them and their respective family members as well as the cultural milieu in which they were raised. Thus, while the novel includes a Vietnam veteran, its focus is not so much on Harvey's war experiences as on his efforts to deal with his postwar community, especially his family, though it is Paul who more clearly inhabits the traditional protagonist role.

Going After Cacciato rapidly achieved critical acclaim. It received the National Book Award in 1979 and quickly became labeled as the definitive Vietnam War novel. Typical of O'Brien's works, the book is difficult to classify; it has been called a combat novel, metafiction, a fantasy, a picaresque adventure, and a work of magic realism. The forty-six chapters are divided into several distinct groupings: there are chapters entitled "The Observation Post," where Paul Berlin, the protagonist, stands guard duty for six hours one night near the South China Sea; there are chapters that deal with the actual events of the preceding six months of the war and with Paul Berlin's previous life; and finally, there are chapters called "Going After Cacciato," which tell of Paul Berlin's imaginary six-month journey from Vietnam to Paris in search of Cacciato, a soldier absent without leave from the war. However, because this three-part structure is interwoven with the novel's epistemological and ontological concerns, it is difficult for the reader to know exactly which events are imagined and which, if any, are real. If the journey to Paris is only imagined, then do the other events actually occur, and does Paul Berlin really stand guard duty in an observation post by the South China Sea? Or is nothing in the novel real? O'Brien's refusal to allow the reader final knowledge, the suspension of judgment through the very ending of the novel, is deftly executed and contributes to the book's uniqueness. Its surrealistic approach links it to the 1979 film *Apocalypse Now*, although this is a connection to which O'Brien would likely object. As he noted in an interview with Eric James Schroeder:

> For me Vietnam wasn't an unreal experience; it wasn't absurd. It was a cold-blooded, calculated war. Most of the movies about it have been done with this kind of black humorish, *Apocalypse Now* absurdity: the world's crazy; madman Martin Sheen is out to kill madman Marlon Brando; Robert Duvall is a surfing nut. There's that sense of "well, we're all innocent by reason of insanity; the war was crazy, and therefore we're innocent." That doesn't go down too well.   (*Vietnam* 138)

Less popular was *The Nuclear Age*, which takes the theme of the cold war—an underlying motif of *Northern Lights*—and expands it into a major concern. The novel alternates among three sections—"Fission," "Fussion," and "Critical Mass"—as it explores the maturation of its protagonist, William Cowling, a young man who grows up during the Cuban missile crisis and the Vietnam War. Like Paul Perry of *Northern Lights*, Cowling does not go to war; however, unlike Paul Perry, he dodges the draft, immersing himself instead in a revolutionary counterculture whose grueling Cuban boot-camp exercises ironically mimic the United States military's basic training. The novel follows Cowling's life for four decades as he tries to escape the impending doom that he feels is imminent at the close of the twentieth century. *The Nuclear Age* would be a useful text in a course that focuses on the anxieties of life in an era of rapidly expanding technology and its potentially toxic elements, perhaps in conjunction with a novel like Don DeLillo's *White Noise* and perhaps with one that reflects post-9/11 fears. It might also serve a course focused on the Vietnam War as merely a dimension of the larger "war" between the United States and the Soviet Union.

O'Brien's fourth novel, *The Things They Carried*, was a Pulitzer Prize finalist, the recipient of France's Prix du Meilleur Livre Etranger, and winner of the Chicago Tribune Heartland Award for fiction. The book, which consists of twenty-two chapters, some as short as a few pages, centers on the soldiers of Alpha Company, a fictional platoon of American foot soldiers in Vietnam in 1969. Like *Going After Cacciato*, *The Things They Carried* examines the physical and emotional burdens borne by soldiers, while considering the nature of the Vietnam War, the role of the imagination, and the process of writing—although this novel goes beyond the earlier one to consider the burdens common to the soldier returning home after the war. Also like *Going After Cacciato*, *The Things They Carried* is difficult to place in any one genre; it is a collection of stories, a work of metafiction, a combat novel, a short-story cycle, a series of narrative fragments, a composite novel, and even, perhaps, nonfiction. Autobiographical overtones emerge as a result of Tim O'Brien the author giving Tim O'Brien the narrator some—but not all—of the same factual details of his own life. For instance, both Tim O'Brien the author and Tim O'Brien the narrator graduate from Macalester College, serve in Vietnam, and write books titled *If I Die in a Combat Zone, Box Me Up and Ship Me Home* and *Going After Cacciato*. Yet Tim O'Brien the author had no children at the time he wrote *The Things They Carried*, while Tim O'Brien the narrator has a ten-year-old daughter, who makes a return journey to Vietnam with him many years after the war's end.

Of all of O'Brien's works, *The Things They Carried* is probably the one most frequently taught in both high school and college. The title story has been anthologized widely, along with other individual chapters, including "How to Tell a True War Story," "Sweetheart of the Song Tra Bong," "The Man I Killed," "In the Field," and "The Lives of the Dead." Whether considered individually or collectively, these stories comment on the power of storytelling in our lives—showing the nature of good and evil, revealing the impact of history, demonstrating the ambiguous nature of life, and anxiously exploring whether the telling of stories might be a cathartic process that offers hope for the future.

In the Lake of the Woods received both the Society of American Historians' James Fenimore Cooper Prize for best historical novel and the novel of the year award from *Time* magazine, and it was chosen by Fox for a made-for-television movie. Like *Going After Cacciato* and *The Things They Carried*, it is taught on a regular basis. As in many of his novels, O'Brien is structurally innovative here, dividing *In the Lake of the Woods* into three types of chapters: those that focus on the protagonists, John and Kathy Wade; "Evidence" chapters, which present information indicating that John Wade murdered Kathy, his wife; and "Hypothesis" chapters, which present the many possibilities of what may have happened to Kathy. Underlying the novel is the horrific presence of the Vietnam

War—John Wade participated in the My Lai massacre, a fact that does not emerge until he is running for political office and that ultimately dooms his aspirations. Like other postmodernist writers, such as DeLillo and E. L. Doctorow, O'Brien creates an ontological puzzle by juxtaposing characters of his own creation with actual historical figures as he probes the mystery of love, the effects of the past on the present, the human tendency to engage in both good and evil, and the atrocities that are generated by warfare.

Tomcat in Love and *July, July*, O'Brien's sixth and seventh novels, mark the author's shift from more serious subject matter to material of a lighter tone. In *Tomcat in Love*, O'Brien moves away from the male-dominated Vietnam War novel to offer a cast of female characters and a comedic look at the universal struggle between the sexes. The novel focuses on Thomas Chippering, a professor of linguistics at the University of Minnesota, who is obsessed with getting revenge on the many people who betray him: his wife, Lorna Sue, who leaves him for a tycoon; his childhood friend, Herbie, who intrudes on his marriage with Lorna Sue (coincidentally, Herbie's sister); a group of Green Berets with whom he served in Vietnam and who haunt him for many years after the end of the war; and a young female student after whom he lusts and for whom he writes a thesis. *Tomcat in Love* works best in a senior or graduate-level seminar, where students are more likely to comprehend O'Brien's underlying spoof of academia and his revenge on the feminist backlash that some of his earlier novels inspired (see the Calloway essay on *Tomcat in Love* in this volume).

O'Brien regards *July, July* as an ensemble novel, one that includes the voices of a large cast of characters, many of them women. The book focuses on the July 2000 reunion of the Darton College class of 1969, which is finally holding its thirtieth reunion a year late. Like many of O'Brien's other works, the novel is structurally distinctive. Half of the twenty-two chapters are entitled "Class of '69" and view the characters as they interact with one another at the reunion. Interspersed between the "Class of '69" chapters are the postcollege stories of individual classmates, each of whom is facing a crucial moment in his or her life: the guilt of infidelity to a spouse, chemotherapy and recovery from breast cancer, the blackmail of a former war protestor, the trauma of the Vietnam War, the rapid approach of middle age. The characters include a Vietnam veteran as well as a draft dodger who deserted to Canada, but *July, July* goes beyond the war to focus on the entire era and to demonstrate the war's effect on a group of students who graduated shortly after the Tet offensive and who have been haunted by one type of war or another for most of their adult lives.

In addition, O'Brien has helped write a collaborative novel, *The Putt at the End of the World*, to which he contributed "Tight Lies," one of ten chapters by nine known authors, including Les Standiford, Dave Barry, Ridley Pearson, and Richard Bausch. The book is a mystery story set at a golf tournament in Scotland.

Short Stories

O'Brien has published several dozen short stories, most of them precursors to his novels. *Northern Lights* appeared as an entire text without the prior publication of its various components; all of O'Brien's other books include pieces published earlier. Some of his short stories were written with a final book in mind, some were written as independent short stories without further destination, and some were rewritten later for inclusion in a book. While only one story in *Tomcat in Love* ("Faith") and just two in *In the Lake of the Woods* ("The People We Marry" and "How Unhappy They Were") were published separately as short stories, many of the chapters in *Going After Cacciato*, *The Things They Carried*, and *July, July* were published independently before being incorporated into the novels. Stories such as "The Ghost Soldiers," "How to Tell a True War Story," "The Lives of the Dead," "Sweetheart of the Song Tra Bong," and the title story "The Things They Carried" are referred to collectively as "the *Esquire* stories," as all were published in *Esquire* magazine in the decade preceding the publication of the book *The Things They Carried*. Similarly, many stories related to *July, July* can be referred to as *Esquire* stories or *New Yorker* stories, as most were published in one or the other before the release of the novel.

The publication of chapters of novels as separate short stories has enabled O'Brien to comment extensively on the process of writing fiction. For instance, "Speaking of Courage," a story initially related to the protagonist of *Going After Cacciato* and published in *Massachusetts Review* in 1976, reemerged in 1990 as part of *The Things They Carried*. In the novel, the protagonist of "Speaking of Courage" is Norman Bowker, not Paul Berlin, as in the original. O'Brien uses this situation to comment metafictively on the nature of writing. In a different chapter, "Notes," he explains directly why the main character and certain details from the original version of "Speaking of Courage" have been changed for a novel published fourteen years later. Similarly, "Loon Point," which was published in 1993 in *Esquire*, reappeared almost a decade later as a chapter in *July, July*, with some variations from the original text. Because O'Brien changes details in many of his short stories between their initial publication and their book-length versions, he further illustrates his thematic interest in the subjective nature of reality. Readers are challenged to determine which version of an event or a character is true, if any.

Published but Uncollected Stories

O'Brien has published several stories that have never appeared in a book-length work. These are rarely cited by critics, but teachers find them extremely useful. "Claudia Mae's Wedding Day," O'Brien's first published short story, although independent in terms of character and plot from his other works, is linked thematically with them in its themes of war and gender. "A Man of Melancholy Disposition" contains characters from *Northern Lights* but was not included as a chapter in that novel. Fruitful discussions can arise from the fact that O'Brien changes Paul Perry's occupation between the two texts. In the story, Paul Perry follows in the footsteps of his father, the domineering Pehr Lindstrom Pehri; in the novel, he becomes a farm extension agent. "Keeping Watch by Night," published in *Redbook* in 1976, contains characters that later appear in *Going After Cacciato*. In the story, the character of Jim Pederson is developed more fully; in fact, he is presented in dual roles, which casts doubt on the veracity of his actions and on his moral stance.

Nonfiction

Memoir

O'Brien has thus far written only one book-length work of nonfiction, his memoir (and first book) *If I Die in a Combat Zone, Box Me Up and Ship Me Home*, an account of his year as a foot soldier with Alpha Company in Vietnam in 1969–70. In it, O'Brien reveals that he considered going to Canada and deserting, a notion he explores in many of his other works, along with the question of courage, the nature of good and evil, the notion of war and peace, and the futility of the Vietnam War. Like his novels, *If I Die in a Combat Zone* is difficult to classify. It is a series of vignettes or sketches, an autobiography, a journal, and even, perhaps, fiction. O'Brien published excerpts from *If I Die in a Combat Zone* separately in various forums, including the *Washington Post*, *Playboy*, the *Worthington* (Minnesota) *Daily Globe*, and the *Minneapolis Tribune*. One chapter, "Step Lightly," was published while he was serving in Vietnam. *If I Die in a Combat Zone* is a precursor to all of O'Brien's work in more than chronology; the book has been crucial to his later craft. Both O'Brien and scholars observe that had he not written *If I Die in a Combat Zone*, he might not have been as successful with the fiction that has followed it (Schroeder, *Vietnam* 141; Vernon, *Soldiers* 177–78; Heberle, *Trauma Artist* 65). As Heberle points out:

> *Combat Zone* is significantly productive of O'Brien's subsequent fiction. Its representation of the author as bystander or observer may reflect his actual experience of the war, but it also creates a quasi-authorial subject position and tendency toward detachment, avoidance, or evasion that will characterize protagonists in all the later books. The internalization of the narrative and its elaborately repetitive formal structure—particularly striking for an autobiographical account—anticipates the self-conscious writerliness that marks all of the later Vietnam writing.
>
> (*Trauma Artist* 65)

Essays and Articles

While O'Brien has published numerous book reviews, his most significant nonfiction works, aside from *If I Die in a Combat Zone*, are his essays and articles. Some of his earliest articles were published during his time as a journalist, in the early to mid-1970s. "The Crumbling of Sand Castles," his defense of John F. Kennedy, appeared in the *Washington Post*, and "The Youth Vote," a discussion before the 1972 McGovern-Nixon presidential election about the impact that young voters can make, was published in the *New Republic*. Three articles — "The Vietnam Veteran: The GI Bill — Less than Enough," an argument that the services offered by the GI Bill were inadequate; "Prisoners of Peace," an essay about the importance of Vietnam veterans, who had been forgotten by Americans; and "Revolt on the Turnpike," an account of a strike by independent truck drivers targeting the Nixon administration — all appeared in *Penthouse*. "Medals! Medals! Everyone's Got Medals," published in the *Los Angeles Times*, complements many of O'Brien's books, as it explains the ultimate lack of value of the medals that so fascinate his protagonists. "All Quiet on the Western Front," published in *TV Guide*, argues that Erich Maria Remarque's work by that same name is a novel of peace as well as a novel of war.

Of the later essays, perhaps the best known are "The Violent Vet," which was published in *Esquire* and debunked the notion of the returning Vietnam veteran as psychotic and dangerous (a notion espoused in many of the films about the war), and "The Vietnam in Me," O'Brien's account of his return journey to Vietnam in 1994, which appeared in the *New York Times Magazine*. Both are useful classroom tools in discussions of the war and its aftermath, as is his keynote address to the 2005 Thirty Years After conference, reprinted in Mark Heberle's *Thirty Years After: New Essays on Vietnam War Literature, Film, and Art*. "Darkness on the Edge of Town," O'Brien's account of a trip to Rock, Kansas; Little Rock, Arkansas; and New York City "to touch the nuclear age" (42) through interviews with those who live near and work in underground missile silos, serves as a good companion to *The Nuclear Age*. "The Mystery of My Lai," a discussion of why soldiers at My Lai crossed the line between anger and murder to slaughter Vietnamese civilians and why those soldiers have remained unpunished, is insightful material to incorporate in classroom discussions of *In the Lake of the Woods*, as is "The Whole Story," O'Brien's companion essay to H. Bruce Franklin's "Kicking the Denial Syndrome: Tim O'Brien's *In the Lake of the Woods*." "Ambush" (not to be confused with either the chapter by that title in *If I Die in a Combat Zone* or the story by that name in *The Things They Carried*), published in *Boston* magazine, generates a discussion of the parallels between the Battle of Concord in the American Revolution and the Vietnam War. Since the ordeal of the British redcoats reflects that of the common foot soldier, "Ambush" makes a good companion to *Going After Cacciato*, *The Things They Carried*, and *In the Lake of the Woods*, especially in discussions of what soldiers in any war "carry," what they know or do not know, what they endure in a surreal environment with an enemy they cannot see, why they focus on survival, why they participate in atrocities, and why history repeats itself.

Other essays, some rather brief, consider a variety of topics. In "The Magic Show," O'Brien explores the process of writing and storytelling and its connection to the art of magic. His fear that America has been too quick to forget the lessons of Vietnam is expressed in "We've Adjusted Too Well." His introspective comments on a war photo by David Burnett in "A Letter from Home" in *Under Fire: Great Photographers and Writers in Vietnam*, edited by Catherine Leroy, indicate his concern with aging and his awareness of warfare as a universal condition. "A Letter to My Son" reveals his love of parenting and his worry that aging will shorten his active role as a father. In "The Best of Times," O'Brien considers the process of memory and how its fallibility will affect his sons' recollections of him as their dad. His anecdotal "Telling Tails" deals with "the centrality of imagination in enduring fiction." Reflections on his return to his childhood hometown of Worthington, Minnesota, several decades later in "My Kind of Town: Fenced In" provide a refreshed perspective from O'Brien's treatment of it in the memoir and help to reference the hometown setting in *The Things They Carried*.

Interviews and Lectures

O'Brien's generosity toward scholars has resulted in the publication of dozens of interviews in various forums, including newspapers, magazines, online sources, and radio. In particular, instructors may wish to consult the work of the following interviewers. (The interviews are listed in Works Cited under the name of the interviewer rather than under the name of the interviewee, Tim O'Brien.) The interviewers are Catherine Calloway, Tobey Herzog, Patrick Hicks, Steven Kaplan, Larry McCaffery, Brian McNerney, Martin Naparsteck, Scott Sawyer, Eric James Schroeder, Jim Schumock, Debra Shostak and Daniel Bourne, Anthony Tambakis, Edward Tarkington, and Lynn Wharton. A 2010 interview with Neal Conan focused on the twentieth anniversary of *The Things They Carried*.

"Writing Vietnam," a lecture that O'Brien gave at Brown University in Providence, Rhode Island, on 21 April 1999 is well known and is frequently cited by scholars. In addition to talking about writing, the role of the imagination, and war stories, O'Brien participated in a question-and-answer session with the audience. Instructors and students will find the transcript readily available online.

Film and Dramatic Adaptations, Readings, and Panel Discussions

Two of O'Brien's works have been turned into films: "The Sweetheart of Song Tra Bong" (as *A Soldier's Sweetheart*) and *In the Lake of the Woods*. *Going After Cacciato* was turned into a play by Romulus Linney, who published it in the *Kenyon Review* in 2005. *The Things They Carried* has been adapted for a number of amateur productions, including the culminating event of a first-year college experience, as described by Eric Waggoner in this volume. In addition, some of O'Brien's personal appearances have been captured on videotape or videodisc, including speeches and readings at George Mason University; Appalachian State University; the Chicago Public Library; Florida Community College, Jacksonville; Radford University; Hendrix College; and the State University of New York College at Brockport. Also available are panel discussions on combat films, the process of writing, and the Vietnam War.

Editions

All of O'Brien's books are available in paperback editions. *If Die in a Combat Zone, Northern Lights, Going After Cacciato,* and *Tomcat in Love* are published by Broadway Books. *July, July* is published by Penguin, and *The Things They Carried* and *In the Lake of the Woods* by Mariner Books. For the twentieth anniversary of the *The Things They Carried* in 2010, Houghton Mifflin reissued the book in both paperback and hardcover. *The Things They Carried* and *Tomcat in Love* have been published in autographed leather-bound editions by the Franklin Library, and *Going After Cacciato* by Easton Press. Many of O'Brien's works are available as e-books as well.

O'Brien's books have been translated into at least a dozen languages, including Czech, French, German, Italian, and Polish. A Latin American or Korean instructor offering a course on global fiction would be able to use *En el lago de los bosques* or *Supsok ui hosu,* the respective Spanish and Korean editions of *In the Lake of the Woods,* and a teacher in Japan could include *Honto no senso no hanashi o shiyo,* the Japanese translation of *The Things They Carried.*

Several of O'Brien's short stories, including "Speaking of Courage," "Enemies/Friends," and "The Nuclear Age," have been published in book format as special editions. While they are more difficult to acquire than the novels in which they also appear, they are useful in showing students how even a single story may merit publication as an independent text.

Copies of previous editions of O'Brien's books, such as those published by Houghton Mifflin, Dell, and Delta, are available from online distributors and from bookstores that sell used books. However, readers are advised to keep in mind that O'Brien continually revises; as he has indicated in conversations with the editors of this volume, he prefers that scholars cite the most recent book edition of his work. The revisions consist primarily of slight line editing and "wordsmithing" of significant interest only to textual scholars.

Secondary Sources

The Works of Tim O'Brien

The primary book-length studies of Tim O'Brien's writing are Steven Kaplan's *Understanding Tim O'Brien,* Tobey Herzog's *Tim O'Brien,* Patrick Smith's *Tim O'Brien: A Critical Companion,* and Mark Heberle's *A Trauma Artist: Tim*

O'Brien and the Fiction of Vietnam. The first three provide biographical and contextual information and review the major elements of O'Brien's work; these insightful introductory texts are quite accessible. Heberle's book is driven by the thesis that wartime trauma informs all of O'Brien's writings and is the most thorough and significant of the four. High school teachers may find useful Barry Gilmore and Alexander Kaplan's *Tim O'Brien in the Classroom: "This Too Is True: Stories Can Save Us,"* a volume of pedagogical materials designed for grades 9–12. None of our respondents mentioned Mats Tegmark's *In the Shoes of a Soldier: Communication in Tim O'Brien's Vietnam Narratives,* which is a book that few libraries carry and which is hampered by its narrow focus and specialized discourse.

Instructors will find a wealth of essays on O'Brien in scholarly journals and books; we note here two essays recommended by several survey respondents that serve as excellent critical introductions: Steven Kaplan's "The Undying Uncertainty of the Narrator in Tim O'Brien's *The Things They Carried*" and Maria Bonn's "Can Stories Save Us? Tim O'Brien and the Efficacy of the Text." Other helpful essays not mentioned elsewhere in these pages are Tom Bowie's "Reconciling Vietnam: Tim O'Brien's Narrative Journey"; Catherine Calloway's "Pluralities of Vision: *Going After Cacciato* and Tim O'Brien's Short Fiction"; G. Thomas Couser's "*Going After Cacciato*: The Romance and the Real War"; Tobey Herzog's "Tim O'Brien's 'True Lies'(?)" and "*Going After Cacciato*: The Soldier-Author-Character Seeking Control"; Clara Juncker's "Not a Story to Pass On? Tim O'Brien's Vietnam"; Donna Pasternak's "Keeping the Dead Alive: Revising the Past in Tim O'Brien's War Stories"; David Piwinski's "My Lai, Flies, and Beezlebub in Tim O'Brien's *In the Lake of the Woods*"; Daniel Robinson's "Getting It Right: The Short Fiction of Tim O'Brien"; Stefano Rosso's "Labyrinths and Tunnels, from the Jungle to Sewage"; Angieszka Salka's "Re-visioning the Democratic Imagination: Tim O'Brien's Vietnam Fiction"; James Schramer's "Magical Realism in Tim O'Brien's Vietnam War Fiction"; Kyung Seok Shim's "The Journey of Dream: Tim O'Brien's Metaphysical Exploration in *Going After Cacciato*"; Robert Slabey's "*Going After Cacciato*: Tim O'Brien's 'Separate Peace'"; Claire Stocks's "Acts of Cultural Identification: Tim O'Brien's *July, July*"; Mark Taylor's "Tim O'Brien's War"; John Timmerman's "Tim O'Brien and the Art of the True War Story: 'Night March' and 'Speaking of Courage'"; and Lynn Wharton's "Hand, Head, and Artifice: The Fictive World of Tim O'Brien" and "Tim O'Brien and American National Identity: A Vietnam Veteran's Imagined Self in *The Things They Carried*." In addition, William Spanos includes a substantial chapter on *Going After Cacciato* in his *American Exceptionalism in the Age of Globalization: The Specter of Vietnam.*

Also available are Catherine Calloway's two bibliographies, "Tim O'Brien (1946–): A Primary and Secondary Bibliography" and "Tim O'Brien: A Checklist." These pieces, although somewhat dated, provide useful lists of textual editions, theses and dissertations, and book reviews.

In addition, the chapters on O'Brien in *Short Story Criticism*, *The Columbia Companion to the Twentieth-Century American Short Story*, *Contemporary Literary Criticism*, *Contemporary Authors*, *Notable American Novelists*, *A Reader's Companion to the Short Story in English*, and *The Dictionary of Literary Biography Yearbook: 1980* provide substantial supplementary material for instructors and students, as do the entries on O'Brien and his work in the *Encyclopedia of American Literature*, the *Encyclopedia of American War Literature*, *War and American Popular Culture*, and *The Vietnam Experience: A Concise Encyclopedia of American Literature, Songs, and Films*. Especially noteworthy are the O'Brien entries in the *Dictionary of Literary Biography*: "Tim O'Brien" in *American Writers of the Vietnam War* and Thomas Myers's "Tim O'Brien" in *American Novelists since World War II*.

The Vietnam War

New nonfiction work about the United States war in Vietnam continues to appear on a regular basis. Recent books include Mark Moyar's *Triumph Forsaken: The Vietnam War, 1954–1965*, Robert Brigham's *ARVN: Life and Death in the South Vietnamese Army*, and Michael Sallah and Mitch Weiss's *Tiger Force: A True Story of Men and War*—about a platoon from the 101st Airborne Division operating in Quang Ngai Province before the My Lai massacre and before O'Brien's tour of duty in the area.[2] (Specific texts on My Lai recommended by our survey participants are Michael Bilton and Kevin Sim's book *Four Hours in My Lai*; Nancy Gentile Ford's essay "The My Lai Massacre: Crossing the Line in Vietnam," in *Issues of War and Peace*; and Philip Beidler's essay "Calley's Ghost.")[3] Other recent books include Robert Stoffey's *Fighting to Leave: The Final Years of America's War in Vietnam, 1972–1973*, John Bahnsen's *American Warrior: A Combat Memoir of Vietnam*, Van Nguyen Duong's *Tragedy of the Vietnam War: A South Vietnamese Officer's Analysis*, Dwight Jon Zimmerman and Wayne Vansant's *The Vietnam War: A Graphic History*, Stephen Atkins's *Writing the War: My Ten Months in the Jungles, Streets, and Paddies of South Vietnam, 1968*, Tony Lazzarini's *Highest Traditions: Memories of War*, and Xiaobing Li's *Voices from the Vietnam War: Stories from American, Asian, and Russian Veterans*.

Two chief pedagogical resources are already somewhat dated. William Griffin and John Marciano's *Teaching the Vietnam War: A Critical Examination of School Texts and an Interpretive Comparative History Utilizing the Pentagon Papers and Other Documents* appeared in 1979, only four years after the fall of Saigon. Marc Jason Gilbert's *The Vietnam War: Teaching Approaches and Resources* was published in 1991, which was well before the normalization of relations between the United States and Vietnam and thus before all the work that was made possible by the new opportunities for exchange and research, as well as before the current trend to include texts by Vietnamese writers in classes and scholarship. Barry Kroll's *Teaching Hearts and Minds: College Students Reflect on the Vietnam War in Literature* is quite helpful for teaching the historical context of the literature. We have included in this book Benjamin Goluboff's "The Vietnam War: A Very Short History."

Internet Resources

Texas Tech University's *Vietnam Center and Archive* is an excellent gateway Web site for teachers. Its wealth of information and resources includes a page, "The Teachers' Resources Web," that is

> intended to assist teachers and students at all levels—from primary school to college. Site materials are designed to accommodate a range of teaching and learning situations from a single 50-minute lecture that is part of a general US history class to a semester or quarter-long dedicated course focusing exclusively on the Vietnam War.

William Joseph of Wellesley College has *Vietnam War Internet Links*, a site that includes numerous links about teaching the war. Teachers should also visit the Web site *Vietnam Studies Group*; the group is a subcommittee of the Southeast Asia Council of the Association for Asian Studies, which "exists to provide resources and information for scholarly research, study, and teaching about Vietnam."

Edwin Moïse, of Clemson University, maintains an extensive online bibliography. *Vietnam War Bibliography* is organized by subject, and many of the entries include helpful annotations. One might direct students to his section on My Lai, as they research that event in their study of O'Brien's *In the Lake of the Woods*. Moïse provides a succinct history of the war that students can review in preparation for a single class meeting.[4] The Web site *Encyclopedia of American Studies* has a brief essay on the Vietnam War that is available online to members of the American Studies Association and in a print edition to nonmembers; there are eighty-six entries that make some reference to the war, including "The Draft," "War and the Representation of War," "The Sixties," "Veterans," "Cold War," "Vietnamese Americans," "Pacifism," "Nuclear Age," "Patriotism," and "Feminism: An Overview." *American Experience: Vietnam Online*, PBS's companion Web site to its thirteen-hour 1983 documentary *Vietnam: A Television History*, features a time line; a who's who; a guide to the weapons, controversies, and language of the war ("In the Trenches"); a list of primary sources; several maps; and a teacher's guide. The Vietnam section of the Web site *Veterans History Project* at the Library of Congress is another good online source.[5]

Short Histories

Among the short printed histories of the war, several respondents mentioned George Herring's *America's Longest War: The United States and Vietnam, 1950–1975* as the standard, although some teachers find it too expensive for classroom adoption. *The Columbia Guide to the Vietnam War*, by David Anderson, narrates the war and its roots and aftermath in eighty-six pages, followed by a glossary of terms, chronology, resource guide, extensive bibliography, and a miscellany of documents and statistics. This book is an excellent if less complex primer and clearly has a student audience in mind—its narrative emphasizes key terms and guides the reader with leading questions like "What was the source of Ho Chi Minh's success in gaining support of the Vietnamese?" Another short introduction appropriate for the literature classroom is Andy Wiest's *Essential Histories: The Vietnam War, 1956–1975.* It is ninety-six pages long and follows the same useful structure of all the titles in this series: introduction, chronology, "Background to War," "Warring Sides," "Outbreak," "The Fighting," "Portrait of a Soldier," "The World around War," "Portrait of a Civilian," "How the War Ended," "Conclusion and Consequences."

Other histories of modest length are *A Short History of the Vietnam War,* edited by Allan Millet (169 pages); *The 25-Year War: America's Military Role in Vietnam,* by Bruce Palmer, Jr. (248 pages); *Portrait of a Tragedy: America and the Vietnam War,* by James Warren (206 pages); *Vietnam,* by Spencer Tucker (244 pages); *The Vietnam War,* by Mitchell Hall (168 pages); *America's War in Vietnam: A Short Narrative History,* by Larry Addington (192 pages); and *Where the Domino Fell: America and Vietnam, 1945–2004,* by James Olson and Randy Roberts, which covers the war in 255 pages and its legacy in approximately 50 pages (including the chapters "Oliver Stone's Vietnam" and "'Nam,' Islam, and the American Future"). Philip Caputo's *10,000 Days of Thunder: A History of the Vietnam War* (128 pages) targets middle school and junior high school students and is of particular interest to those who teach Caputo's memoir or his fiction about the war.

An abundance of photographs makes the following short histories particularly attractive: *The Eyewitness History of the Vietnam War, 1961–1975,* by George Esper and the Associated Press, and *The Vietnam War: The Story and Photographs,* by Donald Goldstein, Katherine Dillon, and J. Michael Wegner. Three almost entirely photographic "histories" are Larry Burrows's *Vietnam*; *Requiem: By the Photographers Who Died in Vietnam and Indochina,* edited by Horst Faas and Tim Page; and Page's *Another Vietnam: Pictures of the War from the Other Side,* which can be contrasted with Philip Jones Griffiths's *Viet Nam at Peace* or either of the two earlier books in Griffiths's photographic trilogy, *Vietnam Inc.* and *Agent Orange: "Collateral Damage" in Viet Nam.* National Geographic created a documentary version of *Another Vietnam* called *Vietnam's Unseen War—Pictures from the Other Side.*

Respondents also recommend the 146-page section on the Vietnam War in Barbara Tuchman's *The March of Folly: From Troy to Vietnam*; the coverage of the war in Howard Zinn's *A People's History of the United States: 1492–Present*; the chapters "Vietnam" and "A Nation at War" in David Farber's *The Age of Great Dreams: America in the 1960s*; and the historical chapters in Neil Sheehan's *A Bright Shining Lie: John Paul Vann and America in Vietnam,* a brilliant blend of history, first-person reportage, and biography that unfortunately concludes before the end of the war, with the death of its subject. One could also use the relevant chapters from any number of general studies of the United States or American military history. A genre-blurring book popular among respondents is Frances Fitzgerald's *Fire in the Lake: The Vietnamese and the Americans in Vietnam.* Edward Doyle and Stephen Weiss's *Collision of Cultures: The Americans in Vietnam, 1954–1973* puts forth a thesis similar to Fitzgerald's, about the American misunderstanding of Vietnam; it is only 192 pages long. *Understanding Vietnam,* by Neil Jamieson, is longer, at 428 pages, but it will appeal to literature teachers and students because of its substantial use of Vietnamese literary texts in its explanation of Vietnamese culture and America's failure to understand it during the war.

Longer Histories

Longer histories include Robert Schulzinger's *A Time for War: The United States and Vietnam, 1941–1975*; Michael Lind's *Vietnam: The Necessary War*; Michael Maclear's *The Ten Thousand Day War: Vietnam, 1945–1975*; Guenter Lewy's *America in Vietnam*; Marvin Gettleman, Jane Franklin, Marilyn Young, and H. Bruce Franklin's *Vietnam and America: A Documented History*; and Michael Hunt's *A Vietnam War Reader: A Documentary History from American and Vietnamese Perspectives.* Gerard De Groot's *A Noble Cause? America and the Vietnam War,* although long, is quite readable and includes a helpful annotated bibliography. The standard long work is Stanley Karnow's *Vietnam: A History,* the companion book to the 1983 PBS series. A few respondents observe that the updates since the book's initial publication in 1983 are minimal. Respondents describe Marilyn Young's *The Vietnam Wars, 1945–1990* as "highly readable" but also as "polemical."

Major Problems in the History of the Vietnam War, edited by Robert McMahon and Thomas Paterson, is a collection of documents and essays useful for its flexibility, though it is expensive and potentially less appropriate for the literature classroom because of its focus on policy rather than the military aspects of the war. Additional collections of essays by historians and others are Marilyn Young and Robert Buzzanco's *A Companion to the Vietnam War,* John Prados's *The Hidden History of the Vietnam War,* Marc Jason Gilbert's *Why the North Won the Vietnam War,* Jayne Werner and Luu Doan Huynh's *The Vietnam War: Vietnamese and American Perspectives,* Andrew Rotter's *Light at the End of the Tunnel: A Vietnam War Anthology,* and David Anderson and John Ernst's *The War That Never Ends: New Perspectives on the Vietnam War.*

Teachers and students alike will find the six-volume *The United States and the Vietnam War: Significant Scholarly Articles,* edited by Walter Hixson, a valuable resource because of the stand-alone nature of the articles and the volumes' topical organization, as indicated by their titles: *The Roots of the Vietnam War, Military Aspects of the Vietnam War, Leadership and Diplomacy in the Vietnam War, The Vietnam Antiwar Movement, The Lessons and Legacies of the Vietnam War,* and *Historical Memory and Representations of the Vietnam War.*

Documentaries and War Correspondence

In terms of documentary histories, several teachers like to use excerpts from the PBS series *Vietnam: A Television History*. We should not forget *Vietnam: The Ten Thousand Day War*. *Hearts and Minds* won an Academy Award for Best Documentary. Several early but revealing and still available documentaries are *The Anderson Platoon*, which follows a platoon for six weeks in 1966; Emile De Antonio's *In the Year of the Pig*, which depicts the history of Southeast Asia in the twentieth century through the first half of the American war there (all in 103 minutes); *Dat Kho: Land of Sorrows*, which focuses on a single Vietnamese family during the war; Joris Ivens's leftist wartime work, including *Le 17ème Parallèle*; and *Winter Soldier*, which documents the Vietnam Veterans against the War movement.

Professional actors read actual letters from the war in *Dear America: Letters Home from Vietnam*. In *Regret to Inform*, Barbara Sonneborn visits the place her husband died and interviews widows from both sides—her translator, Xuan Ngoc Nguyen, also lost her husband in the war. Other documentaries include *Return with Honor*, about the American POW experience, and Werner Herzog's *Little Dieter Needs to Fly*, which tells the story of one POW and his escape. *The Fog of War: Eleven Lessons from the Life of Robert S. McNamara* presents United States military strategy in Vietnam as a legacy of its World War II experience.

There are two documentaries that focus on the riots at the University of Wisconsin: *The War at Home* and *American Experience: Two Days in October*, which is a half-hour adaptation of David Maraniss's excellent *They Marched into Sunlight*. Both the film and the book juxtapose the Wisconsin riots and a disastrous battle for an American unit during the same days in 1967. (Like Sheehan's *A Bright Shining Lie*, Maraniss's book weaves together personal accounts with military and political history.)

Vietnam: An American Journey follows Robert Richter, the first American filmmaker allowed in the country after the war, as he travels through Vietnam. It includes footage from the war and an interview with a survivor of the My Lai massacre. Coco Schrijber's *First Kill* interviews Vietnam veterans and witnesses, including Michael Herr, in an attempt to explore the psychology of combat. Eugene Jarecki's *Why We Fight* investigates the political and financial context of America's modern wars.

The three collections of war correspondence we recommend are Bernard Fall's *Viet-Nam Witness, 1953–66*, the pieces about Vietnam in Martha Gellhorn's *The Face of War*, and either the one-volume or the two-volume college edition of the Library of America's *Reporting Vietnam*. Many of the selections in this last work are more commentary than strict journalistic reporting. Included is the entire text of Michael Herr's *Dispatches*, a work of literary nonfiction taught by a number of respondents (although one notes that students are frequently turned off by this book). Three prominent literary figures of the day turned their visits to Vietnam into books: James Jones's *Viet Journal*, Mary McCarthy's *Vietnam*, and Susan Sontag's *Trip to Hanoi*.

Oral History

For the United States soldier's perspective, the standard oral histories are Al Santoli's *Everything We Had*, Mark Baker's *Nam: The Vietnam War in the Words of the Men and Women Who Fought There*, and Wallace Terry's *Bloods: An Oral History of the Vietnam War by Black Veterans*. Jen Dunnaway's article "Approaching a Truer Form of Truth: The Appropriation of the Oral Narrative Form in Vietnam War Literature" argues that three canonical Vietnam war literary texts—O'Brien's *The Things They Carried*, Herr's *Dispatches*, and Gustav Hasford's *The Short-Timers*—incorporate the oral war story "to convey the 'truth' of the Vietnam War experience more compellingly than the more typically coherent structure of the literary narrative alone" (27). In addition to Santoli's and Baker's books, Dunnaway uses Lieutenant General Harold Moore and Joseph Galloway's *We Were Soldiers Once . . . and Young*, a history drawn largely from interviews. See also *The Soldier's Story: Vietnam in Their Own Words*, by Ron Steinman, and *Eyewitness Vietnam: Firsthand Accounts from Operation Rolling Thunder to the Fall of Saigon*, by Donald Gilmore and D. M. Giangreco.

The earliest major work to employ interviews from various perspectives, including those of the Vietnamese, grieving parents, and both prowar and antiwar Americans, is Gloria Emerson's *Winners and Losers: Battles, Retreats, Gains, Losses, and Ruins from the Vietnam War*, which won the 1978 National Book Award (beating fellow-nominee *Dispatches*). Christian Appy's *Patriots: The War Remembered from All Sides* in a sense updates Emerson's book, though while Emerson works the other stories into what becomes her story, Appy keeps out of the way. There is a passage from O'Brien in the final pages, and it includes this relevant comment:

> It stuns me how ignorant young people are about the war, not just in high school, but in college. They kind of know the music and they've seen *Apocalypse Now* or one of the other movies, but the actual issues that were at stake back then and remain at stake now, they know very little about. I don't think it's their fault so much as the teachers' or the curriculum. It's said to me all the time that school terms run out and they teach Vietnam in a day. And it's a lengthy, complex history! You have to go way back to really understand it. . . . It makes me feel pretty shitty because to understand my books you do have to know at least some of the history.
> (544–45)

Memoirs

The memoirs written by American soldiers in Vietnam are scarcely represented by the few we teach: Caputo's *A Rumor of War*, Tobias Wolff's *In Pharaoh's Army*, Robert Mason's *Chickenhawk*, Robert McNamara and Brian VanDeMark's *In Retrospect: The Tragedy and Lessons of Vietnam*, and David Parks's *GI Diary*. Parks's book is notable as one of only a handful of memoirs by African Americans (eleven are surveyed by Jeffrey Loeb in "The African American Autobiography of the Vietnam War" in Vernon's *Arms and the Self*). O'Brien's own memoir, *If I Die in a Combat Zone*, is rarely taught; indeed, *The Things They Carried* as quasi-autobiography receives more attention than his actual memoir—this despite its clear designation as a work of fiction. Recent American memoirs include Heinemann's *Black Virgin Mountain: A Return to Vietnam* and the television correspondent John Laurence's *The Cat from Hue: A Vietnam War Story*, a fine book with the pedagogical disadvantage of its length (850 pages). Wayne Karlin's *War Movies: Journeys to Viet Nam — Scenes and Out-takes* is a fascinating mélange of genres: a memoir of Karlin's return to Vietnam to work on a Vietnamese film about the war, scenes from the film and its production, poetry, and short fiction. Some anthologies provide first-person accounts: Walter Capps's *The Vietnam Reader* brings together thirty-six essays from veterans, diplomats, theologians, and others; Stewart O'Nan's *The Vietnam Reader* includes poetry, drama, and songs to provide a similar array of perspectives. Catherine Leroy's *Under Fire: Great Photographers and Writers in Vietnam* matches war photographs with writing by the likes of O'Brien, Caputo, Sheehan, David Halberstam, and Wayne Karlin.

Fiction

The novels by other American veterans of the war taught by our respondents are Hasford's *The Short-Timers*; Larry Heinemann's *Paco's Story*; James Webb's *Fields of Fire*; John Del Vecchio's *The Thirteenth Valley*; Philip Caputo's novella "In the Forest of the Laughing Elephant"; John Williams's *Captain Blackman*, a novel primarily about the black American experience; and Joe Haldeman's *The Forever War* and *1968*. *The Forever War* gets at Vietnam obliquely, through science fiction, and the reader-friendly *1968* provides an excellent window on that monumental year, discussing in-country events like the Tet offensive, the attack on Khe Sanh, and My Lai and also domestic ones: hippies and the generation gap, the assassinations of Martin Luther King, Jr., and Bobby Kennedy, the presidential election and the Chicago convention riots, the sexual revolution and the abortion debate, the civil rights movement and the Washington, DC, riots. The mental trauma suffered by Spider, the main character, allows Haldeman to comment on the changing scientific understanding of post-traumatic stress disorder and also on homosexuality. The psychologist's efforts to interpret Spider's character might amuse students who are suspicious of their teacher's efforts to interpret literary texts. Like *The Forever War* and other fiction by Haldeman, *1968* brings science fiction into the conversation about war and so invites comparison with the work of Kurt Vonnegut. Most of Haldeman's war writing can be found in *War Stories*.

  The two canonical novels depicting pre–Vietnam War global blustering by the United States are Graham Greene's *The Quiet American* and William Lederer and Eugene Burdick's *The Ugly American*, both of which are taught as frequently as any of the wartime fiction. One of our participants prefers the

2002 film version of *The Quiet American* to the novel for classroom use and suggests having students compare it with the 1958 film, which is highly sanitized. Though published after the war, Anthony Grey's *Saigon* surveys the history of the Vietnamese war for independence from the 1920s to 1975, but at nearly eight hundred pages it is long for classroom use (unless read in sections). Norman Mailer, while not a Vietnam veteran, has two titles that are sometimes taught: *Armies of the Night*, his oddly autobiographical account of the 1967 antiwar march on Washington, and *Why Are We in Vietnam?*, a short novel about a hunting trip taken just before a character's departure for Vietnam.

In addition to Stewart O'Nan's book, the major anthologies are Wayne Karlin, Larry Rottmann, and Basil Pacquet's *Free Fire Zones: Short Stories by Vietnam Veterans*, the first and so an essential book for anyone teaching the evolution of the field; Nancy Anisfield's *Vietnam Anthology: American War Literature*; H. Bruce Franklin's *The Vietnam War in American Stories, Songs, and Poems*; and J. A. Smith's *Voices from the Wall: Anthology of Short Stories from the Vietnam War*.

Although our respondents did not mention these pairings, we recommend Stephen Wright's *Mediations in Green* in conjunction with *In the Lake of the Woods* and Larry Heinemann's *Close Quarters* in conjunction with any O'Brien Vietnam War text. Also of note are any of Tobias Wolff's stories ("Wingfield," "Soldier's Joy," "The Other Miller," "Casualty," and the novella *The Barracks Thief*). New works continue to appear that could easily be used in a classroom, like Marti Leimbach's *The Man from Saigon*, Karl Marlantes's *Matterhorn: A Novel of the Vietnam War*, and Tatjana Soli's *The Lotus Eaters*. Also worthwhile are two earlier works, *The Fearless Man*, by Donald Pfarrer, who previously gave us *Neverlight*, and Tim Farrington's *Lizzie's War*, a good companion to *Neverlight*. The Vietnam veteran Stephen Wright's Civil War novel *The Amalgamation Polka* can be read in the context of Vietnam War literature.

Poetry

Of the American poets from the Vietnam War, the one taught most often is Yusef Komunyakaa. Our respondents also teach John Balaban (*Remembering Heaven's Face: A Story of Rescue in Wartime Vietnam*), W. D. Ehrhart, Walter McDonald, Michael Casey, and Bruce Weigl. Philip Jason believes Weigl's *Song of Napalm* is "one of those few" works from the war destined "to become a permanent part of our literary culture" (*Acts and Shadows* 138). Teachers might prefer an anthology: *Winning Hearts and Minds: War Poems by Vietnam Veterans*, edited by Larry Rottman, Jan Barry, and Basil Pasquet; *Carrying the Darkness: The Poetry of the Vietnam War* or *Unaccustomed Mercy: Soldier-Poets of the Vietnam War*, both edited by Ehrhart; or the Vietnam section of Lorrie Goldensohn's *American War Poetry*. Two anthologies offer works of Vietnamese as well as American poets: *From Both Sides Now: The Poetry of the Vietnam War and Its Aftermath*, edited by Phillip Mahony, and *Writing be-*

tween the Lines: An Anthology on War and Its Social Consequences, edited by Kevin Bowen and Bruce Weigl.

Drama

David Rabe, the author of *The Basic Training of Pavlo Hummel, Sticks and Bones,* and *Streamers,* is the primary dramatist taught by our respondents, though Donald Ringnalda would have it otherwise. The "paradoxical premise" of Ringnalda's essay "Doing It Wrong Is Getting It Right: America's Vietnam War Drama" is that "drama is best suited for grappling with the Vietnam War (or any war) precisely because it is the least suited. . . . It is real because it is so blatantly artificial" (68). James Reston collects several dramatic works in *Coming to Terms: American Plays and the Vietnam War.* We should note that there have been several amateur stage productions of *The Things They Carried* and that Jill Taft-Kaufman's essay "How to Tell a True War Story: The Dramaturgy and Staging of Narrative Theatre" addresses the issues of adapting this novel to the stage.

Film

The films taught by respondents are *The Green Berets; Go Tell the Spartans; Hamburger Hill; Full Metal Jacket; Platoon; The Deer Hunter; Apocalypse Now; Coming Home; 84 Charlie MoPic; The Killing Fields; Casualties of War; Good Morning, Vietnam; Born on the Fourth of July; Forrest Gump; Jacob's Ladder;* and *We Were Soldiers.* Teachers also report showing episodes and excerpts from the television series *Tour of Duty* and *China Beach* and the television miniseries adaptation of Caputo's *A Rumor of War.*

Teachers should consider having students read essays written by veterans about Vietnam war films. O'Brien's own essay "The Violent Vet" debunks the myth of insanity promulgated by films like *Apocalypse Now* and *Taxi Driver.* For O'Brien, dismissing the war as an insane venture and a historical aberration allows us to avoid facing the real questions the war poses about humanity, morality, and nationality. William Broyles's "Vietnam: How the War Became the Movie" reflects on several films and compares them with films about other wars and from other nations, on *The Things They Carried,* and on Broyles's own experiences as a veteran and as the coproducer of the television show *China Beach.* Philip Beidler reconsiders *Platoon* and other films in his personal essay "Late Thoughts on *Platoon*" in *Late Thoughts on an Old War: The Legacy of Vietnam.*

Music

Music was certainly an integral part of the war era, generating such well-known tunes as Country Joe McDonald's "I-Feel-Like-I'm-Fixin'-to-Die Rag"; Staff Sergeant Barry Sadler's "The Ballad of the Green Berets"; Crosby, Stills, Nash, and Young's "Ohio"; and Creedence Clearwater Revival's "Fortunate Son." Survey participants also recommend Bruce Springsteen's "Born in the U.S.A."; "The Big

Parade," by 10000 Maniacs; and Pete Seeger's "Waist Deep in the Big Muddy." Useful studies of the music of the war are Lee Andresen's *Battle Notes: Music of the Vietnam War* and James Perone's *Songs of the Vietnam Conflict*, David James's "The Vietnam War and American Music" in Rowe and Berg's *The Vietnam War and American Culture*, and Ray Pratt's "'There Must Be Some Way Outta Here!': The Vietnam War in American Popular Music" in Kenton Clymer's *The Vietnam War: Its History, Literature and Music*. Beidler's "The Music of the Nam" in *Late Thoughts on an Old War* surveys its subject in the form of a personal essay. O'Brien once told one of this book's editors that his personal theme song for the war, the song that plays in his head, the song his unit sometimes sang while moving through rice paddies, was the Beatles' "Hey Jude."

Essays

Teachers should consider having students read essays that reflect broadly on American literature from the war. "The Beauty and Destructiveness of War: A Literary Portrait of the Vietnam Conflict," by Pat Hoy II, is an engaging examination of O'Brien's works as well as Caputo's and Wolff's memoirs, Mailer's *Armies of the Night* and *Why Are We in Vietnam?*, Robert Olen Butler's story collection *A Good Scent from a Strange Mountain*, and Jade Ngoc Quang Huynh's *South Wind Changing*. Hoy's observation that Wolff's book evokes all the war's clichés but "never mentions them," so that "we see where such clichés might have come from," suggests a way of thinking about how O'Brien's narratives work ("Beauty" 182). His thoughts on war's "beauty" and on gender also give much to readers of O'Brien to ponder.

Respondents recommend Jerome Klinkowitz's "Writing under Fire" and two Tobey Herzog articles, "John Wayne in a Modern Heart of Darkness: The American Soldier in Vietnam" and "Writing about Vietnam: A Heavy Heart of Darkness Trip." See also Ringnalda's "Fighting and Writing: America's Vietnam War Literature," the forerunner to his book *Fighting and Writing the Vietnam War*. Philip Beidler's "Thirty Years After: The Archaeologies" provides a nifty trajectory, with personal reflection. His essay "Viet Pulp" in his *Late Thoughts on an Old War* is a refreshing examination of texts literature professors don't normally teach or even read: popular, mass-market paperback war fiction. Beidler has done a great service by digesting for us this enormous genre; interested students should also be directed to H. Bruce Franklin's "The Vietnam War as American Science Fiction and Fantasy" and especially to his *Vietnam and Other American Fantasies*, a study of American culture through the intersection of the war with genres such as science fiction and comic books.[6] There are two chapters on representations of the war in detective fiction ("Hard-boiled Nam I: The Vietnam War in Detective Fiction" and "Hard-boiled Nam II: James Lee Burke's Dave Robicheaux") in Philip Jason's *Acts and Shadows: The Vietnam War in American Literary Culture*. Two other chapters in the book serve as stand-alone introductory analyses: "Vision and Tradition" and "Vietnam War Writing and Authenticity."

Criticism

In addition to Ringnalda's and Jason's books, other book-length criticism of the literature of the war includes Timothy Lomperis and John Clark Pratt's *"Reading the Wind": The Literature of the Vietnam War*; Philip Melling's *Vietnam in American Literature*; Philip Beidler's *American Literature and the Experience in Vietnam* and *Re-writing America: Vietnam Authors in Their Generation*; Thomas Myers's *Walking Point: American Narratives of Vietnam*; Jim Neilson's *Warring Fictions: American Literary Culture and the Vietnam War Narrative*; Tobey Herzog's *Vietnam War Stories: Innocence Lost*; Lloyd Lewis's *The Tainted War: Culture and Identity in Vietnam War Narratives*; Brenda Boyle's *Masculinity in Vietnam War Narratives: A Critical Study of Fiction, Films, and Nonfiction Writings*. Mark Taylor's *The Vietnam War in History, Literature, and Film*; James Wilson's *Vietnam in Prose and Film*; Katherine Kinney's *Friendly Fire: American Images of the Vietnam War*; Jinim Park's *Narratives of the Vietnam War by Korean and American Writers*; and four edited volumes of essays — Philip Jason's *Fourteen Landing Zones: Approaches to Vietnam War Literature*, William Searle's *Search and Clear: Critical Responses to Selected Literature and Films of the Vietnam War*, Robert Slabey's *The United States and Viet Nam from War to Peace*, and Owen Gilman, Jr., and Lorrie Smith's *America Rediscovered: Critical Essays on Literature and Film of the Vietnam War*. Gilman is the author of the more specialized study *Vietnam and the Southern Imagination*. A valuable study of the war and the home front is Maureen Ryan's *The Other Side of Grief: The Home Front and the Aftermath in American Narratives of the Vietnam War*.

Two works that place the war in a classical tradition are James Tatum's *The Mourner's Song: War and Remembrance from the* Iliad *to Vietnam* and Lawrence Tritle's *From Melos to My Lai: War and Survival*. See also Christopher Michael McDonough's "'Afraid to Admit We Are Not Achilles': Facing Hector's Dilemma in Tim O'Brien's *The Things They Carried*" and Thomas Palaima's "Courage and Prowess Afoot in Homer and the Vietnam of Tim O'Brien." Mark Heberle's edited collection of thirty-four essays, *Thirty Years After: New Essays on Vietnam War Literature, Film and Art*, is the new indispensible book in the field.

Three general critical essays on American poetry of the war are Lorrie Smith's "Resistance and Revision in Poetry by Vietnam War Veterans," Lorrie Goldensohn's long chapter "American Poets of the Vietnam War" in her *Dismantling Glory: Twentieth-Century Soldier Poetry*, and the chapter "Fragging the Chain(s) of Command: Mutilation and GI Resistance Poetry" in *Hearts and Minds: Bodies, Poetry, and Resistance in the Vietnam Era*, by Michael Bibby. Book-length criticism includes *Memories of a Lost War: American Poetic Responses to the Vietnam War*, by Subarno Chattarji, *Radical Visions: Poetry by Vietnam Veterans*, by Vince Gotera, and *Out of the Vietnam Vortex: A Study of Poets and Poetry against the War*, by James Mersmann.

Jeffrey Fenn's *Levitating the Pentagon: Evolutions in the American Theatre of the Vietnam War Era*, and Nora Alter's *Vietnam Protest Theatre: The Television*

War on Stage are the primary studies of drama. For short guides, see (along with the Ringnalda essay) Weldon Durham's "Gone to Flowers: Theatre and Drama of the Vietnam War" and Toby Silverman Zinman's "Search and Destroy: The Drama of the Vietnam War."

For studies of film, see Jeremy Devine's *Vietnam at 24 Frames a Second*, Linda Dittmar and Gene Michaud's *From Hanoi to Hollywood: The Vietnam War in American Film*, Gilbert Adair's *Hollywood's Vietnam: From* The Green Berets *to* Full Metal Jacket, and Albert Auster and Leonard Quart's *How the War Was Remembered: Hollywood and Vietnam*. See also Michael Anderegg's *Inventing Vietnam: The War in Film and Television*, the Vietnam chapters of Lawrence Suid's *Guts and Glory: The Making of the American Military Image in Film*, Emmett Early's *The War Veteran in Film*, Marilyn Matelski and Nancy Lynch Street's *War and Film in America: Historical and Critical Essays*, and Robert Eberwein's *The War Film*. Jon Volkmer reads O'Brien against one particular film in "Telling the 'Truth' about Vietnam: Episteme and Narrative Structure in *The Green Berets* and *The Things They Carried*."

Catherine Calloway's "American Literature and Film of the Vietnam War: Classroom Strategies and Critical Sources" remains a thorough, although early, coverage of the field, including many of the cultural interpretations of the war and its legacy. It appears in Gilbert's *The Vietnam War: Teaching Approaches and Resources*, which offers a helpful guide to curriculum development resources and sample syllabi. See also Larry Johannessen's *Illumination Rounds: Teaching the Literature of the Vietnam War* and Ann Kelsey and Anthony Edmonds's *Resources for Teaching the Vietnam War: An Annotated Guide*. A more recent pedagogical essay is Philip Jason's "Coda: Teaching War Literature" in *Acts and Shadows*. The chapter "Learning about the War" in Arnold Isaacs's *Vietnam Shadows: The War, Its Ghosts, and Its Legacy* is a critical discussion of the war's classroom presentation. (The book also contains a bibliographic essay.)

References

General bibliographies are John Newman, David Willson, David DeRose, Stephen Hidalgo, and Nancy Kendall's *Vietnam War Literature: An Annotated Bibliography of Imaginative Works about Americans Fighting in Vietnam*, Carl Singleton's *Vietnam Studies: An Annoted Bibliography*, Lester Brune and Richard Dean Burns's *America and the Indochina Wars, 1945–1990: A Bibliographical Guide*, and Louis Peake's *The United States in the Vietnam War, 1954–1975: A Selected Annotated Bibliography of English-Language Sources*. Also see Philip Jason's *The Vietnam War in Literature: An Annotated Bibliography of Criticism*.

A much shorter and more recent survey is Lucas Carpenter's entry "Vietnam War" in the *Encyclopedia of American War Literature*. The seventy-page chapter "The War in Vietnam" in M. Paul Holsinger's *War and American Popular Culture: A Historical Encyclopedia* offers a hodgepodge of information on films, television shows, songs, and comic books; select people (e.g., Muhammad Ali); events (e.g., teach-ins); and novels and poetry and their creators. Kevin Hillstrom and Laurie Collier Hillstrom have given us *The Vietnam Experience: A Concise Encyclopedia of American Literature, Songs, and Films*, with over fifty entries of more than one page. The entry on O'Brien's *The Things They Carried* is titled "The War in Quang Nai Province." (Another short look at the area of operations in which O'Brien fought is Benjamin Goluboff's "Tim O'Brien's Quang Ngai.")

Beidler's "The Language of the Nam" in *Late Thoughts on an Old War* is a personal essay that could have been subtitled "The Words We Carried." Other useful references are Spencer Tucker's *Encyclopedia of the Vietnam War: A Political, Social, and Military History*; Stanley Kutler's *Encyclopedia of the Vietnam War*; John Bowman's detailed chronology, *The Vietnam War: An Almanac*; James Olson's *Dictionary of the Vietnam War*; Bruce Lockhart and William Duiker's *Historical Dictionary of Vietnam*; Marc Leepson and Helen Hannaford's *Webster's New World Dictionary of the Vietnam War*; Edwin Moïse's *A Historical Dictionary of the Vietnam War*; and Gregory Clark's *Words of the Vietnam War: The Slang, Jargon, Abbreviations, Acronyms, Nomenclature, Nicknames, Pseudonyms, Slogans, Specs, Euphemisms, Double-Talk, Chants, and Names and Places of the Era of United States Involvement in Vietnam*. One respondent recommends the glossary at the back of Eric Hammel's *Khe Sanh: Siege in the Clouds — An Oral History*.

Vietnamese Voices

The book-length memoir from the "other side" that is taught most often is *A Vietcong Memoir: An Inside Account of the Vietnam War and Its Aftermath*, by Truong Nhu Tang, a former minister of justice for the Provisional Revolutionary Government. Other book-length memoirs are the former ambassador Bui Diem's *In the Jaws of History* and Bui Tin's *Following Ho Chi Minh: The Memoirs of a North Vietnamese Colonel*. Bui Tin is also the author of *From Enemy to Friend: A North Vietnamese Perspective on the War*. Jade Ngoc Quang Huynh's *South Wind Changing* tells the story of a young South Vietnamese boy during the war who was later imprisoned by the Communists; he eventually escaped and made his way to America. As Pat Hoy II writes, "Huynh's only crime in Vietnam was that he was an intellectual, a student at the university following the war. . . . We see here no confirmation of the wisdom of our Domino Theory, but we do see what, once upon a time, long ago, our nation believed it was combating" ("Beauty" 185). *Don't Burn*, the diary of Dang Thuy Tram, a Viet Cong doctor, was a sensation in Vietnam when it was published posthumously in 2005; it has since been turned into a film by Dang Nhat Minh and was published in the United States as *Last Night I Dreamed of Peace*. In addition to the Vietnamese perspectives collected in these books, see David Chanoff and Doan Van Toai's *"Vietnam": A Portrait of Its People at War*. See also *Even the*

Women Must Fight: Memories of War from North Vietnam, by Karen Gottschang Turner. Teachers should refer students to the Web site *People's War and Tran Van Tra*, a course study module prepared by Ernest Bolt and Amanda Garrett in 1999 that includes information on and excerpts from Nguyen Tan Thanh, Nguyen Thi Dinh, Tran Van Tra, and Truong Nhu Tang, as well as a section on Vietnamese women in the war.

Memoirs by Vietnamese women include the popular *When Heaven and Earth Changed Places*, by Le Ly Hayslip, a woman who supported the Vietcong against the South Vietnamese army only to be accused by the Vietcong of treason, sentenced to death, and raped before being released. This book and her second memoir, *Child of War, Woman of Peace,* were made into a feature film by Oliver Stone titled *Heaven and Earth*, the final installment of his Vietnam trilogy. A more recent and quite compelling memoir is *Ao Dai: My War, My Country, My Vietnam*, by Xuan Phuong and Danièle Mazingarbe. Phuong lived a life of privilege until 1946, when, at the age of sixteen, as the reviewer Margaret Bodemer wrote, "dressed in her school uniform, a purple *ao dai* or tunic dress . . . she literally and figuratively crossed the river from life as a member of the bourgeois class to join the revolution" against the French—though she remained ambivalent about the Communists (46). That episode alone would be worth having students read against O'Brien's "On the Rainy River." (Phuong later fought against the Americans, lived through the postwar poverty, worked as a documentary filmmaker, and, finally, ran her own art gallery.) Another woman's memoir, Duong Thi Thoa's essay "Changing My Life: How I Came to the Vietnamese Revolution," enjoys a practical classroom length of thirteen pages. Memoirs by two other Vietnamese women are Nguyen Thi Dinh's *No Other Road to Take* and Duong Van Mai Elliott's *The Sacred Willow: Four Generations in the Life of a Vietnamese Family*. Elliott's book brings the family to America. A multigenerational work of fiction also rich in historical perspective and ending in the United States is Uyen Nicole Duong's *Daughters of the River Huong*. Sandra Taylor's history *Vietnamese Women at War: Fighting for Ho Chi Minh and the Revolution* draws heavily on interviews and archived primary sources. The documentary *The Long Haired Warriors,* by Mel Halbach, interviews Vietnamese women who fought in the wars.

Literary anthologies about this era include John Clark Pratt's *Vietnam Voices: Perspectives on the War Years, 1941–1975,* a collection of prose, music, and poetry, and Kevin Bowen, Bruce Weigl, and Nguyen Ba Chung's *Mountain River: Vietnamese Poetry from the Wars, 1948–1993*. One should also be aware of Huynh Sanh Thong's *An Anthology of Vietnamese Poems: From the Eleventh through the Twentieth Centuries* and the dated but still useful *An Introduction to Vietnamese Literature,* by Maurice Durand and Nguyen Tran Huan. In addition, teachers interested in introducing students to the important informing literary tradition should consider *The Tale of Kieu* from 1813, by Nguyen Du; the oral folk poetry that John Balaban collected when he was in Vietnam during the war, *Ca Dao Viet Nam: Vietnamese Folk Poetry*; and Balaban's translations of the provocative eighteenth-century female poet Ho Xuan Huong in *Spring Essence*. Kien Nguyen's two historical novels also take us back—*Le colonial,* to French missionaries in 1773, and *The Tapestries*, to the turn of the twentieth century. (Kien, the child of an American businessman and a Vietnamese woman, grew up in Vietnam and immigrated to the United States a decade after the fall of Saigon. He tells the story in *The Unwanted: A Memoir of Childhood.*)

Le Luu's *A Time Far Past: A Novel of Viet Nam* follows its protagonist from the French military's defeat in 1954 into the 1980s. Andrew X. Pham's nonfiction *The Eaves of Heaven: A Life in Three Wars*, creatively tells his father's story from the 1940s to 1976, just after the end of the country's civil war, though its nonlinear unfolding weaves the family's history into Vietnam's history from the early nineteenth century. Two books reveal prewar Vietnam from the Vietnamese perspective: the 1936 novel *Dumb Luck*, by Vu Trong Phung, and *Red Earth: A Vietnamese Memoir of Life on a Colonial Rubber Plantation*, by Tran Tu Binh. The standard early discussion by an American is Bernard Fall's *The Two Viet-Nams: A Political and Military Analysis*. The French perspective is sometimes demonstrated in class with the epically long film *Indochine*, which one respondent described as "a view of Vietnam from a romanticized, nostalgic French perspective," and Marguerite Duras's two books *The Sea Wall* and *The Lover*, the second of which was made into a film and is unusual for its reversal of the myth. Instead of symbolizing Vietnam as an innocent young woman beloved and "saved" by a Western man (e.g., *The Quiet American*), Duras gives us an innocent young French woman who is seduced by a worldly Chinese man. The works of the Vietnamese writer Son Nam, an adviser for the film production of *The Lover*, have yet to be translated, though the Vietnamese film *Buffalo Boy* is based on three of his stories and, like *The Lover,* is set during the French occupation of the 1940s. The film *The Scent of Green Papaya* follows chronologically, focusing on a Vietnamese orphan from the early 1950s to the early 1960s. Two stories by Nhat Linh, a Hanoi writer during the 1920s and 1930s, are available in translation at the Viet Nam Literature Project Web site: "The Dream of Tu Lam" and "Going to France." Monique Truong's *The Book of Salt* takes us to 1930s Paris by imagining the life of Gertrude Stein and Alice B. Toklas's Vietnamese cook. (Ho Chi Minh makes a cameo appearance in this novel.)

Fall's *Street without Joy: The French Debacle in Indochina* gives an early historical perspective on these fictions. Secondary sources focusing on art and culture of this era include *Phantasmatic Indochina: French Colonial Ideology in Architecture, Film, and Literature*, by Panivong Norindr, which treats the French construction of its colony as the eroticized feminine, and *Vietnamese Voices: Gender and Cultural Identity in the Vietnamese Francophone Novel*, by Nathalie Huynh Chau Nguyen. *Between Sacrifice and Desire: National Identity and the Governing of Femininity in Vietnam*, by Ashley Pettus, explores how postcolonial Vietnam from the 1950s into the 1990s employed constructs of the feminine in the service of cultural unity, and *Imagining Vietnam and America: The Making of Postcolonial Vietnam, 1919–1950*, by Mark Philip Bradley, brings the United States into the process during the colonial era. Among the many works on Vietnamese history are titles that will provide teachers with solid background material for understanding its complexity: Shelton Woods's *Vietnam: An Illustrated History* and three essay collections: Nhung Tuyet Tran and Anthony Reid's *Viet Nam: Borderless Histories*; Hue-Tam Ho Tai's *The Country of Memory: Remaking the Past in Late Socialist Vietnam*; and Van Huy Nguyen and Laurel Kendall's *Vietnam: Journeys of Body, Mind, and Spirit*, about contemporary life.

The Sorrow of War, by Bao Ninh, and *Novel without a Name*, by Duong Thu Huong, a woman who fought for the North Vietnamese, are the two canonical novels, if responses to our survey are representative. In "'Incense and Ashes': The Postmodern Work of Refutation in Three Vietnam War Novels," Steven Liparulo analyzes these texts with *The Things They Carried*. *The Sorrow of War* works as both a trauma text and a metafiction. Derek Maus's essay in this volume discusses teaching *Novel without a Name*; Huong has also written two stirring postwar novels: *Memories of a Pure Spring* and *No Man's Land*. Indications of her books' worth are the Vietnamese government's opposition to their publication and her status as internal exile—she is not allowed to leave the country. Also of note is *The Other Side of Heaven: Post-war Fiction by Vietnamese and American Writers*, edited by Wayne Karlin, Le Minh Khue, and Truong Vu. An early novel of interest is Tran Van Dinh's *Blue Dragon, White Tiger*. Le Minh Khue's *The Stars, the Earth, the River* works quite well in class, as its stories cover the periods before, during, and after the war. Curbstone Press, which published Khue's book, has brought out a number of contemporary Vietnamese texts in English, including another important collection, *Behind the Red Mist*, by Ho Anh Thai, and the anthology *Love after War: Contemporary Fiction from Viet Nam*, edited by Wayne Karlin and Ho Anh Thai. Kevin Bowen and Nguyen Ba Chung edited and translated contemporary poetry in *Six Vietnamese Poets*. Linh Dinh published the shorter *Night, Again: Contemporary Fiction from Vietnam* in addition to his own story and poetry collections—his *Fake House* sets its postwar stories in both Vietnam and America. Three noteworthy Vietnamese films about contemporary life are *Cyclo*, *The Vertical Ray of the Sun*, and *Three Seasons*, which includes a United States veteran of the war searching for the daughter he left behind. *Cyclo*, an urban jungle film set in Hanoi, places the war as the shaping background, even though its characters rarely admit it. *The Vertical Ray of the Sun* contrasts traditional Hanoi, "western" Ho Chi Minh City (Saigon), and a bucolic coastal bay.

The war displaced thousands of Vietnamese, many of whom came to reside permanently in the United States. Numerous works provide insight into the life of Vietnamese Americans, or "Vietnamerica." The major anthology, the first resource here, is *Watermark: Vietnamese American Poetry and Prose* (1998), edited by Barbara Tran, Monique Truong, and Luu Truong Khoi. Lan Cao's *Monkey Bridge*, a novel of a Vietnamese girl's assimilation into American life, has become the most recognized diaspora novel. Le Thi Diem Thuy's *The Gangster We Are All Looking For* tells the story of a refugee family, and though the book is identified as a novel on the cover, portions of it were previously published as nonfiction. The novel *Grass Roof, Tin Roof* and the story collection *The Gentle Order of Girls and Boys*, both by the Vietnamese American writer Dao Strom, can be supplemented in class with some of her music. T. C. Huo has written two novels about young American immigrants from Southeast Asia, *A Thousand Wings*, with a gay male protagonist, and *Land of Smiles*. A gay Vietnamese American poet, Truong Tran, has published two volumes: *Placing the Accents* and *Dust and Conscience*. Not all the short stories in Nam Le's *The Boat* feature the Vietnamese American experience, so that the book expresses a tension, a pushing and pulling, of this aspect of the author's identity.

Andrew Lam's essay collection *Perfume Dreams: Reflections on the Vietnamese Diaspora* and his several as-yet-uncollected short stories give insight into the generation that was born in Vietnam and transplanted to the United States as children. Lam is one of the talking heads in the documentary *Saigon, U.S.A.*, a fine examination of generational differences among Vietnamese Americans, as well as the focus of *My Journey Home*, a documentary about his return visit to Vietnam. He was also one of the coeditors of the San Jose Mercury News's *Once upon a Dream . . . : The Vietnamese-American Experience*. The film *American Experience: Daughter from Danang* recounts a woman's troublesome journey back to Vietnam.

Andrew X. Pham writes of his travels from the United States to Vietnam in *Catfish and Mandala: A Two-Wheeled Voyage through the Landscape and Memory of Vietnam*. The protagonist of the film *The Beautiful Country* travels from Vietnam to the United States with a woman who becomes yet another version of Kieu, the Vietnamese heroine who suffers for her beauty and whose pain and survival are held by many Vietnamese to be emblematic of their country. Quang X. Pham's *A Sense of Duty: My Father, My American Journey* tells the story of a refugee, the son of a South Vietnamese air force fighter pilot, who grew up and fought as a helicopter pilot for the United States Marines in the Gulf War. See also James Freeman's *Hearts of Sorrow: Vietnamese-American Lives*, Paul James Rutledge's *The Vietnamese Experience in America*, Jane Bradley Winston and Leakthina Chau-Pech Ollier's *Of Vietnam: Identities in Dialogue*, and Shirley Geok-lin Lim and Cheng Lok Chua's *Tilting the Continent: Southeast Asian American Writing*.

Philip Jason's survey "Vietnamese in America," which also appears as chapter 6 of *Acts and Shadows*, examines American writers' novelistic representations of Vietnamese refugees in America and addresses the question of authority for any non-Vietnamese writer who attempts to tell the refugees' story. Renny Christopher's *The Viet Nam War / The American War: Images and Representations in Euro-American and Vietnamese Exile Narratives* includes an attack on O'Brien for ethnocentrism and solipsism; one respondent uses it for generating class discussion. Critiques of O'Brien for failing to convey a Vietnamese per-spective can be considered in relation to non-Vietnamese writers who presump-tively—according to some readers—give voice to Vietnamese characters. In this vein, Robert Olen Butler's Pulitzer-winning collection *A Good Scent from a Strange Mountain* works nicely with O'Brien's *The Things They Carried* or even *July, July*.

Postwar Lives and Legacies

All war stories by veterans and witnesses are, in fact, postwar stories, even when set entirely during the war; many of the books regularly taught in courses on war literature focus on, or are framed by, the veteran's memories. One anthology emphasizes the American postwar experience: *Aftermath: An Anthology of Post-Vietnam Fiction*, edited by Donald Anderson. A survey respondent sug-gested the special issue of *Granta* that was published in March 1985, on the tenth anniversary of the fall of Saigon. Edited by James Fenton, it presents a way of looking at how the war's legacy was being constructed. Maxine Hong Kingston's important and timely *Veterans of War, Veterans of Peace* collects nar-ratives written in workshops she conducted, narratives from veterans and civil-ians profoundly affected by Vietnam and other wars.

Mark Heberle's *A Trauma Artist* is the primary authority for examining O'Brien's work in terms of post-traumatic stress disorder. Read Heberle's essay in this volume to see how he incorporates his research into the classroom. Essays on trauma in O'Brien's writing include David Jarraway's "'Excremental Assault' in Tim O'Brien: Trauma and Recovery in Vietnam War Literature," Timothy Melley's "Postmodern Amnesia: Trauma and Forgetting in Tim O'Brien's *In the Lake of the Woods*," Brad Lucas's "Traumatic Narrative, Narrative Genre, and the Exigencies of Memory," and Brian Jarvis's "Skating on a Shit Field: Tim O'Brien and the Topography of Trauma." Book-length works focusing on trauma and the Vietnam War are Jonathan Shay's *Achilles in Vietnam: Combat Trauma and the Undoing of Character* and Hebert Hendin and Ann Pollinger Haas's *Wounds of War: The Psychological Aftermath of Combat in Vietnam*. For an essay-length introduction to the topic, see Kalí Tal's "Speaking the Language of Pain: Vietnam War Literature in the Context of a Literature of Trauma." But as Jeremy Green in his essay in this book wisely reminds us:

> Notions of post-traumatic stress disorder, disseminated to the point of cliché, are both germane and curiously unhelpful. There is a danger in the discussion of literary texts, particularly in the classroom, that psychologi-cal models of explanation can displace close reading to the point where the text becomes illustrative of or ancillary to the categories and terms of abnormal psychology.

Mindful of this risk, we can nevertheless productively pursue with our students investigations into the relation between trauma and literary expression, as Green himself does with *In the Lake of the Woods*.

Kalí Tal is also the author of an essential text on expressions of trauma in literature, *Worlds of Hurt: Reading the Literatures of Trauma*. Other recommended studies of trauma are Judith Herman's *Trauma and Recovery: The Aftermath of Violence*, Cathy Caruth's *Trauma: Explorations in Memory* and *Unclaimed Experience: Trauma, Narrative, and History*, Laurie Vickroy's *Trauma and Survival in Contemporary Fiction*, Ruth Leys's *Trauma: A Genealogy*, and Sigmund Freud's *Beyond the Pleasure Principle*. See also Ben Shephard's *A War of Nerves: Soldiers and Psychiatrists in the Twentieth Century*. For the more theoretically inclined, there is Elaine Scarry's *The Body in Pain: The Making and Unmaking of the World*.

One survey respondent teaches the course Literature, Memory, Trauma, which studies O'Brien alongside Primo Levi's *Survival in Auschwitz*, Pat Barker's *Regeneration*, Toni Morrison's *Beloved*, Robert Graves's "Recalling War," Siegfried Sassoon's "Repression of War Experience," Wilfred Owen's "Dulce et Decorum Est," Elizabeth Bishop's "In the Waiting Room," and Dori Laub's essay "Bearing Witness or the Vicissitudes of Listening." Other trauma texts taught by respondents and not elsewhere mentioned include Irena Klepfisz's "Bashert"; Primo Levi, Marco Belpoliti, and Robert Gordon's *Voices of Memory*; Sylvia Plath's "Daddy"; Paul Celan's "Todesfuge"; and Elie Wiesel's *Night*.

Jeremy Green teaches *In the Lake of the Woods* with Toni Morrison's *Beloved* and *Paradise* and Cormac McCarthy's *Blood Meridian* to explore how contemporary American literature expresses repressed historical traumas and their return. In the context of O'Brien's representation of My Lai, Green asks students to research cultural histories of the American frontier, "from Frederick Jackson Turner to Richard Slotkin's *Gunfighter Nation*." (See the chapter "The Frontier War" in Milton Bates's *The Wars We Took to Vietnam: Cultural Conflict and Storytelling*.) Brenda Boyle, another contributor, offers a unit on history and memory that supplements examinations of literary texts with such short pieces as Toni Morrison's "Memory, Creation, and Writing," Pierra Nora's "Between Memory and History," Joan Scott's "The Evidence of Experience," selections from Jerry Lembcke's *The Spitting Image: Myth, Memory, and the Legacy of Vietnam*, Paul Connerton's *How Societies Remember*, Daniel Schacter's *Searching for Memory: The Brain, the Mind, and the Past*, and Martin Evans and Ken Lunn's *War and Memory in the Twentieth Century*.

Examining media distortions of war also complicates what O'Brien refers to as "happening-truth." See Rob Kroes's "Mediated History: The Vietnam War as a Media Event" in *If You've Seen One, You've Seen the Mall*; another survey participant suggests analysis of media coverage of the Gulf. Derek Maus, a survey participant and contributor, suggests comparing the useful distortion of facts leading to the Gulf of Tonkin Resolution with Rat Kiley's useful distortion of facts in his storytelling; one is reminded of John D'Agata's use of classical rhetoric in defending the slippery nature of veracity in memoir:

> Cicero, nonfiction's first true master, discussed in several letters that were later published publicly how he and his contemporaries frequently invented facts in their senatorial speeches — speeches that we have since inherited as the foundation of literary nonfiction. "As I see it, it is the strength of the argument that matters most," Cicero wrote to his friend Atticus, and then to the larger world, "not the precision of its evidence."
> ("Joan Didion's Formal Experiment" 10)

Is there a difference between fudging facts for literary effect and for casus belli? Less morally problematic is John Huston's 1944 documentary *Let There Be Light*, about a nine-week in-patient transition program for emotionally troubled soldiers returning from World War II, which is so hammy that it bothers today's expectations of objectivity and nonfiction authenticity in documentary. It serves the classroom by opening discussion about the historical development of our understanding of trauma, about the nature of wartime and postwar propaganda (Who is the audience? Whom is the film attempting to placate?), and about the genre's tradition of blurring the line between fiction and nonfiction (a topic dear to O'Brien's readers). A provocative discussion on this tradition is Louis Menand's *New Yorker* essay-review of Michael Moore's film *Fahrenheit 9/11*.

Individual and collective memories of, responses to, and recovery from events like war inform one another. Just as a writer's story is shaped by the myths, ideologies, and legacies of the war (pick your term), it also interprets them and creates its own versions of the larger story, versions informed as much by the era of its writing as by the era of its setting. As Heberle has observed in *A Trauma Artist*, O'Brien's memoir *If I Die in a Combat Zone* might well have been a far different book had it been written a decade later, after some of the myths of the war had taken root. Nonfiction studies of the war's legacy bear the same complications. Rather than passively transmit discovered cultural truths, they interpret and create meaning, a process that is influenced by the circumstances of the study's production. As De Groot has commented about Loren Barritz's *Backfire: A History of How American Culture Led Us into Vietnam and Made Us Fight the Way We Did*, "[T]he book ultimately reveals that there are few scholars who are adept at both military and cultural history" (qtd. in McNay). As the subtitle of Marita Sturken's *Tangled Memories: The Vietnam War, the AIDS Epidemic, and the Politics of Remembering* reminds us, even memory is political.

Some of the other books that play the tricky, fascinating game of interpreting the Vietnam War's cultural significances are Myra MacPherson's *Long Time Passing: Vietnam and the Haunted Generation*; John Hellman's *American Myth and the Legacy of Vietnam*; Fred Turner's *Echoes of Combat: The Vietnam War in American Memory*; Philip West, Steven Levine, and Jackie Hiltz's *America's*

Wars in Asia: A Cultural Approach to History and Memory; John Carlos Rowe and Rick Berg's *The Vietnam War and American Culture*; H. Bruce Franklin's *M.I.A.; or, Mythmaking in America*; Alf Louvre and Jeffrey Walsh's *Tell Me Lies about Vietnam: Cultural Battles for the Meaning of the War*; Andrew Martin's *Receptions of War: Vietnam in American Culture*; and Jeffrey Walsh and James Aulich's *Vietnam Images: War and Representation*. Philip Beidler provides an early essay-length discussion in "Re-writing America: Literature as Cultural Revision in the New Vietnam Fiction."

Women and Gender

Of the memoirs written by women, *Home before Morning: The Story of an Army Nurse in Vietnam*, by Lynda Van Devanter, is taught most often. In addition, Lynda Van Devanter has compiled, with Joan Furey, the anthology *Visions of War, Dreams of Peace: Writings of Women in the Vietnam War*. Four other collections are Keith Walker's *A Piece of My Heart: The Stories of Twenty-Six American Women Who Served in Vietnam*, Dan Freedman and Jacqueline Rhoads's *Nurses in Vietnam: The Forgotten Veterans*, Kathryn Marshall's *In the Combat Zone: Vivid Personal Recollections of the Vietnam War from the Women Who Served There*, and Elizabeth Norman's *Women at War: The Story of Fifty Military Nurses Who Served in Vietnam*. Also of interest is *War Torn: Stories of War from the Women Reporters Who Covered Vietnam*, by Tad Bartimas and eight other writers. Similar experiences are turned into a history in Virginia Elwood-Akers's *Women War Correspondents in the Vietnam War, 1961–1975*.

Two relatively recent books by nurses who served in the war have not yet made it to the classrooms of our respondents, but they must be noted: Mary Reynolds Powell's memoir, *A World of Hurt: Between Innocence and Arrogance in Vietnam*, and Susan O'Neill's *Don't Mean Nothing: Short Stories of Vietnam*. Then there is Lady Borton, who worked in a hospital for Vietnamese civilians in Quang Ngai Province during the time that O'Brien was there, 1969–71, and who has written two memoirs: *Sensing the Enemy: An American Woman among the Boat People of Vietnam* and *After Sorrow: An American among the Vietnamese*. Several of Borton's poems, including "A Boom, a Billow," "Row upon Endless Row," and "Walking Class," appear in Van Devanter and Furey's anthology. Nor should we forget accounts by soldiers' wives. Bettina Hofman's essay "On the Battlefield and Home Front: American Women Writing Their Lives on the Vietnam War" analyzes Van Devanter's memoir with two other memoirs: *Lonely Girls with Burning Eyes*, by Marian Faye Novak, a Marine officer's wife, and *In Love and War*, cowritten by a former prisoner of war and his wife, Jim and Sybil Stockdale.

The four novels written by women and taught by our respondents are Bobbie Ann Mason's *In Country*, Susan Fromberg Schaeffer's *Buffalo Afternoon*, Danielle Steel's *Message from Nam*, and Sigrid Nunez's *For Rouenna*. Another story collection to be considered is Diana Dell's *"A Saigon Party" and Other Vietnam War Short Stories*.

An essay by a male veteran that works nicely with O'Brien's fiction, especially "How to Tell a True War Story," is William Broyles's "Why Men Love War." One respondent contrasts O'Brien's work with the "more sexually charged, masculinist prose" of Larry Heinemann's *Paco's Story*—which, like *Going After Cacciato*, won the National Book Award. William Eastlake's *The Bamboo Bed* is another highly sexualized novel, written during the height of the war by a World War II veteran. Three other texts our respondents mentioned are Chinua Achebe's *"Girls at War" and Other Stories*; Charlotte Perkins Gilman's "The Yellow Wall-paper," written in 1892; and Jamaica Kincaid's "Girl," which one respondent teaches with "The Things They Carried" to describe the burdens young women bear. One might also consider teaching a story from the Spanish Civil War about women combatants, Ralph Bates's "Brunete Ballad," which Ernest Hemingway rejected for his 1942 anthology *Men at War* for being implausible, and the memoir of a woman from the Iraq war, *Love My Rifle More than You: Young and Female in the U.S. Army*, by Kayla Williams. (For this war, see pages 47–48 as well as the essays by Vernon and Perel.)

For general, accessible essay-length discussions of gender issues in the literature of the Vietnam War, see Milton Bates's "Men, Women, and Vietnam"; Lorrie Goldensohn's "Men and Women and Women"; Philip Jason's "Sexism and Racism in Vietnam War Fiction" in *Acts and Shadows*; Katherine Kinney's "Humping the Boonies: Women and the Memory of War" in *Friendly Fire*; Jacqueline Lawson's "'She's a Pretty Woman . . . for a Gook': The Misogyny of the Vietnam War"; Lorrie Smith's "Back against the Wall: Anti-feminist Backlash in Vietnam War Literature"; Carol Acton's "Diverting the Gaze: The Unseen Text in Women's War Writing"; and Kalí Tal's "The Mind at War: Images of Women in Vietnam Novels by Combat Veterans." The bibliographic guide is Deborah Butler's *American Women Writers on Vietnam: Unheard Voices*. Several respondents also assign selections from Susan Jeffords's *The Remasculinization of America: Gender and the Vietnam War*. See also Cynthia Enloe's *Does Khaki Become You? The Militarization of Women's Lives*, Carol Burke's *Camp All-American, Hanoi Jane, and the High-and-Tight: Gender, Folklore, and Changing Military Culture*, Shelley Saywell's *Women in War: First-Hand Accounts from World War II to El Salvador*, Major General Jeanne Holm's *Women in the Military: An Unfinished Revolution*, Vicki Friedl's *Women in the United States Military, 1901–1995: A Research Guide and Annotated Bibliography*, and Susan Brownmiller's *Against Our Will: Men, Women, and Rape*.

Several survey participants remarked that the issue of gender in O'Brien's works leads to some of the liveliest and most sustained class discussion and some of the most interesting student writing. Lorrie Smith's "'The Things Men Do': The Gendered Subtext in Tim O'Brien's *Esquire* Stories"—stories that became part of *The Things They Carried*—is the favorite critical essay to assign students, and many libraries use databases that make it available online.

Much of the essay concerns O'Brien's story "Sweetheart of the Song Tra Bong" and how it provocatively raises the issue of gender difference. As O'Brien has often said, he wanted the story to propose that women and men can be equally bellicose and brutal. More recently, images of female United States soldiers participating in the abuses at Abu Ghraib, Iraq, provided fodder for classroom conversation. Consider reading O'Brien's imagined naturally militant Mary Anne against the women in the ranks in Iraq, using texts such as the documentary film *Lioness*; the essay collection *One of the Guys: Women as Aggressors and Torturers*, edited by Tara McKelvey; or Coco Fusco's creative nonfictional *A Field Guide for Female Interrogators*. One might productively contrast "Sweetheart of the Song Tra Bong" with O'Brien's early "Claudia Mae's Wedding Day," in which the soldier withholds all information about the war from his sweetheart back home. Other critical discussions of "Sweetheart of the Song Tra Bong" are Elisabeth Piedmont-Marton's essay in this volume, the section in Kinney's *Friendly Fire* (150–56), and Terry Martin and Margaret Stiner's "'Sweetheart of the Song Tra Bong': Tim O'Brien's (Feminist?) *Heart of Darkness*." (While O'Brien's rewriting of Joseph Conrad's novella is commonly discussed, one respondent instead compared *Heart of Darkness* with *Going After Cacciato*.) Alex Vernon's chapter "O'Brien's War, O'Brien's Women" in *Soldiers Once and Still* focuses on the story as well. One should also look at Susan Farrell's "Tim O'Brien and Gender: A Defense of *The Things They Carried*," Pamela Smiley's "The Role of the Ideal (Female) Reader in Tim O'Brien's *The Things They Carried*: Why Should Real Women Play?," and Tina Chen's "'Unraveling the Deeper Meaning': Exile and the Embodied Poetics of Displacement in Tim O'Brien's *The Things They Carried*."

One survey participant has studied "Sweetheart of the Song Tra Bong" in a class on American literature and the environment, in the unit on gender and nature. His students compared it with other tales of women who disappear into the land—namely, Margaret Atwood's *Surfacing* and "Death by Landscape" and Margaret Fuller's 1841 story "Leila." (The students have previously worked through ecofeminist readings about the cultural association of women with nature; see also Lee Schweninger's "Ecofeminism, Nuclearism, and O'Brien's *The Nuclear Age*" and Jacqueline Foertsch's "Not Bombshells but Basketcases: Gendered Illness in Nuclear Texts.")

A woman also disappears into the landscape in *In the Lake of the Woods*. Critical discussions of gender hostility in this novel include William Young's "Missing in Action: Vietnam and Sadism in Tim O'Brien's *In the Lake of the Woods*" and the review of the novel by Pat Hoy II.

The Cold War, the 1960s, and Postmodernism

For many students of the era, its foundational condition was the cold war, with its threats of mutually assured destruction and governmental intrusion and conspiracy. In addition to the numerous sources described by Doug Davis in his essay in this volume on teaching O'Brien's *The Nuclear Age*, another respondent who teaches the literature of the cold war uses Kurt Vonnegut's *Cat's Cradle*, Walter Miller's *A Canticle for Leibowitz*, and Pat Frank's *Alas, Babylon*. For background he has his students read excerpts from H. W. Brands's *The Devil We Knew: Americans and the Cold War*, Margot Henriksen's *Dr. Strangelove's America: Society and Culture in the Atomic Age*, and Stephen Whitfield's *The Culture of the Cold War*. They also watch *The Manchurian Candidate*, *Dr. Strangelove*, and *Wargames* and read Arthur Miller's *The Crucible* and Leslie Marmon Silko's *Ceremony*.

Several respondents teach O'Brien and the Vietnam War in the context of the social upheaval of the 1960s—see, for example, the Web site *The Sixties Project*. For some, O'Brien's (and his characters') decision to submit to the draft becomes an occasion to debate the demands placed on a democratic citizenship. One respondent pairs O'Brien's "On the Rainy River" with Thoreau's *Civil Disobedience*, because the O'Brien story "complicates and illuminates Thoreau's ideas about resistance to government by considering the consequences of compliance and resistance." O'Brien's later story "Winnipeg," about a man who flees from the draft to Canada, could be added to this discussion. Another respondent uses "Letter from a Birmingham Jail," by Martin Luther King, Jr., as well as essays by William Mahedy (*Out of the Night: The Spiritual Journey of Vietnam Vets*), Erich Fromm (*The Essential Fromm: Life between Having and Being*), Haig Bosmajian (*Freedom Not to Speak*), and J. William Fulbright (*The Vietnam Hearings*). The many writings of Daniel Berrigan (e.g., *The Trial of the Catonsville Nine*) would also fit such a course.

One survey participant uses Susan Sontag's *Trip to Hanoi*, and another teaches a unit on morality that groups *The Things They Carried* with Vonnegut's *Cat's Cradle*, Maxine Kumin's "Woodchucks," Carolyn Forché's "The Colonel," Randall Jarrell's "The Death of the Ball Turret Gunner," Wilfred Owen's "Dulce et Decorum Est," Michael Harper's "Debridement," David Foster Wallace's "Lyndon," and John Balaban's "Story." Another teacher juxtaposes *Going After Cacciato* with Joan Didion's *Democracy*, while still another uses selections from Fredric Jameson's *The Political Unconscious: Narrative as a Socially Symbolic Act*. See also Agnieszka Salka's "Re-visioning the Democratic Imagination: Tim O'Brien's Vietnam Fiction."

An excellent study of the cultural conditions surrounding the war is Milton Bates's *The Wars We Took to Vietnam*, with its chapters "The Frontier War," "The Race War," "The Class War," and "The Generation War." Michael Bibby's *Hearts and Minds*, a study of the era's poetry, has chapters on the struggles of blacks and women in America. Also consider using Sara Evans's "Sources of the Second Wave: The Rebirth of Feminism" in *Tidal Wave: How Women Changed America at Century's End*, Clyde Taylor's "Black Consciousness in the Vietnam Years," and an excerpt from Christian Appy's *Working-Class War: American Combat Soldiers and Vietnam*. A contemporary essay on the war's class gap recommended by another survey respondent is James Fallows's "What Did You

Do in the Class War, Daddy?," a narrative of a bus trip with Harvard students who successfully dodged the draft.

One respondent lists as helpful Terry Anderson's *The Movement and the Sixties: Protest in America from Greensboro to Wounded Knee* and Alexander Bloom and Wini Brienes's primary-document collection *"Takin' It to the Streets": A Sixties Reader*, and he uses Appy's statistics about the average age of United States soldiers in Vietnam — nineteen — when analyzing the characters of *The Things They Carried*. Another survey participant likes Appy's book for its examination of "both the mechanism of the draft and the experience of veterans" in "explicating the pressures on the characters in O'Brien's fiction and the fraught relationship between the personal and the political." For teachers, these respondents recommend David Farber's *The Sixties: From Memory to History* and direct our attention in particular to the essays "Sexual Revolutions," by Beth Bailey, and "The Politics of Civility," by Kenneth Cmiel.

Considering this era the main moment of postmodernism, one respondent finds Phillip Brian Harper's *Framing the Margins: The Social Logic of Postmodern Culture* a good resource on the social dynamics and John Carlos Rowe's essay "Postmodernist Studies" a good argument for locating the Vietnam War at the heart of postmodern culture. The most thorough discussion of this topic is Michael Bibby's edited essay collection *The Vietnam War and Postmodernity*. Alex Vernon's *Soldiers Once and Still: Ernest Hemingway, James Salter, and Tim O'Brien* challenges presumptive characterizations of either the Vietnam War or Tim O'Brien's writing as postmodern (4–18, 53–62). Teachers might have success engaging students in a debate about the postmodern label frequently attached to *In the Lake of the Woods* by using the contentions made by Jeremy Green, Christopher Kocela, and Jennifer Peterson in this book.

For many scholars, novels like *Going After Cacciato*, *The Things They Carried*, and *In the Lake of the Woods* are indisputably postmodern. Several early commentators remarked on the magic realism of *Going After Cacciato* as a postmodern trait, though O'Brien's repeated insistence that the novel is a realistic depiction of a daydream — and his turn to metafiction in his later two Vietnam novels (*The Things They Carried* and *In the Lake of the Woods*) — has somewhat muted that conversation. Catherine Calloway's "'How to Tell a True War Story': Metafiction in *The Things They Carried*" never uses the term *postmodern*, but its discussion of metafiction clearly points in that direction; see also John Clark Pratt's "Tim O'Brien's Reimagination of Reality: An Exercise in Metafiction." Michael Kaufmann's "The Solace of Bad Form: Tim O'Brien's Postmodernist Revisions of Vietnam in 'Speaking of Courage'" contrasts the postmodern example of this story with the modernist practice of Hemingway. Lucas Carpenter's "'It Don't Mean Nothin': Vietnam War Fiction and Postmodernism" reads O'Brien with Stephen Wright's *Meditations in Green* and Michael Herr's *Dispatches*. See also the portions on O'Brien in Christopher Donovan's *Postmodern Counternarratives: Irony and Audience in the Narratives of Paul Auster, Don DeLillo, Charles Johnson, and Tim O'Brien*.

Additional student-friendly discussions of postmodernism, beyond the short definitions in various reference sources (such as the *Encyclopedia of American Studies*), can be found in the introduction to Paula Geyh, Fred Leebron, and Andrew Levy's *Postmodern American Fiction: A Norton Anthology*, Derek Maus's *Readings on Postmodernism*, and Lois Tyson's *Critical Theory Today: A User-Friendly Guide*. Respondents also mentioned several other studies in particular relation to O'Brien, many of which are rather dense primary theoretical texts: Hayden White's "The Question of Narrative in Contemporary Historical Theory" and "Storytelling: Historical and Ideological"; Hans Kellner's *Language and Historical Representation: Getting the Story Crooked*; Jane Flax's "Postmodernism and Gender Relations in Feminist Theory"; Brian McHale's *Postmodernist Fiction* and *Constructing Postmodernism*; Michel Foucault's *The Archaeology of Knowledge and the Discourse on Language*; Fredric Jameson's *Postmodernism; or, The Cultural Logic of Late Capitalism*; Linda Hutcheon's *A Poetics of Postmodernism: History, Theory, Fiction* — in particular, chapter 7, "Historiographic Metafiction"; Slavoj Žižek's *The Sublime Object of Ideology* and *Tarrying with the Negative: Kant, Hegel, and the Critique of Ideology*; John Barth's "The Literature of Exhaustion" and "The Literature of Replenishment"; Jean-François Lyotard's "What Is Postmodernism?" from *The Postmodern Condition: A Report on Knowledge*; and Catherine Belsey's *Poststructuralism: A Very Short Introduction* and *Critical Practice*.

The literary texts most often taught with O'Brien in terms of postmodernism are Norman Mailer's *Armies of the Night* and Joan Didion's *Democracy*, in order, as one survey participant remarks, "to discuss authorial intrusion and self-aware textuality in postmodernism." Other mentioned texts are Jack Kerouac's *On the Road*; Nathanael West's *Miss Lonelyhearts*; E. L. Doctorow's "The Writer in the Family"; Grace Paley's "A Conversation with My Father"; Maxine Hong Kingston's "No Name Woman"; Leslie Marmon Silko's *Storyteller*; Hisaye Yamamoto's "Seventeen Syllables"; Alice Walker's "Everyday Use"; Margaret Atwood's "Happy Endings"; John Edgar Wideman's *Philadelphia Fire*; Robert Coover's "The Babysitter"; Ishmael Reed's *Yellow Back Radio Broke-Down*; Thomas Pynchon's *The Crying of Lot 49* and "The Secret Integration"; John Barth's *Lost in the Funhouse* (particularly, "Life-Story"); Joyce Carol Oates's "The Turn of the Screw"; Don DeLillo's *White Noise*; Louise Erdrich's *Tracks*; Toni Morrison's "Recitatif," *Sula*, and "Unspeakable Things Unspoken"; Kathy Acker's *Great Expectations*; and Kurt Vonnegut's *Bluebeard*.

Other War Literature

Two major editions of war literature are John Keegan's *The Book of War* and Paul Fussell's *The Norton Book of Modern War*. A shorter, more affordable anthology is Sebastian Faulks's *The Vintage Book of War Stories*. The chief anthology of poetry has already been mentioned, Lorrie Goldensohn's *American*

War Poetry. Hemingway's *Men at War*, though dated, is a significant text in the history of war literature (the introduction alone is worthwhile). Jeffrey Fischer's "Killing at Close Range: A Study in Intertextuality" is a pedagogical piece on teaching O'Brien's "The Man I Killed" with chapter 9 from Erich Maria Remarque's *All Quiet on the Western Front* and Thomas Hardy's poem "The Man He Killed."

The chief Civil War works taught and studied with O'Brien are the obvious ones: Ambrose Bierce's *Tales of Soldiers and Civilians*, especially "Occurrence at Owl Creek Bridge," and Stephen Crane's *The Red Badge of Courage*, "The Veteran," "The Little Regiment," and select poems. See also Christopher Campbell's "Conversation across a Century: The War Stories of Ambrose Bierce and Tim O'Brien." For a good poetry anthology, we suggest the Library of America's *Poets of the Civil War*, edited by J. D. McClatchy.

The recommended literature from World War I also consists of many familiar works: John Dos Passos's *Three Soldiers*, E. E. Cummings's surrealistic *The Enormous Room*, Remarque's *All Quiet on the Western Front* (in both the print and the screen versions), the film *Gallipoli*, Pat Barker's *Regeneration*, Dalton Trumbo's *Johnny Got His Gun* (both the novel and the film), Herbert Asquith's poem "The Volunteer," the famous war poems of Rupert Brooke, Siegfried Sassoon, and Wilfred Owen, and, of course, the work of Hemingway. *In Our Time* ("Soldier's Home" and "Big Two-Hearted River") and *The Sun Also Rises* speak to postwar life and trauma. *In Our Time* works quite well with *The Things They Carried* as metafictional story collections if we treat Nick Adams as the author of the tales, some of which include a character named Nick Adams. (The chief evidence for the Nick-as-author reading is the excised ending of "Big-Two Hearted River" published in *The Nick Adams Stories*; see Debra Moddelmog's "The Unifying Consciousness of a Divided Conscience: Nick Adams as Author of *In Our Time*.") Some teachers (as well as some published criticism) group an O'Brien text with *A Farewell to Arms* and *The Red Badge of Courage* to address issues of courage—see Tobey Herzog's essay in this volume, as well as Milton Bates's "Tim O'Brien's Myth of Courage," Carl Horner's "Challenging the Law of Courage and Heroic Identification in Tim O'Brien's *If I Die in a Combat Zone* and *The Things They Carried*," James Hughes's *Fear and Courage in Tim O'Brien's* If I Die in a Combat Zone, Going After Cacciato, *and* The Things They Carried, and the two essays placing O'Brien in a classical tradition cited previously: Christopher Michael McDonough's "'Afraid to Admit We Are Not Achilles': Facing Hector's Dilemma in Tim O'Brien's *The Things They Carried*" and Thomas Palaima's "Courage and Prowess Afoot in Homer and the Vietnam of Tim O'Brien."

One survey respondent teaches a seminar on Hemingway and O'Brien to

demonstrate how conversations in *A Farewell to Arms* resemble some in O'Brien's works, how style in *Lake of the Woods* appears to model Hemingway's clipped sentence, how the use of the baby water buffalo story resembles Hemingway's use of bullfighting in *In Our Time* as a metaphor for war, how in both *A Farewell to Arms* and [*The Things They Carried*] the love story subsumes the war story or becomes yet another metaphor for talking about war.

Another respondent teaches Hemingway's "A Natural History of the Dead" with O'Brien's "The Man I Killed" as "examples of how writers deal with the inclusion of graphic violence in their writing about war." Zivah Perel, both a survey participant and a contributor to this volume, teaches *The Things They Carried* in a unit on literature about death alongside Emily Dickinson's "Because I could not stop for Death" and "I heard a fly buzz when I died," Don DeLillo's story "Videotape," and Gabriel García Márquez's "The Handsomest Drowned Man in the World." Works of fiction by women about World War I that are sometimes taught in conjunction with the "male" texts are Katherine Anne Porter's "Pale Horse, Pale Rider" and Edith Wharton's *One of Ours*.

As Perel notes in her essay, the literature of World War II poses a challenge for teachers in that many of the major texts are rather long. The book mentioned most often by respondents is Joseph Heller's *Catch-22*; as John Clark Pratt argues in "Yossarian's Legacy: *Catch-22* and the Vietnam War," Heller's novel "should properly be seen as a paradigm for the Vietnam War itself" (89). The other frequently taught darkly comic text about the war fought by the "greatest generation" is *Slaughterhouse-Five*. Published in 1969 and peppered with references to Vietnam, Kurt Vonnegut's novel can be read as Vietnam protest literature. Both it and *The Things They Carried* include metafictional reflections, a veteran's struggle to defy time and mortality, significant scenes of human excrement, and peculiar allusions to Christianity (see David Jarraway's "'Excremental Assault' in Tim O'Brien" and Alex Vernon's "Salvation, Storytelling, and Pilgrimage in *The Things They Carried*").

One respondent observes that the cast of *The Things They Carried* rehashes the diversity of characters standard in literary representations of platoon-sized units since World War II and so provides a familiarity disrupted by the presence of Mary Anne in "Sweetheart." That standard can be demonstrated in class with the refreshingly short novel *A Walk in the Sun*, by Harry Brown, its film version or a film like *The Dirty Dozen*, and the more contemporary *Saving Private Ryan*, along with, of course, Vietnam films like *Platoon*. One might use John Horne Burns's *The Gallery* as a subversive use of this convention and also as a challenge to the linking of fragmented postmodern narratives chiefly to books from the war in Vietnam.

Other World War II texts taught by survey participants are Bruno Bettelheim's "Returning to Dachau"; Paul Fussell's "My War: How I Got Irony in the Infantry," in *The Boy Scout Handbook and Other Observations*, "Thank God for The Atom Bomb," in *"Thank God for the Atom Bomb" and Other Stories*, and *Wartime*; Leslie Marmon Silko's *Ceremony*; Martha Gellhorn's *The Point of No Return*; Thomas Pynchon's *Gravity's Rainbow*; and James McBride's *Miracle at*

St. Anna. Respondents also recommend the Holocaust film *Shoah*, the conventionally heroic film *Sands of Iwo Jima,* and the postwar film *The Best Years of Our Lives.* Poetry from World War II is not as canonical as that from World War I, or even as that from Vietnam, though interested students and teachers should see the relevant sections in Goldensohn's anthology and in her companion study and in Harvey Shapiro's anthology *Poets of World War II.* Kalidas Misra places O'Brien and Herr in the literary context of Mailer, Heller, and Vonnegut in "The American War Novel from World War II to Vietnam." For a survey of issues and critical discussions, see "Reading Twentieth-Century American War Literature" in Vernon's *Soldiers Once and Still* (29–62). See also Barbara Wiedemann's "American War Novels: Strategies for Survival."

Other recommended war texts, which fall outside this tradition of modern American war literature, are Homer's *Iliad, The Sovereignty and Goodness of God by Mary Rowlandson with Related Documents* by Mary White Rowlandson, the Kenneth Branagh film version of *Henry V,* and two books by the Chinese American writer Ha Jin: *Ocean of Words,* his story collection about the Chinese army, and *War Trash,* his imagining of Korean prisoners of war in an American internment facility.

The legacy of Vietnam War literature in the Persian Gulf War can be explored in Gabe Hudson's story collection *Dear Mr. President,* a darkly comic book with a strong and acknowledged indebtedness to Vonnegut; in the David Russell film *Three Kings;* and in the most famous memoir to come out of the war, Anthony Swofford's *Jarhead.* As the DVD box for the film version of *Jarhead* dramatically insists, "Swoff and his fellow Marines sustain themselves with sardonic humanity and wicked comedy on blazing desert fields *in a country they don't understand against an enemy they can't see for a cause they don't fully grasp*" (emphasis added).[7] Teaching the book and the film versions of *Jarhead* provides a remarkable opportunity for exploring O'Brien's famous distinction between "happening truth" and "story-truth." The film takes such astonishing liberties with the memoir that it arguably transforms the story into fiction—yet it preserves the memoir's title, and the packaging presents it as a film version of Swofford's book. Assuming that the book is a good-faith representation of Swofford's experiences—there is some debate about its nonfictionality—teachers can use the film to explore the legitimacy and efficacy of Rat Kiley-esque exaggerations.

From the Iraq war, begun in March 2003, survey respondents mentioned Kayla Williams's *Love My Rifle More than You* and Evan Wright's three-part special report in *Rolling Stone,* "The Killer Elite." It must be said, however, that the survey was conducted when the war was only a few years under way and not many narratives had emerged. Wright's three articles have since been transformed, first into a book, *Generation Kill,* and then into a dramatic series for cable television, comparable in genre with HBO's earlier World War II series, *Band of Brothers.* Since the survey, a multigenre collection of veterans' writings, Andrew Carroll's *Operation Homecoming: Iraq, Afghanistan, and the Home Front, in the Words of U.S. Troops and Their Families* has appeared.

John Crawford's memoir *The Last True Story I'll Ever Tell* would make a good companion to teaching *The Things They Carried*. While we have numerous memoirs by journalists and soldiers, at this time the prevailing narrative form is the documentary: *Fahrenheit 9/11, Gunner Palace, The War Tapes, Off to War: From Rural Arkansas to Iraq, Occupation: Dreamland, The Ground Truth, Combat Diary: The Marines of Lima Company, Baghdad ER, When I Came Home, Control Room, The Dreams of Sparrows, Little Birds, Lioness, Taxi to the Dark Side, No End in Sight, Brothers at War, Standard Operating Procedure,* and *Restrepo.* Dramatic motion narratives are the feature films *The Situation, Stop-Loss, Redacted, The Kingdom, Green Zone,* the series *Over There,* and *The Hurt Locker,* the Academy Award Winner for best picture of 2009. Some films of the homefront are *Rendition, Lions for Lambs, In the Valley of Elah, The Visitor, Brothers,* and *The Messenger.* (For a thorough list see Jack Shaheen's *Guilty: Hollywood's Verdict on Arabs after 9/11.*)

Journalists have given us *Hocus Potus,* by Malcolm Cook Macpherson, *We Are Now Beginning Our Descent,* by James Meek, and the slightly futuristic graphic novel *Shooting War,* by Anthony Lappeé. Books of poetry include *Here, Bullet,* by Brian Turner, a veteran, and several volumes from civilians: Jorie Graham's *Overlord* frames the 2003 invasion of Iraq through memory of the D-Day invasion of Normandy, the poems in C. D. Wright's *Rising, Falling, Hovering* are of a citizen's grappling with her nation's warmaking, and Frances Richey presents a mother's verse memoir of her son's deployment in *The Warrior.* The title of the anthology *Poets against the War,* edited by Sam Hamill, leaves no doubt about its contents.

The ground campaigns of the war on terror in Afghanistan and Iraq have seen the creation of an entirely new genre, the soldier's blog, a diurnal form that, because of its public nature and the author's status as a member of the military, typically resists the intimate aspect of diaries, journals, and letters. Students are especially responsive to Colby Buzzell's *My War: Killing Time in Iraq* and G. B. Trudeau's Doonesbury.com's *The Sandbox: Dispatches from Troops in Iraq and Afghanistan.* Men and women in uniform have also created videos set to music and posted them online. Works presenting Iraqi perspectives include Yasmina Khadra's novel *The Sirens of Baghdad,* the nonfiction chronicle *Baghdad Burning: Girl Blog from Iraq,* by Riverbend, and Dunya Mikhail's poetry collection, *The War Works Hard.*

Genre Issues

Classroom discussions of *The Things They Carried* inevitably address the distinction between happening-truth and story-truth, a distinction that actually plays out as a blurring of fiction and nonfiction in the service of "truth." The strength of the narrator's argument has led readers and critics to question the happening-truth of other O'Brien texts. His memoir, *If I Die in a Combat Zone*, is written in such a novelistic manner that it has fallen under suspicion, and Mark Heberle even suggests that O'Brien's most famous essay, "The Vietnam in Me," might contain some fabrication. The same suspicion has also touched Tobias Wolff's Vietnam memoir, *In Pharaoh's Army* — see, for example, "The Beauty and Destructiveness of War," by Pat Hoy II. But if O'Brien and Wolff truly have spun their memoirs into texts that approach the fictionality of novels, they are not doing so without precedent, as made clear by Paul Fussell's chapter on the fictional nature of Robert Graves's *Good-Bye to All That* in his seminal *The Great War and Modern Memory*. And John Ransom's *Andersonville Diary* from the Civil War is an earlier nonfiction text so historically unreliable, as one colleague informs us, that it potentially qualifies as fiction. Marilyn Wesley addresses this issue in her article "Truth and Fiction in Tim O'Brien's *If I Die in a Combat Zone* and *The Things They Carried*." See also Daniel Lehman's "Reading Outside In: Over the Edge of Genre in the Case of Private O'Brien."

Another text that blurs the issue that two respondents listed is *Into the Black Sun: Vietnam, 1964–1965*, by Takeshi Kaiko, a Japanese correspondent during the Vietnam War. As Mark Heberle has observed about this novel and Kaiko's postwar novel, *Darkness in Summer*,

> Both works seem to be autobiographical first-person narratives in which there is little or no distinction between the author and the central character, a traditional Japanese narrative form known as *shishosetsu* or "I-novel." . . . As a result, both novels appear to be unmediated and completely authentic reactions to Vietnam rather than fabricated fictions or reified historical or ideological analyses.   ("Darkness" 190–91)

These two novels would be right at home in a course on autobiography taught by one of our survey participants. It includes, along with *The Things They Carried*, Dorothy Allison's *Two or Three Things I Know for Sure*, Dionne Brand's *A Map of the Door of No Return: Notes to Belonging*, Wayson Choy's *Paper Shadows: A Chinatown Childhood*, Dave Eggers's *A Heartbreaking Work of Staggering Genius*, Lucy Grealy's *Autobiography of a Face*, Mary Karr's *The Liar's Club*, David Sedaris's *Naked*, and Lauren Slater's *Lying*. All these texts "deal in some way with the rhetorical construction of subjectivity." Another respondent teaches *Not So Quiet: Stepdaughters of War*, a novel in the guise of a memoir, written in 1930 by Evadne Price under the pseudonym Helena Zenna Smith. See also Le Thi Diem Thuy's *The Gangster We Are All Looking For*, discussed earlier.

The major study of autobiographical writing about war is Samuel Hynes's *The Soldiers' Tale: Bearing Witness to Modern War*. See also Mary McCay's

"The Autobiography of Guilt: Tim O'Brien and Vietnam" and Alex Vernon's "Submission and Resistance to the Self as Soldier: Tim O'Brien's Vietnam War Memoir."

Finally, *The Things They Carried* is frequently taught in courses devoted to the short story. The chief critical resource here is Farrell O'Gorman's *"The Things They Carried* as Composite Novel"; see also the chapter on that work in James Nagel's *The Contemporary American Short-Story Cycle: The Ethnic Resonance of Genre*. There are many examples of this form, from early works like James Joyce's *Dubliners*, Sherwood Anderson's *Winesburg, Ohio*, Sarah Orne Jewett's *The Country of Pointed Firs*, and William Faulkner's *Go Down, Moses* to the more recent *The Women of Brewster Place*, by Gloria Naylor, Amy Tan's *The Joy Luck Club*, John Updike's *Too Far to Go: The Maples Stories*, and Denis Johnson's *Jesus' Son: Stories*. Catherine Calloway's essay in this book applies the term *ensemble novel* to O'Brien's *July, July*. The films of Robert Altman and Quentin Tarantino also play with this means of storytelling.

NOTES

[1] All quotations from books by Tim O'Brien have been taken from and checked against the most recent paperback edition.

[2] "The operation degenerated into a nightmare as the U.S. grunts 'ignored the rules of war. They went berserk.' Spurning strenuous efforts by the sober to check their rampage, they stormed villages, randomly torched flimsy thatch-roofed hutches, and tortured and murdered helpless peasants, including women, children, the elderly and even the blind. . . . [The] unit was founded in November 1965 by the leathery Maj. David Hackworth, the model for the demented Col. Kilgore (played by Marlon Brando) in 'Apocalypse Now,' to 'outguerrilla the guerrillas'" (Karnow, *Tiger Force*).

[3] One might encourage students to research the history of such atrocities, in Vietnam and other wars, to help frame the events of My Lai, including events from the Iraq War (e.g., at Haditha, Iraq, 19 November 2005).

[4] An even shorter introduction to the war can be found in Dan Ford's *The Warbird's Forum*. The section "I Need to Know Everything about the Vietnam War by Thursday!" appears targeted to a high school level, and opens with the following: "You're writing a paper about Vietnam? Well, you have a problem, because very likely most of what your teacher believes about the Vietnam War is wrong. . . . There was a wall between those who served in Vietnam and those who formed public opinion about the war, and for the most part the wall still exists. You'll have to decide for yourself whether you should trim your homework to suit the likely prejudices of your teacher."

[5] Two other sites with good links are the Vietnam War subcategory of Donald Mabry's *Historical Text Archive* and Robert Eng's Web site *East and Southeast Asia: An Annotated Directory of Internet Resources.*

[6] Franklin's first chapter, "From Realism to Virtual Reality: Images of America's Wars," appears in the widely used *Norton Reader*, 12th edition.

[7] See Elisabeth Piedmont-Marton's essay "Writing against the Vietnam War in Two Gulf War Memoirs." Three other noteworthy memoirs from the war are Joel Turnip-

seed's *Baghdad Express*; *The Eyes of Orion: Five Tank Lieutenants in the Persian Gulf War*, by Alex Vernon with Neal Creighton, Jr., Greg Downey, Rob Holmes, and Dave Trybula; and Vernon's *Most Succinctly Bred*. This last book could work well in composition classes alongside either *If I Die in a Combat Zone* or *The Things They Carried*—it's short, its chapters are stand-alone essays, it takes the reader from the Cold War and Vietnam through the Persian Gulf War and into the Iraq War, and much of it focuses on the author's college years. For an essay-review about select fiction from that war, including Hudson's collection, see Vernon's "Fiction from the First Gulf War."

Part Two

APPROACHES

Introduction

Alex Vernon

Kalí Tal's pedagogical essay "When History Talks Back: Using Combat Narratives and Vietnam Veteran Speakers to Teach the Vietnam War" does not refer specifically to Tim O'Brien. Nevertheless, it can help us think about how we approach teaching O'Brien's work:

> The very thing that makes veterans' testimony so attractive to us—the *authenticity* of it—makes that testimony suspect as history. The Vietnam veteran has a tremendous personal investment in his version of the story. Retelling the war is his way of rebuilding personal and national myths that have been shattered by the wartime experience.

Tal is concerned with the complex process of telling and receiving nonfiction war stories, in print or in person. (Fictional accounts often share this complexity.) Writers write to make sense. They impose narrative; even seemingly chaotic texts, like Michael Herr's *Dispatches*, possess a controlling logic—the madness is the method. Mark Heberle in this volume uses Tal's essay "Speaking the Language of Pain" to note the incommunicability of trauma, an incommunicability that demands oblique—that is to say, to some degree fictional—expression.

With this frame, the two Tim O'Briens of *The Things They Carried*, narrator-character and author, interest me less in their blurring of truth and fiction, and their assertion of story-truth's challenge to happening-truth, than in their dramatization of a veteran's unceasing task of "rebuilding personal and national myths." The narrator-character in any text, fiction or nonfiction, is always both fictional and nonfictional in the author's ongoing negotiation for meaning among personal memory, collective history, and present needs of self and audience. *The Things They Carried* gives us several episodes that change in the retelling, such as Curt Lemon's death, the Norman Bowker and Kiowa stories, and the ambush stories—retellings in which O'Brien dramatizes the process of oblique expression. The title and opening chapter-story launches this process by ending timorously: Lieutenant Jimmy Cross tells us—tells himself—a story about his failure of leadership and about his resolve to forget Martha in order to regain professional focus. But we know better than to believe that this particular story is fixed, resolved, finished, forgotten. The same holds true for the final chapter-story, "The Lives of the Dead," whose insistence on keeping the dead alive and preserving little Timmy's innocence renders it an exercise in storytelling's active and uncertain effort to shape and control Tim the narrator-character's emotional life.

That O'Brien revises stories from publication to publication reinforces this idea of constant shaping and controlling. *Going After Cacciato* offers another story in which a soldier creates a narrative to make sense of his present self.

Like most journey narratives, Paul Berlin's imagined one ultimately serves as self-discovery (even as it participates in the complicated mythology informing all American road narratives, as Russell Morton Brown reveals in his essay in this volume). *In the Lake of the Woods* portrays the darker side of self-invention, when public denial of past events produces two narratives of the self, a division that cannot be sustained. We should always bear in mind that O'Brien maintains the difference between nonfiction and fiction in his own work. While his fiction asserts the power of story-truth, he does not fictionalize his nonfiction (as far as we know, Heberle's suspicion is still just a suspicion), his fictional characters remain aware of their own storytelling practices, and the distinction between story-truth and happening-truth becomes a way of talking about narratives of identity. (The amount of personal material O'Brien included in his donation to the Harry Ransom Center suggests that he is not fully committed to shrouding the historical actualities of his life.)

Tal writes:

> We must, as teachers, find a way to cope with the fact that the Vietnam War, as depicted by the veterans whom we invite to our classrooms, may not be the same Vietnam War which we have uncovered through our research, or even which the soldier himself survived some fifteen years earlier.   ("When")

After all, most veterans aren't historians. I've had students express supreme dissatisfaction when they realized that *The Things They Carried* was mere fiction. Yet I hope that they learned to appreciate this particular message about the relation between experience and narrative. Students might gain from thinking about the glut of documentary films released during the Iraq and Afghanistan war, the failure of these films to thrive at the box office, and the lack of successful creative novelistic treatments of the war. By 2010 the war had not yet produced its *Three Soldiers*, its *The Naked and the Dead*, its *Going After Cacciato*. It's as if, however valuable as historical documents and as art, the documentaries stopped satisfying—if you saw one or two, you felt you'd seen them all—and caring citizen-audiences longed for the revitalization afforded only by the imagination through new language and new vision.

Tal's frame also encourages us to use the story-truth versus happening-truth rhetoric to deprivilege the veteran's experience, thereby granting a measure of imaginative and critical authority to nonveterans, such as our students. Even if soldiers and veterans in *The Things They Carried* appear to have the moral edge in creating story-truth, anyone can tell a compelling story, and anyone can mine narratives and histories to shape a rich version of the truth. As Zivah Perel writes in her essay in this book, "By exposing the reader to the process of putting together a story-truth," O'Brien "encourages the reader to create his or her own resonance, meaning, or moral." This invitation to participate is especially important if the teacher, or any student, is a war veteran and thus a presumed authority simply for having been there. I am a veteran of the Persian Gulf War, but I keep my experiences out of the classroom and avoid admitting my service for as long as the students let me. Janis Haswell, whose essay appears in this volume, encourages her upper-level literature students to explore not only the relation between experience and its expression but also the reader's role in authenticating—or authorizing—the author. Brenda Boyle, another contributor, has found that the foregrounding of competing perspectives, rhetorical positioning, and formal play in *The Things They Carried* can serve as a model for composition students. The effect is legitimatizing and liberating. David Magill, another contributor, reports that his experience with O'Brien's fictions and essays in the writing class corroborates Boyle's testimony: "O'Brien's struggles both as a man and as a writer allow students to see that they are not the only ones who are language-deficient, that even the best writers struggle with a language that controls and constructs them as they construct it."

The depriviléging of the veteran's experiential authority over the historical truth presents an odd corollary to the strong possibility that the appeal of *The Things They Carried* for students derives largely from its ahistorical nature. Tal notes that the war "is merely interesting history" for students and their "lack of passion, lack of moral involvement in the issues of the war, means that their real fascination is usually with the soldiers who fought, rather than the causes they fought for" ("When"). The book's title story fits the bill perfectly, as do the stories that follow. The Vietnam War is the setting; it is not the story. "On the Rainy River" comes the closest to "moral involvement in the issues of the war," yet even it works primarily on issues of character. One could teach *The Things They Carried*, and teach it successfully, without teaching the war: students do not need maps or time lines or lectures on the political situation to appreciate and learn from the text; perhaps this fact helps explain its teachability and its widespread classroom use. The book's lack of heroic deaths, its acts of barbarity and stupidity by the "good guys"—there is nothing new here, nothing in the text that characterizes these experiences as particular to this war. Jennifer Peterson's investigation in this volume of postmodern identity by way of *In the Lake of the Woods* depends not on the specific terms of the war but on the general coinciding of the war with high postmodern aesthetics.

Indeed, O'Brien aims to generalize his war stories. Kathleen Puhr writes in her essay about how, for her high school students, the "essential premise" of O'Brien's fiction is that "the more we tell a story, the better we tell it, because the less the facts matter," as "the art of storytelling involves tracing and retracing experiences, elevating them to the universal." When her colleagues introduce some aspect of the war's history, such as draft dodging, they appear to be seizing an opportunity to present additional material rather than providing a direct interpretive strategy. In his fiction, nonfiction, and interviews, O'Brien insists on the ahistorical sameness of the soldiering experience, and he wants to connect with nonveteran lives as well. Even *Going After Cacciato* and *In the Lake of the Woods*, while seemingly more historically and politically grounded than

The Things They Carried, turn on issues of character, not on issues of the war. O'Brien is a writer, he insists, not a Vietnam War writer. Of course he knows that the American Revolution, the world wars, and the wars in Korea, Vietnam, and Iraq have been very different for soldiers and citizens alike; but ultimately his purpose is the very humanistic one of seeing beyond difference—of history, of participant status, even of nationality, gender, and race.

The story-truth versus happening-truth rhetoric that many essays in this volume discuss plays here too. In conversations and lectures, O'Brien likes to use *The Iliad* as his example of how story-truth trumps historicity. Generations hence will have forgotten the author, he argues, will have forgotten the war's actualities, and will have only the stories that have compelled themselves into our inheritance. Interestingly, what will survive will not necessarily be a soldier's tale; rather, it will be a story that the collective imagination has preserved, adapted, found useful. Thus the contingent, evolving nature of narrative in *The Things They Carried* becomes a metaphor for this larger process. Jen Dunnaway's use of intertexts in the classroom shows O'Brien's novel "to be rich in history without rendering it literally historical. It is one of those texts that dramatizes the ways in which the Vietnam War has been and continues to be processed within American cultural consciousness."

The works of Tim O'Brien are not universally admired. Some readers find them pretentious and full of literary trickery. Eric Waggoner, who reports on using *The Things They Carried* as the primary text in West Virginia Wesleyan's interdisciplinary first-year seminar program, acknowledges in his essay how "especially infuriating" the novel can be for students "with a personal or family history of military service." He continues:

> [I]n one memorable class session, a student whose father, uncles, and brothers were all Vietnam or Gulf War veterans actually threw her copy of the book across the room after she learned of the high degree of fictional embellishment in this work of fiction.

For such readers, the text's active and happy defiance of "what happened," of historical accountability even within a fictional treatment, offends. For other readers, the character-driven plots do not obfuscate, do not mitigate, what they think is O'Brien's too liberal antiwar, or at least anti–Vietnam War, position. His war has not shaken historical disagreement; its label as the "bad war" has not achieved consensus. O'Brien himself has argued against dismissing the war without bothering to study it, and he often expresses surprise at how little postwar youth knows of its prehistory, causes, players, and evolution. Oddly, though, his own fictions avoid explicit incorporation of the realities to which he wants readers to attend.

Do O'Brien's stories avoid the complexities of ethical analysis of war? In privileging character and relegating the war to the backdrop, can an accusation of irresponsibility actually stick? I'm reminded of the film *We Were Soldiers*, advertised as being an apolitical presentation of wartime suffering, violence, and courage, and of my immediate reaction—an accusation of the irresponsibility of that approach. Do we consider the Vietnam War bad only because we lost? Are soldiers like Mad Mark in *If I Die in a Combat Zone* and Azar in *The Things They Carried* necessary to win wars? Why do politically neutral narratives like *We Were Soldiers* attract a jingoistic reception, while antiwar narratives tend to be the ones to win canonical status?

I am being deliberately contentious. The essays that follow approach O'Brien through the same issues, if on different terms and in varied spirits, and through many others. Waggoner challenges his students to look past the apparent resistance to history of *The Things They Carried* and work "from the assumption that the book cannot be understood outside its sociohistorical context." Zivah Perel's and Edward Rielly's essays, which place O'Brien's fictions in the context of literary works about other wars as well as the Vietnam War, similarly find that O'Brien's writing—even his literary techniques—cannot be separated from his war. Elisabeth Piedmont-Marton's approach to "Sweetheart of the Song Tra Bong" as a story about the "rules" of storytelling, of gender, and of war is unusual in locating the story in its proper time and place—in the military situation. This context creates a tension between the story's imaginative element and the actual war—ironically, what my students find to be the most unrealistic moment in *The Things They Carried*, Mark Fossie's importing his girlfriend by helicopter to the combat zone, has a factual basis for the nonurban legend on which O'Brien drew. This tension, I suspect, one could constructively juxtapose with the tension between the real and the imagined in *Going After Cacciato*. Tobey Herzog pursues the fight-or-flight dilemma that nags many of O'Brien's characters as an ahistorical and acultural issue of character and also as an opportunity for "interesting comparisons of cultures, wars, characters, narrative strategies, [and] definitions of courage and cowardice."

We should not fault O'Brien, or any war novelist, for failing to present the larger context beyond . . . well, beyond what the soldiers carried. As Tal notes, soldiers frequently don't know the full story of their situation—they often know very little about the political, the strategic, or even the operational purposes for which they are being used. O'Brien does not enlist characters to talk or think about Bao Dai or President Diem or Robert McNamara, for example, because those characters would not have done so. O'Brien also avoids enmeshing his readers in the complicated political situation, as one might accuse Hemingway of doing in *For Whom the Bell Tolls* (even though, for some readers, especially among Hemingway's contemporaries, the novel was not political enough). A novel is not a history primer. Instead, O'Brien allows readers to respond on different levels. The title "July '69" tells us a great deal about that powerful story if we know something of the war's development or if we care to learn; but one's emotional response does not depend on that knowledge. We should, however, heed Jen Dunnaway's warning that if we permit an O'Brien work "to teach itself," then "important pedagogical opportunities can be missed." It was Hemingway's Krebs, in the chapter-story "Soldier's Home" from *In Our Time*, who taught us that it's only after the war, when veterans read and study other people's histories and stories, that they begin to craft a coherent story of their war and of their selves. (Hemingway's decision to call him "Krebs" rather than "Harold," in military fashion, underscores the war's impact on the character's identity.)

The issue of an evolving collective story about the war—even an evolving pair of codependent, opposing stories about the war (an evolving story about conflicting stories) raises an interesting question: What if the war and its consequences had turned out differently? I pose this question not to elicit alternative histories but to guide students to a different line of inquiry about the literature.

The way the war progressed after O'Brien returned to civilian life has shaped his fictions and our reception. *If I Die in a Combat Zone*, which was published before the war's end, is not stridently antiwar. The memoir, while reflecting O'Brien's antiwar attitude and hesitation to fight, acknowledges that others might know better about the war's justification, and O'Brien openly admires one of his company commanders for being a wise warrior. Had the war turned out differently, we would not have the same *Going After Cacciato* or the same *In the Lake of the Woods*. We might not have had these works at all. The "truth" of O'Brien's experiential authority involves factors outside O'Brien and factors that postdate his wartime experiences. Rielly's essay notes that most of his student-readers of *Going After Cacciato* prefer the lazy Lieutenant Corson to the gung-ho Lieutenant Martin because Corson refuses to risk his soldiers to accomplish his assigned missions, a dereliction of duty that the students appreciate. Yet we can and should push back: Would readers respond the same way in the context of a different war? In *Saving Private Ryan*, a film about the "good war," World War II, the captain orders an assault on an enemy position that could have been bypassed, and his action results in the death of one of his soldiers. The film suggests that his order, while controversial, was the right, even heroic, course of action. How might audiences have reacted if Private Ryan had been a character less apparently noble than the one played by the attractive blue-eyed actor Matt Damon?

Several of the essays in this book contextualize O'Brien's work by invoking subsequent wars—specifically, the Gulf War, of 1990–91, and the Iraq war, which commenced March 2003. Derek Maus suggests that comparing O'Brien's *The Things They Carried* with the Vietnamese writer Duong Thu Huong's *Novel without a Name* helps students appreciate the complexity of war in general, its language and representation (including that of dissent). Perel finds that the David Russell film *Three Kings*, not unlike O'Brien's narratives, asserts the power of the individual through rewriting. Russell's film is divided into two halves; the first half represents the media's unreliability and naiveté surrounding the Gulf War, and the second, after the men give up their pursuit of the bullion in favor of helping the Iraqi rebels, rewrites the narrative of the war more ideally. Gates, Barlow, Elgin, and Vig serve as the potential for what could have been a just—or less unjust—war.

Comparisons between the Iraq and Afghanistan war and the Vietnam War will continue to be drawn but also disputed. There are convenient parallels; there are great differences. Doug Davis argues for another potentially instructive comparison by assessing O'Brien's Vietnam novels as perhaps less helpful in thinking through the new millennium's war on terror than his cold war novel (whose protagonists are classifiable as domestic terrorists):

> Reading *The Nuclear Age* in the second nuclear age connects the present age of terror to the past age of nuclear threat by showing how the sense of global threat that drives William into the basement and that drove the American military to acquire tens of thousands of nuclear weapons and to fight in Vietnam still drives the nation to war today.

We should not restrict class discussion to such "content" as historical actualities, claims, and comparisons or to the morality of behavior by nation-states or individuals. As *Dispatches* reminded us, one way of saying something new about war is to find a new way to say it, to push language and form in new directions (or wildly further in known ones) and, in doing so, say new things. Jeremy Green's discussion of Paul Wade's traumatic witnessing of the My Lai massacre argues that *In the Lake of the Woods* "emphasizes . . . the resistance of certain events to narration, to the explanatory logic of cause and effect on which the historian and detective depend. Here the novelist has an advantage over the historian." Fictional representations are at once less than and more than historical accounts. Christopher Kocela's essay highlights art's defamiliarizing function, in which literary technique works to challenge the reader's perceived knowns, a function Kocela adopts for the classroom. Milton Bates tackles the stories concerning Kiowa's death in *The Things They Carried* by providing a lesson sequence using those stories to illustrate narrative theory. Catherine Calloway engages her students with the complex structure of *July, July*; her essay about that engagement should serve to call more readers and scholars to attend to that novel. When I taught a seminar devoted to O'Brien's works, my students enjoyed *July, July* most of all. The framing story of a college reunion allowed these college seniors to think about their own futures, and the assortment of characters leading civilian lives in a generally realistic narrative afforded moments of sympathy. The students found that the book raised many of the issues of the earlier texts without frustrating their desire for stories with determinate plots. *July, July* came as welcome relief from the postmodern storytelling of the earlier O'Brien works.

As all teachers know, classroom context makes an enormous difference. Reita Gorman shows her Memphis inner-city high school students how literature matters by encouraging them to connect personal experiences with the situations dramatized in *The Things They Carried* and *A Farewell to Arms*. The students connect with the texts in ways that both overlap and depart from the personal connections drawn by Waggoner's students at West Virginia Wesleyan. Calloway's essay on *Tomcat in Love* argues for a different interpretive context altogether, one that students acquainted with feminist literary criticism can appreciate. For Calloway, this novel invokes Vietnam, semantic acrobatics, and male chauvinism only to make fun of them. O'Brien uses *Tomcat in Love* to poke a little fun at himself and his critics.

Indeed, we tend to overlook, in approaching literature as significant as the works of Tim O'Brien, the spirit of play. *Going After Cacciato*, *The Nuclear Age*, *The Things They Carried*, and *July, July* are serious texts. They are also fun. And for all of Tim O'Brien's commitment to personal and collective memory and to studying the lessons of his war, a mischievous book like *Tomcat in Love* might prove a better solution—at least for O'Brien personally if not for readers aesthetically—than the grim puzzle that is *In the Lake of the Woods*. Even collectively, historical-political particularities can perhaps be made to matter too much; maybe one generation should not demand that future generations become too mired, drowning like Kiowa in the shit fields of its own past.

If I were to teach a course devoted to the literature of the Vietnam War, I might end it with *Rushmore*, a playful film about an adolescent boy, Max Fischer, and a Vietnam veteran, Herman Blume, vying for the same woman, two lost souls struggling for opposite reasons. Max in his youth cannot find his place in the world; Blume in his youth had his—the war—thrust on him. Max's generally flippant attitude toward life is applied to Blume's military experience: "Were you in the shit?" Yet this flippancy doesn't hide his respect. At the end of the movie, Max stages a play about Vietnam, starring himself in a Rambo-like getup and complete with flamethrowers and explosions. It's ludicrous; it also brings Blume to tears. Why? Because Max upsets the conventions of manliness that so disturb Blume? Because Max turns Blume's war into something fresh and fun? Because Max, daring not to presume to tell a "true" story, creates the only valid homage possible? Because Max teaches the lost, divorced drunkard of a veteran that it's okay to be a cliché?

Blume gets the woman. She's Max's teacher, after all, and British, name of Cross—a good representative of the old order. Max finds love with a bespectacled, bookish Asian American classmate, defying the war's racial component and upending the familiar war-story plot of competition for the girl.

Rushmore, which came out in 1998, is not a war movie; it's not even a wartime movie. I have difficulty imagining its coming into being after the United States went to war in Afghanistan and Iraq. Interestingly, it deliberately alludes to *The Graduate*, a wartime movie that referred to the war in Vietnam not at all. But the film contributes to the passing of the war from the generation that fought it to the generation that lives after, and carries on.

The Vietnam War: A Very Short History

Benjamin Goluboff

Vietnamese history has been, from the beginning, a story of warfare—both internal and against a variety of neighboring or colonial states. For this brief historical sketch it is best to join that story in progress, in 1945, with Japan's surrender to the Allies at the conclusion of World War II. In 1940 the Japanese had occupied Vietnam, a French colonial holding since the 1860s; by 1945 they had largely dismantled the French colonial administration. Defeated, the Japanese transferred power to the Vietminh, a Communist movement formed in 1941 by Ho Chi Minh to oppose the Japanese occupation. A dedicated Vietnamese nationalist with ties to the Soviet Union, Ho, "the Grandfather of the Revolution," declared Vietnam's independence on 2 September 1945, quoting from Thomas Jefferson, among others.

Weeks later, however, British troops landed in Saigon and returned power to the French. There was a brief period of negotiation during which Ho sought to persuade the French to designate Vietnam a unified free state within the French colonial apparatus, but by the winter of 1946 a full-fledged war had broken out between the French and the Vietminh. The war, known as the First Indochina War, lasted nine years, and it contributed to anti-Communist sentiment in the United States during the cold war. Ho was considered the puppet of either China or the Soviet Union, or both; the belief that his victory in Vietnam would contribute to the global spread of Communism prompted presidents Truman and Eisenhower to support the French with funds and equipment.

The war ended in 1954 with a stunning victory by the Vietminh, who had laid siege to a French stronghold in North Vietnam called Dien Bien Phu. The fall of Dien Bien Phu was a triumph of logistics coordinated by Vo Nguyen Giap, Ho Chi Minh's chief general, who would later be responsible for the guerrilla strategies that ultimately defeated American forces in Vietnam. Giap showed extraordinary resolve in the battle for Dien Bien Phu, incurring roughly eight thousand casualties — four times the number of French dead — in taking the stronghold (Karnow, *Vietnam* 540). Immediately after the French defeat at Dien Bien Phu, talks on the future of Vietnam began in Geneva among representatives from the warring parties and from several Western powers. What came to be known as the Geneva Accords of 1954 set the stage for a conflict in which American forces would play an increasingly central role.

The Geneva Accords called for a cessation of hostilities in Vietnam, Cambodia, and Laos and established a line of demarcation at the seventeenth parallel, between what would shortly become Communist and non-Communist states. North of the line was Ho Chi Minh's Democratic Republic of Vietnam. South of the line was the Republic of Vietnam, always referred to in the American media as South Vietnam; here Bao Dai, Vietnam's last hereditary emperor, installed Ngo Dinh Diem as president, pending a popular election — which Diem would subsequently avoid. A vigorous anti-Communist, Diem was much admired by United States political and military leaders, at least at first. But he became unpopular among the South Vietnamese as a result of attacks on their civil rights, raids on Buddhist pagodas, and a rural anti-insurgency program that forced many from their ancestral homes.

Diem survived several abortive coups and even an assassination attempt in which two South Vietnamese Air Force pilots bombed the presidential palace. American support for him began to erode, and when Diem was finally deposed and executed by a group of generals from the Army of the Republic of Vietnam (ARVN) in 1963, it was with the complicity of Henry Cabot Lodge, the American ambassador to Vietnam, and President John F. Kennedy (Karnow, *Vietnam* 277). During the nine years of Diem's presidency, political and military tensions had escalated significantly. In 1955 Ho Chi Minh instituted a bloody and unpopular land reform campaign in the north. In 1959 North Vietnam began improving and enlarging the network of jungle pathways that would come to be known as the Ho Chi Minh Trail, a jungle route through Laos and Cambodia that the North used to infiltrate men and supplies into South Vietnam.

In 1960 a group of South Vietnamese nationalists made common cause with North Vietnamese Communist cadres to form the National Liberation Front (NLF). Originally dedicated to civil disobedience against the Diem regime, the NLF eventually formed guerrilla military units (the so-called Vietcong) that fought against ARVN and the Americans. Relations between northern Communist and southern nationalist elements within the NLF are a matter of historical conjecture. One key South Vietnamese organizer of the NLF considers the northern party to have cynically manipulated the Front in order to achieve its "imperialistic revolution" (Truong Nhu Tang 268). By the end of 1963 there were fifteen thousand American military advisers in South Vietnam, training and leading ARVN units as they engaged both NLF guerrillas and North Vietnamese Army regulars.

In the years after Diem's death, South Vietnam's political leadership was in flux, with one general or junta succeeding another until 1967, when Nguyen Van Thieu was elected president. Despite continued American financial and military support, Thieu presided over an increasingly chaotic government and over a military that was (with some heroic exceptions) corrupt and ineffective, until the fall of Saigon in 1975.

The Lyndon Johnson years, from 1963 to 1968, saw American involvement in Vietnam transformed from an advisory to a combatant role. The Tonkin Gulf incident of 1964 was the first significant step in this transformation. Twice in August 1964 North Vietnamese torpedo boats attacked an American destroyer patrolling the Gulf of Tonkin to conduct electronic espionage and to support a South Vietnamese commando mission in North Vietnam. The destroyer sustained no significant damage, and the second incident may not have actually happened, but the event was interpreted as provocative by the United States media and military (Santoli 15). Largely through the persuasiveness of Secretary of Defense Robert McNamara, who covered up the destroyer's role in the commando mission, President Johnson convinced Congress to pass the Gulf of Tonkin Resolution, which gave the president unrestricted power to conduct the war against North Vietnam (Karnow, *Vietnam* 365). By March 1965 the first American combat troops had arrived in Vietnam.

General William Westmoreland, a distinguished veteran of World War II and Korea, was commander of all United States military forces in Vietnam from 1964 until 1968. Because he shared with Johnson the belief that overly aggressive tactics in Vietnam would draw China into the war, Westmoreland pursued a policy of limited warfare. His field commanders had orders not to pursue the enemy into sanctuaries or base areas in Cambodia or Laos. Their mission was typically "search and destroy," which meant patrolling rice paddies and trails in the hope of confronting the enemy or searching villages to flush out guerrillas from the civilian population among whom they hid. Westmoreland believed that search and destroy and limited use of force would make for a war of attrition that would gradually wear down the enemy's will to fight in South Vietnam. Concurrent with this strategy, Westmoreland was committed to a variety of civic action programs collectively known as pacification. Digging wells, inoculating children, teaching villagers advanced agricultural techniques—all were supposed to win the "hearts and minds" of the South Vietnamese and keep them from joining the Communist insurgency. Whatever effects they may have had on Vietnamese society, one undeniable result of Westmoreland's tactics was the creation of an extraordinarily large refugee population—by the end of the war, perhaps a quarter of the total Vietnamese population had been driven from its homes (Herring 178).

The Westmoreland years also saw Operation Rolling Thunder, a relentlessly destructive air campaign against North Vietnam. Johnson believed that bombing the capital city of Hanoi and the port city of Haiphong would persuade the North Vietnamese to enter into peace talks. Indeed, the first round of peace talks, which took place intermittently until 1973, began in Paris in May 1968, but by that time the Vietnam War had entered a new phase. On 31 January 1968, during Tet, the celebration of the lunar New Year, North Vietnamese Army regulars and NLF guerrillas launched a massive attack against virtually all the major cities of South Vietnam. The Tet offensive was the result of years of planning by General Giap, who oversaw a huge and silent infiltration campaign against the south. There were pitched battles in the ancient imperial city of Hue and at Khe Sanh, a fortified marine outpost in the central highlands where Westmoreland, deceived by Giap, had long expected an enemy push. Fighting erupted in areas of Saigon that had been considered secure, and Vietcong commandos briefly occupied the American embassy there.

Eventually, United States forces rolled back the advances the NLF and NVA made during Tet and inflicted staggering casualties on the enemy. But because it discredited Westmoreland's optimistic predictions of success, the Tet offensive was a political and psychological victory for the north. After Tet, Creighton Abrams relieved Westmoreland as top American commander in Vietnam, and he was responsible for implementing President Richard M. Nixon's new strategy for Vietnam. Vietnamization, or the Nixon Doctrine, involved increased resources and training for ARVN forces, phased withdrawals of United States troops, heightened pacification efforts, and continued air strikes intended to bring Hanoi to the bargaining table. The Nixon years saw an intensification of the antiwar movement at home and a collapse of morale among United States soldiers in Vietnam. Abrams presided over an army troubled by drug abuse, racial tension, and breaches of discipline that ranged from mutinies (the army called them "combat refusals") to the murder, or "fragging," of commanding officers.

Tim O'Brien's tour of duty in Vietnam took place at this low ebb in the American war effort. O'Brien served with the Fifth Battalion of the 46th Infantry, 198th Infantry Brigade of the Americal Division from February 1969 to February 1970 ("Vietnam in Me" 48). The Americal Division operated largely in Quang Ngai Province, the southernmost of the five provinces that made up Vietnam's narrow and mountainous central highlands region. Quang Ngai was a heavily populated agricultural region and one that since the war with the French had been a stronghold of the Communist insurgency. The Americal Division's mission was to seek out Vietnamese guerrillas sheltering among the civilian population and in the jungles away from the coast. This involved patrolling heavily mined pathways, exploring and blowing up the network of tunnels that honeycombed the countryside, and searching and sometimes destroying villages. The defoliant Agent Orange was used extensively in Quang Ngai to eliminate the foliage cover that rendered the enemy invisible to aircraft. The army also relied heavily on artillery, establishing free-fire zones—areas assigned for randomly scheduled bombardment, where anyone moving would automatically be considered the enemy. All this resulted in tragic disruption in the lives of Quang Ngai's civilian population. An American journalist who knew the province well, and memorably characterized the Americal Division's war there as "a reprisal against houses," estimated that 50,000 civilian casualties occurred there annually following the arrival of American forces (Schell 209).

The Americal Division conducted a number of large search-and-destroy operations. The operation that seems to have had the largest impact on O'Brien's imagination was a "population control" initiative called Russell Beach. Undertaken on the Batangan Peninsula and involving O'Brien's Fifth Battalion just before his arrival in Vietnam in February 1969, Operation Russell Beach entailed removing the civilian population from the peninsula, sweeping it for guerrillas, then resettling the people. Both Russell Beach and the Batangan are named in O'Brien's *If I Die in a Combat Zone* (118). The peninusula is named four times in *The Things They Carried*, most strikingly as the place where Alpha Company shakes hands with the corpse in "The Lives of the Dead" (209). Paul Berlin's observation post is on the Batangan, putting the peninsula squarely at the center of *Going After Cacciato*, because all the action of that novel is either remembered or dreamed as Berlin stands watch there. In November 1969 guerrilla representatives to the Paris peace talks claimed that 1,200 Vietnamese civilians had been murdered during Operation Russell Beach (Middleton). Other sources do not substantiate this claim (Goluboff 57).

O'Brien's tour of duty took place as the best known of United States atrocities in Vietnam was coming to light. In March 1968 Lieutenant William Calley, commanding an infantry company from the Americal Division's 11th Brigade, ordered the murder of more than three hundred civilians at My Lai, a village in Quang Ngai near the Batangan. The American press quickly became aware of the event, and by fall 1969 the army had assigned General William Peers to investigate the atrocities, which included torture, mutilation, and rape. Calley was eventually convicted of the murder of twenty-two people; his sentence was commuted in 1971, and he served little time. My Lai and the Peers investigation figure in *If I Die in a Combat Zone*. The narrators of O'Brien's Vietnam novels, however, are often reluctant to name the place directly. Typically they name associated places (e.g., My Khe, Pinkville) or speak of the 48th Vietcong Battalion, the enemy unit thought to have been operating around My Lai and the Batangan Peninsula (Goluboff 54). Even in *In the Lake of the Woods*, a novel preoccupied with My Lai, the narrator only speaks of the place as Song My—the village of which My Lai hamlet was one component—until the story of Kathy Wade's disappearance is well advanced.

My Lai deepened antiwar sentiment at home, and the fall of 1969 saw massive demonstrations in Washington, DC, to end the war. Nixon continued to reduce troop numbers in Vietnam while extending the war elsewhere, seeking to disrupt enemy sanctuaries and resupply lines through a "secret" bombing of

Cambodia and ground "incursions" into Cambodia and Laos. The Paris peace talks entered a new phase in 1970, as Nixon's national security adviser (later the secretary of state), Henry Kissinger, entered into secret negotiations with Le Duc Tho, a North Vietnamese general and diplomat. These talks continued, soon in a more public way, until January 1973, when Kissinger and Tho (who would share the Nobel Peace prize that year) signed the Paris Peace Accords. Nixon had sought to hasten the progress of the talks by renewed bombing raids against North Vietnam and by mining Haiphong Harbor in 1972. In March of that year, sensing the end of the American war, North Vietnam launched another major offensive against the cities of the south.

Not long after the signing of the Paris Peace Accords in January 1973 and the departure of the last American troops from Vietnam, Congress passed the War Powers Act, legislation intended to limit the president's power to wage war without congressional approval. In 1974 Hanoi designed a final offensive, the Ho Chi Minh Campaign, to be led by Le Duc Tho during the dry season of 1975. As the campaign began, Cambodia's capital, Phnomh Penh, fell to the Communist Khmer Rouge insurgency, initiating the four-year genocidal rule of the Cambodian dictator Pol Pot. With Hanoi's armored columns advancing on Saigon, President Thieu fled to Taiwan, transferring power to General Duong Van Minh, one of the original conspirators against Diem. Minh surrendered the capital, which was later renamed Ho Chi Minh City, on 30 April 1975.

In addition to its impact on the cultures and landscapes of Southeast Asia, the Vietnam War had a transformative effect on American society, embroiling Americans in a series of conflicts, some of which have not yet been resolved. Many of these involved what Americans of the period called the credibility gap, which referred to the inconsistency between the pronouncements of government and the military and the way events played out on the ground. The credibility gap, exacerbated by Nixon's Watergate scandal, reasserted itself during the immediate postwar years when General Westmoreland initiated a $120 million libel suit against CBS over a 1982 documentary entitled "The Uncounted Enemy: A Vietnam Deception." The documentary claimed that, in order to create the impression that American forces were winning in Vietnam, Westmoreland had intentionally underestimated enemy troop strength in the years leading up to Tet and had disregarded CIA reports of the North Vietnamese infiltration of the south. Westmoreland eventually dropped the suit when CBS issued a statement that he considered an apology, but controversy persists about the degree to which Westmoreland was aware of conditions leading up to the Tet offensive. Some media historians consider *Westmoreland v. CBS* to have contributed to the decline of the TV documentary as a vehicle for investigative journalism (Mascaro).

The military draft was the focus of bitter conflict during the Vietnam years. Many draft-age men fled to Canada and elsewhere to avoid conscription; others burned their draft cards as an act of civil disobedience. The first organized "burn-in" took place at the University of California, Berkeley, in 1965. In 1968 the Yale chaplain, William Sloane Coffin, and the activist physician Benjamin Spock were prosecuted for encouraging young men to burn their cards. In the same year Daniel and Philip Berrigan, activist priests, used pig's blood to deface records at several local draft boards in Maryland.

Opponents of the draft argued that the Vietnam War was an illegal, "aggressive" war, according to principles of international law upheld in the Nuremberg tribunals after World War II (T. Taylor, *Nuremberg* 15). Some criticized the Selective Service System for granting local draft boards overly broad discretionary powers and decried a policy of student deferments that penalized low-income Americans, who were less likely to enroll in college. During the Nixon years significant reforms were made to the draft. In 1970 a lottery was instituted, severely limiting the powers of local draft boards. Changes to the Selective Service laws in 1971 made student deferments shorter and harder to obtain and sought to make the draft more representative of national population demographics. The draft was discontinued in 1973 with the departure of the last American troops from Vietnam. In 1977, one day after his inauguration, President Jimmy Carter gave amnesty to the many young men who had fled the country to avoid conscription.

Other significant postwar controversies included the status of Vietnam War veterans and the debate over American prisoners of war left behind in Vietnam. The POW controversy reached its climax in 1993, when the Select Senate Committee on POW Affairs, chaired by Senator John Kerry, announced its finding "of no compelling evidence" to prove the existence of live Americans still captive in Vietnam, Laos, or Cambodia (United States). The committee had been formed in 1991, after decades of speculation that a significant number of POWs had been left behind by Nixon's Operation Homecoming, a prisoner-exchange program undertaken with the North Vietnamese in 1973. Meanwhile, American veterans returning from Vietnam faced a variety of difficulties. Many complained that instead of receiving the heroes' welcome that veterans of earlier wars had enjoyed, they were rejected for bearing the stigma of an unpopular and unsuccessful conflict. Others struggled with health problems believed to be side effects of exposure to Agent Orange or with post-traumatic stress disorder (first recognized as a legitimate psychological diagnosis in 1980) as a result of their combat experiences (Karnow, *Vietnam* 25). In 1967 a group of combat veterans founded Vietnam Veterans against the War, an advocacy and protest group that sponsored an investigation of war-time atrocities, opposed the war's expansion into Laos, and staged numerous antiwar demonstrations, including a two-day occupation of the Statue of Liberty.

When American troops ousted Iraqi forces from Kuwait in 1991, President George H. W. Bush declared, "By God, we've kicked the Vietnam syndrome once and for all" (Apple). The president's remark is one of many examples of how the Vietnam War has remained a touchstone in American political discourse long after the close of the cold war. Debate over candidates' Vietnam-era military service was a significant feature of the 2000 and 2004 presidential campaigns. Bill Clinton, Americans learned, circumvented the draft through a variety of methods, including Arkansas political connections and a special defer-ment for his 1968 Rhodes scholarship; George W. Bush may or may not have discharged his military obligations through his association with the Texas Air National Guard from 1968 to 1973. Opponents of Senator John Kerry's 2004 presidential bid produced a series of television ads intended to discredit the senator's war record as the decorated commander of a United States Navy swift boat in Vietnam; the advertisements gave rise to "swiftboating," a new term for political smear tactics. Memories of the Vietnam War abide in the press and the national imagination as the Iraq war continues. David Halberstam, a principal *New York Times* correspondent during the Vietnam War, spoke for many Amer-icans when he said in an interview not long before his death, in 2007, "I thought that in both Vietnam and Iraq, we were going against history" (Filkins).

The consequences of the Vietnam War may never be fully reckoned. One conservative estimate of the war's financial cost to the United States places it at $167 billion—not to mention the years of crippling inflation that followed (Herring 304). Approximately 58,000 American servicemen and -women died in Vietnam; the death toll for North and South Vietnamese soldiers and civilians is incalculable but must surely be measured in the millions. For many Ameri-cans the most serious costs of the war were personal or spiritual: families divided over questions of national service, a lingering distrust between the generations. Some have lamented a loss of national honor or prestige, regretting the coun-try's failure to honor its promise of support to South Vietnam, mourning a loss of national innocence or moral integrity. However various, the war's effects on the American society were transformative. One distinction of Tim O'Brien's work is to have captured something of this transformation.

The Things We Carry:
Lessons from O'Brien in
American National Mythology

Jen Dunnaway

The pleasure of teaching *The Things They Carried* derives in part from the fact that the text is an exercise in the creation of national myth. In both content and structure, Tim O'Brien's Vietnam War masterwork performs a still-unfolding narrative of the status of the Vietnam War in American culture; a transparently didactic text, it cues readers' emotional reactions and even scripts the correct and appropriate responses to its own dark revelations. Just as there is a right way to "tell a true war story," the text hints that there is a right way to consume and absorb the disquieting reality of the Vietnam War. *The Things They Carried*—from its emphasis on male suffering to its lexicon of trauma to its elliptical skirting of atrocity—is as much about the ways in which the war has been mythologized in the national imagination as it is about the war itself. Teaching this text, we thus offer our students a glimpse of the inner workings of popular culture. In their encounter with *The Things They Carried*, students can in effect bear witness to the creation of national myth, and their awareness and critical appraisal of this experience can facilitate a more nuanced understanding not only of O'Brien's complex work but also of the cultural rhetoric of their own time.

Nonetheless, I have often found my students overly eager to take *The Things They Carried* at face value, to default to the most superficial reading and "lessons" of the text. Out of an abundance of enthusiasm for the book, a sense of empathy for O'Brien's narrative persona, and occasionally a post-9/11 jingoism that discourages the questioning of anything to do with war, a good number of students may be reluctant to engage this work in a manner they perceive to be critical. As an instructor in a freshman writing program that emphasizes the development of students' cultural literacy as well as their writing skills, I have learned to adapt my approach to help ease students past the roadblock of their problematically uncritical enjoyment of the text, with the ultimate goal not of diminishing pleasure or of transforming them into sniping critics but of making accessible to them a more richly contextualized understanding of O'Brien's work and the mythical narratives in which it is implicated. In a seminar course I teach, The Vietnam War and American Culture, I have obtained positive results by assigning sections of *The Things They Carried* alongside certain carefully chosen "intertexts" that shed light on crucial elements of O'Brien's work. When two texts are placed in dialogue, students are more resistant to O'Brien's manipulations and less resistant to broader, more contextualized ways of understanding *The Things They Carried* that place it within the larger landscape of American national mythology. My contribution to the body of knowledge on teaching this rewarding and multifaceted text is an introduction to teaching with intertexts, using as examples the two combinations I've found most productive in the seminar classroom.

Marita Sturken's excellent piece "The Wall and the Screen Memory," which appears in her book *Tangled Memories*, provides an intriguing commentary on the Vietnam Veterans Memorial in Washington, DC, covering the effort and conflict surrounding various aspects of its planning, construction, unveiling, and reception. When assigned in conjunction with "The Things They Carried," the first story in O'Brien's eponymous collection, it provides students with an illuminating introduction to the controversy at the heart of Vietnam War memory. In her article, Sturken suggests that "public commemoration is inextricably tied to the question of how war is brought to closure in American society" and goes on to ask, "How does a society commemorate a war whose central narrative is one of division and dissent, a war whose history is still formative and highly contested?" (44). This contested nature of Vietnam War memory persists at the center of her inquiry and informs her analysis of the public's interaction with the Vietnam Veterans Memorial wall. One aspect of this interaction, discussed in detail, is the unique "artifact ritual" that the memorial has engendered: the tendency of visitors to leave objects at the wall that are both decidedly idiosyncratic and publicly meaningful. She catalogs the most commonplace of these objects, which include "photographs, letters, poems, teddy bears, dog tags, combat boots and helmets, MIA/POW bracelets, clothes, medals of honor, headbands, beer cans, plaques, crosses, playing cards" (76), as well as the more cryptic and unusual: a shot glass of whiskey, a Vietnamese wedding ring, a Harley-Davidson motorcycle. The names engraved in the memorial's granite slabs, Sturken observes, are visually uniform, equalized by the absence of rank or other distinguishing information; it is the personal objects that invest the names with individual significance (61).

Perceptive students are quick to link this public artifact ritual with O'Brien's cataloging of individual soldiers' possessions in his opening story and his use of these possessions to foreground each soldier's character. In a manner that echoes both the personalizing impulse of artifact ritual and the elegiac tone of the memorial, O'Brien lists the things each man carries in the field, using long, repetitive, fluid sentences, creating a compendium of "things" that continues through the entirety of the story:

> P-38 can openers, pocket knives, heat tabs, wristwatches, dog tags, mosquito repellent, chewing gum, candy, cigarettes, salt tablets, packets of Kool-Aid, lighters, matches, sewing kits, Military Payment Certificates, C rations, and two or three canteens of water. (2)

In a sense, then, O'Brien and Sturken represent opposite ends of a chronology, O'Brien describing items carried into the field by soldiers during the war itself and Sturken discussing analogous items relinquished many years later at the memorial to the soldiers' deaths. To be pushed beyond this basic eureka moment, students might be asked to ponder why remembrance of the war is framed in both instances in such explicitly material terms. Why this emphasis on artifacts? What role do artifacts play in our understanding of the war and the individuals who took part in it?

At this point I find it useful to have students list and examine a few of the objects mentioned by Sturken and O'Brien. Getting students to think about the artifacts themselves and to look at the authors' lists for patterns and similarities tends to lead them toward more probing questions about the materiality of memory, the constructedness of our understanding of a war that ended over thirty years ago. The objects common to both accounts tend to be those that have become most firmly associated with the Vietnam War in popular imagining: dog tags, helmets, boots, cigarette lighters—humble, generic items from any war that have attained an almost iconic status in relation to Vietnam. We relate to the war through its relics, and this may strike some students as odd, considering the relative abundance of both historical documentation and surviving veterans. Part of the reason for this "artifactual" quality might lie in Sturken's original premise concerning the contestedness that defines the war's history, from which the apolitical solidity of material things may provide a measure of reprieve. As O'Brien's narrator quips, "[F]or all the ambiguities of Vietnam, all the mysteries and unknowns, there was at least the single abiding certainty that they would never be at a loss for things to carry" (16). It would seem that the concrete realm of physical things is the one place where history is certain, unambiguous, "factual"—a notion that O'Brien emphasizes in his meticulous cataloging of the exact weights of each of the items carried by the men.

However, the instructor might ask if this is actually the case, if the material realm is really as incontestable as O'Brien's preoccupation with physical and experiential details suggests. Sturken contends that each object left at the memorial is a communication of some sort and that visitors who relinquish things there are imagining their audience "variously as the American public and the community of veterans" (78). Yet the meaning of these communications is often mysterious, ambiguous. As in O'Brien's story, these things signify—but can they possibly mean the same thing to every "reader"? Are their meanings stable over time, or do they vary as a function of the historical or political context or audience? I have students choose an item from each author's list and brainstorm its possible meanings. I then ask them to separate their findings into two categories: individual or personal meanings and public, national, or cultural meanings. A pair of dog tags left at the wall, for example, communicates in the public realm the basics of military identification; to the individual relinquishing them, they might represent a very specific narrative of friendship, of a promise fulfilled, or of the harsh consequences of bravado or carelessness. In "The Things They Carried," the narrator similarly makes the point that every object carried has a story and a meaning, a meaning that might be obscure or even contradictory depending on the character of the person carrying it. Norman Bowker, "otherwise a very gentle person," incongruously carries a severed thumb (13). Lieutenant Jimmy Cross carries a pebble whose meaning is specifically predetermined by its sender, who writes that she found it on the beach "precisely" at the high-tide mark, signifying a "separate-but-together quality" that prompted her to send it to him "as a token of her truest feelings for him" (8). For Cross, however, the pebble's meaning changes irrevocably when one of his men is killed, after which it comes to signify his negligence, his lack of "soldierly discipline," and the guilt he will "carry like a stone in his stomach for the rest of the war" (20, 16). Students begin to realize that even within the realm of physical reality, meanings are subjective and unstable, displacing one another as contexts shift and versions of history contend for prominence.

Indeed, as Sturken points out, the "mystery" of the artifacts relinquished at the wall is a part of what enables the memorial, and by extension the war itself, to resist decisive, clear-cut narratives of healing or closure. Moreover, the memorial marks a crossover point where "objects are transposed from personal to cultural artifacts" (76), and in this context the items take on compound meanings as both personal and public signifiers. Students may be led to view in a similar light O'Brien's segue from personal effects into nationally meaningful abstractions toward the end of "The Things They Carried." Enjoying continual resupply and "stunning" resources, what the soldiers carry is ultimately "the great American war chest—the fruits of science, the smokestacks, the canneries, the arsenals at Hartford, the Minnesota forests, the machine shops, the vast fields of corn and wheat—they carried [them] like freight trains" (16). Thus carrying "things" is not just a personal matter; it represents the larger issue of exporting America itself, of superimposing its history, culture, ideologies, and commodities onto other nations: the project of war.

This interplay among personal and national meanings in O'Brien's work is more easily understood by students who have studied Sturken's account of the Vietnam Veterans Memorial, and the pairing of these texts marks a turning point at which students begin to make sense of the question I ask on the first day of class: "*How* do we know what we know about the Vietnam War?" Entering freshmen are often still surprised and perturbed by the notion that history can be "contested," and these two texts together can help give a human, comprehensible reality to this concept. They also introduce the notion that Vietnam War representation itself forms an observable trajectory, with its own chronology and conventions; students or instructor might suggest in discussion that O'Brien, writing several years after the dedication of the memorial and with the accompanying artifact ritual well established, might have been responding to this new mode of history making in a way that a Vietnam War text written earlier could not. By understanding Vietnam War representation as a chronology, where events occurring since the war influence the way we remember it, students gain the opportunity to observe their own role as readers from a critical distance and to experience consciously the perspective(s) they bring to the table. The pairing of "The Things They Carried" and "The Wall and the Screen Memory" thus exerts a synergistic effect on their understanding of both texts at multiple levels. As each text gives greater dimensionality to the other and opens up avenues of inquiry not previously apparent, students find increasingly innovative ways to approach the central issues of O'Brien's craft and the (re)creation of history.

What makes a text like Sturken's so useful as an intertext is the way it highlights central themes of O'Brien's without offering a specific reading that might foreclose more expansive student responses to "The Things They Carried." It can be a challenge to discover a secondary source that engages with primary material in such a productive manner without preemptively interpreting it. However, teaching with intertexts can also be as uncomplicated as pairing a story from *The Things They Carried* with an excerpt from another of O'Brien's works. To do so goes to the heart of a central theme of this text: repetition and the retelling of stories. Typically understood in the context of traumatic reenactment or metafiction, the idea of repetition is often the subject of analysis only insofar as it operates within *The Things They Carried*—as in, for example, the various accounts of Ted Lavender's death and its aftermath that span several chapters in the collection. On the other hand, to show how repetition and retelling operate *across* O'Brien's texts not only affords students a broader perspective on the theme's importance to his work but moreover dramatizes the changing status of the Vietnam War in the American cultural consciousness.

The way in which the stories, fragments, and images that make up *The Things They Carried* are recycled from O'Brien's previous work complicates the already vexed questions of truth, accuracy, authenticity, and autobiography in which O'Brien purposefully entangles his narrative. In some instances—as in "The Man I Killed"—the author has been straightforward about the actual incident on which the story is based. Other stories represent more subtle and perhaps unconscious retellings that nonetheless speak volumes about our culture's changing attitudes toward the war. A charge that my students hotly contest is that *The Things They Carried* represents a sentimental or even sugar-coated rendition of the war, one that depicts atrocity and carnage only in elaborately circumscribed ways and in which it is more important for the reader to develop an overdetermined sympathy for O'Brien's lovable characters than to confront the realities of the conflict. I believe this argument is supported by the much more uncompromising stance that O'Brien takes toward violence and "evil" in his work both immediately following *The Things They Carried*—*In the Lake of the Woods*—and from previous years, such as his 1973 memoir *If I Die in a Combat Zone*. To explore these issues, I have my students compare an excerpt from "Spin," the third chapter in *The Things They Carried*, with a chapter entitled "The Man at the Well" from *If I Die in a Combat Zone* that is nominally unrelated but strikingly similar to "Spin" in setting and detail.

In "Spin," O'Brien narrates an uplifting and only gently ironic tale of cross-cultural bonding in which the squad enlists an old Vietnamese man, "slow and stooped over," to guide them through the Bantangan Peninsula's deadly minefields, where every day they would "troop along after him, tracing his footsteps, playing an exact and ruthless game of follow the leader" (33). The troops come "to love the old man" for keeping them safe and honor him with a marching song they make up to accompany their excursions: *"Step out of line, hit a mine; follow the dink, you're in the pink"* (33). The day of the squad's departure is a "sad scene": the soldiers "loaded him up with boxes of C rations" (33). The old man started to cry. "'Follow dink,'" he said to each of us, "'you go pink'" (34).

How jarring to discover that the autobiographical antecedent to this sweet tale is one of sadistic brutality. "The Man at the Well" begins with an ancient Vietnamese man, blind, "his spine bent into a permanent, calcified arc" (99). O'Brien's company spends the afternoon at the old man's village, where he welcomes the Americans and draws up water from the village well for them to drink and bathe in. "To be ingratiating he said, 'Good water for good GI's.' Whenever there was occasion, he repeated the phrase" (99). Then, at the end of an idyllic and relaxing afternoon, one "blustery and stupid soldier . . . picked up a carton of milk and from fifteen feet away hurled it, for no reason, aiming at the old man and striking him flush in the face" (100). Though the old man recoils from the attack, tottering precariously, drenched in milk and blood, "[n]o one moved to help" (100). The narrative makes it clear that his survival depends on his continued deference to the Americans, even if it means enduring humiliation and violence: recovering, the old man, "with the ruins of goodness spread over him, perfect gore . . . dunked into the well and came up with water, and he began showering the next soldier" (100).

In contrast to the uplift offered by "Spin," this anecdote grabs the reader by the throat in the worst possible way, eliciting feelings of horror, pity, and shame. Clearly, however, despite their almost opposite conclusions, these are versions of the same story. The archetypal figure of an old man who offers kindness and care, the focus on his eyes and his spinal deformity, the single pidgin English phrase that is repeated: all these similarities identify the "Spin" fragment as a rewriting, nearly two decades later, of the horrifying incident at the well. The milk of human kindness that is literally thrown in the old man's face in *If I Die in a Combat Zone* has become the C rations with which the man is generously "loaded up" in *The Things They Carried*. I ask my students to think about what could possibly have happened in the intervening eighteen years between the publication of these two texts to account for such a profound transformation—even a reversal—of this story. "Spin" has not replaced "The Man at the Well"; on the lecture circuit, O'Brien still tells the original story, which haunts him both as emblematic of the "small, everyday acts of atrocity and evil" that marked the war and as indicative of his own complicity in his failure to intervene (O'Brien, Hendrix Coll., Ithaca Coll.). However, it is clear that these two texts are versions of the same incident, thematically twinned, with different meanings but a common root.

To facilitate students' exploration of the relation between these two texts, any number of additional intertexts might be inserted into the interval between them. A slide show of Ron Haeberle's photos of the My Lai massacre for *Life* magazine or Nick Ut's iconic 1972 shot of the nine-year-old Kim Phuc fleeing her napalmed village can help remind students that images of grisly horror and American or American-funded atrocity were both fresh and familiar in 1973 when *If I Die in a Combat Zone* was published. Where did the public's consciousness of atrocity go? O'Brien ponders this very question in his 1994 article "The Vietnam in Me," an account of his postwar return trip to his old unit's area of operations, a region that included the village that was to become a household name after the publication of Haeberle's photographs. Describing the "null stares" he now receives from college students when he speaks about the My Lai massacre, O'Brien concludes that "evil has no place, it seems, in our national mythology" (52). Students might consider whether American atrocity reentered the realm of taboo during the so-called war on terror, amid such developments as abuse at United States military prisons and efforts by the Bush administration to circumvent international laws prohibiting torture. The text of Ronald Reagan's "noble cause" speech, addressed to the Veterans of Foreign Wars in 1980 and marking a turning point in the renarrativization of the Vietnam War, may be additionally helpful in demonstrating how American conduct has been wiped clean through successive reimaginings of the war's purpose and execution. Post-9/11 Hollywood treatments such as *We Were Soldiers*, with its ambivalently triumphalist tone and echoes of a "just" war, are also useful in this respect.

Of course, perhaps not all students (or teachers) would agree that the "Spin" segment is, in fact, a retelling of "The Man at the Well." But as is often the case, productive discussions can arise out of disagreement. How else might the student account for the thematic similarities between these two pieces? Does anything even remotely like the event described in "The Man at the Well" occur in *The Things They Carried*? If it does (students might cite Azar's mockery of a traumatized Vietnamese girl in "Style" or Rat Kiley's torture and slaughter of a baby water buffalo in "How to Tell a True War Story"), how is physical violence by Americans depicted and justified, and against whom is it directed? What is the impact of this carefully mediated violence on our understanding of the story or on our sympathy for the characters? Students might additionally be asked whether such a blunt, withering account of brutality as that in "The Man at the Well" would even be possible in the context of *The Things They Carried* in the light of its specific thematic concerns, moral tone, and narrative objectives. Students might contemplate, in other words, what aspects of the Vietnam War have become unspeakable in the context of our contemporary understanding.

To students, *The Things They Carried* is arguably the most likable and accessible of O'Brien's works, and it can thus appear to be almost effortlessly teachable: students will always have something to say about it. If the instructor allows it to teach itself, however, important pedagogical opportunities can be missed.

Fortunately, students tend to enjoy discovering connections between texts in a course, between courses in their programs of study, between history and their contemporary milieu; teaching *The Things They Carried* with intertexts helps open up the metacultural and indeed mythic dimensions of O'Brien's art, revealing the book to be rich in history without rendering it literally historical. It is one of those texts that dramatizes the ways in which the Vietnam War has been and continues to be processed within American cultural consciousness, and as such, it affords students an inside perspective on how the sustaining myths of a nation are generated out of specific, charged historical events. Intertexts provide the most direct way to render this perspective accessible to students, and in my experience their incorporation provides the most rewarding possible encounter with *The Things They Carried* for both students and instructor.

Teaching *The Nuclear Age* in the Second Nuclear Age

Doug Davis

I like to begin my class discussions of *The Nuclear Age* with a bang. I give in-class screenings of two short animated films produced for the Federal Civil Defense Administration (FCDA) in the early 1950s, *Target You* and *Duck and Cover*. Both provide practical advice on how to protect oneself in the case of a nuclear attack: one should hide under a blanket, duck into a doorway, or—of course—build a bomb shelter. The films visualize the nightmare scenario that drives O'Brien's protagonist William Cowling deep into his own hole: the realization that he, an ordinary person growing up in the security of his own home in the heartland of America, is a target who can suddenly die in a nuclear blast.

Students enjoy these films for different reasons. Many laugh in disbelief that anything can save someone from an atomic blast; others see sensible, if overly hopeful, advice from a more innocent era. I use these cartoons to provide a jumping-off point for discussing what O'Brien describes as his "big cartoon of the nuclear age," in which characters and events "are blown way out of proportion" (F. Kaplan 100). I ask students how the advice given in the films resembles their own experiences, for they live in a world with many similarities to William Cowling's nuclear age. Even before the terrorist attacks of 9/11, historians and military planners were thinking of the 1990s and the twenty-first century as a second nuclear age, defined by the threat of nuclear attack from terrorists and inimical regimes. The long-defunct FCDA has since been reborn as the Department of Homeland Security (DHS). *Target You* has accordingly become the DHS's new online guide for homeland security, *Preparing Makes Sense. Get Ready Now.*

Once considered by many reviewers to be an odd relic of cold war history, *The Nuclear Age* is more relevant than ever in the classroom. The three realms of threat that O'Brien describes in the three sections of his novel—the threat of nuclear attack in "Fission," the threat of a long-running, ill-defined war of containment in "Fusion," and the threat of nuclear terrorism in "Critical Mass"—are all a part of our students' lives. Reading the book as a representation of the history of the nuclear threat helps students understand the extent to which the destructive capabilities of nuclear technologies are realized in imaginary images, scenarios, and narratives about the future that pervade their everyday lives. O'Brien's nonlinear writing style, jumping about from 1995 to 1958 to 1968, helps connect what students may otherwise think of as very different moments in history. Reading *The Nuclear Age* in the second nuclear age connects the present age of terror to the past age of nuclear threat by showing how the sense of global threat that drives William into the basement and that drove the American military to acquire tens of thousands of nuclear weapons and to fight in Vietnam still drives the nation to war today.

I see the challenges of teaching O'Brien in the second nuclear age as three-fold. First, as educators we must demonstrate the connections between two very different areas of scholarly inquiry: foreign affairs and literary practice. Second, we must link the history of the cold war to the history of the war on terror. Finally, we must show students how their understanding of O'Brien's cold war literary practice can be used to make sense of American global strategy as a deeply literary practice in its own right.

To use *The Nuclear Age* in the classroom to crack open the nut of American nuclear history, I first communicate to students the novel's form as a nuclear war story and its relation to other prominent works of nuclear war artistry. O'Brien's story is different from others in that it does not dramatize nuclear war or its aftermath in the mode of a military thriller or a postnuclear tragedy. Instead, it offers a darkly comic, character-driven consideration of what it means to be a nuclear subject—a subject of a "total war" machine that does not distinguish between civilians and combatants.

Accordingly, in my American literature and cold war culture classes I put O'Brien's text in a tradition that begins with narratives about bombing campaigns in World War II written in the mode that novelist Bruce Jay Friedman dubbed "black humor." I draw class readings and film viewings from a constellation of texts that represent nuclear subjects. Prominent postwar authors who use black humor to represent the condition of being a subject of a total war machine in World War II include Thomas Pynchon in *Gravity's Rainbow*, Kurt Vonnegut in *Slaughterhouse-Five*, and Joseph Heller in *Catch-22*. Nuclear war films use similar doses of black humor and polluted mixtures of love and war to represent the inhumanity of the nuclear condition—in particular, Sidney Lumet's *Fail-Safe*, Stanley Kubrick's *Dr. Strangelove*, and Joseph Sargent's *Colossus: The Forbin Project*. Two other texts that treat nuclear fear in a personal narrative form similar to O'Brien's are Ross McElwee's darkly comedic documentary *Sherman's March*, which traces the filmmaker's search for love in the midst of nuclear fear, and John McPhee's nonfiction book *The Curve of Binding Energy*, which follows the story of a nuclear engineer who is in many ways William Cowling's counterpart and who tries to reform the nuclear weapons complex from within. Finally, it is interesting for students to read *The Nuclear Age* alongside two postnuclear novels, Russell Hoban's *Riddley Walker* and Denis Johnson's *Fiskadoro*, both of which take O'Brien's project beyond the end to imagine the condition of the postnuclear subject.

While utilizing the black humor common to many literary nuclear war narratives, O'Brien ultimately deploys it within the narrative form of the bildungsroman (Herzog, *Tim O'Brien* 131). He makes the political situation of the nuclear age personal through his protagonist, William Cowling. I emphasize to my students that it is a common practice for American writers to emphasize aspects of national identity in their treatment of individual protagonists, from Mark Twain's Huck Finn and Tom Sawyer and the poet-persona of Walt Whitman to Jack Kerouac's Sal Paradise and Pynchon's Oedipa Maas. Yet through William

Cowling, O'Brien presents an American identity not just in national but also in geopolitical terms. William, as Patrick Smith observes, is "a cold-war everyman," (89) working through the lived contradiction between threat and security known as nuclear deterrence. Only a quantum jump to a new state—a state of denial in which the physics of nuclear explosions become merely "a cunning metaphor" (O'Brien, *Nuclear Age* 312)—saves the lives of his family at the novel's end. I find that when I discuss the book's conclusion it is useful to ask students questions that go beyond it. While his family members' individual lives may be saved, is William's nuclear family saved too? Or is the nuclear family also a casualty of the nuclear age?

In discussing the plot, I begin at the end and ask students to chart how William got into his personal hole in the first place. The answer to that question necessarily turns to issues of cold war history, for it is entwined with the issue of how the United States became dependent on nuclear weapons. Students soon see how William's development as a person mirrors the development of the nation over the course of the cold war, from a threatened state (the novel's "Fission" section), to a nation at war both abroad and with itself ("Fusion"), and ultimately to a nation of global wealth and power under a technological system of mass death that is facing new threats of terrorism ("Critical Mass"). As we chart William's personal history on a time line, supported by passages from the text, I ask students to identify two influences that shape his personal life: global political events and his imagination of a future war. While unpacking the plot, students discover how politics and imagination work in tandem to propel William's passage through the nuclear age. For instance, William describes his decision to dodge the draft and go underground as "the dynamic decid[ing] for me" (121). Enigmatic pronouncements such as this are good topics for class discussion. What are the properties of this dynamic? Where did it come from? Likewise, working from descriptive passages, such as William's childhood visions of nuclear war (29–30) and his college visions of the combat in Vietnam (71), I ask, How does William's imagination of the threat posed by serving in Vietnam compare with his imagination of the threat posed by nuclear war?

I use descriptive questions such as these to turn William's private story back into a public one in class discussions that foreground the relation between literature and history. I present the novel as a part of an intertextual multimedia module, using William's personal history to explore cold war cultural and political history. I assign readings from Paul Boyer's cultural study of the first years of the nuclear age, *By the Bomb's Early Light*, asking students to report on different chapters that discuss reactions to the invention of the atomic bomb across American society, from advertising to science. I supplement the historical reading with short films and songs drawn from new cold war multimedia collections, such as the six-disc music and film anthology *Atomic Platters* (which also contains *Target You* and *Duck and Cover*). I use primary policy texts from the anthology *The American Atom: A Documentary History of Nuclear Policies from the Discovery of Fission to the Present* (Cantelon, Hewlett, and Williams) and I direct students to find vintage civil defense manuals and memorabilia at various Web sites, including those for Eric Green's Civil Defense Museum, the Cold War Museum, and Conelrad. All these supplementary materials help students learn how thoroughly nuclear fear permeated American culture.

For the "Fission" section I use several primary documents to help students understand the origins of the nuclear threat. It is instructive to read *The Nuclear Age* alongside foundational policy documents, including Albert Einstein's 1938 letter to President Roosevelt urging the construction of an atomic bomb to ward off the threat of a German bomb; George Kennan's so-called Long Telegram of 1947, "The Sources of Soviet Conduct," which first articulated the policy of Soviet containment; the full text of the once top-secret National Security Council document 68 (May), which in 1950 became the guide for American nuclear strategy for the next fifty years; and Secretary of State John Foster Dulles's so-called Massive Retaliation Speech of 1954, "The Evolution of Foreign Policy," which introduced the concept of assured destruction. The rhetoric of these texts is hair-raising, and they communicate to students the passion and sense of mortal danger that fueled the cold war. Two historical works help frame my classroom discussion of these primary texts: Lawrence Freedman's comprehensive study *The Evolution of Nuclear Strategy*, and Fred Kaplan's history of the early days of nuclear strategy and the creation of the nuclear war think tank RAND, *The Wizards of Armageddon*, which is written in a gripping narrative style that makes for good reading.

For the "Fusion" section, I supplement classroom readings with primary texts by leading postwar cultural critics as well as lectures on the place of the Vietnam War in cold war history. I draw from a selection of texts from the 1950s and 1960s to help students understand the Vietnam era's counterculture of protest and how William's sense of America's insanity was "in the air" at the time: Erich Fromm's "Can a Society Be Sick?" in *The Sane Society*; chapters on college life in *The Organization Man*, by William Whyte, Jr.;[1] Theodore Roszak's "Technocracy's Children"; and Paul Goodman's *Growing Up Absurd*. In cold war cultural studies and postwar literary survey classes, I often teach *The Nuclear Age* alongside Norman Mailer's *Armies of the Night*, since each concerns the narrator's place in the counterculture as both a participant and an outsider. I ask students to analyze how O'Brien's darkly humorous novel contrasts with Mailer's New Journalism novel and how Mailer and O'Brien-William understand the threats that motivate the counterculture as well as its political efficacy. It is eye-opening at this point to view Sam Green and Bill Siegel's documentary, *The Weather Underground*, which provides a firsthand look at the historical figures on which O'Brien's committee is based. In the announcements that pepper "Fusion," O'Brien discusses the development of the air war in Vietnam (73, 110–11); I use these sections to make connections between the Vietnam War and the nuclear threat. I draw a class lecture from the historian

Mark Clodfelter's *The Limits of Air Power*, which contains a detailed account of how the threat of nuclear retaliation determined President Johnson's limited approach to the war.

For "Critical Mass" I ask students to detail the reasons why William abandons his earlier antinuclear principles. I emphasize the irony of his situation—that in turning his back on his principles, William may have enriched himself, but he is now an agent of a new kind of threat confronting the reader's future: nuclear terrorism. "Where on earth," he asks in the final "Quantum Jump" chapter, his comrades dead and a detonator in his hand, "is the happy ending?" (298). It is a question we may very well ask ourselves in the second nuclear age. I address this exact question to my students, for the result of William's decades of fighting his state of fear is yet another kind of nuclear fear. At this point I direct my students to the final primary text of my multimedia module, the new National Security Strategy for the United States of America (NSS), produced by President Bush's National Security Council (NSC) in 2002 in response to the 9/11 terrorist attacks and then revised in 2006. I ask students to compare this document's fearful futures with those described in NSC 68 by using such concepts of literary analysis as imagery, rhetoric, narrative, characterization, and theme. Students soon see how the enemy characters have changed from NSC 68's Soviet slave state to the NSS's rogue evildoers. Yet they also find that the assumption of a nuclear threat and the prioritizing of American military power remain grand themes in both texts.

An understanding of the threatening power of William's imagination ultimately helps students connect the literary to the political. They see for themselves the power that William's fearful imagination wields not only over himself but also over American global strategy. They discover that the fearful imagination that guided his life is much the same as that which guided the United States through permutations of the policy of nuclear deterrence in the cold war. It is the same imagination that justified the global nuclear arsenals whose loose components now haunt our collective futures. The ever-threatened quality of national character that O'Brien identifies in his national bildungsroman remains a part of American culture and global strategy. I end the class discussion of O'Brien's novel by asking my students if they can imagine a better future than William can.

NOTE

[1] I find it instructive to discuss with my students how much Whyte's analysis of cold war college life resembles their own experience and how much they think that their life plans conform to Whyte's paradigm of the organization man. I then ask them, Is William an organization man? How does his college experience shape his future relationships with the institutions of the family, the state, and the economy?

"Thinking Seriously about Canada": Defamiliarizing O'Brien's Work from a Canadian Perspective

Christopher Kocela

Having taught O'Brien's works in large urban universities in both Canada and the United States, I have found that strategies developed to help Canadian students come to terms with O'Brien's fiction have also proved successful with students in the American South. The teaching focus I describe in this essay was originally intended to challenge and complicate what I perceived as two significant trends in Canadian undergraduates' reception of O'Brien's work. On the one hand, although most of the students were encountering O'Brien for the first time in my survey of contemporary American literature, many described his work as familiar because it confirmed their general expectations about Vietnam War fiction. These expectations, I discovered, were shaped in large part by the postmodern presentation of the war in films like *Apocalypse Now* and *Full Metal Jacket*, to which my students compared O'Brien's "How to Tell a True War Story" (in *The Things They Carried*) and "Night March" (in *Going After Cacciato*) with (I thought) problematic ease. On the other hand, there was a smaller but quite vocal minority who took the difficulty of O'Brien's work as an occasion to question whether Canadians would ever be able to (or, more pointedly, should ever need to) understand the war and its legacy. The simple truth of the Vietnam War, as voiced by some of these students, was that Canada had had the good sense not to fight in it and had generously harbored young American men seeking to escape the draft.

The refusal of students to entertain the relevance of American cultural anxieties and values in the Canadian classroom was rare in my teaching experience (particularly in a course dedicated to American literature), and it caused me to reflect critically on my own understanding, as a Canadian, of the ongoing legacy of the Vietnam War in Canada. I realized that while Vietnam is, according to H. Bruce Franklin, "no longer really a country or even a war but a 'syndrome'" for many Americans (*Vietnam and Other American Fantasies* 3), the war exists in the minds of some Canadians as a clear historical marker of Canada's difference from the United States—a difference on which much of Canadian national identity depends. My pedagogical emphasis on defamiliarization when teaching O'Brien's works is not simply an effort to challenge belief in the cultural differences between the United States and Canada. Instead, I hope to make my students more critical of their culturally received ideas about the war—especially the idea that Vietnam, as the first "postmodernist war" (Jameson, *Postmodernism* 44), demands a correspondingly postmodern treatment as a fragmented, decentered, schizophrenic, and ultimately unknowable conflict. Because the idea that Vietnam is "always already unrepresentable" (Bibby, "Post-Vietnam Condition" 148) continues to circulate in various forms in the United States and

Canada, I believe my approach will prove useful to teachers of O'Brien's work on both sides of the Rainy River.

In my undergraduate survey of post-1945 American literature, I teach O'Brien as the final author in a midterm unit called Metafiction as Social Commentary. The unit aims to expose students to a variety of contemporary authors (Thomas Pynchon, Ishmael Reed, Robert Coover, Donald Barthelme, Maxine Hong Kingston, Kathy Acker, and David Foster Wallace are featured on a rotating basis) through whom they come to observe general traits of postmodernist fiction and their employment for social criticism. To establish a framework for reading these difficult texts, I rely on the influential theses about postmodernist fiction developed by Brian McHale and Linda Hutcheon, and I also use our course texts to illustrate points of connection between contemporary theory and fiction (Pynchon's *The Crying of Lot 49* as a primer on poststructuralism, Acker's texts as *ecriture feminine*, etc.).

As the capstone to this unit, I typically teach two O'Brien stories: "How to Tell a True War Story" and "On the Rainy River," both from *The Things They Carried.* For instructional purposes, these two stories are complementary. "How to Tell a True War Story" masquerades as an instructional booklet for telling true stories about combat and life in the jungle, but as students quickly discover, the story's metafictional form and repetition of events subvert the simple step-by-step teleology of the how-to manual. "On the Rainy River" is a much more straightforward and linear narrative about a young man's temptation to flee to Canada to escape the draft, concluding with his decision to go to Vietnam and fight. But the end of the story defies expectations by portraying this decision as a cowardly act, thereby reversing the poles of a certain conventional, nationalistic morality that depicts war veterans as heroes and draft dodgers as cowards. Both stories build toward what, in the terms of early Russian formalist criticism, can be called a defamiliarizing effect on the reader, in which the initial frameworks for understanding Vietnam are rendered problematic. In teaching these stories, I try to make students aware of how O'Brien's fiction achieves these defamiliarizing effects and what his work suggests about our ability—and responsibility—to understand and represent Vietnam.

I focus first on "How to Tell a True War Story," and I begin by posing a question about the story's end: Why does the narrator feel so hostile to the "older woman of kindly temperament and humane politics" (84) who approaches him in tears? This question effectively launches class discussion because many students are put off by the narrator's reaction to this woman—particularly his description of her, in Rat Kiley's language, as a "dumb cooze" (68). As debate about the overall likability of the narrator heats up, I redirect discussion by asking the class to consider how the exchange between this woman and the narrator reflects our own relationship, as readers, with O'Brien's story. After his encounter with the woman, the narrator claims that "[y]ou can tell a true war story if you just keep on telling it" (85); but the meaning of "tell" is ambiguous here, implying the ability both to express and to discern a true war story. Have we, by the end of O'Brien's story, learned how to tell a true war story in either of these senses?

To test our ability to tell a true war story, I ask my students to close their texts and describe what happens to Curt Lemon. Most students recall that the story of Lemon's death is repeated with minor variations several times in "How to Tell a True War Story" (in fact, there are four tellings in the story and a total of six throughout *The Things They Carried*). As they begin to discuss the events of Lemon's death, I observe reactions to the details they put forward: invariably some cringe while others laugh self-consciously, particularly at mention of Dave Jensen's singing "Lemon Tree" as he removes parts of his friend's body from the foliage. I interrupt the process of recollection to reiterate the goal of the exercise. Which details enable us to tell the truth about Lemon's death? I then ask four volunteers to read aloud the various versions of the story. Afterward, students generally agree that the four narratives of Lemon's death are distinct in tone, ranging from the almost romantic sensibility of the first version (70) to the absurdity and gore of the "Lemon Tree" account (83). Yet since none openly contradicts the others, we doubt the historical fact of Lemon's death (as we come to doubt, for example, virtually every event in Coover's repetitive postmodernist text "The Babysitter"). Instead, what students realize through this exercise is that repetition in O'Brien's story, while reinforcing the fact of Lemon's death, makes the event less familiar with each subsequent telling because of the shifts in tone and context.

It is at this point that I introduce the concept of defamiliarization to describe the effect of repetition in O'Brien's text. I begin by presenting defamiliarization in the terms established by the Russian formalist critic Viktor Shklovsky. For Shklovsky, defamiliarization describes the process by which literature challenges our view of the world, rejuvenating our relationship with things that have ceased to attract our attention in everyday life. In his 1917 essay "Art as Technique," Shklovsky describes defamiliarization as the transformation of habitual knowledge into perception: "The purpose of art is to impart the sensation of things as they are perceived and not as they are known" (18). Literary texts effect this transformation through the unique devices at their disposal. In poetry, elevated language, rhyme, and meter defamiliarize our common use of language, thereby altering our perceptions; in artistic prose works, the inherent difference between the events in a narrative and the way in which the narrative orders and represents those events (in tone, with flashbacks, etc.) makes us reevaluate our conventional notions of causality and temporality.[1]

Returning to O'Brien, I ask my students to consider whether the specific forms of defamiliarization that we have examined in "How to Tell a True War Story" amount to a broader defamiliarization of our habitual knowledge concerning the Vietnam War. After his first attempt to tell the truth of Lemon's death, the narrator describes his efforts in terms that recall Shklovsky's definition of defamiliarization as a transformation of knowledge into perception: "And then afterward, when you go to tell about it, there is always that surreal seemingness, which makes the story seem untrue, but which in fact represents the hard and exact truth as it *seemed*" (71).[2] If "surreal seemingness" has become a convention in films and literature about the Vietnam War, does O'Brien's fiction reinforce or defamiliarize that convention and the cultural knowledge it propagates?

Students are frequently divided over this issue, so it is at this point that I segue into an analysis of "On the Rainy River," which more clearly addresses the issue of defamiliarization in a cultural register. As with "How to Tell a True War Story," our study of "On the Rainy River" begins with a consideration of the ending. After the narrator decides not to flee to Canada, the story concludes with the following paragraph:

> The day was cloudy. I passed through towns with familiar names, through the pine forests and down to the prairie, and then to Vietnam, where I was a soldier, and then home again. I survived, but it's not a happy ending. I was a coward. I went to the war. (61)

Given our discussion so far, students are quick to identify the defamiliarizing effects of this final paragraph. Many note the way in which the final two sentences reverse expectations by portraying cowardice not as a flight from Vietnam to Canada but as a flight from Canada to Vietnam.[3] Some students also call attention to the radical compression of the narrator's wartime experiences in the final paragraph. In retrospect, the narrator portrays traveling to and fighting in Vietnam as historically equivalent to passing through "towns with familiar names" in northern Minnesota. The implication is that the most significant and haunting moment in his experience of the Vietnam War takes place not in Vietnam at all but in a boat on the Rainy River between Minnesota and Ontario, twenty yards from the Canadian shore. The narrator suggests that to understand this reversal of expectations, we need to place ourselves in the moment of his indecision about fleeing to Canada:

> I want you to feel it—the wind coming off the river, the waves, the silence, the wooded frontier. You're at the bow of a boat on the Rainy River. You're twenty-one years old, you're scared, and there's a hard squeezing pressure in your chest.
> What would you do? (56)

Given the clear emphasis here on the narrator's various sensations and perceptions when faced with the reality of Canada, I ask the class whether we can view this passage as the narrator's direct invitation to defamiliarize our habitual knowledge about Canada. If so, what knowledge are we being asked to transform through this new perceptual framework?

I go on to ask my students what they know about Canada in relation to the Vietnam War. Of course, many immediately point to the fact that Canada served as a safe haven for young American men fleeing the draft, but beyond this, their historical knowledge is sketchy at best (and no less so, in my experience, in Canada than in the United States). Students tend to vastly underestimate the number of deserters who actually fled to Canada during the course of the war: as many as 500,000 by some estimates—approximately nine times the number of Americans killed in Vietnam. Students also tend to know little about how Canada and the Canadian government reacted to this tremendous influx of war resisters. Some of my Canadian students point with pride to the fact that the Liberal prime minister of Canada during the war, Pierre Elliott Trudeau, actively encouraged young American men to come to Canada. In a March 1970 press statement, Trudeau famously announced, "The government is welcoming U.S. draft dodgers and deserters to Canada. . . . I hope Canada will become a refuge from militarism" (Dickerson 55). Yet students are generally unaware of the indirect economic role Canada played in the Vietnam War and of the fact that major media sources at the time of Trudeau's announcement were accusing the government of tracking down and questioning American war deserters. To provide some historical context,[4] I point out that many Canadian businesses profited (to the tune of billions of dollars) from the Vietnam War through the Canada–United States Defense Production Sharing Agreement—an agreement that allowed Canadian firms to compete for American contracts for ammunition, clothing, and other military equipment. (Students are surprised to learn that the caps worn by the Green Berets were manufactured in Toronto.) Canada wasn't always as welcoming of war resisters as Trudeau's open invitation would suggest. The same year that Trudeau issued his statement, Canada's major news magazine, *Maclean's*, ran a story focusing on how the Royal Canadian Mounted Police (RCMP) were cooperating with the FBI in tracing and interrogating deserters in Canada. In bringing these details to light in the Canadian classroom, I was not trying to deflate nationalistic pride; instead, my aim was to defamiliarize habitual knowledge about Canadian history and to establish the importance of attending to the legacy of the Vietnam War in Canada. That legacy is both economic and cultural, since a great number of American men and women who fled to Canada between 1963 and 1974 never returned to the United States.

Teaching now in the United States, I continue to find that defamiliarizing Canada's role in the Vietnam War has a valuable impact on student understanding of O'Brien's story. To begin with, information about the RCMP's role in tracing the movements of war resisters lends historical justification to the narrator's fear of fleeing through the Canadian woods, "the law closing in on all sides—my hometown draft board and the FBI and the Royal Canadian Mounted Police" (50). This image supports the story's conclusion that, contrary to the view of some, fleeing to Canada was no cowardly act.[5] But in the light of the estimated number of men and women who went to Canada during the war, the more significant impact of historicizing "On the Rainy River" is that students come to see the narrator's conflict as representative of a broad cultural movement. I encourage my students to view the narrator's reflections on Canada as an oblique commentary on American cultural values and ideals. Does the narrator's ultimate decision to reject Canada and go to Vietnam speak to the reasons why the United States went to war?

As students begin "thinking seriously about Canada" in O'Brien's text (44), it becomes apparent that the narrator, at the start of the story, knows very little about his neighboring country ("the idea seemed purely abstract") despite living fairly close to the border (44). I then ask how, or if, the narrator's understanding of Canada changes through the course of the narrative. To try to answer this question, we identify every reference to Canada in the text, eventually focusing our attention on three passages from the last pages of the story. The first describes the narrator's initial approach to the Rainy River after fleeing his job at the meatpacking plant (47); the second and third occur six days later, in Elroy Berdahl's boat, when the narrator realizes he is in Canadian waters for the first time (55, 57). Students quickly identify a common strain in the narrator's musings about Canada: though essentially unknown to him, the country threatens to engulf him in difference so threatening that he can comprehend it only as another life, another world, or as sheer fantasy. On one level, this reaction emphasizes the courage required by war deserters to leave their country for unknown prospects. But the end of the story also sheds an ironic light on the narrator's understanding (or lack of understanding) of Canada. As he continues to wrestle with the idea of going to Canada, his past life comes back to him in a hallucination that takes the form of a "weird sporting event" attended by American heroes ranging from Abraham Lincoln to Huck Finn to Gary Cooper (58). As I point out to my students, this is the only passage in "On the Rainy River" that approaches the "surreal seemingness" we generally associate with representations of the Vietnam War. But why is that convention used to construct a fantasy about American history and cultural values? And why is this American fantasy described only after the narrator has recognized Canada as a "pitiful fantasy" (57)?

Though I prefer to let students form their own conclusions about the significance of the narrator's hallucination, I make one final observation about the end of the story in hope of tying together some key threads of our class discussion. Regardless of how we interpret the implied relation between the narrator's "pitiful fantasy" of Canada and his reveries about the United States, I submit that the end of "On the Rainy River" dramatizes myth making on another level. The Rainy River and Elroy Berdahl can be read as analogues to the mythical river of Lethe and its silent boatman, Charon, the figure in Greek myth responsible for ferrying souls to the underworld. I mention this analogy to my students not only because they have encountered this mythic reference twice already in the course (in Allen Ginsberg's "A Supermarket in California" and John Cheever's "The Swimmer") but also because I believe O'Brien's recourse to mythology here reflects his view of what "true" war stories are able to teach their readers.

In an interview with Eric James Schroeder, O'Brien describes what he calls the "fullness of the word 'story'" in relation to communal value and myth:

> How do you gather a lesson from *The Iliad* or *The Odyssey*? They're stories. They have no single moral, no single lesson. Not even a set of lessons or morals. The word you used was "myth." The story should have a *mythic* quality to it, even a short story that isn't reducible to a parable from the Bible. . . . I don't expect the reader to draw any single moral out of it either; but rather, by going through the process of having imagined something, one gathers a sense of the *stuff* that's being imagined, a sense of what a war is and what escape from war is. And that sense can't be pinned down to a message or a moral. ("Two Interviews" 130)

For O'Brien, the didactic function of a well-crafted story cannot be reduced to a single moral instruction but resides, instead, in its ability to simulate the process of imaginative experience for the reader. This emphasis on process and perception over accepted values is in keeping with Shklovsky's theory of the defamiliarizing role of literature, and in the light of that theory, it is tempting to read the analogy between O'Brien's Rainy River and Lethe, the river of forgetfulness, as a self-reflexive comment on the "mythic" aspect of O'Brien's fiction. Although the narrator of "On the Rainy River" describes his turning back from Canada as a cowardly act, his story provides the reader with a vivid sense of "what a war is and what escape from war is" (Schroeder, *Vietnam* 130). Without reducing "On the Rainy River" to a single moral message, one can say that a didactic function of the story is to encourage imaginative engagement with historical events over the forgetfulness that inevitably attends habitual knowledge. The aim of my attempts in the classroom to place O'Brien's stories in historical context and to call attention to their defamiliarizing effects is to draw out this didactic or mythic dimension of his works.

NOTES

[1] In the later work of Roman Jackobson, Shklovsky's formalist account of defamiliarization becomes a structural model for explaining the historical development of literary forms. See Steiner; Erlich.

[2] Steven Kaplan describes the objective of O'Brien's writing in terms that recall Shklovsky's definition of defamiliarization: "Tim O'Brien tries to make his readers believe that what they are reading is true because he wants them to step outside their everyday reality and participate in the events he is portraying" (*Understanding* 178–79).

[3] Heberle (*Trauma Artist* xxii–xxiii) and Herzog (*Tim O'Brien* 1–2) discuss O'Brien's use in public lectures of "On the Rainy River" as a personal confession (later revealed to the audience as fictional) of his own cowardice in going to Vietnam. As I mention to my students, the painful question about whether to go to Vietnam or flee to Canada is also dramatized

in chapter 9 of *July, July*, entitled "Winnipeg" (originally published as a short story in the *New Yorker* in August 2000). "Winnipeg" tells the story of Billy McMann, a young man who succeeds in escaping to Canada in 1969 but who ends up with a lifelong bitterness toward the woman who promised to flee with him but backed out at the last moment.

4 Historical details here are from Dickerson 55–57.

5 Billy McMann, the protagonist of "Winnipeg" (see n3) also fears being tracked by the Mounties shortly after he arrives in Canada (112).

6 To my knowledge, no one has commented on the mythic analogy between the Rainy River and Lethe in O'Brien's story, although Carpenter compares O'Brien's Rainy River with Hemingway's "Big Two-Hearted River" ("'It Don't Mean Nothin'" 48), and Herzog compares Elroy Berdahl with Claude Rasmussen in *In the Lake of the Woods*, which is also set on the Rainy River (*Tim O'Brien* 116–17).

Teaching *The Things They Carried* with Duong Thu Huong's *Novel without a Name*

Derek C. Maus

Years after its initial publication, *The Things They Carried* continues to be a staple of undergraduate literature courses. Following the United States–led invasion of Iraq in 2003, Tim O'Brien was frequently invoked, usually to harness what were seen as his credentials as an antiwar writer. Although O'Brien spoke out against the invasion and subsequent occupation of Iraq—often noting its similarities to the Vietnam War—the cultural discourse into which his comments (and quotations from his earlier books) were introduced is a relatively impoverished one, a condition that I believe severely hobbles examination of his writing. The war in Iraq has exacerbated the polarization of discourse in the United States into prowar and antiwar camps, which leaves little room for nuanced analysis of conflict, either contemporary or historical. It should not be surprising that students who have been steeped in such an oversimplified rhetoric echo its language when they first encounter O'Brien's fictions about war and its participants. The discernment of fine distinctions is generally estimable in the study of literature but is especially important when dealing with O'Brien's fiction, which presents its readers with thematic, structural, ontological, and emotional challenges at every turn.

Pairing O'Brien with thematically similar writers is a common strategy for enhancing students' awareness of the complexity of his work. The most frequent comparisons have included either other American writers of war fiction (e.g., Ernest Hemingway, Robert Olen Butler) or non-American "soldier-poets" (e.g., Erich Maria Remarque, Wilfred Owen). I have found that students' discussions of the works in such linkages are generally vigorous but tend to remain proscribed by received notions about the specific conflicts being depicted (e.g., "The Vietnam War was shameful and immoral" or "World War II was a 'good' war") or about war in general (e.g., "War is Hell" or "Dying for one's country as a soldier is the ultimate glory").

Alternatively, coupling *The Things They Carried* with Duong Thu Huong's 1995 *Novel without a Name* (*Tiêu thuyêt vô dê*) creates a potentially rich discursive dynamic for three reasons. First, both works examine the Vietnam War, but they do so from ostensibly opposing perspectives, thereby broadening the scope of what constitutes Vietnam War fiction beyond its customary American boundaries. Duong's protagonist-narrator, Quan, a platoon commander in the North Vietnamese Army, is the enemy of O'Brien's company of American soldiers. Second, both O'Brien and Duong write with the authority of having participated in the war they depict, albeit in different circumstances. O'Brien spent fourteen months in Vietnam as part of the United States Army's 46th Infantry, and Duong served in the Communist Youth Brigade for seven years during the war, organizing cultural events to maintain morale and further political education among the front-line troops. Third, since departing the battlefield, both writers have earned their reputations in part because of their criticism of the forces—political, ideological, cultural, and even personal—that put them there in the first place. *If I Die in a Combat Zone* marked the beginning of this process for O'Brien in 1973, while Duong began an outspoken career as a public dissident a decade or so later. She was expelled from the Vietnamese Communist Party in 1989 for her scathing written critiques of the party and its leaders. She was imprisoned in 1991 for seven months for attempting to smuggle her manuscripts—including *Novel without a Name*—out of the country.

Each of these three points requires students to examine their preconception that O'Brien and Duong were enemies in the war they both fictionalize. When teaching the novels together, I begin by having students discuss their underlying presumptions about the relationship between the two authors. This discussion usually involves some rather emotional exchanges regarding the extent to which soldiers owe allegiance to their country after their return from war, a topic that stirred especially strong reactions during the spring 2004 semester, when debate over the military service of George W. Bush and John Kerry during the Vietnam War dominated the national political discourse. Individual students' attitudes correlated closely with the extent to which they presumed that soldiers uncritically and unconditionally agreed with the orders they received from their civilian and military commanders.

Immediately before our formal reading, I provide the students with biographical details about O'Brien and Duong and ask them to describe in a few sentences what message they expect the two books to convey. They submit these writings to me anonymously so that we can use them to seed our discussions once we have read both works. Their responses tend to be colored by the binary contemporary discourse about war, as well as lingering reverberations of the cold war's geopolitical dichotomies. They generally expect Duong, as a dissenting victim of a repressive Communist government, to be sympathetic toward the United States. Some students take this expectation further, predicting that *Novel without a Name* will resemble Alexander Solzhenitsyn's *One Day in the Life of Ivan Denisovich* in exposing the horrors of Communism from within. Others expect that Duong will relate the tale of a soldier who sees the error of his ways and changes sides to fight against the Communists.

Whereas the students' preconceptions about Duong tend to be fairly uniform,[1] their predictions about O'Brien are generally more polarized, almost wholly in keeping with the contemporary antiwar discourse. The class divides between those who think that *The Things They Carried* will condemn the Vietnam War in the manner of *Apocalypse Now* or *Full Metal Jacket* and those who believe that O'Brien will reveal himself as a traitor to the sacrifice made by his fellow soldiers. The students tend to conceptualize dissent as a purely oppositional function, given that a substantial number of them expect both O'Brien and Duong to betray the nation they served during the war. That one can dis-

sent against a society's actions without adopting or extolling the values of its
adversary is rarely understood as a possibility in advance, yet it is precisely such
a reading that I believe affords greater insight into the works.

Steven Liparulo's 2003 article "'Incense and Ashes': The Postmodern Work
of Refutation in Three Vietnam War Novels"[2] exemplifies the kind of non-
dichotomous critical perspective I wish to foster. Liparulo claims that both *The
Things They Carried* and *Novel without a Name*—in addition to Bao Ninh's
The Sorrows of War—engage in

> a Socratic refutative literary practice that seeks to unsettle its reader's
> sense of certainty, to challenge the reader's understanding of the obliga-
> tions of citizenship and belief in myths of national "exceptionalism," and to
> emphasize its own complicity in creating scenes of harm and suffering.
>
> (72)

Liparulo's reading of the works offers useful commentary on each of the three
points of comparison between O'Brien and Duong enumerated above. His association of both novels with a postmodern rhetorical function ("refutations
of powerful master narratives" [90]) helps categorize them as nonideological
statements of dissent—that is, critiques that do not inherently validate their
opposites. His claim that the novels "represent anxiety and ambivalence to-
wards love, patriotism, religion, the obligations of citizenship—those passions
and capacities necessary for life beyond mere survival that also create in us all
profound and intractable vulnerabilities" (90)—strongly echoes the humanistic didacticism that has marked each author's career since leaving the battlefield. Finally, Liparulo states that both O'Brien and Duong intend to move
beyond "liberal-humanist revisions" (83) that regard the soldiers as victims of
circumstance rather than morally complicit agents in war. He asserts that their
characters—and by extension their readers—are faced with more difficult social and personal issues: "It is not simply a matter of going to war or not—the
responsibilities run deeper than that, citizenship is more than an abstraction,
communities make material and contradictory demands" (83). While Liparulo's
article is a welcome addition to the scholarship on both O'Brien and Duong, my
classroom experiences indicate that the students are capable of arriving independently at a similar conclusion.

In formulating such a critical middle path, students need to recognize the
treatment of themes common to both works, with the larger goal of comprehending the ways that dissent against the status quo of one's culture need not in-
vert it in the process. As an example of the many possible thematic comparisons
between the books, I illustrate the ways in which O'Brien and Duong explicitly
claim that the principles supposedly motivating the soldiers in their stories are,
at best, vaguely understood and, at worst, cynically debased by their political
and military leaders. In diagnosing these pathologies, O'Brien and Duong are
not perfectly in alignment, but their attitudes coincide in transcending simplistic

accusations of purely external guilt. O'Brien attributes the war's aimlessness to a pervasive lack of honest introspection in the broader American culture that produced everyone (including O'Brien himself) involved in the war on his side. On the other hand, Duong blames both the self-interest of the party cadres for manipulating the Vietnamese people and the people themselves (including herself) for accepting such manipulation even after they became aware of it. Furthermore, both O'Brien and Duong depict moments during which characters speculate that processes similar to those they observe in their own culture are also taking place in that of their enemies, thereby problematizing any claim that O'Brien or Duong desire to just "switch sides."

To illustrate this comparison, I first ask students to look at two sets of fictional and nonfictional passages by O'Brien. In a 1999 keynote address on writing about the Vietnam War, O'Brien described his hometown of Worthington, Minnesota, as

> a town that congratulates itself, day after day, on its own ignorance of the world: a town that got us into Vietnam. Uh, the people in that town sent me to that war, you know, couldn't spell the word "Hanoi" if you spotted them three vowels. They couldn't do it.   ("Writing Vietnam")

These comments are echoed in the story "On the Rainy River" in *The Things They Carried*, as O'Brien's fictionalized self is debating whether to dodge the draft:

> I'd be screaming at [the people of Worthington], telling them how much I detested their blind, thoughtless, automatic acquiescence to it all, their simpleminded patriotism, their prideful ignorance, their love-it-or-leave-it platitudes, how they were sending me off to fight a war they didn't understand and didn't want to understand. I held them responsible. By God, yes, I *did*. . . . They didn't know Bao Dai from the man in the moon. They didn't know history. They didn't know the first thing about Diem's tyranny or the nature of Vietnamese nationalism, or the long colonialism of the French—this was all too damned complicated, it required some reading—but no matter, it was a war to stop the Communists, plain and simple, which was how they liked things, and you were a treasonous pussy if you had second thoughts about killing or dying for plain and simple reasons.   (45)

By themselves, these two passages reinforce the notion that O'Brien is exonerating himself by blaming Worthington, and based on their in-class responses, the students generally tend to accept or reject this according to their preconceptions about protest literature.

A second juxtaposition of passages, however, complicates either a wholly sympathetic or a wholly antagonistic reading. In a 1980 interview, O'Brien recalled his personal war experience as follows:

My time in Vietnam is a memory of ignorance and I mean utter ignorance. I didn't know the language. I couldn't communicate with the Vietnamese except in pidgin English. I knew nothing about the culture of Vietnam. I knew nothing about the religion, religions. I knew nothing about the village community. I knew nothing about the aims of the people, whether they were for the war or against the war. . . . No knowledge of what the enemy was after. . . . and I compensated for that ignorance in a whole bunch of ways, some evil ways. Blowing things up, burning huts as a frustration of being ignorant and not knowing where the enemy was.

(qtd. in Klein)

O'Brien transfers this recognition of ignorance to the story "The Things They Carried" by describing with similar language the group of American soldiers to which his fictionalized self belongs:

Their principles were in their feet. Their calculations were biological. They had no sense of strategy or mission. They searched the villages without knowing what to look for, not caring, kicking over jars of rice, frisking children and old men, blowing tunnels, sometimes setting fires and sometimes not, then forming up and moving on to the next village, then other villages, where it would always be the same. (15)

O'Brien repeatedly reinforces the thematic associations of willful ignorance among Worthington (a metonym for the United States), the soldiers, and himself, as in this passage from "In the Field" in which a young lieutenant reflects upon his preparation for combat:

Jimmy Cross did not want the responsibility of leading these men. He had never wanted it. In his sophomore year at Mount Sebastian College he had signed up for the Reserve Officer Training Corps without much thought. An automatic thing: because his friends had joined, and because it was worth a few credits. . . . He was unprepared. . . . [E]ven after all these months in the bush, all the days and nights, even then he did not know enough to keep his men out of a shit field. (167–68)

O'Brien emphasizes the "automatic" nature of Jimmy Cross's decision, which recalls both the "automatic acquiescence" of his fictionalized Worthingtonians and the instinctual "calculations" of his fellow soldiers. In each instance, he shows that the moral implications of killing and possibly being killed remain unconsidered.

This last point is indispensable to expanding understanding of the book, since O'Brien acknowledges that his greatest personal failing was that he *had* considered the moral implications but had been unwilling or unable to act upon them. As the narrator of "On the Rainy River" agonizes over escaping to Canada, he expresses his seeming conundrum:

> It was a kind of schizophrenia. A moral split. I couldn't make up my mind.
> I feared the war, yes, but I also feared exile. I was afraid of walking away
> from my own life, my friends and my family, my whole history, everything
> that mattered to me.   (44–45)

He condemns himself unambiguously when he ultimately rejects exile:

> I passed through towns with familiar names, through the pine forests and
> down to the prairie, and then to Vietnam, where I was a soldier, and then
> home again. I survived, but it's not a happy ending. I was a coward. I went
> to the war.   (61)

Although Worthington and characters such as Jimmy Cross are reproached for
their willing moral ignorance, O'Brien reserves one of the vilest insults in the
martial lexicon—coward—for himself.

Finally, O'Brien's suggestion that even the enemy lacks ideological conviction
threatens the very casus belli for the war since it invalidates the domino theory.
In "The Man I Killed" O'Brien imagines the biography of a Vietcong soldier
whom he has just killed. The vision is a far cry from the caricature of the battle-
hardened, amoral monster conjured by the epithet "Charlie":

> Frail-looking, delicately boned, the young man would not have wanted to
> be a soldier and in his heart would have feared performing badly. . . . In the
> presence of his father and uncles, he pretended to look forward to doing
> his patriotic duty, which was also a privilege, but at night he prayed with his
> mother that the war might end soon. Beyond anything else, he was afraid
> of disgracing himself, and therefore his family and village.   (127)

Like O'Brien and like the soldiers in his platoon who "killed, and died, because
they were embarrassed not to" (21), this soldier participates in the war not to
uphold deeply held convictions but simply to avoid disgrace. Avoidance, ignorance, and transference of shame seem to be the predominant purposes of the
war O'Brien describes, whether among the officers, the enlisted men, those on
the home front, or even the enemy.

Although William Searle has argued that in *Novel without a Name* Communism "is overshadowed by Vietnamese patriotism, dwarfed by it, shamed by it"
("Dissident Voices" 234), several passages contradict such a straightforwardly
nationalistic reading. For example, when Quan returns briefly to his native village, he visits Mr. and Mrs. Buu, whose house is "one of the most luxurious in
the village" (128–29). They serve him a meal that he describes in stark contrast
with the extreme privations of the soldiers he has lived among for ten years: "If
it hadn't been for the rustic ceramic cups and the peasant crockery, it would
have looked like a feast described in one of the Chinese classics" (130). Midway
through the meal and its accompanying discussion of "the problems of the vil-

lage and the country" (130–31), the diners are joined by Mr. Ly, a local party
official who invites Quan to speak as a "heroic combatant" at the meeting to
which he is headed: "Party cadres just repeat the same old speeches. Speak,
the people will believe you. Speak to us about your victories. It will inspire the
people for the next harvest season" (131–32). When Quan resists, Mr. Ly reas-
sures him that they will "discuss the main points beforehand. The important
thing is to understand the Party line" (132). After Mr. Ly's departure Mr. Buu
angrily denounces him and the ideology he serves: "Now the ones who hold the
reins are all ignoramuses who never even learned the most basic morals. They
study their Marxism-Leninism, and then come and pillage our vegetable gar-
dens and rice fields with Marx's blessing" (133). Searle interprets this as Duong
"distinguish[ing] between those who sacrifice" and "those who benefit from the
misery of others, between those who protect the ancestral altars" and "those
who merely seek applause" (234). But such a dichotomous reading ignores
other aspects of this scene that reveal Duong's broader intent. The Buu family's
opulence is jarringly disproportionate to the rest of the village and presumably
has required currying favor with the same party leaders against whom Mr. Buu
rails. This hypocrisy is exposed when his wife admonishes him after his out-
burst: "Please, now don't you go looking for trouble. After all, they're the ones
in power. We can't do anything about that" (133). Furthermore, although Mr.
and Mrs. Buu's thoroughly solicitous behavior toward Mr. Ly while he is in their
house can be partly attributed to traditional Vietnamese hospitality, it also appears sycophantic in the light of Mr. Buu's subsequent snarling condemnation.
Duong undercuts Mr. Buu's self-righteousness—Mr. Buu identifies himself as
"the most rebellious person in the village" (137)—by noting his passive and
self-interested assent to the powers that be.

Duong repeatedly delivers her criticisms of the system through unsympa-
thetic or amoral characters, a technique that (as Liparulo notes) destabilizes
any sense of moral certainty and also implicates any participant in a corrupt
system, especially those who willingly ignore their recognition of its corruption.
For instance, Duong depicts two party officials traveling on a ramshackle train,
contrasting their corpulence with the other passengers' poverty and emaciation
while also emphasizing the passengers' ambiguous deference:

> The two men were fat, their skin as pale as crickets left too long in a match-
> box. They sat like masters in the middle of the crowd. The other passengers
> only gave them sidelong glances, frightened, fawning looks. Even the mer-
> chants with their sharp tongues didn't dare chatter in their vulgar slang.
> Everyone was stiff, frozen, paralyzed by some invisible force.   (158)

Any sense that this paralysis results from being in the presence of exemplary
Communists is immediately shattered by the men's conversation, in which the
older of the two openly acknowledges the self-serving artifice behind the ideology used to justify the extreme privations of the war:

Building a civilization is difficult. But guaranteeing a small number of people a civilized existence, why, there's nothing easier. Like I say, civilization is a long, hard, road, and—on top of it all—at the end you have to share power. For a people as primitive as ours, using a religion to guide them through some shortcuts to glory is a hundred times easier than trying to civilize them. . . . We demolished the temples and emptied the pagodas so we could hang up portraits of Marx, enthrone a new divinity for the masses.   (162–63)

When a military officer confronts them, accusing them of slandering Marx and the government, the older man quickly chastens him, saying, "When it comes to defending Marxist thought, that's *our* business, not yours" (166). The officer walks away shamed, and the party official returns to his seat, exclaiming to his companion, "Did you see that? A nation of imbeciles. They need a religion to guide them and a whip to educate them" (167). The two Communists are morally reprehensible, but the military, as exemplified by the browbeaten officer, continues to serve them out of fear.

The ramifications of such submissive complicity are made brutally clear when Quan recalls a story told to him by a fellow soldier named Tien:

The captain was off on some mission. That bastard Huu wanted to impress division headquarters, so he decided to launch an operation. Since the colonel was also gone, Huu's subordinates approved his plan. Huu was secretary of the regimental Party cell. The comrades voted unanimously in favor of the operation. Half to please him, half out of negligence, the scout platoon concocted some fantastic report about the situation. All false. . . . The next day it took three platoons to retaliate and remove the corpses.   (231)

Tien becomes increasingly angry as he relates how the "kids" were killed "because of some idiot's ambition. They're *all* dead because of that bastard" (232). But the mention of the subordinates' toadying participation implicates more than just Huu in these deaths. As Tien weeps bitterly, Quan mechanically asks him to "think of morale, of the other comrades" but also fears "a time when no one will want to say anything to anyone anymore" (232). The moral muteness he imagines pervades the novel and makes it impossible for him to perceive any glory in his side's ultimate victory. Quan's interrogation of a captured ARVN soldier near the end of the novel illustrates his distance from the ideology that sustained the war:

In war, everyone kills. I'd also shoot at you like I'd shoot at an animal, without even thinking about it. Perhaps all this misery comes from worshipping different gods. Why don't you ask your lieutenant to advise his government to worship the god Marx? . . . Or we could all just agree to choose any old god. Take, for example, the god Tho Dia, who lounges around with his big belly in the corner of the kitchen. . . . Nobody would even think of going and killing someone over such a lousy god. (245–46)

Quan has long since ceased to believe in the religion proffered by the likes of the two men on the train, but he can replace it only with an amoral survival instinct. The terrified prisoner fails to understand and returns to his cell as Quan falls into a reverie about a battlefield populated by insectlike armies:

> On both sides you screamed, you killed in mad, frenzied bursts, shrieking for joy when the blood gushed, the brains shattered; you went at one another like savages under the dense rain of machine-gun fire. Then the survivors limped off the battlefields to swell the reserves, to join the ranks of future combatants. The dead offered their bodies to carnivorous birds and worms. (247)

He emerges from his reverie with the comment that "[w]e had forgotten everything" and laments especially the loss of a traditional Vietnamese creation myth (247).

The strong temptation to read this passage simply as a sort of nationalist call for a return to Vietnamese unity is undermined by the extent to which the two men on the train are proved correct in their assessment of the pacification of the Vietnamese populace by religion, whether Marxist ideology or ancestral beliefs. As Quan notes, "On both sides you died believing that you had attained your ideal" (247). Duong implicates herself indirectly in the spread of such "religion" when Quan attends a rally featuring a political education group much like the Communist Youth Brigades with which she was involved (259–60). Like O'Brien, Duong criticizes not only the officers and soldiers who participated in the war but also the wider society (including herself) that assented to it.

The scholarly vocabulary of Liparulo's article likely limits its value to all but the most advanced undergraduates.[3] However, even if one does not present it to students in advance of their discussions of the novels, it illustrates the potential value of surpassing the contemporary discourse on war. The approach outlined here does not seek blithe acceptance of Liparulo's reading (or mine) as an authoritative compromise between polarized preconceptions but rather intends to generate a less prescribed interpretation of the two works, which students can then consider on its own merits. In this way the students will engage in a critical process that heeds both works' fictionalized warnings against unexamined convictions.

NOTES

[1] The concept of a writer remaining devoted to the precepts of Communism while condemning a government that is nominally Communist is not one that the students have volunteered, perhaps not surprisingly, since the popular conception of Communism

as a monolithic philosophy remains relatively undimmed even after the end of the cold war.

[2] Liparulo's article is available on the Internet at the home page for *War, Literature, and the Arts* (www.wlajournal.com).

[3] I have had only one opportunity to teach *The Things They Carried* and *Novel without a Name* together since Liparulo's article appeared. I made students aware of the article as a potentially useful resource for their written assignments only after we had concluded our in-class discussion of the two novels. I did this expressly to encourage the students to generate, rather than simply respond to, a nonpartisan reading of the two books.

O'Brien in an American War Literature Class

Alex Vernon

For several years now I've taught a course called American War Literature to first- and second-year undergraduates. Now that narrative representations of the current global war waged chiefly in Iraq and Afghanistan have begun appearing, this course enjoys a relevancy for the students that few of my other literature courses do.

Hendrix College is a private, Methodist-affiliated liberal arts institution in central Arkansas with a student body of about 1,400. Because its writing-across-the-curriculum program does not involve a composition course, students typically satisfy their lower-level writing requirement in their introduction-to-literary-studies class, of which American War Literature is one. The goals of the course are to explore America's complicated relation to its military history through narrative expressions of that relation, introduce students to the interpretation of literature at the college level, and teach students how to write an academic essay. The focus of this essay is on the first of these goals, though I should repeat here the epigraph to the course description, from an interview with Tim O'Brien: "The environment of war is the environment of life, magnified" (qtd. in McNerney, "Responsibly" 23).

As the only literature course many of my students will take, American War Literature includes several genres and media, and it surveys as much American literary history as it can. Beginning with the Civil War and progressing to the war in Iraq and Afghanistan, I move my students from nineteenth-century sentimentalism through realism and naturalism, modernism, postmodernism, and into contemporary works, and we touch on the relation between history and literary history.

The Civil War

For the first day of class, students read several stories and poems that appeared during the Civil War in various papers and popular publications from both sides, many titles of which can be found in Alice Fahs's excellent study *The Imagined Civil War: Popular Literature of the North and South, 1861–1865*. I divide the class into groups and assign each group the task of summarizing the plot and message of one of these short texts. It does not take long for the groups to begin repeating the same messages: that mothers see raising their sons for war as their highest purpose and that young women prefer not only soldiers but wounded soldiers: men with lost limbs get the girls. But the conversation quickly turns to the nature of propaganda and to the function of literature in reflecting and shaping (or reinforcing) public sentiment. I also use these texts to establish the literary context against which writers like Ambrose Bierce and Stephen Crane operated.

Crane's *The Red Badge of Courage*, the course's first novel, opens by challenging Henry Fleming's acceptance of the gender roles promulgated by the popular press. His mother does not want Henry to go, and while one girl ridicules him as he marches off to war, he fancies that another one admires him, and he cherishes this fancy during his campaigns. Students inevitably debate about the novel's—or rather Henry Fleming's—preoccupation with war and about being wounded as the means to manhood. Does Crane intend us to take Fleming at his word or to question his self-characterization? The novel thus introduces the course's semester-long investigation into the relation between gender and war.

The Red Badge of Courage is an accessible text for the students (some have previously read it or something else by Crane), so it eases them into the course, into class discussion, and into the practice of literary interpretation aimed at narrative ambiguity and complexity rather than thematic simplicity and clarity. Sometimes I complicate matters by having students read "The Veteran," Crane's short story coda to *Red Badge*, with its difficult-to-discern opinion of Fleming's heroism, both during the war and decades later. The novel also introduces students to other course-long concerns, such as authorial experiential authority, unreliable narrators and protagonists, psychological realism and literary naturalism, and the relation of religion and Christianity to war.

World War I

From Henry Fleming to Frederic Henry: Ernest Hemingway's *A Farewell to Arms* revisits some of the same ground as Crane's novel — authorial experiential authority (Hemingway did not witness the retreat from Caporetto), the gap between author and protagonist and the potential for an unreliable narrator, literary naturalism, and the issues of religion and gender in war. I always open the last discussion day with the question, "Why do Catherine and the baby die?" What interpretations can we posit? The students usually fill the chalkboard.

The potential for a critical distance between Hemingway and Frederic centers on the book's reputation as antiwar. Suggesting that any of Frederic's actions might not have received Hemingway's approval—say, the killing of the engineering sergeant—encourages us to question Frederic's character, including his antiwar statements. By viewing *A Farewell to Arms* as a fictional memoir written some ten years after the end of World War I, can we see Frederic as exaggerating his antiwar position because it was the trendy literary move? This particular question, though it will strike some as far-fetched, models aggressive, inquisitive contextual reading. Thinking of the book as a fictional memoir becomes an important step for class consideration of Frederic's perspective and begins a conversation about the memoir genre.

A Farewell to Arms also serves to introduce modernism. We begin, on the first day, remarking on the novel's style, and the students' observations lead to a minilecture on modernism in general and World War I's effect on modernist culture. At the 2008 International Hemingway Society Conference in Kansas City, Steven Trout, of Fort Hays State University, noted the oddity of the status of *A Farewell to Arms* as the American novel of World War I, given that the situation of a volunteer ambulance lieutenant on the Italian front departs markedly from the typical doughboy experience. The next time I teach the book, I plan to raise Trout's question, What does this departure say about the nature or the absence of a received metastory about the war in the United States?

One year I followed *A Farewell to Arms* with the film version of Dalton Trumbo's *Johnny Got His Gun*, another work about gender and war, shattered male bodies, religion and jingoism, and a problematic antiwar expression. The novel, originally published in 1939, is widely accepted as stridently antiwar, and the film (which Trumbo wrote and directed) reinforces this position—as do the 2007 edition of the book with a foreword by Cindy Sheehan, an antiwar protester whose son was killed in the war in Iraq, and a fall 2008 release of a filmed stage adaptation (in time for the presidential election) starring one of the college generation's television heartthrobs at the time, Ben McKenzie. As with *A Farewell to Arms*, we can scrutinize the antiwar position of *Johnny Got His Gun*. I do this in class by discussing Trumbo's refusal to reprint the novel until after World War II, by looking at excerpts from Trumbo's introduction to the 1959 edition (in which he distinguishes between the "value" of the two world wars), and by reading aloud the resounding, revolutionary call to arms in the novel's final pages.

World War II

If *A Farewell to Arms* observes a lackadaisical character who comes to reject World War I's wastefulness, Martha Gellhorn's *Point of No Return* (originally published as *The Wine of Astonishment*) gives us a reluctant soldier who comes to embrace World War II's necessity.

After we watch the segment on the Spanish Civil War in PBS's *Reporting America at War* series as a way of introducing Gellhorn and as a way of familiarizing the students with a war many of them know nothing about, I broach the subject of the canon, a subject to which we return as we continue studying this text. Who has a say in creating the canon? Why have the students never heard of Gellhorn, and why has this novel has never received canonical status? We speculate together: Because of its lack of experiential authenticity—a nonsoldier, and a woman, wrote it at a time (1948) when veterans were publishing their books. (How are we to assess the fictionalized witnessing efforts of war correspondents?) Because it features a Jewish protagonist and because not all the character portraits of soldiers are flattering. Because it reveals a nonchalance about—even an ignorance of—the war among soldiers just when the United States was committing itself to the myth of the "good" war. Because the reading public wasn't ready for a Holocaust novel (it ends at Dachau, after the liberation). Because it depicts emotional and sexual relations between men and women too frankly, with one woman basically date-raped and another finding it all very ho-hum, in sex scenes that I contrast with those in Hemingway's *For Whom the Bell Tolls*. Because it simply is not as good as Norman Mailer's *The Naked and the Dead* or Irwin Shaw's *The Young Lions*, the two monumental texts that appeared the same year and quickly dominated the canon of that war's literature.

Point of No Return is a fine book. It portrays battalion dynamics and the different demands made on officers and on soldiers more accurately than anything else we study. And it brings to the course its first female writer since those Civil War pieces. Some students, including one Iraq war veteran, love the book for its quiet and potent realism. Others find its characters and plot not vital enough—merely carriers for the ideas Gellhorn wants to convey.

From the ground to the air, from print to screen: *The War Lover*, a film based on John Hersey's novel of the same name, is the story of a bomber squadron. Its rejection of war lust serves its postwar audience exactly what it needs, and its linking of war lust and male sexuality advances the course's ongoing dialogue about gender. (A James Salter novel or a section from his memoir *Burning the Days* would be another way of including air combat as well as the Korean War.)

The allied bombing campaign of Germany, dramatized in *The War Lover,* receives a different treatment in Kurt Vonnegut's *Slaughterhouse-Five*, an excellent segue to literary postmodernism as well as to Vietnam. Published in 1969, the book makes references to the new war and perhaps might not have been written otherwise. (I have been tempted to show clips from *The Fog of War*, in which Robert McNamara discusses how war makers applied the carpet bombing and attrition logic of World War II to Vietnam.) Gender is very much at stake in this novel, in terms both of men and women's romantic relationships and of war's emasculating and infantilizing effects. Christianity receives negative attention, connecting this text with others in the course. I also needle the class by asking if this novel is truly antiwar or simply anti–carpet bombing and anti–crusade rhetoric. *Slaughterhouse-Five* is the first book of the semester to tackle what we today understand as post-traumatic stress disorder, a condition that earned its name and place as a result of the Vietnam War.

The Vietnam War

We begin the Vietnam War section of the course with the 2002 film version of *The Quiet American*. This remarkable and visually compelling work helps me communicate the historical background to the United States' involvement in the war. Though set in the 1950s, the film ends with a sequence of newspaper headlines charting the United States' gradual military immersion in Vietnam. The gender troubles in *The Quiet American* take on a new dimension, as the young Vietnamese woman at the heart of the conflict between the two men, Thomas Fowler (representing the last gasp of European colonialism) and Alden Pyle (the first breath of American neocolonialism) symbolizes Vietnam itself. The film not only involves a feminizing (and eroticizing) of the colonial, oriental other but also plays into the Vietnamese literary tradition of seeing Vietnam as a victimized woman (*The Tale of Kieu*). The male competition for the young woman echoes that of *The War Lover*; both films participate in the split-hero motif in American war literature, featuring two characters on the same side whose rivalry represents a larger moral debate, which dates at least as far back as Maxwell Anderson and Laurence Stallings's play *What Price Glory?* and includes such works as James Salters's novel *The Hunters*; the films *Coming Home*, *Apocalypse Now*, *Platoon*, *Brothers*, and *The Hurt Locker*; and the novels *We Pierce*, by Andrew Huebner, and *Dog Soldiers*, by Robert Stone.

In *The War Lover*, the British woman Daphne chooses between two men, and her choice becomes the film's moral compass. In *The Quiet American*, however, the Vietnamese woman, Phuong, has her fate decided for her: by the men, by her older sister, by her country's plight. The difference is telling, because the film also lacks a clear moral position. Demonizing Pyle, the American, is too easy, especially if the alternative is Fowler's expatriated, drugged, dropped-out complacency and his several betrayals to preserve his personal status quo: of his wife, his Vietnamese lover, and his friend Pyle. Finally, the story of the film's delayed release in response to the 9/11 terrorist attacks leads to an interesting comparative discussion—the film's climactic event is a car bombing of a busy Saigon intersection, orchestrated by the American and causing a great number of civilian casualties.

Which brings us to Tim O'Brien. I have considered teaching the underappreciated novel *The Nuclear Age* as a way of doing a cold war text. I've also considered teaching *In the Lake of the Woods*, because happening-truth trumps story-truth, thereby turning the novel into a critique of that strain of postmodernism allied with the triumph of spin. That John Wade is a politician has a particular resonance with the infamous line from one of President George W. Bush's aides during the Iraq war, dismissing the "reality-based community" and asserting the administration's right to "create our own reality" (qtd. in Suskind).

But inevitably we read and study *The Things They Carried*. *Slaughterhouse-Five* began our conversation about postmodern literature; *The Things They Carried* complicates it. The Tim O'Brien narrator-character is not Tim O'Brien; the writer "invented 90 percent of a new Tim O'Brien, maybe even more than that" (S. Kaplan, "Interview" 95). Does the novel truly comment metafictionally? Does it deny the modernist romanticization of soul by rendering selfhood a social construction, by being ironic? Does it blur the line between reality and fiction? As I've written elsewhere:

> Declaring that story-truth can achieve a greater truth than happening-truth, as O'Brien's mantra goes, hardly dissolves the distinction between fiction and reality: By asserting the different kinds of truth each accesses, O'Brien preserves the distinction, just as naming a fictional character after himself underscores the work's fictionality.   (*Soldiers* 59)

The narrator of *Slaughterhouse-Five* is more ambiguously "real" than O'Brien's narrator. These two texts work well together beyond the terms of their relation to postmodernism. The nature of evil, the problem of religion, even the major presence of excrement brings them in direct conversation.

The Things They Carried raises issues of form as it plays with the novel, the story collection, and the memoir. It also wonders about the purpose of storytelling. Assuming the fictional O'Brien narrator-character as the author of all the stories—even those in which he does not appear—do we read his aim as bearing witness or as attempting to move beyond the war in his emotional life? The two aims, I want students to realize, affect our interpretation. They condition how we think about memory and selfhood, which additionally speaks to the fragmented nature of the book as well as to the confusion between fiction and nonfiction. I've lately come to wonder if two of the book's final stories undercut the narrator's project of salvation through storytelling, with "The Ghost Soldiers" providing a comically literal metaphor for the effort to resurrect and preserve the spirits of the past—"Sorriest fuckin' case I ever seen," Azar calls Tim O'Brien the character right before kicking him in the head (216)—and "Night Life" portending darkly as Rat Kiley, the medic and symbol of healing, comes unhinged.

Finally, I ask the students to read Lorrie Smith's article "'The Things Men Do': The Gendered Subtext in Tim O'Brien's *Esquire* Stories" to initiate discussion of how gender and romance function in the war context. As best I can, I defer conversations related to the article to this final period. Smith charges that O'Brien's fiction excludes female participation, and this claim expands the concern about experiential authority from simply a matter of authorship to one of audience. Her article always makes for a spirited class period. It serves too as a model for academic writing.

Like Tim O'Brien's *The Things They Carried*, Yusef Komunyakaa's *Dien Cai Dau* presents a series of individual pieces — in this case, poems — that function as a whole and tell a story. The book opens with combat soldiers in the field, in full sensory detail, and closes back in the United States. Along the way, the pieces admit their status as a veteran's retrospection to varying degrees. *Dien Cai Dau*'s poems have different apparent narrators, but the book becomes even more interesting when we presume a common narrator behind these personae (much as we've done with *The Things They Carried*). In addition to the usual interpretive suspects, such as gender and trauma, Komunyakaa's poetry brings race into the conversation. I ask my students to pretend ignorance of Komunyakaa's race and locate where in the text any racial signals enter, an exercise I follow with the question, "Why there?" Some of the poems never clearly indicate the author's race. In these particular cases, I've found it rewarding to ask whether, and if so how, race matters. Finally, I see both O'Brien's and Komunyakaa's books as reflecting on — even questioning — the value and efficacy of art in confronting the ghosts and comforting the haunted.

Lynda Van Devanter's *Home before Morning* poses different questions about art. The memoir starts by asserting the book's origin as an effort to deal with Van Devanter's postwar troubles; it makes no claim to artistry. It encourages trust and connection in perhaps the same way that O'Brien's posturing encourages suspicion and distance. Yet the opening chapter is skillfully woven, and the book pushes an agenda. There is art, and artifice, in nonfiction. And while *The Things They Carried* and *Dien Cai Dau* operate in history only generally, at some point and place during and after the war, *Home before Morning* engages history directly — the history of American Catholicism, of post-traumatic stress disorder, of women in uniform. Indeed, this is the only text in the course written by a female veteran, the only opportunity to see how one woman performs her gender in a traditionally male profession at the same time. The homecoming experience is particularly valuable in querying gender, partly because in the last third of the book Van Devanter is less conscious about depicting the challenges of being a woman in uniform. Is the postwar life, is post-traumatic stress disorder, in experience or expression, at all a function of gender?

The Gulf War and the War in Iraq

The work of fiction to gain the most critical traction from the Gulf War is Gabe Hudson's *Dear Mr. President*. Hudson joined the United States Marines after the war, a fact that once again raises the issue of authenticity and authority, and the likely reason for the book's extremely imaginative approach. Perhaps it's safe to say that most war veterans would be too committed to the actual, especially for their first book; indeed, O'Brien himself has attributed *Going After Cacciato*'s flight of fancy to his already having published his memoir, to his having gotten the actual out of his system.

So class begins by asking not about authenticity or experiential authority but about why this war produced such a paucity of literary response. And as we work our way through the text, I suggest that *Dear Mr. President* is less about the war than about the institution of the United States armed forces in that era. The book is as absurd and dark as *Catch-22* and *Slaughterhouse-Five*, but is it definitively antiwar? Even more than O'Brien's, Hudson's book invokes Vonnegut's. We think through the connections, and we find ourselves returning to the now familiar concerns: patriotism, propaganda, gender, trauma, religion, bodily violence. What makes Hudson fascinating to study at this point in the semester is his obvious awareness of these concerns (and others), such that he appears to play with them and to play with his readers' expectations for them.

Some seven years after its beginning, the war in Iraq still had not produced significant literature from United States veterans. Indeed, the war's signature genre is the documentary film. The course spends its last week watching instead of reading. *War Tapes* is remarkable in that it merges the actual soldiering experience with the nonparticipant documentary art. Several soldiers carried cameras during their yearlong deployment, filming as much as they could; afterward, the film's producers turned those thousands of hours into the final product. Many of the course's concerns find expression in this text, most notably the general challenge of faithful and compelling representation, and including Crane's wrestling with manliness and Vonnegut's and O'Brien's excremental displays. *War Tapes* brings the course home, to the present, and connects the present with the past in a way that I hope inspires in my students a continuing appreciation for how the narrative arts engage history and inform their own living in the world.

Teaching O'Brien
in the Context of War Narratives

Zivah Perel

Apocalypse Now's Captain Benjamin L. Willard has in many ways become the popular representation of a Vietnam War veteran. The first scene of the 1979 film shows him drunk in his room, explaining in a voice-over his desire to return to the United States and his inability to do so. With the eerie "This Is the End" by the Doors as a soundtrack, Willard self-medicates, getting so drunk that his Tai Chi practice ends with a broken mirror and splattered blood. The audience is implicitly asked to imagine him standing next to a film-hero version of the men who returned home from Europe and the South Pacific at the end of World War II, the men who inspired Tom Brokaw to write *The Greatest Generation*. As the myth holds, these men were noble, served their country, and helped defeat one government that was genocidal and another that attacked American soil. The contrast between these representations points to the power of narrative to shape perceptions of a given war and the people who fight it and how the Vietnam War differs from previous American wars.

Tim O'Brien is widely read as a canonical Vietnam War author, and his books rightly occupy a prominent place in the literature of the war. The ways O'Brien's work illuminates the Vietnam War experience for students is valuable, yet reading it within the larger tradition of war stories is what truly elucidates his narrative and structural choices. I encourage my students to make the connections O'Brien proffers by recognizing the references to the act of writing, other authors, and previous wars that permeate his work. O'Brien claims that *If I Die in a Combat Zone* and *Going after Cacciato* are not exclusively about the Vietnam War but about the individual and his role in the political world (Naparsteck 6). This claim becomes my rationale for asking students to utilize the connections they see between O'Brien's work and the narratives of other wars as a primary method for understanding his writing. Yet the political world O'Brien explores in his literature is uniquely post–Vietnam War and as such refers to and differs from earlier representations of American wars.

To help my students understand the resonance of these choices, I assign readings that illustrate the trajectory of American war literature. The narrator of Dalton Trumbo's World War I novel *Johnny Got His Gun* reels from his devastating injuries in part because he suffers them at the hands of unprecedented and brutal warfare absent from Civil War texts like Ambrose Bierce's "An Occurrence at Owl Creek Bridge" and Stephen Crane's poem "War Is Kind," texts that illustrate the brutality of warfare but lack the magnitude of Trumbo's novel. By the time my students read sections of *The Things They Carried*, they are ready to discuss how O'Brien's representation of the Vietnam War compares with what they have read from and about earlier wars.

The Vietnam War inspired service narratives that, taken as a whole, contrast greatly with those from World War II in their rejection of the possibility for redemption for either the military in general or the individual soldier. Representations of the enemy in Vietnam create a stark contrast for any student who has seen *Schindler's List* or a film from the Indiana Jones series—movies that invoke the cruelty of the Nazis and turn them into the quintessential enemy. The belief in a just war evaporates in the ambiguities O'Brien describes, and students can better understand O'Brien's personal—and for O'Brien everything is personal—issues with the war. In *If I Die in a Combat Zone*, he writes:

> Kill and fight only for certain causes; certain causes somehow involve self-evident truths; Hitler's blitzkrieg, the attack on Pearl Harbor, these were somehow self-evident grounds for using force . . . but the war in Vietnam drifted in and out of human lives, taking them or sparing them like a headless, berserk taxi hack, without evident cause, a war fought for uncertain reasons.   (138)

The Vietnamese America fought against were not the Nazis or the Japanese. They were battling to gain their independence and to form their own government. As O'Brien sees it, the Vietnam War was based on questionable politics and on immoral grounds, as he makes clear earlier in the memoir when he likens American combat assaults in Vietnam to Hitler's blitzkrieg (*If I Die* 110). Blame shifts, and the enemy becomes not only the Vietnamese people but also the American systems that mired men like O'Brien, Kiowa, and their friends in Vietnam. The dichotomy students are used to working with when dealing with war fiction, "us" versus "them," breaks down, and the moral justification for the war disappears along with this dichotomy, a point O'Brien repeatedly illustrates in *The Things They Carried*.

Students recognize the motif of finding a moral appearing and reappearing throughout *The Things They Carried*. Unlike the situation in prior American wars, the morals of the war in Vietnam are as varied as the ambiguities and individual experiences of the war, and this contrast is critical to understanding O'Brien's book. O'Brien succeeds in making my students' search for the moral frustrating and elusive. In the essay "The Past and the Possible: Tim O'Brien's Dialectic of Memory and Imagination," Eric James Schroeder makes a point about *If I Die in a Combat Zone* that also serves as an observation about *The Things They Carried*: "[M]oral ambivalence" permeates the book, and "whereas a moral order *does* exist, the text itself cannot decode it; the reader must find it for himself" (122). For instance, during class we often debate whether Jimmy Cross is truly responsible for Ted Lavender's death—is O'Brien's moral that Cross should have burned Martha's letters as punishment for recklessly leading his men? Or is it that Cross took Lavender's death too personally? Does he have to remember that things like this happen in Vietnam, that war is hell, and that burning Martha's letters only punishes him further? My students are left to decipher the moral, and our discussion is interesting because no answer is ever entirely clear.

We also spend a significant amount of class time on O'Brien's concepts of truth. He defines happening-truth as what "really happened" and story-truth as dedicated to "mak[ing] the stomach believe" (qtd. in Herzog, *Tim O'Brien* xi). Story-truth may or may not be "truthful," as the word is traditionally defined, but for O'Brien it is every bit as honest and real as happening-truth if it expresses a larger point about a war or life experience. The slippage between these definitions motivates students to question the truth, both as abstract concept and in application to O'Brien's texts. Their process of questioning, which mirrors the one O'Brien presents in the book, is crucial when examining the Vietnam War through O'Brien's work or any other lens.

The subjectivity implied by O'Brien's definitions of truth encourages students to reexamine the reliability and subjectivity of other texts, and it often rattles their innate desire to believe as truth whatever is presented to them. Just as O'Brien as an author can manipulate happening-truth into story-truth, students begin to take liberties in their interpretations of O'Brien, using their personal epistemologies to inform their readings. They tap into their experiences of hardship and views of the world as shaped by their families or cultures to grapple with the questions O'Brien poses. Recognizing the subjectivity of their own opinions illuminates the subjectivity of everything they read and is an important step in understanding literature and the materials they encounter in their other courses.

O'Brien's distinction between story-truth and happening-truth inevitably leads students to question the veracity of his stories and his role in them. At that point, I encourage them to explore the parts of *The Things They Carried* they might otherwise overlook: the wording on the title page and the dedication. We talk about what it means that the title page reads, "a work of fiction by Tim O'Brien," yet the narrator of the stories is named Tim O'Brien. In interviews, O'Brien repeatedly reminds interviewers that the narrator Tim O'Brien is as fictional as the men he describes in the book—and yet the dedication is to "the men of Alpha Company, and in particular to Jimmy Cross, Norman Bowker, Rat Kiley, Mitchell Sanders, Henry Dobbins, and Kiowa," the very characters who appear in the stories and who O'Brien claims are based on his imagination. My students now wonder about the seemingly autobiographical notes about writing that they had relied on as insight into the real-world author's construction of the book. Students often focus on the topic of truth when reading *The Things They Carried*, and our discussion motivates them to explain how they see truth in O'Brien's world and in their own. Although the discussion sometimes gets away from the book, explaining O'Brien's view of truth from their perspective encourages them to digest the concept and examine the role of truth and authenticity in literature, especially war narratives.

For O'Brien, story-truth is preferable to happening-truth because it can more powerfully convey an experience to the reader; it is not bound to reality.

O'Brien is able to retain control of and give meaning to his experience in Vietnam by dissociating from his actual experience—his happening-truth—and rewriting it as a story-truth that attempts to explain and recapture for his readers the Vietnam War experience. The fictional experience of *Going After Cacciato* and the repeated return to the subject of writing in *The Things They Carried* highlight the important role that representing, rather than reporting, plays in O'Brien's work.

O'Brien's invocation of World War II in *If I Die in a Combat Zone* reveals why a character like Mitchell Sanders is so preoccupied with looking for, and failing to find, a moral in his experience in Vietnam and why his preoccupation becomes a major narrative theme in *The Things They Carried*. Herzog notices that Tim O'Brien the narrator gives the reader incremental details about Curt Lemon's death, alluding to Joseph Heller's method of revealing Snowden's death in *Catch-22* (*Tim O'Brien* 107). Herzog continues to find evocations of prior war literature in *The Things They Carried*:

> This death-recognition story, told in "The Man I Killed" and repeated with variations in two other sections, seems a prose version of Thomas Hardy's famous World War I poem "The Man He Killed." It connects with a tradition in war literature of a protagonist engaging in a sympathetic identification with the enemy, but an experience always presented from the protagonist's point of view. (110)

Finding a moral in World War II narratives is generally easy. Erich Maria Remarque's *All Quiet on the Western Front* demonstrates that even in as violent and often senseless a war as World War I, a degree of common humanity linked soldiers and their enemies. The Tim O'Brien narrator does attempt to identify with the man he may or may not have killed, yet Mitchell Sanders has more trouble. I have my students read aloud O'Brien's description of the thumb Sanders cuts off a dead Vietnamese boy, which he gives to Norman Bowker as gift. As usual, Sanders claims that "there's a definite moral here" (13). The following is the end of an exchange between Sanders and Henry Dobbins about the thumb:

> Henry Dobbins thought about it.
> Yeah, well, he finally said. I don't see no moral.
> There it *is*, man.
> Fuck off. (14)

My students have various reactions. They are disgusted by Sanders's gesture yet intrigued by what the war must have been like to elicit such an action. They are comforted by Dobbins's response, since his inability to find a moral and his frustration with the question mirror their own. Inevitably, students offer what they think Sanders is getting at, ranging from the brutality of war to the ruthlessness required to kill to the desire to find humor even in the terrible. As a class, we never agree on a moral, and I try to make my students feel comfortable allowing for a range of responses and feelings.

Because as a group we cannot quite figure out what is moral and what is not in the stories O'Brien tells—not to mention what is fact and what is fiction—students begin to realize that their struggle mirrors O'Brien's characters' struggle to form a coherent and authentic narrative about the war and that this in turn mirrors O'Brien's own struggle. His commitment to story-truth gets the reader as close as possible to the experiences Sanders describes as ineffable. O'Brien comments on his expectations of his readers, "I don't expect the reader to draw any single moral out of it. . . . [It] can't be pinned down to a message or a moral. It's a story, and you finish a story with a whole cluster, a constellation, of emotions and yearnings and whimsies" (qtd. in Schroeder, *Vietnam* 130). O'Brien seeks to elucidate the Vietnam War experience for the reader. And the search for a moral that runs through the stories of *The Things They Carried* parallels O'Brien's search for a story-truth in the rewriting of his own experience. By exposing the reader to the process of putting together a story-truth, he encourages the reader to create his or her own resonance, meaning, or moral. Evan Carton notes the tendencies of Vietnam War narratives to rely on a "personalist epistemology" (296), which explains the privileging of the individual voice that occurs in *The Things They Carried*. By debating with one another what did and did not happen in the story and what each occurrence means, my students realize that O'Brien is instructing them not only on how to read the Vietnam War (i.e., to question what they read or what they are told) but also on how to *read*. They are each like Mitchell Sanders, who spends the bulk of *The Things They Carried* preoccupied with his search.

O'Brien's instructions for reading are particularly valuable to first- and second-year students. Whereas in an upper-level course, I spend some time talking about postmodernism and how O'Brien might fit into the literary movement, I find that this kind of specific literary background is overwhelming for first- and second-year students who are challenged and motivated by what O'Brien does in the novel regardless of how it fits into literary history. I focus instead on the larger philosophical and representational issues that arise in O'Brien's work. Students are quick to notice the lack of a linear plotline in *The Things They Carried*, and this leads into a discussion of how O'Brien uses structure to create meaning. O'Brien's different accounts of the same events and the ways in which his narratives jump in time trouble my students, as many crave the order a linear plotline ostensibly provides. I push them to examine why O'Brien might write that way by asking them how his stories make them feel. When they answer that they are confused and disoriented and feel disconnected from some of the characters and action, they start to realize that the meaning and form are the same for O'Brien.

The fictional O'Brien who narrates *The Things They Carried* is an effort on the writer O'Brien's part to rewrite his service experience in a way that creates some kind of truth for both himself and his readers. That his book discusses the writing process in as much depth as it discusses the Vietnam War demonstrates how important a role writing and rewriting is to the substance of his narrative. In rewriting his experience in a way that invests it with meaning, O'Brien actualizes the potentially redemptive aspects of the service experience in Vietnam. This is not to say that *The Things They Carried* looks to validate either America's objectives and actions in Vietnam or O'Brien's (and the other men's) behavior there. However, O'Brien does attempt to rewrite the narrative of his experience to present it in a way that has resonance. Why he spends so much of *The Things They Carried* writing about writing becomes clearer to my students. O'Brien's philosophy on truth and the role of storytelling links the discussions of war and writing that often appear to students as unrelated.

When I assign *The Things They Carried* to a class, I focus on "The Lives of the Dead," the story that closes the book. It begins with an anecdote about Cross, Lemon, Kiowa, and the other men but finishes with a memory about O'Brien's youth and a young girl, Linda, with whom he was friends. The story cuts back and forth between the two narratives. Linda died from cancer when she was nine years old, and O'Brien explains the power of storytelling in bringing him comfort. He writes that a story can make "the dead seem not quite so dead" (238). Here, he is at his most obvious; writing is restorative and even regenerative (Linda's hair grows back, and she looks more alive than ever in his stories). By juxtaposing Linda's narrative with that of the platoon, O'Brien emphasizes the restorative and regenerative effects he sees his writing as having for his war experience. The story is important for understanding why O'Brien writes and why other war authors may write. For first- and second-year students, who are often discussing literature for the first time in their college careers, "The Lives of the Dead" helps solidify for them why studying literature is important. They can relate closely to this story because it is about losing a loved one, a more common experience for college students than serving in a war.

In *The Things They Carried* the power to tell a war story emerges as the power of the individual voice, a voice that struggled for legitimacy during the war in Vietnam. The preoccupation with telling personal stories arises in response to the lack of a coherent and trustworthy collective narrative of the war. The merging of fiction and nonfiction Schroeder observes in Vietnam War literature (*Vietnam* 125) mirrors the methods of reporting that contaminated official government reports throughout the war. Just as the government mixed fact with a constructed narrative, many individual narratives about the war similarly blend real experience and fiction to create a story-truth. Although the motivations may be different—the government aimed to garner public support for the war even if it required deception, whereas individual storytellers aim to explode the official versions of the war—they mix both fiction and nonfiction to create a story with resonance. By self-consciously fictionalizing his own experience, O'Brien refuses to let the reader forget this aspect of his narrative.

Although this historical background is important to reading O'Brien, I take care to not frontload our discussion of his work with too much history about the war. Instead, I fill in gaps in the information my students provide when the particular book requires it. O'Brien's work stimulates discussion so easily that I try not to dampen it by lecturing. I do explain to students, some of whom already know the information and are happy to step in when they can, that the Vietnam War is widely recognized as the first war in which the media functioned without censor. T. Louise Brown explains that censorship would have "necessitated different jurisdictions for US civilians and third country nationals and, as the war was never officially declared, it would have been hard to justify politically" (113). Consequently, journalists were able to accompany the military without worry of censorship. News stories, however, often were generalized and incomplete. Despite the potential for accuracy afforded the media, the information disseminated to the public was often deficient. President Johnson's troubled relationship with journalists, a result of his belief in "the duty of journalists to support the president in foreign policy matters" and the need Johnson felt to curry favor, led to the adoption of a "policy of controlled optimism" that promised, through progress reports, more than it could deliver (Brown 113). Moreover, journalists couldn't be everywhere, and they had to rely heavily on official military and government accounts. The results of this type of coverage and the subsequent representations of the war frustrate O'Brien, and his books attempt to recover a truthful story.

Our class discussion about how O'Brien works into his texts the accuracy of news reporting and the general public's dissatisfaction surrounding the Vietnam War provides a segue into a discussion of the Gulf War and the war in Iraq. I like to show my class David Russell's *Three Kings* (1999), a film that, like O'Brien's work, attempts to rewrite the war or service experience in a way that imbues it with meaning. *Three Kings* follows four soldiers — Gates, Barlow, Elgin, and Vig — as they chase after the gold bullion Saddam Hussein stole during his invasion of Kuwait. The soldiers plan on stealing the bullion and leaving Iraq as rich men. Instead, they become entangled in a conflict in a small village between Hussein's militia and the civilians living under its tyrannical rule. *Three Kings* asserts the power of the individual through rewriting. The film is divided into two halves. The first half represents the media's unreliability and naiveté during the Gulf War, and the second, after the men give up their pursuit of the bullion in favor of helping the Iraqi rebels, rewrites the narrative of the war more ideally. Gates, Barlow, Elgin, and Vig serve as the potential for what could have been a just — or at least a less unjust — war. Although less overtly, the motif of writing and representing that my students explored in O'Brien's texts appears in *Three Kings*, and our class discussion addresses the connections between the Gulf War and the conflict in Iraq.

Depending on the semester and the amount of time I have to spend on war narratives, I may include an excerpt of Anthony Swofford's memoir *Jarhead* and a screening of the film. Near the beginning of the memoir, Swofford talks about watching war movies with his platoon before they ship out to Iraq for what will become Operation Desert Storm. (This scene appears nearly identically in the film.) It is a short section and speaks directly to the influence that war films have on soldiers. I also include a section from the end of the memoir, where Swofford writes, "I remade my war one word at a time, a foolish, desperate act" (254). In this section, students see how a soldier from the Gulf War views writing about war and his role in telling its story. Many students are already familiar with the film *Jarhead* and are excited to see how a contemporary film fits into the context of O'Brien and the other war texts we have examined in class.

It is impossible in any given semester to read O'Brien with perfect completeness. By focusing course discussions on O'Brien's work alongside that of others from various American conflicts, I can achieve some of the context I feel they require. It is when my students move from Dalton Trumbo's soapbox discussion of the meaninglessness of World War I to O'Brien's discussion of the justness of World War II versus the ambiguous motives of America's involvement in Vietnam and relate both to a war they are trying to interpret now that they learn the most from O'Brien's work. When I was an undergraduate at Cornell University, a professor of mine began a course titled British Modernism and Two World Wars with E. M. Forster's epigraph to *Howards End*: "Only connect." I often use this quotation in my own literature classes, and it could work equally well for O'Brien's work. O'Brien's work is important in the context of war narratives, but it also requires students to think in a way that is crucial for them as college students. By making connections among different wars, war texts, authors, and time periods and seeing how they all come together, students achieve what I believe is a primary goal of the literature classroom.

Going After Cacciato in a Course
on the Literature of the Vietnam War

Edward J. Rielly

I teach Tim O'Brien's *Going After Cacciato* in a course called Literature of the Vietnam War. English majors and students from a variety of departments take the course. It is open to sophomores through seniors, although the twenty-five-student limit usually means the course closes before many sophomores can register. The readings include short stories, usually two novels, at least one memoir, poetry, songs, and films. Students also read about and are tested on the history of the war, and they study the impact of the war on Americans—e.g., the effects of post-traumatic stress disorder (PTSD). In addition, service learning is an option that students may choose rather than a traditional research paper.

The course is designed, as the syllabus states,

> to deepen our understanding of the literature that has come out of the Vietnam War; to develop a basic knowledge and understanding of the war; to increase our awareness of the historical, political, and social ramifications of the war; and to examine the relationship of historical events to literary and film depictions of those events.

I approach these objectives chronologically, so that students can follow the progression of the war. The texts vary somewhat from year to year; in its most recent iteration, the course began with a viewing of the film *Go Tell the Spartans*, which depicts the war in its early stages, when the United States military was engaged largely as advisers.

Students began their reading along two parallel paths: in *The Vietnam War: A History in Documents*, by Marilyn Young, John Fitzgerald, and A. Tom Grunfeld, and in the literary texts. The initial literary assignment was Lynda Van Devanter's memoir, *Home before Morning*, which recounts a young woman's life before the war, her decision to serve in the conflict as a nurse, and her life after the war, including her struggle with PTSD. In addition to class meetings devoted to the literature, I set aside sessions to discuss the historical reading.

As we made our way through America's military buildup and reached the late 1960s, we considered events such as the Tet offensive, viewed the film *Platoon*, and discussed *Going After Cacciato* (with Paul Berlin's arrival in Vietnam occurring in the summer of 1968). Then the class read *Song of Napalm*, Bruce Weigl's collection of poetry, and, while studying the final stages of the war, viewed *The Killing Fields*. The film reminded students that the Vietnam War was part of a broader conflict in Indochina and that its effects continued long after the final battle. We ended the semester with Bobbie Ann Mason's novel *In Country*, which is about a teenager trying to get to know her father, who died in the war at about her current age. In some ways, her search is analogous to what my entire class does as we try to understand the Vietnam War, the people who fought in it, and some of the literature that the war produced.

Going After Cacciato is a major reading assignment in this course. I hope students will appreciate the book as the great novel that I believe it is, but it also contributes to their understanding of the war and a variety of issues that we discuss during the semester. Our examination of *Going After Cacciato* typically includes, among other matters, the topics enumerated below.

1. The three-part structure of the novel and how it relates to O'Brien's use of time, the author's assessment of the war experience, and ways in which soldiers respond to combat, including various efforts to try to escape the horrors of war

Explaining the three-part structure while students are reading the novel and before classroom discussions lessens frustration for the students and enables them to understand the novel more effectively than if they read it without any preparation. I explain that the novel contains three types of chapters, all identified at least as early as 1982 in an article by Dennis Vannatta: chapters that recount the main narrative action, which is the pursuit of Cacciato; chapters in which a wide range of past events not directly part of the main action are recalled; and the chapters entitled "The Observation Post."

Each type, I explain, has a different temporal focus. The chapters narrating the pursuit of Cacciato occur in a reasonably typical past progressive, the action completed and narrated chronologically. The second type of chapter recalls past events that Paul Berlin, the protagonist, has experienced, although these events do not occur in strict chronological order. These retrospective chapters continue throughout the book, contributing to the fictional world of the novel while also offering insights into aspects of the war that we encounter in other readings, including our history text.

Within the temporal context of the novel, the "Observation Post" chapters occur in the present, as Paul stands guard from about midnight to six o'clock in the morning. During these hours, he remembers past events, including the pursuit of Cacciato, attempts to order events correctly, and reflects on what might have happened had he and others made different decisions.

My students initially find the first type of chapter the most straightforward, but that perception proves illusory. As they read about the pursuit of Cacciato, the story steadily falls away from realism—literally so, in the plummet through the hole in the road. Wanting to prepare my students to read effectively without short-circuiting their individual discoveries, I leave for classroom discussion such matters as when the "real" pursuit of Cacciato ends and Berlin's imaginative continuation of the story picks up. Classroom discussions also explore the interrelations among the content of the three types of chapters and what Berlin is actually attempting during his six hours standing guard.

*2. The failures of reason (and sometimes imagination) in the novel as repre-
sented by deliberate narrative collapse and the inability of soldiers, as the war
progressed, to discern clear reasons for the war, for their officers' decisions, and
for their own involvement in the conflict*

At times in the novel, reason fails to provide an avenue forward. Again, the fall
through the hole in the road—by Paul Berlin, Sarkin Aung Wan (Paul's love
interest), and the other soldiers pursuing Cacciato—is illustrative, demonstrating a collapse of reason and imagination. The incident disrupts the logical development of the narrative and follows what Paul Berlin describes as a "lapse of
imagination" (75). He wants Sarkin to accompany him to Paris, but Lieutenant
Corson decides that Sarkin and her two aunts must be left behind. Paul finds
no logical or credibly imaginative solution to the problem, instead substituting a
deus ex machina intervention that serves different roles, including keeping the
young couple together and introducing the character of the Vietcong major Li
Van Hgoc. It is important for students to understand that this is not the author's
failure but the character's, for it is Paul Berlin who is attempting to imagine
most of the pursuit narrative.

Similarly, no logical continuation seems possible when the soldiers are rescued
by Cacciato from an Iranian jail only to find themselves in their 1964 Impala
caught in a traffic circle surrounded by tanks and armored personnel carriers.
There is no logical way out, but abandoning logic, Oscar throws the car into
reverse and suddenly they are out of the rotary and onto a highway. Near the
end of the novel, Sarkin decides to leave Paul Berlin. He seeks a compromise
solution, but the integrity of the narrative offers none. As he watches her move
away, he notes again his failure: "He tried to imagine it differently, he tried hard,
but the power to make a wish was no longer the power to make it happen. It was
a failure of imagination" (313).

We consider in class the significance of these failures. We remember that
Paul Berlin is imagining this narrative while standing guard at the observation
post, and sometimes he just comes up short imaginatively. There are limitations
to the fictional character's imagination as there are limits to the imaginative
powers of each student and instructor.

More broadly, Berlin's failure also represents the inability of American soldiers, as the Vietnam War progressed, to understand the rationale for the war
and the reasons for the orders they were expected to carry out. We study a real
battle, such as the attempt to take Hamburger Hill, to see the apparent illogic
that characterized many efforts during the war—in this case, the heavy death
toll from taking the location, the discovery that by the time Americans reached
the summit most of the enemy had slipped away, and the subsequent return of
the enemy once the Americans had moved on. The increasing number of American soldiers who refused to obey orders from the late 1960s on was a logical
response to a situation in which the perception of a lesser danger (penalty for
disobedience) replaced the greater danger (death). Paul Berlin's story making,

we conclude, is his attempt to escape, however temporarily, the war and its many horrors.

3. The theme of heroism versus cowardice in the novel and its relation to the question of duty

The previous discussion leads naturally to the matter of duty and bravery. A good focal point for our classroom discussion of this topic is the dialogue in chapter 29 between the American soldiers and the Iranian captain, Fahyi Rhallon. The debate moves through related subjects: the meaning of war, the importance of perceived purpose, the choice between staying and running, the motivations of self-respect and fear, and the necessity for the war to be seen as just in order for soldiers to commit themselves to it.

Discussion of these issues inevitably turns to Paul Berlin's personal alternatives and choices. We notice, for example, his subtle physical movement when Rhallon raises the choice between deserting and staying to fight: "Paul Berlin looked away. He watched the dancing students" (198). The subject, students conclude, is particularly sensitive for Paul, who has been considering his own fear.

Early in the novel, he is described as frightened of the war and uncertain how he will respond to it. He thinks of returning home after the war with his medals in place, shaking his father's hand, and saying, "I did okay" (47). As much as he would like to flee the way Cacciato did, he cannot do so and also realize his homecoming dream. So he stands guard at the observation post hour by hour, trying to do two things to keep his fear in check and sustain his sense of duty. He tries to recall the chronology of past events—when and how individuals died—so he can make sense of the war, so he can understand a logic and a purpose behind it. Second, he creates a counter-narrative, rooted, up to a point, in reality (Cacciato's desertion and the men's short-lived pursuit of him) but extending far beyond reality, all the way to Paris. So he escapes in this fantasy narrative without making his father, family, and friends ashamed of an actual desertion. By this time, the class usually is coming to not only an intellectual but also an empathic understanding of Paul Berlin.

4. Depictions of the enemy, centering on Li Van Hgoc, as human, and the relationship of this characterization to Vietnam combat and to how demonization of the enemy contributes to development of PTSD

During the chapters set in Li Van Hgoc's tunnel, 13 and 15, both Paul Berlin and my students learn a great deal about the enemy. They realize that the enemy is much like us. Van Hgoc is from a good family and was an excellent student. He was drafted, went to war reluctantly, lost his future, and even deserted—only to be returned finally to the war and condemned to remain in the tunnel where Berlin finds him. All these experiences he shared with American soldiers—less commonly, of course, desertion. Even the penalty of confinement in the tunnel is applicable when understood metaphorically. A collection of poetry, *Poems from Captured Documents*, selected and translated by Thanh T. Nguyen and the poet Bruce Weigl, supplements this discussion of likeness. Particularly poignant are the poems expressing love for individuals from whom the soldiers are separated because of the war, especially as my students come to understand that many of these soldier-poets never survived to return to the homes and loved ones—just like so many American soldiers.

The service-learning project comes into play with this topic. Students who choose service learning rather than the research paper devote at least twenty hours during the semester to tutoring students in grades 3–12. The tutoring occurs at after-school study centers operated by the Portland Housing Authority in Portland, Maine. The service-learning students keep a journal, with an entry for each day at the center, and write an essay about their experiences. In addition to providing an obvious service, they learn about people from other countries. Many of the students at the centers are children of Vietnamese immigrants, and most are from families who were allied with the South Vietnamese government and the United States during the war, rather than children of Vietcong or North Vietnamese Army regulars. Yet larger than the issue of political ideology is a sense of community that stretches across racial and national boundaries, and my students working at the centers become part of that community-building effort.

Our consideration of how Americans often saw the enemy—as an evil, even subhuman, creature—and their ways of responding to the enemy leads us to explore post-traumatic stress disorder. I have used Jonathan Shay's *Achilles in Vietnam* in this course, and even when I do not, I present Shay's conclusions about the causes and effects of PTSD.

5. *Ways in which* Going After Cacciato *delineates characters*

Two pairs of characters—the two lieutenants (Corson and Sidney Martin) and Paul Berlin and Cacciato—yield especially perceptive classroom analyses. Students find Corson a failed leader in numerous ways. Martin, on the other hand, is knowledgeable, enthusiastic, and dedicated to victory.

Yet virtually every student in the class much prefers Corson, whose ultimate goal is keeping his men alive, even if that means allowing the enemy to live as well. The touchstone for this character contrast is the sharp difference in how the two lieutenants approach standard operating procedures, principally regarding Vietcong tunnels. After Frenchie Tucker and Bernie Lynn die in tunnels following Martin's orders, the men frag Martin, an action that leads to our analysis of Paul Berlin and Cacciato. Corson's protectiveness of the soldiers under his command compels them not only to follow Corson but also to accept his limitations and support him in his illness.

Paul Berlin and Cacciato are possibly the least warlike soldiers in the novel. Students are likely to conclude, though, that Cacciato is truer to his convictions than Paul Berlin. When the soldiers have had enough of Martin's death-inducing directives and resolve to murder him, they try to persuade everyone to commit to the act by touching the grenade that will kill Martin. Paul Berlin agrees to touch it; Cacciato refuses. Finally, Paul Berlin pries Cacciato's hand from the fishing line and presses the grenade against his palm, perhaps feeling that even forced unanimity justifies his own participation.

This exploration of character differences dovetails with further consideration of the progress (or lack of it) of the war effort and the increasing rebellion that plagued the American military as the war lumbered through its final stages. We talk about the increasing numbers of fragging incidents, growing drug use, and open defiance of orders in the years after the Tet offensive. The novel invites consideration of numerous what-ifs, or, to use Paul Berlin's term, "possibilities" (323). Or, as Paul Berlin also put it, wondering especially about Cacciato's attempt to walk to Paris, "What had really happened and what merely might have happened? How did it end?" (27). Similarly, we consider the possibilities of the war. Was there a chance to win? What would winning have meant? What if a sense of purpose had been clearly articulated and maintained? Both the novel and the war leave many questions unanswered, although one question that the class answers by the end of our treatment of the novel is where the actual pursuit ends and Paul Berlin's fantasy narrative begins.

In chapter 46, after Corson has left with Sarkin, the remaining American soldiers prepare to crash through the door of the apartment in which they expect to find Cacciato, whom they will then capture. Oscar Johnson smashes the door down, and they rush into the room only to discover it empty. Paul Berlin suddenly finds himself on his knees shaking, repeatedly and automatically firing his rifle. He hears someone whimpering, then learns that the sound is coming from himself. The men are back on the hill where Cacciato had camped out on an early leg of his journey to Paris, at the conclusion of chapter 1. At this point, the class understands that the many intervening chapters have chronicled Paul Berlin's imaginative continuation of the story, his attempts to reestablish continuity and meaning within his actual war experiences, and his guard duty at the observation post, where he engaged in his acts of memory and imagination.

Going After Cacciato consistently proves to be an excellent choice as a classroom text. A richly dense novel, it offers no end of topics for discussion, and its deeply humanistic perspective provides a context for exploring the Vietnam War, in particular, and, more broadly, a range of other timeless issues.

Teaching *In the Lake of the Woods* as a Historical Novel

Jeremy Green

It is a truism dear to newspaper pundits and postmodernism theorists alike that contemporary culture lacks a strong sense of history. When it comes to the cultural memory of the Vietnam War, this truism is both thoroughly apt and oddly misleading. On the one hand, images of the war circulate in popular culture to the point that they have become clichés, a visual shorthand disseminated by Hollywood; on the other hand, Vietnam remains unassimilated, a historical disaster that still shadows United States culture and politics. William Gibson's *Pattern Recognition*, a sharp-eyed novel about contemporary ultraconsumerism, features a Californian-Vietnamese fusion restaurant called Charlie Don't Surf, the interior of which is decorated with grainy blowups of authentic Vietnam War Zippo lighters inscribed by GIs with pungent, often obscene, slogans. This mélange of movie allusion—the restaurant's name comes from a line of dialogue in *Apocalypse Now*—and authentic artifact blends the fictional and the real with postmodern insouciance, shrewdly illustrating the superficiality of historical reference in a style-fixated culture: even the insignia of traumatic violence scratched onto the army-issue lighters become a brand. At the same time, the memory of Vietnam continues to shape present political realities. The presidential race of 2004 was toxic with rumor and innuendo about Senator John Kerry's service in Vietnam and President George W. Bush's record in the Texas Air National Guard. Equally, echoes of Vietnam reverberated in the news about the United States occupation of Iraq. The atrocities, falsehoods, and geopolitical fantasies of the newer conflict inescapably recalled the disastrous involvement in Southeast Asia.

The vagaries of cultural memory inform the classroom experience. Today's college-age students will likely be familiar with the Vietnam War primarily from the movies; they may know little of the historical reality and the context in which the war was fought. Tim O'Brien's Vietnam narratives, from *If I Die in a Combat Zone* to *In the Lake of the Woods*, provide an unmatched resource for examining the meaning of the war, exploring the psychology and ethics of combat, and interrogating historical representation. This essay focuses on ways to approach the last of these through the analysis of *In the Lake of the Woods*. Many of the most compelling historical novels of the 1990s and the first decade of the twenty-first century, novels that might profitably be taught alongside O'Brien's, deal with traumatic moments in American history. For example, Toni Morrison's *Beloved* and Don DeLillo's *Libra*, two of the great novels of the 1980s, weave their fictions around documented events—the case of the escaped slave Margaret Garner and the enigmatic life of Lee Harvey Oswald, respectively—that challenge historical understanding. Similarly, O'Brien's John

Wade, the protagonist of *In the Lake of the Woods*, participates in one of the darkest episodes of the Vietnam War, the My Lai massacre. When news of this atrocity reached the United States, revulsion and recrimination came quickly and contributed to the altered public perception of the war. But in subsequent years My Lai has been "erased almost entirely from the national consciousness" (Bilton and Sim 4). O'Brien asks how such an event came about in the first place and why it has since been kept out of the national imaginary. John Wade's strategies, both crafty and pathological, for dealing with his involvement in My Lai vividly illustrate the way Vietnam lives inside and outside the historical consciousness.

Rather than adopt a direct, straightforward documentary approach to his historical materials, O'Brien obliges the reader to piece together a narrative out of fragmentary memories, snippets of information and dialogue, suggestive analogues, and hypotheses. Reading the novel is a process of detection, of collecting clues to solve a mystery—or, rather, several related mysteries. Classroom discussion of *In the Lake of the Woods* might usefully pursue the tendency of the novel to invite forensic attention, such that the reader is at once a detective and a historian, the former being a type of the latter. What kind of activity does detection—or indeed historiography—involve? As will be apparent from the first reading assignment, the novel has five different kinds of chapter titles. There are chapters that offer a direct statement of affairs, a more or less straightforward narration ("How Unhappy They Were," "How the Night Passed," "How He Went Away"). A more reflective, interrogative mode appears in chapters with titles that open with "What" or "Where" ("What He Did Next," "Where They Searched"). These two variations on direct presentation—how and what—are the initial questions an investigation might pose to establish the basic facts: What happened? How did it happen? But clearly the mysteries in the novel cannot be solved by this method alone. Hence, readers find themselves engaged in three other kinds of writing: there are chapters headed simply "Hypothesis," which speculate on possible sequences of action to fill in the gaps in knowledge; there are philosophical meditations, which examine the nature of something ("The Nature of Marriage," "The Nature of the Beast"); and finally there are "Evidence" chapters, which offer snippets of witness testimony, excerpts from documents, and exhibits (photographs and objects). Understanding the story of John and Kathy Wade draws on different kinds of intellectual activity: evidence must be judged; hypotheses entertained; and large, abstract issues examined.

To dwell on the formal variety of O'Brien's novel raises two further questions: What activities are involved in writing a history? And, further: What kind of history can in fact be written about the events in question—events that elude understanding? The novel solicits the activity of a detective of sorts, but the questions the detective must entertain grow in scope and difficulty as the evidence accumulates. Making sense of the mystery of Kathy Wade's disappearance demands that the reader-investigator make sense of John Wade's life—his political vocation, his marriage, his childhood, and, above all, his service in Vietnam, at the heart of which lies his participation in the My Lai massacre. The novel implies that all these pieces are connected. But it also forces the reader to recognize that the events in question are, at a fundamental level, resistant to comprehension. *In the Lake of the Woods* refuses to grant the satisfaction typical of a detective story or cohesive history: the events the narrator brings to light raise questions that cannot be answered. That Kathy's disappearance remains a mystery—the reader never learns whether she has been murdered by John Wade, staged her own vanishing, or simply was swallowed up by the vast wilderness of Lake of the Woods—symbolizes the greater mysteries of motive, ethics, and historical understanding that reach back into the American experience in Vietnam.

The most direct way to approach the problem of historiography in the novel is to look at the chapters of evidence. Here the narrator is present, with a couple of important exceptions (he writes in the first person in the footnotes late in the novel), as an editor rather than as a distinctive voice. Discussion might develop from the following questions: How has the evidence been selected? Is such evidence offered in Wade's defense or incrimination, as if the book could be considered an inquest or trial? And what in fact constitutes evidence? The narrator-editor presents significant statements from people who knew John Wade—witnesses to his life if not to his crimes—and exhibits that might have a bearing on the disappearance of Kathy. As the book progresses, the evidence comes to include excerpts from various kinds of text—works of psychology, political biography, and even fiction. (Thomas Pynchon's *The Crying of Lot 49*, for instance, offers a passage that seems applicable to Kathy's situation in her strange, airless marriage.) Clearly, the idea of evidence must be expanded to include thought-provoking analogues and parallels; the hermeneutic quest extends far beyond the perusal of obvious material clues. Thus the "Evidence" chapters open the story of John Wade to the history and psychology of warfare and politics. Fiction—not least the novel under study—can sit honorably beside the nonfiction sources O'Brien incorporates.

It is worth pausing here to ask how the evidence chapters shape the experience of reading *In the Lake of the Woods*. The various perspectives—some hostile to Wade, others sympathetic—are presented without comment from the narrator and thus convey the idea that the truth is dialogical: it will emerge through the reader's own active interpretation of multifarious sources. As differing views of Wade rub up against each other, the reader gains not only a deeper appreciation of his complicated, secretive life but also a sense that a monocular view of events is insufficient. This point underscores the distinctive postmodern tenor of O'Brien's novel. The term *postmodern* might set off alarm bells—perhaps rightly so. Classroom discussion of the historical novel frequently brings up the charge that history is itself a kind of fiction, a "postmodern" observation of a heedless kind. While this claim may be offered in justification of the novel, it propagates a casual relativism that undercuts the enterprise of a novel like *In the Lake of the Woods*. The massacre at My Lai is part of the historical record, as are the attempts to cover it up, and O'Brien's novel engages with that record in a deliberate and unsettling way. To recognize, as the reader must, that the events of John Wade's life—the events of Vietnam itself—are particularly complicated and refractory is not to succumb to the slack relativism by which all accounts are fictions, one as good as the next. Indeed, the remarks of certain witnesses collected in the "Evidence" chapters demonstrate how inadequate perceptions can be. The material gathered as evidence supplements the narrative by tracing its events beyond the diegetic frame, into the future—the period after the Wades' disappearance, when the book was ostensibly researched—and out into the public world of recorded events, notably through the excerption of the Peers Commission hearings on the My Lai massacre. At the same time, the evidence points to an insufficiency in the narrative proper. As the reader learns more about John Wade, the novel casts its net further and further afield in search of analogues and suggestive parallels, among them Custer's Last Stand and the Revolutionary War. Wade's encrypted past comes to light, but it remains elusive, elliptical, a series of gaps and blanks that constitute lacunae in the historical understanding.

Such gaps occur at the intersection of psychology and history. The two major enigmas the novel investigates, Kathy's disappearance and the atrocities at My Lai, are connected through a night of delirium John Wade spends in the holiday cottage after his defeat in the primary. From the horrifying day in My Lai and the troubling night in Minnesota only fragments remain, slippery little pieces of memory, images both tantalizing and scarifying. With the exception of shooting Private First Class Weatherby, which he remembers vividly, John Wade is uncertain about his actions at My Lai, just as he remains in the dark about what exactly happened that night in the cottage. Notions of post-traumatic stress disorder, disseminated to the point of cliché, are both germane and curiously unhelpful. There is a danger in the discussion of literary texts, particularly in the classroom, that psychological models of explanation can displace close reading to the point where the text becomes illustrative of or ancillary to the categories and terms of abnormal psychology. John Wade's actions, as far they can be known, may indeed be linked to trauma, but this notion should be the starting point for an examination of the novel that pursues its tropes, themes, and strategic silences through a literary reading.

Post-traumatic stress disorder has been a subject of much media attention, particularly in relation to the Gulf War and the war in Iraq. Trauma has also lately attracted marked interest among literary theorists. Works by Cathy Caruth and Dominick LaCapra offer a rich resource to the reader of O'Brien's novel, but they should perhaps be approached with caution and a light touch in the classroom. The peculiarity of trauma—its strange logic—might be drawn into the discussion through questions about John Wade's experience. Conventional thinking about trauma situates the subject as the victim of a life-threatening accident or violence that leaves a wound in the psyche (the word *trauma* derives from the Greek for *wound*). Sigmund Freud, who found *traumatic neurosis*, as he termed it, a particularly challenging puzzle, compared the after-effects of warfare—shell shock—with those of an accident such as a train crash. The subject of trauma is one whose psychic wound stems from a violent threat, whether by chance or design, to his or her survival. John Wade's trauma seems different in etiology. Although his Vietnam experiences placed his life in peril on numerous occasions, the events that he seems unable to encounter in conscious memory are those in which he was more the aggressor than the victim—or in some sense both victim and aggressor. Wade emerges from his trance to find himself in the drainage ditch where the bodies of the murdered villagers have been thrown, and from there he shoots PFC Weatherby. Why is he in the ditch in the first place? Does it suggest a perverse identification with the slaughtered? Or is he practicing some further violence on their corpses—killing the dead, so to speak? And why does he shoot Weatherby? These questions remain rhetorical because the moment, like much of Wade's memory of the massacre, is opaque, unintelligible, as befits "a place where the air itself was both reality and illusion, where anything might instantly become anything else" (72). Similarly, the events of the night Kathy disappears survive in his memory as hallucinatory instants stranded between nightmare and reality.

The perplexity of trauma, as Caruth has argued, stems from the fact that past events of extreme intensity cannot be registered by consciousness yet continue to exert a destructively powerful influence on the subject. Because these events elude memory, they cannot be directly represented in narrative. Thus trauma belongs less to sober historical reconstruction than to the uncanny, to haunting and fraught repetition, to inexplicable behavior and insoluble mysteries. Historical detection in O'Brien's novel bears the scars of this difficulty: as the search for Kathy Wade and for the truth about her husband widens in scope both geographical and historical—covering thousands of acres of the Minnesota wilderness and reaching back into Wade's past—it moves not toward resolution but toward greater uncertainty, especially when John Wade stages his own disappearance in an apparently suicidal simulacrum of his wife's vanishing. What the novel emphasizes, therefore, is the resistance of certain events to narration, to the explanatory logic of cause and effect on which the historian and detective depend. Here the novelist has an advantage over the historian. O'Brien's fictional investigation of Wade's life and disappearance opens onto the historical events of Vietnam in 1968, including the massacre at My Lai; it also opens simultaneously onto the unknown, the inconclusive and speculative.

Introducing the idea of trauma to the discussion need not—indeed, should not—entail fitting O'Brien's protagonist into a template from an abnormal-psychology textbook, nor does it mean smuggling some much-derided Freudian notion into the analysis of the book. Instead, the point is to explore the way trauma disrupts historical narrative as much as it ruptures psychic integrity. In comprehending the character of John Wade, as a historian labors to explain an enigmatic chain of events, the reader makes use of rich conceits that repay careful analysis in the classroom. One must serve here as an example. Throughout the novel, Wade's psyche is described in terms of a mirror image. At first blush, this seems a conventional figure for introspection, a standard trope for narcissistic self-absorption. Yet in O'Brien's novel the mirror serves John Wade as a prop to manipulate reality. As a boy he practices magic tricks as a way of constructing a new self:

> In the mirror, where miracles happened, John was no longer a lonely little kid. He had sovereignty over the world. Quick and graceful, his hands did things ordinary hands could not do—palm a cigarette lighter, cut a deck of cards with a turn of the thumb. Everything was possible, even happiness.   (65)

The mirror becomes a place where a superior self can be manufactured—made by hand, so to speak, since the conjuring tricks Wade perfects, and which give access to the world of miracles, must be rehearsed time and again in front of a mirror.

Magic gives John Wade power over the physical world and also the immaterial attributes he craves, including the love and approval of his father. And it is this magic that he tries to perpetuate through trickery and sleight of hand in his subsequent life as a husband to Kathy, a soldier in Vietnam, and a political candidate seeking office. But the manipulation of reality becomes an internal principle as well. In one of several images of incorporation and corporeal engulfment in the novel, Wade takes this mirror—the magical surface that miraculously corrects an insufficient reality—into his mental processes:

> [H]e secretly kept the old stand-up mirror in his head. Pretending, of course—he understood that—but he felt calm and safe with the big mirror behind his eyes, where he could slide away behind the glass, where he could turn bad things into good things and just be happy.   (65–66)

The formidable optics—eyes that conceal a mirror that screens and alters an unpalatable reality—suggest that the most significant magic trick of all lies in sustaining the illusion of a coherent self.

John Wade constructs this elaborate illusion in situations both promising and refractory, including politics, combat, and marriage. Yet unlike a die-hard postmodernist, for whom simulation can replace reality altogether, Wade struggles time and again with a reality that cannot be manipulated because it cannot be acknowledged as reality in the first place. This impossible reality is trauma. Trauma seems to be at home in neither reality nor illusion. It presents some unmanageable third category that undoes the carefully doctored reality in which John Wade lives. It shapes the psyche as its unacknowledged truth, and it shapes the form of the narrative, which circles around an absence.

The novel's refusal to give up its secrets can prove frustrating to students. Yet the crucial point is that the secrets the investigation divulges, the secrets of John Wade's past, point only to an irreducible unknown. The traces of this unknown are perhaps most obvious in two repeated pieces of evidence—the maddening flies that Richard Thinbill recalls from My Lai and the anguished cry of George Armstrong Custer (*"John! John! Oh, John!"*). Custer's cry in particular marks the place where historical inquiry runs up directly against the violence and horror of events. At this point, historical detection, which engages the reader for much of O'Brien's novel, must acknowledge its lack of mastery. And this acknowledgment, finally, raises questions about the kind of historical novel O'Brien has written, a novel powerfully animated by the desire to understand but driven also to explore the limitations of understanding. Such limitations, it seems, are a necessary corollary of the struggle to remember Vietnam.

Teaching *Going After Cacciato*
as an American Road Narrative

Russell Morton Brown

> The road was red. It climbed the mountain at a bad angle for the march,
> not winding with the mountain's natural contours but instead going straight
> up. For hiking or strolling it would have been a good road. The view was
> magnificent, and along the road grew many forms of tropical foliage, and
> everywhere it was wild country and pure.   (*Going After Cacciato* 160)

Going After Cacciato illustrates how we seek structures that give coherence and
meaning to events. Paul Berlin, standing on guard duty in Vietnam in 1968, creates a story in which a deserting soldier, Cacciato, is leading him and his squad
out of Vietnam and all the way to Paris.[1] This fantasy helps Paul Berlin get
through the night; it also provides the narrative line that carries the reader
through the book. But in constructing his story of Cacciato, Paul Berlin is uncertain how to give it shape, a challenge he connects with the shapelessness of
war:

> Waiting, trying to imagine a rightful but still happy ending, Paul Berlin
> found himself pretending, in a wishful sort of way, that before long the war
> would reach a climax beyond which everything else would seem bland and
> commonplace. . . . He pretended he had crossed that threshold.   (25)

Realizing that raw data do not yield meaning, Paul Berlin later imagines Doc
Peret, the squad's medic, reminding him that "[f]acts are one thing. . . . Interpretation is something else" (226). The source of meaning is "[p]utting facts in
the right framework. And we're counting on you to get us off the hook" (226).

The uninterpreted data in an English course are the texts on the syllabus:
they gain meaning for students from the course's form and framework. Because what gives a course its shape is what *Going After Cacciato* calls "a story
that makes sense" (293), I want to show how using *Going After Cacciato* as
the closing text in a seminar on the American road narrative both contributed
to the shape of that class—providing my students a more complete understanding of how the road functions as a rich cultural and literary symbol in
America—and made that novel part of the larger framework that governed
their understanding.

To show students the tradition of the American road narrative, a tradition
that subsequent authors become aware of and are shaped by, I initially focus
on three foundational texts: Mark Twain's *The Adventures of Huckleberry Finn*,
John Steinbeck's *The Grapes of Wrath*, and Jack Kerouac's *On the Road*. I supplement these with a substantial selection from Francis Parkman's *The Oregon
Trail* and the first sixteen pages of Sinclair Lewis's *Free Air*.[2] In the second

part of the course, students read three late-twentieth-century texts that self-consciously reply to these narratives about America as a developing nation still completing its move into nationhood and that express anxieties about the nation America has become: Jim Harrison's *A Good Day to Die*, Bobbie Ann Mason's *In Country*, and O'Brien's *Going After Cacciato*. I did not, when I first designed the course, make a conscious decision to end it with novels of the Vietnam era, but these books have proved especially useful in examining the road narrative in later American fiction.[3]

Beginning the course with the first eleven chapters of *The Oregon Trail* (a bit more than a third of the book) shows students the mythic American road, which was first a saddle trail. E. N. Feltskog, the editor of the 1969 edition of *The Oregon Trail*, observes that while the road west had already gained symbolic value in American writing before *The Oregon Trail* was published in 1849, it was Parkman who "understood how the road, stretching westward in vast isolation and terrifying loneliness, dominated the imagination of those who traveled it" (12a). Having established the road as a symbolic site, Parkman added crucial features that will appear in the later works we read: the westward trek; the soon-to-be familiar pattern of the young man leaving behind his too-binding family to travel, most often with a young male companion; and—in Parkman's frequent references to his rifle—the presence, and often the prominence, of the gun.[4]

Parkman's need for an experienced guide who will lead him in the wilderness and his fascination with the other (in the figure of the Native peoples) anticipate the way road narratives contain the motifs Leslie Fiedler finds central to classic American novels:

> To "light out for the territory" . . . seems easy and tempting from the vantage point of a chafing and restrictive home; but civilization once disavowed and Christianity disowned, the bulwark of woman left behind, the wanderer feels himself without protection, more motherless child than free man. (26)

Fiedler concludes that there is "a substitute for wife or mother presumably waiting in the green heart of nature: the natural man, the good companion, pagan and unashamed—Queequeg or Chingachgook or . . . Jim." *The Oregon Trail* confirms this, as well as Fiedler's further observation that "the figure of the natural man is ambiguous, a dream and a nightmare at once" (26). We will see later versions of Fiedler's natural man in *On the Road*, when Sal and Dean find their promised land in rural Mexican village life, and, even more strikingly, in *Going After Cacciato*, when Paul Berlin's version of his "natural man" proves to be a woman and a native of Vietnam—Sarkin Aung Wan.

Perhaps the most important aspect of Parkman's text for my course is its celebration of the restlessness of the Westerners he encounters—"that race of restless and intrepid pioneers," whom he idealizes because their "axes and rifles have opened a path from the Alleghanies to the western prairies" (4). Such passages prepare us for the hero of *The Adventures of Huckleberry Finn*, who at the beginning of chapter 2 (long before he has decided to flee with Jim) tells his readers that "miserableness" is the result of the simple act of remaining quiet and stationary, because trying to hold still makes him "itch all over in a upwards of a thousand places" (18). The intensity of Huck's restlessness prepares for the "[a]lways goin' and goin'" of *The Grapes of Wrath* (163) and the sense in *On the Road* that the only thing to do is "to go someplace" (117), and it anticipates *Going After Cacciato*, with Berlin's restless impatience with "the incredible slowness with which time passed" (45)—which is what prompts his fantasy of flight along a western road.

Huck's river journey became an essential expression of the American story of the road, and his famous pronouncement about being prepared "to light out for the Territory" gives my course its theme. Still, I want my students to see that we must not reduce these texts simply to reiterations of the same story. In celebrating the opening of the West and the joy of exploring unsettled territories, *The Oregon Trail* embodied the American quest for new frontiers and became an inspiration to the rapid settlement of the West, unambiguously understood by Parkman and those who followed to require the displacing of the Native peoples who also fascinated them. Twain's novel, in contrast, remains our emblematic expression of the acceptability of running away. It expresses what the novelist Wright Morris described as the "impulse to get away from it all . . . a pattern of flight from a world that will not stand still"; Morris thought Twain showed us "why exile has for the American artist a peculiar charm. . . . like Huck Finn, he slips the noose of Aunt Sally and makes for the territory" (25–26). Thus, from the beginning, two competing ideas—in quest of and in flight from—lie at the heart of the American road story.

We next read the opening of Sinclair Lewis's *Free Air*. This book shows the new role of the motor vehicle in American culture, and its opening suggests that driving will be viewed as a heroic act, a motif continued in the fiction that follows, including *The Grapes of Wrath*, *On the Road* (with Dean Moriarty as the apotheosis of the heroic driver), and *Going After Cacciato*. The opening of *Free Air* also offers unexpected intertextuality: when Claire Boltwood, the protagonist, reflects on the danger of losing momentum on a bad road—which she realizes might mean getting "stuck for keeps" (6)—the novel anticipates the importance of staying in motion in subsequent road narratives (as when Dean passes other cars on the road "on pure momentum") and prepares us for its role in *Going After Cacciato*, where it has implications for the way America and its soldiers have been drawn into the war. More specifically, the first chapter of *Free Air* culminates with Claire driving into "a hole in the road ahead . . . a deep water-filled hole" with "scattered straw and brush" (which causes her to think of the "débris of a battlefield") (8). This makes for a fascinating, if coincidental, connection when we reach the surreal chapter 13 of *Going After Cacciato*, "Falling through a Hole in the Road to Paris."

What is especially useful about the opening of *Free Air* is that it shows how an idea that grew out of Parkman's account—with its unexamined conflation of restlessness with nervousness in the author's observation that "[i]f a man is constitutionally liable to nervous apprehensions, a tour on the distant prairies would prove the best prescription" (Parkman 1849, 128; ch. 7)—has become conventional wisdom. Claire is driving her father west to cure "nervous prostration" brought on by the stress and overwork of the urban East. Not only is his cure effected by the trip, but Claire, through her discovery of the real American West, with its character-building challenges and its ethos of rugged individualism, gains a new hardihood and a more democratic vision. Although *The Grapes of Wrath* will ironize the idea that the road offers a successful escape and suggest that the West can no longer function as the escape valve imagined by Frederick Jackson Turner, taking the road west as a healing cure for neurasthenia and other psychic disturbances has remained surprisingly persistent in the road tradition. It is present in the opening sentences of *On the Road*:

> I first met Dean not long after my wife and I split up. I had just gotten over a serious illness that I won't bother to talk about, except that it had something to do with the miserably weary split-up and my feeling that everything was dead. With the coming of Dean Moriarty began the part of my life you could call my life on the road. (1)

And all three of the Vietnam-era novels we read associate acute emotional distress with the decision to take to the road.[5] Two of these, *A Good Day to Die* and *In Country*, are set in the United States and deal with returned veterans and those who have lost a loved one; the story that Paul Berlin creates also has its sources in emotional trauma, but because it takes place in the midst of the war, it cannot be restorative in the same way.

Although the troubled roads of the Vietnam-era novels are prefigured by *The Grapes of Wrath*, Kerouac, though writing after Steinbeck, manages to have his road both ways in his account of his late 1940s travels, published as *On the Road* in 1957. He is like Steinbeck in suggesting that there has been some kind of loss in American society, but his ecstatic celebration of car travel as pure energy returns the road journey to a positive adventure, one that restores to the twentieth century the possibilities offered by the nineteenth-century West. Dean Moriarty, the boon companion as well as the masculine guide that Kerouac's Sal Paradise needs, embodies the frontier ethos. Sal tells us, "[H]is 'criminality' was not something that sulked and sneered; it was a wild yea-saying overburst of American joy; it was Western, the west wind, an ode from the Plains" (8). Dean looks like a cowboy, "a young Gene Autry—trim, thin-hipped, blue-eyed, with a real Oklahoma accent—a sideburned hero of the snowy West" (2). He brings with him the romanticized imagery of the Old West that pervades *On the Road*. However, even before the conclusion of the first of the novel's five parts, Sal—having reached San Francisco for the first time—does have to learn that there are limits to western travel: "Here I was at the end of America—no more land—now there was nowhere to go but back" (77). It's a sentiment echoed by Dean with his "No more land! We can't go any further 'cause there ain't no more land!" (169). It is surely this awareness of physical limits that makes what Sal calls the "holy road" its own end in a way it has not been in previous accounts. This sense of limitation and the need to transcend it looks ahead to Cacciato's boundary-crossing journey to Paris because it leads us inevitably to Sal and Dean's nation-abandoning trip into Mexico in *On the Road's* conclusion, where they finally find "the magic land at the end of the road" (276).

On the Road thus looks both backward and forward. The quintessential celebration of road travel in America, it takes the romanticizing of car and road further than any previous work and is the last book in which a serious American writer will leave the westward journey so unironized and view the road trip as an unquestioned glorification of unbridled masculinity. At the same time, by embedding allusions to a variety of earlier works, ranging from *The Odyssey* through "books about pioneers" and narratives by Herman Melville, Mark Twain, Jack London, Ernest Hemingway, and others, Kerouac's novel becomes the first of the road books to engage in a struggle with tradition and thus anticipates the self-conscious (and increasingly skeptical) responses to the road that will follow.

On the Road is also transitional in that, while drawing on the appeal inherent in the great American journeys, it doesn't follow the descriptive realist tradition that had been an attraction for readers of earlier road narratives, the promise to show readers landscapes they had not themselves experienced. Instead, *On the Road's* rhapsodic, drug-fueled journeying gives readers a new and subjective vision of an already familiar road—a strategy that will be enlarged on in *A Good Day to Die* and, more particularly, by Hunter Thompson in the opening of *Fear and Loathing in Las Vegas* and Tom Wolfe in *The Electric Kool-Aid Acid Test*. These drug-distilled road trips look forward to the dreamscapes through which Paul Berlin journeys in *Going After Cacciato*.

Enough connections have emerged by this point that I now want my students to think about how they have become sensitized as readers to questions of influence and inherited form and how that allows them to attend to certain features of the texts, ask certain questions, and anticipate patterns. Because their responses are being shaped by their shared history of reading, I want them to see that they are engaged in a discourse—one that has formal characteristics and conventions. I want them not merely to begin to sense the road narrative as a genre but to feel, with Tzvetan Todorov, that "failing to recognize the existence of genres is equivalent to claiming that a literary work does not bear any relationship to already existing works" (8). I have them read a passage from "Forms of Time and of the Chronotope in the Novel" to see how Mikhail Bakhtin connects road narratives with the picaresque: he observes that the road became a valuable narrative device because it is "a particularly good place for random encounters" (243), and he argues that road narratives form a genre distinct from the novel of travel because the "road always . . . passes through familiar territory, and not through some exotic alien world . . . ; it is the sociohistorical heterogeneity of one's own country that is revealed and depicted" (245). I point out that Bakhtin's idea of the road narrative as mapping out our own territory resonates with Benedict Anderson's suggestions that the origins of the novel—which he connects with the origins of the nation—can be found in the "picaresque tour d'horizon," a narrative that is "not a tour du monde," because the "horizon is clearly bounded" (35). The sense that the road journey may allow protagonists to become acquainted with the nation and to learn its limits is useful for the texts we read (though challenged by the inclusion of *Going After Cacciato*). This brief venture into theory allows us to reflect on the works we have read so far as both instances and interrogations of nation building and nation defining, and it prepares us to ask how later works signal their engagement with tradition—and how they must go beyond their inheritance to renew the form or to criticize it as purveying dangerous tropes and outworn conventions.

The idea that the road narrative may become both outworn and dangerous emerges in the novels with which I conclude my course; while Harrison's, Mason's, and O'Brien's works all explore the idea of the road as refuge and the journey as restorative, they also offer a critical view of restless American travel and suggest that the idealization of a road west may be linked to American imperialism. In *A Good Day to Die* a whimsical decision on the part of the cowboylike Tim and the narrator to drive west to destroy a dam that never actually existed shows how the road trip has become a pop fantasy, a movie- and television-induced dream useful for creating false dramas in one's life. And Harrison's book implies that this fantasy resulted in America's involvement in Vietnam. When Tim is killed in the novel's conclusion, his death is connected to the western ethos that he, like Kerouac's Dean, personifies: "I knew Tim would die the moment he turned from the cattle and looked in amazement at the fuse that was no longer there. And then he had tried to run in those gaudy blue cowboy boots" (172).[6]

Mason's *In Country* advances this questioning of the road narrative. Her novel, which makes explicit connections with Twain and Kerouac, shows its young protagonist concluding that America's myth of taking to the road in flight may have led to Vietnam. When the returned vet Emmett finds his niece Sam after she has run away, he tells her:

> Once when I was little and Daddy gave me a whipping because I didn't feed the calves on time, I ran away from home. . . . I thought I was getting revenge, for some reason. It's childish, to go run off to the wilderness to get revenge. It's the most typical thing in the world.   (221)

Sam replies:

> That explains it then. . . . That's what you were doing in Vietnam. That explains what the whole country was doing over there. The least little threat and America's got to put on its cowboy boots and stomp around and show somebody a thing or two.   (221)

When we turn at the end of the course to *Going After Cacciato*, my students observe that it is the only book on the syllabus set entirely outside of the borders of the United States. But because the American road narrative has become so familiar to them as readers, they are also quick to see that the book is filled with signifiers that locate it within that tradition. For example, in addition to the echoing of "on the road" in various chapter headings and the novel's extensive play with various modes of travel, *Going After Cacciato* has a passage that both connects it with the mythic drives of *On the Road* and establishes clearly the gun-and-car connection:

> And Paul Berlin drove. His eyelids hung on speed. Run, rush, recede—a rhyme to keep his eyes open, and he clutched the wheel the way he'd once clutched his rifle, unloving but fearful of losing it. The feeling of being flung over a waterfall, a landfall, spun out to the edge of the speeding dark. No control. (246–47)

O'Brien further associates the fantasy road trip that Berlin creates with the American story of western exploration by emphasizing that Cacciato and the squad that pursues him are continually traveling west. When Paul Berlin encounters the refugees Sarkin Aung Wan and her father (recalling Parkman's encounters with Native Americans), Sarkin says to him, "I shall guide you," to which he replies, "Cacciato. He's our guide. . . . he's out there in front. A scout" (60). Moving the road story from the American West to Southeast Asia allows O'Brien to literalize an idea current in the antiwar rhetoric of the Vietnam era—that, rather than finding the Pacific Coast a limitation to be chafed against, Americans continued their westward trek, carried by their momentum across the Pacific and into a disastrous Asian adventure. That unceasing movement, O'Brien suggests, is still impelling soldiers like Paul Berlin—who (in a memory of his past Vietnam experience) describes himself as "dull of mind, blunt of spirit, numb of history, and struck with wonder that he could not stop climbing the red road" (168).

Not surprisingly, the western imagery in O'Brien's novel is sinister. Paul Berlin is jokingly called "cowboy" by Doc—an appellation that at first seems mere male camaraderie but, because of its association with the western gunslinger, carries a heavy weight once we have read the last chapter. There the story of going after Cacciato, already told in the opening chapter, is retold with new details, most notably the fact that, when the squad first tried to bring Cacciato back, Paul Berlin lost control of his automatic weapon. In a final merging of car and gun, Paul Berlin's fantasy of driving heroically with "no control" is revealed as a displacement of a darker truth:

> How did it start? A kind of trembling, maybe. He remembered the fear coming, but he did not remember why. Then the shaking feeling. The enormous noise, shaken by his own weapon, the way he'd squeezed to keep it from jerking away from him. Simple folly, that was all. (333)

Is this the trauma that Paul Berlin flees in his fantasy journey—the knowledge that he has killed Cacciato?

And what does *Going After Cacciato* suggest about the manifest destiny that the road journey has embodied and that may have taken America into Vietnam? Is there a way to get off the road while acknowledging that the road narrative has become the only meaningful framework for Paul Berlin—indeed, perhaps a way of making sense for America in general? One answer is suggested by Sarkin Aung Wan's aphoristic comment: "The way in is the way out" (98). If going west has paradoxically carried Americans across the Pacific and into the East, they can get out by continuing west . . . and coming full circle, back to Europe. Thus to arrive in Paris would make them ready to repeat the original European journey to the New World—either as their journey home or as a turn of the wheel beginning a new historical cycle.

At the end of my course, quest and flight become one: *Going After Cacciato* suggests that the Vietnam War may have resulted from the continuing venture into unexplored wilds (Parkman's story) and considers, but cannot not fully embrace, the Huck Finn story of flight as an alternative. Paul Berlin's Huck flight is a fantasy that takes him to the end of the road in Paris, even though he remains unmoving, trapped in Vietnam. Still, fantasy and reality do merge in the novel's concluding pages: all the members of the squad, longing to go home, join in collectively imagining a narrative for Cacciato, one in which he makes his journey safely and becomes an image of possibility for them all.

In telling an ambiguous tale that leaves us deeply ambivalent about the road narrative, *Going After Cacciato* reflects the way my students feel at the end of this course. At the last meeting of the term many talk about making their own road trips, yet their discussions show that they have also grown aware of the road as having the power to carry both individuals and nations into troubled places.[7]

NOTES

[1] In this essay, I ignore the reader's initial experience of the novel, in which the relation between fantasy and reality is not at first clear.

[2] In lectures and through the course Web site, I make students aware of the range of other early American road narratives, such as Jack London's *The Road* and Henry Miller's *The Air-Conditioned Nightmare*.

[3] To suggest the breadth of the American road narrative, I ask students to write on one additional work. Fruitful choices have included Tom Wolfe's *The Electric Kool-Aid Acid Test*, Joan Didion's *Play It as It Lays*, Robert Stone's *Dog Soldiers*, Robert Pirsig's *Zen and the Art of Motorcycle Maintenance*, William Least Heat-Moon's *Blue Highways*, Mona Simpson's *Anywhere but Here*, and Stephen Wright's *Going Native*. Robert Kroetsch's *The Studhorse Man* and Guy Vanderhaeghe's *The Englishman's Boy* have been useful for students who want to compare the treatment of road narrative in English Canada with its American counterpart; some students have chosen Jacques Poulin's *Volkswagen Blues*, an explicit response to *On the Road* from a French Canadian that invites us to consider

Kerouac's narrative as a product of his Quebecois inheritance. For more on cultural differences between American and Canadian road narratives, see R. Brown.

[4] The conjunction of the horse (and, in later narratives, the car) with the weapon reminds us that while stories of the road might seem to privilege flight over fight, the distinction is not clear. In addition to the taking of a gun on the road in Kerouac's *On the Road* and Harrison's *A Good Day to Die* — not to mention the heavily armed soldiers in *Going After Cacciato* — even the pastoral innocence of *Free Air* is disrupted by the figure of the threatening hitchhiker on Claire's running board who inquires, "Got a revolver, of course?" (104). And while *The Grapes of Wrath* does suggest that the road offers a peaceful solution to the disastrous disruptions of capital because "there's nobody to shoot" (49), Wright's *Going Native* makes the gun the central character of the road trip.

[5] Consider also the breakdown that sends the protagonist of *Zen and the Art of Motorcycle Maintenance* on his road journey and the opening of *Blue Highways* with its narrator (who has lost both his wife and his job) deciding to see if a "man who couldn't make things go right could at least go" (1).

[6] There is a moment in *Going After Cacciato* that makes one wonder if O'Brien, whose narrative is larded with satiric glances at the myths of the Old West, is recalling this description of Tim's ironic death: "On the long walks Sarkin Aung Wan . . . would ask about Fort Dodge. Was it a true cattle town? Was it difficult to walk in spurs? He told her, . . . yes, many people in Fort Dodge broke their legs and ankles trying to walk with spurs" (170). Of course, many intertexts, popular and literary, are evoked in this novel, including the Bob Hope–Bing Crosby road movies and the flight from the war at the end of Hemingway's *A Farewell to Arms*.

[7] With more time, this course might turn its attention to that most devastating of all post-Vietnam road novels, Cormac McCarthy's *Blood Meridian* — or to his postapocalyptic version of the narrative in *The Road*.

From Short-Story Cycle to Ensemble Novel: Teaching *July, July*

Catherine Calloway

Tim O'Brien is well established as a writer of short stories, having published at least forty, most of them precursor stories to his book-length works of fiction published months or years, sometimes even a decade or more, after the stories first appeared. Chapters from *Going After Cacciato* were first published in such periodicals as *Denver Quarterly*, *Gallery*, *Shenandoah*, *Redbook*, and *Esquire*, and chapters from *The Nuclear Age* first appeared in the *Atlantic*, *Esquire*, *Ploughshares*, and *Granta*.

While most of O'Brien's books are hard to place in one genre, his fifth book, *The Things They Carried*, has been definitively classified as a short-story cycle.[1] Almost half of its chapters appeared in print before its 1990 release, beginning in 1976 with the publication of "Speaking of Courage" (a story initially connected to *Going After Cacciato* but later revised for *The Things They Carried*). O'Brien moved away from the short-story cycle after the publication of *The Things They Carried*, publishing in advance only one chapter from each of his next two books, *In the Lake of the Woods* and *Tomcat in Love*. With *July, July*, however, he not only moved back to the short-story cycle but did so in new ways. Even though *The Things They Carried* remains a worthwhile classroom tool for demonstrating O'Brien's innovative use of the short-story cycle, *July, July* offers valuable challenges and insights of its own.

The most comprehensive definition of the short-story cycle comes from James Nagel, who traces the origins of the genre from the Greek cyclic poets to contemporary literature and distinguishes between the short-story cycle and the short-story sequence, the composite novel, and the novel in general. According to Nagel,

> a cycle is less unified than a novel but has much greater coherence and thematic integrity than a mere collection of unrelated stories. It can focus on the development of a single character, but it is more likely to involve scenes devoted to a series of characters who interact with each other throughout the episodes, so that the major character of one story may function in the background of another. (17)

Furthermore, it is not the sequential order of the stories that is important but the connections among them (12). Each story in a cycle must be able to "stand alone (with a beginning, middle, and end) yet be enriched in the context of the interrelated stories" (15). Nagel emphasizes the importance of the publication history of a particular cycle of stories:

> Because the constituent stories of cycles often appear individually in magazines before being anthologized, they pose special interpretive problems for scholars. These narratives are not always the same in the magazines as they are in the collected volumes, suggesting that adjustments had to be made in setting, character names, and chronology to synthesize independent works into a unified whole. (14)

The process Nagel describes is familiar to readers of O'Brien's works. In *July, July*, ten chapters were published independently as stories, five in *Esquire* and five in the *New Yorker*. With the exception of "Loon Point," all were published between March 1998 and August 2002, shortly before or coinciding with the publication of the book.

To demonstrate the nature of the chapters as separate stories that can stand independently as coherent works, I first assign a selection of the ten stories from *July, July* that were published previously: "Class of '68," "Nogales," "Winnipeg," "July '69," "Too Skinny," "Little People," "Half Gone," "What Went Wrong," "Loon Point," and "The Streak." Students can see that each story focuses on a particular character or set of characters as well as on a certain incident or important moment and that it meets the prerequisite of possessing a beginning, middle, and end. "Half Gone" focuses on Dorothy Stier's half-naked march down the driveway to force her husband, Ron, to acknowledge the reality of her breast cancer; "Nogales," on the events leading up to the abandonment of Karen Burns and a group of senior citizens in the desert by drug smugglers; "Winnipeg," on the desertion of Billy McMann to Canada during the Vietnam War; "July '69," on the ordeal that David Todd endures in Vietnam after being shot in both feet; and "The Streak," on Amy Robinson's gambling wins and her subsequent divorce. Even "Class of '68," a one-page story that can be classified as flash fiction or sudden fiction, is easily recognizable as an independent story, as it records a conflict between Dorothy Stiers and Billy McMann at their class reunion.

Students can note that while O'Brien makes some changes from story to book form, the revisions typically fit the types of changes that Nagel considers usual for stories that are later merged into a longer work:

> the modification of clarifications of family relationships, descriptions of locations and their distances from other places, and explanations of time parameters, matters essential in the appearance of individual stories published in separate places months or years apart from one another but redundant in a collected volume. (14)

Students can readily understand why there may be a difference of two or three years between the ages of the characters from version to version and why David Todd in *July, July* imagines his future residence as Minneapolis—not Edina, as in the original "July '69"—and why Billy McMann in *July, July* leaves the

United States for Canada on 1 July 1969 rather than on 7 July 1969, as he does in the earlier version of "Winnipeg."

The most problematic story in *July, July* is chapter 13, "Loon Point," which was originally published in *Esquire* in January 1993, almost a decade before the book. It challenges readers to question its significance to O'Brien's writing process and its place in the book. In an interview with Karen Rosica shortly after the publication of *Tomcat in Love* and before the writing of *July, July*, O'Brien replied, when asked about future projects, that he might write a story about "a [married] woman who decides to have an affair with her dentist," then takes a trip to northern Minnesota with him, where he drowns. In fact, he had already written and published such a story under the title "Loon Point," and it was already well known to O'Brien scholars. Although Ellie Abbott's husband is named Jack in the 1993 version instead of Mark, as in *July, July*, the story is essentially the same. O'Brien's statement to Rosica casts doubt on the veracity of his account and calls attention to the issue of truth, a thematic concern in much of his writing. Reading the original "Loon Point" and the story of the same name that appears in *July, July* in conjunction with Rosica's interview can raise some interesting questions about storytelling and the nature of truth.

Once students have read a selection of the original short stories, I assign *July, July*, a book that reviewers term "an ensemble novel,"[2] one that contains a large cast of characters. Here students can see how individual short stories have been skillfully interwoven into a much larger text to form a novel. O'Brien juxtaposes eleven chapters set in the present at a class reunion — all entitled "Class of '69" — with eleven chapters that flash back to the past. Nine of the eleven flashback chapters are stories previously published in *Esquire* and the *New Yorker*. ("Class of '68," which first appeared as a story in *Esquire* in March 1998 is recast in the novel as a "Class of '69" chapter.) The two other flashback chapters, "Hearing" and "Well Married," easily could have been published as stand-alone stories but were not.

O'Brien blends the two types of chapters together throughout the book, interspersing the "Class of '69" chapters with stories that tell what he considers a "pivotal, fork-in-the-road, edge-of-the-cliff moment" in the postcollege lives of each of the book's eleven main characters ("Interview"). In an interview with Robin Vidimos, O'Brien noted that each protagonist's life

> is shaped by a handful of critical events or decisions. This insight, boiled down to its essence, is the force driving *July, July*. . . . The challenge was to find a moment of choice and then tell a story about it, hoping the reader would get a sense of the character's history and future.

In interweaving these fork-in-the-road stories with the "Class of '69" chapters, O'Brien skillfully turns what could be classified as a short-story cycle into an ensemble novel with a wide range of voices.[3] Unlike such previous short-story cycles as Ernest Hemingway's *In Our Time* and Sherwood Anderson's

Winesburg, Ohio, O'Brien's *July, July* has many protagonists, not a central figure like Nick Adams or George Willard. O'Brien establishes multiple pairings: Jan Huebner and Amy Robinson, the respective protagonists of "Little People" and "The Streak," share the stories of their divorces with each other; Ellie Abbott, who has had an adulterous relationship and is the protagonist of "Loon Point," confides in Paulette Haslo, a Presbyterian minister and the protagonist of "Hearing"; Marv Bertel, the protagonist of "Too Skinny," spends his time vying for more than friendship with Spook Spinelli, the protagonist of "Well Married," on whom he has always had a crush; Dorothy Stiers, the protagonist of "Half Gone," and Billy McMann, the protagonist of "Winnipeg," continue their postcollege love-hate relationship; and David Todd and Marla Dempsey of "July '69" and "What Went Wrong" ponder both the Vietnam War and the disintegration of their marriage.

I ask students to consider the role of the "Class of '69" chapters in the novel. Why are they important, and how do they contribute to *July, July*? In considering their significance, students can see the relevance of the previously published stories to the complete novel. Using a technique familiar to readers of *Going After Cacciato*, O'Brien skillfully links each "Class of '69" chapter to one or more of the protagonist's individual stories. For example, the second "Class of '69" chapter, which ends with a conversation between the divorcees Amy Robinson and Jan Huebner, is followed by the individual stories of these two women and their failed marriages: first Amy's story in "The Streak" and then Jan's in "Little People." Chapter 6, the third "Class of '69" chapter, which concerns a conversation between Spook Spinelli and Marv Bertel precedes the chapter "Well Married," which describes Spook's bigamous relationship with her two "husbands." In like manner, chapter 8, the fourth "Class of '69" chapter, which focuses on the conflict between Dorothy Stiers and Billy McMann at the class reunion, leads into "Winnipeg," the chapter that details the reason behind their thirty-one-year-old conflict: Dorothy, who later married one of Billy's best friends, would not flee to Canada with Billy when he decided to ignore his draft induction notice and evade the Vietnam War.

In chapter 10, the fifth "Class of '69" chapter, a relationship of trust emerges between Paulette Haslo and Ellie Abbott. The chapter ends with each woman deciding to reveal her secret to the other. Because Ellie tells Paulette that she should go first, the next chapter is "Hearing," the story of how Paulette, who is arrested for breaking into the house belonging to a member of her congregation, is defrocked—relieved of her ministerial rights—and loses her church. Ellie's story of her affair with Harmon Osterberg, a married dentist who dies while on a weekend getaway with her, is told in chapter 13, "Loon Point," after Paulette and Ellie discuss in chapter 12—another "Class of '69" chapter—the situation that Paulette details in "Hearing." Similarly, O'Brien follows an allusion to Dorothy Stiers's breast cancer in chapter 14, a "Class of '69" chapter, with Dorothy's story in chapter 15, "Half Gone." This pattern continues throughout *July, July*. The reference to the death of Karen Burns in chapter 16, a "Class of '69" chapter, is followed by "Nogales," the story of the events that led up to Karen's death. The sigh by Marv Bertel at the end of chapter 18, a "Class of '69" chapter, as he realizes he has yet to be a participant in the game of Truth, precedes his telling of the story of his weight loss, deceit, and marriage in chapter 19, "Too Skinny." Students can see that there is a direct connection between the "Class of '69" chapters and the fork-in-the-road stories to which they are linked, the structural device of a class reunion helping to reinforce and enhance these tales.

While some of the "Class of '69" chapters serve as introductions to individual stories, others provide information that is essential to the novel as a whole over-all. The first "Class of '69" chapter is especially important, as it provides a mini overview of the book. It introduces the major characters, giving readers a peek at their personalities, dreams, emotions, successes, and failures, and alludes to such major themes as "[d]eath, marriage, children, divorce, betrayal, loss, grief, disease" (7), aging, and war. In addition, the opening chapter reveals characters' feelings about each other. At times, the "Class of '69" chapters offer predictions or foreshadow future events. In the first such chapter, David Todd and Marla Dempsey speculate that Ellie Abbott and Harmon Osterberg may have had an affair, which is confirmed later in the chapter as well as throughout the novel. Chapters 16, 18, and 22 foreshadow the crash of a plane on which Spook Spi-nelli and Marv Bertel are passengers.

The "Class of '69" chapters serve other roles as well. For one, they alert stu-dents to the importance of two central off-stage characters, Karen Burns and Harmon Osterberg, who are dead when *July, July* begins and who cannot speak for themselves at the reunion. With the exception of the account of Karen's trip to Mexico in "Nogales" and the recounting of Harmon's drowning in "Loon Point," all the information that readers receive about Karen and Harmon comes from other characters, who may or may not perceive them correctly. While O'Brien uses omniscient narration to bring Karen back to life in "Nogales" long enough for us to realize some of her anxieties, hopes, and dreams, Harmon dies at the beginning of "Loon Point," without ever speaking a word, so his point of view is even more limited than Karen's. Why, I ask students, are these two characters' voices excluded from the text, especially Harmon's? Is the author minimizing their significance by not allowing them to defend their actions, or is he indirectly indicating that they are more important than they seem? Like the father in Tennessee Williams's *The Glass Menagerie*, who is present only through a photograph and the memories of other characters, they perhaps serve a much more important role than is first evident.

"Nogales" and "Loon Point" are central to *July, July*. Both stories incorporate themes common to O'Brien's work, such as betrayal and the things that people will do for love. But they also add information that is crucial to the events sur-rounding the deaths of Karen Burns and Harmon Osterberg, information that would be lacking if the fork-in-the-road stories were absent from the text. By reading "Nogales," students are privy to the details that lead up to the murder of Karen Burns—details that the other characters of *July, July* appear to lack. That Karen's murder is important is clear from page 1, where it is alluded to by Amy Robinson and Jan Huebner. However, it is only by reading "Nogales," which focuses on Karen and not the class reunion, that we receive the intimate details of the last days of Karen's life, where she makes the choice to permit the trip to Mexico as well as reveals the effects of her lifelong rejection by men: "The rejections had been curt and crushing. Twice she had ended up in hospitals" (211). While Amy Robinson in the first "Class of '69" chapter indicates that no one seems to know for sure who murdered Karen, "Nogales" gives us the events that lead up to Karen's death and implies that the man responsible is Darrell Jettie, a driver for Homewood Estates, a retirement community where Karen works. In addition, although Amy and Jan comment on Karen's naïveté, her weight problem, and her lack of luck with men, it is only in "Nogales" that we receive Karen's own feelings about her desperate need for love and realize how badly she wants Darrell Jettie to desire her. The omniscient narrator tells us that Karen wishes she could "find a way to let [Darrell] know how savage she is, how female, how she would claw and wrap herself around him and keep him prisoner forever, make him feel everything she felt, make him crazy with desire and hurt" (214). Significantly, Karen is alive at the end of "Nogales," although stranded in the desert after a trip to Mexico, and the text, while open-ended, implies that Karen and her elderly traveling companions will not survive. "Nogales," which O'Brien strategically places after a "Class of '69" chapter in which the other characters have gathered to eulogize Karen's and Harmon's lives, fills in the gaps that exist between that stand-alone story and the "Class of '69" chapters, providing answers to questions about how Karen may have died as well as adding insight into her character.

"Loon Point," which briefly recounts the story of Harmon Osterberg's death, focuses not so much on Harmon as on Ellie Abbott. In fact, the allusions to Harmon throughout *July, July* serve more as a springboard into the secrets of Ellie's life than they do to characterize him. When asked to reveal what they have learned about Harmon from reading the entire novel, students generally say that he was a dentist, had a good sense of humor, and was obviously married—although not to Ellie Abbott. If asked about Ellie, they are much more forthcoming: Ellie cheated on her husband, Mark; she constantly hears the sound of loons in her head (a reminder of Harmon's drowning) and feels "the lake in her [own] lungs" (204), even though she was not in the water when Harmon drowned; she lives in fear that her affair will be revealed; and she feels the need to confess her affair to Paulette Haslo and later to her husband. It is obvious that O'Brien uses Ellie Abbott as his main example of the psychological burden that is instilled by the weight of secrecy and the threat that a third party—in this case, one of the police officers who investigated Harmon's death—will maliciously reveal that secret. It is a threat that stems partly from Ellie's rejections of the man's overtures and partly from her reminding him of a woman in his own past who had betrayed him. In chapter 10, Ellie asks Paulette, "Did you ever have to keep a secret? Really *have* to. . . . For me it's *always*. Every time the phone rings, every time a car drives by. Never goes away" (133). The psychological toll on her is evident throughout *July, July*, but it is "Loon Point" that reveals the choices that Ellie made in her life to bring about this burden and its consequences. O'Brien expands the story, adding a malevolence to the police officer that is absent from the *Esquire* version. In the novel, the police officer tells Ellie that he will help serve as her "conscience" (173), a conscience that she reveals to Paulette Haslo, who, we learn through the "Class of '69" chapters, is a silent listener in "Loon Point," though not a character in that story itself—just as Ellie is obviously the silent listener of Paulette's own story, "Hearing," and just as the other characters in *July, July* are the silent listeners of other individual tales. O'Brien enriches both the fork-in-the-road stories and the "Class of '69" chapters by interrelating them throughout the text.

The "Class of '69" chapters introduce characters that drift through the background of *July, July* but do not receive individual stories; in fact, these characters are never given names but are referred to by their occupations: the lieutenant governor of Minnesota, a retired librarian, a chemist, a Lutheran missionary. We sense that these characters have their own secrets and engage in silent subterfuges with each other as, for instance, O'Brien shifts a scene just long enough to let us know that "[a] prominent physician and an ex-basketball star, now a mother of three, [are] soap[ing] up in the women's locker room" (41). I ask students to consider the role of these other characters, who are useful for creative writing exercises. Who exactly are they, and what are their individual stories? What are the critical moments in their lives, their own forks in the road? As is typical of O'Brien's work, the ambiguous nature of some of the characters and the open-ended nature of many of the stories permit multiple endings, numerous possibilities, and various angles of vision that offer students the opportunities to create character and even to write alternate endings to certain stories. For example, in another version of "Nogales," perhaps Karen Burns could be rescued from the desert along with her senior citizen friends and given another fate. Perhaps the flames along the desert are not a burning plane carrying Spook Spinelli and Marv Bertel.

A skillful blend of both short-story cycle and ensemble novel, *July, July* gives instructors the opportunity to challenge students to think about the importance of form and technique and to see how a text can incorporate a variety of devices that fold back on each other, unifying, enhancing, and enriching the text as they go.

NOTES

[1] For a thorough discussion of *The Things They Carried* as a short-story cycle, see James Nagel's chapter on that work in his *The Contemporary American Short-Story*

Cycle: The Ethnic Resonance of Genre. See also Farrell O'Gorman's *"The Things They Carried* as Composite Novel."

[2] See, for instance, the reviews of *July, July* by John Habich and Constance Schuller.

[3] Robert Siegel and Jacki Lyden have compared O'Brien's large cast of characters to that of a Greek chorus that "sings . . . a symphony of American life."

Story and Discourse in *The Things They Carried*

Milton J. Bates

The Things They Carried is arguably Tim O'Brien's most powerful response to the Vietnam War. It is also his most teachable work of fiction. Because of its straightforward, colloquial, and seemingly transparent style, *The Things They Carried* is accessible to students with a wide range of literary competence. Whatever their level of expertise, however, they find one aspect of the book unsettling (besides its often grim subject matter): the narrator of the stories, whom students usually identify with the author, frequently invites them to accept as fact events that prove later to have been invented.

Such invention should come as no surprise, considering that *The Things They Carried* is avowedly a work of fiction.[1] Novels and short stories conventionally posit a fictional given, a "Let's suppose this really happened," that remains unchallenged in the works themselves. When the narrator revises essential elements of stories in the same book, however, he violates the implied contract between storyteller and listener.

Experienced readers recognize this strategy as a staple of metafiction. It is also thematically purposeful. In "How to Tell a True War Story" and other pieces, O'Brien distinguishes between what he calls story-truth and happening-truth. He defines a true story as one that "makes the stomach believe," even though some or all of it may be made up (78). Students may agree in principle yet still feel cheated. This response affords the instructor an opportunity to lead them from a sense of betrayal to insight and a better understanding of narrative conventions.

In this essay I describe an approach that I have used in a course on Vietnam War literature for advanced undergraduates (juniors and seniors) and in a course on narrative theory for graduate students. This approach assumes that the instructor can devote three classes, each lasting an hour or two, to a sequence of four stories in *The Things They Carried*. The students also read a theoretical essay by Jonathan Culler and, as an option, a nonfiction article by O'Brien. For each class I indicate the reading and writing to be done in advance and also the general content of class discussion. Though I assume that the class proceeds by discussion, the material can be adapted to a lecture format.

First Class

Reading assignment: "Speaking of Courage" (Things 137–54)
Writing assignment: No more than 200 words on the following topic: In "Speaking of Courage" Norman Bowker does little more than drive around a lake in his hometown, imagining conversations that he might have with various people. What seems to be the point of the story, and how does its setting—that is, where it takes place and when—contribute to its meaning?

The writing assignment, due in class, is meant to focus the students' thinking on a topic to be discussed that day. I usually assign one topic for each class. Each student must write on six topics over the course of the semester and present a five- to ten-minute oral response to one of them. In this way, at least one student, and usually several, can be counted on to move the discussion along. The word limit forces students to distill their thinking and get directly to the point, forgoing a leisurely introduction and conclusion.

The content of the topic determines when it will be considered during the class period. The class on "Speaking of Courage" might begin with the student presentation, for it will elicit responses that can be examined and refined as the discussion develops. At one level, for example, "Speaking of Courage" is about the war. But it is also about Norman Bowker's inability to tell his story (the "speaking" of the title becomes increasingly ironic), his relationship with his father, his postwar aimlessness, the disparity between official rhetoric and firsthand experience, and so forth. Discussion of the setting might focus on activities associated with the Fourth of July (patriotic speeches, fireworks) and the polluted lake; these parallel the flares, mortar rounds, and paddy filth in Vietnam.

As one moves from the story's theme and setting to its organization, one notices the structural as well as thematic function of Bowker's circular route around the lake. More of the past is revealed with each revolution until, thirteen pages into the eighteen-page story, the reader learns about Bowker's failure of courage (149). Once disclosed, it takes on explanatory force, accounting for his mysterious behavior in the present. When Bowker allowed his friend Kiowa to sink into the field of excrement, he too became "part of the waste" (153). Waste, initially a metonymy, gradually becomes the story's controlling metaphor.

According to the criteria of formalist criticism, "Speaking of Courage" is a well-made story. Is it overly tidy? I invite students to recall instances where they felt that elements in the story were being manipulated for the sake of symmetry or symbolism. One of the more intrusive examples is the anonymous voice that comes over the intercom at the A&W root beer stand, speaking the lingo of military radio transmissions: "Fire for effect. Stand by" (152). Some students may feel that the connections between lake and paddy, between fireworks and flares, are likewise too neat.

Second Class

Reading assignment: "Notes" (Things 155–61) and Jonathan Culler's essay "Story and Discourse in the Analysis of Narrative"
Writing assignment: No more than 200 words on the following topic: According to the information provided in "Notes," which parts of "Speaking of Courage" belong to the story and which to the discourse? See Culler's essay for the distinction between story and discourse.

Though Russian formalism and French structuralism did not invent the story-discourse distinction, they undertook to theorize it under the equivalent terms *fabula-sjuzhet* and *histoire-récit*. Gérard Genette discusses the subject at length in *Narrative Discourse* (*Discours de récit*), as does Seymour Chatman in *Story and Discourse*. Culler's essay has the advantages of brevity and accessibility. He also goes a step beyond Genette and Chatman in challenging a premise of their work—namely, that story ("what happened," whether as historical fact or as fictional given) is the stable cause of all recountings of the story and the measure of their value. Reflecting on the examples of Sophocles's *Oedipus*, George Eliot's *Daniel Deronda*, and Sigmund Freud's case history of the Wolfman, Culler demonstrates that in some cases it is discourse that determines story. Sophocles's tragedy, for example, proceeds on the assumption that Oedipus killed his father, even though the testimony of an eyewitness raises the possibility that he is innocent. Culler argues that in *Oedipus* and other narratives the relation between story and discourse is ultimately undecidable, that the two cannot be reconciled in a coherent narratology.

Students do not need to understand the full implications of Culler's argument in order to respond to the day's topic. Together with the metafictional "Notes," it provides them with the means to distinguish story from discourse in "Speaking of Courage." The story is set forth in Norman Bowker's seventeen-page letter, which the character-narrator Tim O'Brien summarizes and quotes selectively in "Notes." We learn that the fictional Tim O'Brien was also present at Kiowa's death in the sewage field but came away emotionally unscathed. In contrast to Bowker, he shifted easily—so he claims—to graduate school and a career as an author.

This Tim O'Brien goes on to explain how he transformed events (story) in "Speaking of Courage" (discourse), substituting his Minnesota hometown for Bowker's Iowa. He added the lake for literary effect, as a counterpoint to the paddy, and compressed Bowker's cruising to a single day, the Fourth of July. In the first published version, he neither identified Bowker by name nor mentioned the key event, Kiowa's death. Another letter from Bowker, followed by Bowker's suicide, prompted him to revise the story as we have it in "Speaking of Courage."

The student who is assigned to present the writing topic in class will, together with other members of the class during the ensuing discussion, make most of these points. The instructor may need to intervene occasionally to clarify aspects of Culler's argument. Sooner or later, though, the class will have to address the provocative conclusion of "Notes." There, reflecting on the composition of "Speaking of Courage," O'Brien says:

> It was hard stuff to write. Kiowa, after all, had been a close friend, and for years I've avoided thinking about his death and my own complicity in it. Even here it's not easy. In the interests of truth, however, I want to make it clear that Norman Bowker was in no way responsible for what happened to Kiowa. Norman did not experience a failure of nerve that night. He did not freeze up or lose the Silver Star for valor. That part of the story is my own.   (160–61)

In what sense "my own"? Whether the phrase refers to the story or to the discourse—that is, to what really happened or to Bowker's and O'Brien's accounts of what happened—it casts doubt on the version of the story that we have so diligently reconstructed.

Third Class

Reading assignment: "In the Field" and "Field Trip" (Things 162–78, 181–88). Optional: "The Vietnam in Me"
Writing assignment: No more than 200 words on the following topic: How do "In the Field" and "Field Trip," as discourses, force us to revise the story told in "Speaking of Courage" and "Notes"? (If the optional reading is assigned, another question can be added: How does "The Vietnam in Me" compel us to revise further the story that we extract from the four sewage-field stories in The Things They Carried?)

Because "In the Field" follows "Notes" and deals with the same key events, we expect the story to continue in the first-person confessional mode of "Notes" and to answer the questions raised by its conclusion. Instead, it reverts to the anonymous narration used in "Speaking of Courage." Not until the opening sentence of "Field Trip" do we learn that the fictional Tim O'Brien wrote it. The setting of the story shifts from the United States in the late 1980s to Vietnam in the late 1960s. The events in the story are seen through the eyes of two characters in addition to the narrator: Lieutenant Jimmy Cross and a "young soldier" who remains conspicuously unnamed (the lieutenant, who prides himself in remembering the names of the men in his platoon, cannot recall the soldier's name). This triangulation in points of view makes it harder to arrive at a consistent version of events.

The student presenter and class members are certain to notice Norman Bowker's marginal role in this retelling of the story. He is one of three soldiers who wade through the paddy, searching for Kiowa's body. Though it is he who finds the body, he does not appear deeply affected by the death. Rather than assume personal responsibility for it, he takes the philosophical view: " 'Nobody's fault,' he said. 'Everybody's' " (176).

The person closest to Kiowa in the story, and the one who feels the greatest burden of guilt, is the nameless young soldier. The passage describing his effort to hold on to Kiowa's boot echoes a passage in "Speaking of Courage." Indeed, the two are identical in places (149, 171). This suggests that much of what we have been told about Bowker belongs to discourse rather than to story. It was the young soldier—not Bowker—who lost his best friend in the sewage field that night and blamed himself for the loss.

Is the young soldier Tim O'Brien? It is hard to avoid this conclusion, inasmuch as no one else is identified as Tim O'Brien in the story. O'Brien, who claims that he was present, exonerates Bowker at the end of "Notes" and hints at his own complicity in Kiowa's death. Like the young soldier, he says that he was Kiowa's close friend. The match is far from perfect, for the young soldier seems considerably younger than the college graduate who speaks of his writing career in "Notes" and never mentions a girlfriend (or ex-girlfriend) named Billie. However, unless we identify O'Brien as the young soldier, we will find it difficult to account for his behavior in "Field Trip."

The narrator of "Notes" professes to have glided easily from Chu Lai to Harvard and a successful writing career (157). He concedes that his fiction, though not undertaken as therapy, did have therapeutic value. He also acknowledges that he has tried to avoid thinking about Kiowa (160). So it is not entirely out of character for the narrator to return to Vietnam twenty years after Kiowa's death to perform a ritual of atonement. He has brought Kiowa's moccasins (a hunting hatchet in the first edition of *The Things They Carried*) to bury at the spot where his friend disappeared into the muck. The O'Brien of "Field Trip" seems scarcely the same person as the one in "Notes" who prided himself in leaving the war behind. "This little field," he reflects, "had swallowed so much. My best friend. My pride. My belief in myself as a man of some small dignity and courage. . . . For twenty years this field had embodied all the waste that was Vietnam, all the vulgarity and horror" (184–85).

Sorting story from discourse, the class may arrive at a sequence of "real" events much like the following: Soon after graduating from college, the protagonist Tim O'Brien was drafted into the army and sent to Vietnam, where he was assigned to an infantry platoon operating near Chu Lai. During a particularly horrifying rainy night, the platoon took mortar fire while bivouacked in a paddy that served as the village toilet. He watched helplessly as his best friend and foxhole mate was struck by shrapnel and sank into the ooze. Years later he dealt with his guilt by writing about the episode. Initially unable to speak candidly of his failure of courage, he projected it onto a fictionalized version of another platoon member. Finally, however, he mastered his shame and fear and returned to Vietnam with his daughter. There, in the same paddy where he had failed his friend, he was at last able to forgive himself.

Within the fictional world of *The Things They Carried*, this version of the story could serve as the true north from which to measure discursive declinations. During the third class on the sewage-field stories, the class might consider how the discourse seems in places to "cause" the story in much the same way that Culler describes in his essay. That is, the aesthetic requirements of the narrative and the emotional requirements of the narrator seem to demand that certain episodes be invented—for example, that Norman Bowker wade into a polluted lake at the end of "Speaking of Courage" and commit suicide in "Notes."

When the fictional world is located in the world of historical fact, the story-discourse relation becomes more complicated. Students who read O'Brien's memoir "The Vietnam in Me" learn that the Tim O'Brien who appears as a character in *The Things They Carried* is to some extent a fictional creation. In real life, Tim O'Brien did not return to Vietnam until 1994, four years after the publication of the book. "The Vietnam in Me" echoes elements in "Field Trip": O'Brien writes about losing a comrade named McElhaney in a paddy much like the one in *The Things They Carried*, under similar circumstances (56).[2] Life imitates art when, revisiting the site, he finds momentary peace of mind (57). But there are differences: O'Brien, who had no daughter in 1994, returned to Vietnam with a lover who left him shortly afterward. While writing the memoir, he was nearly as suicidal as the fictional Norman Bowker.

One can teach the selections in *The Things They Carried* without reference to the author's biography. However, "The Vietnam in Me" underscores the lesson that one learns from applying Culler's "Story and Discourse in the Analysis of Narrative" to the fictional works—namely, that discourse is always a variation on (and sometimes even an invention of) story. We can easily imagine a future narrative that will compel us to revise the story told in "The Vietnam in Me."

Once students have learned how to apply the story-discourse distinction to the sewage-field sequence, they can apply it to other parts of *The Things They Carried* as well, either in class or in an assigned essay. The sequence having to do with the killing of an enemy soldier ("The Man I Killed," "Ambush," and "Good Form") offers the same challenge, as do the anecdotes in "How to Tell a True War Story."

Storytellers, Culler reminds us, seek constantly to ward off the listener's "So what?" Rather than tell a pointless story, they may alter its content — by inventing characters, events, and speeches — for the sake of meaning and coherence. In this way the moral of the story becomes a function of the story rather than of the discourse. When the evaluative function of discourse is transferred to the story, we have O'Brien's story-truth, a truth that does not require an explicit statement of the moral.

Consequently, one question should run like a golden thread through the fabric of class discussions: Why might the narrator have altered the happening-truth in his account? For example, does Tim O'Brien, a character in *The Things They Carried*, gain anything by representing his own experience as though it were Norman Bowker's? Does "Speaking of Courage" "[make] the stomach believe" more effectively than the "truer" version disclosed in the rest of the sequence? Or is it the process of disclosure, the reluctant unveiling of a shameful secret, that we find viscerally compelling?

However students respond to these and similar questions, they will come away from the discussion with a greater appreciation of the art that informs O'Brien's apparently artless storytelling. Would *The Things They Carried* be easier to read if it conformed to the familiar conventions of storytelling? Of course it would. But the book would also have less to teach us about the pleasures and predicaments of narrative.

NOTES

[1] In the first edition (Houghton, 1990), the page opposite the copyright notice bears the statement "This is a work of fiction. Except for a few details regarding the author's own life, all the incidents, names, and characters are imaginary." This caveat was subsequently moved to the copyright page, where it appears in greatly reduced type.

[2] The name "Rodger D McElhaney" appears on the Vietnam Veterans Memorial wall, panel 20W, row 7. He was killed in Quang Ngai Province on 16 July 1969, during O'Brien's tour of duty in Quang Ngai.

Teaching *Going After Cacciato*
and *The Things They Carried*
in the Context of Trauma

Mark Heberle

The broadening of English studies to include nonliterary discourses and my greater awareness of Tim O'Brien's personal experience and fictional representations of psychic and ethical disfigurement have led me to focus on trauma when I teach *Going After Cacciato* and *The Things They Carried*. Because none of the courses in which I teach O'Brien allows extensive coverage of his entire career, I have deliberately chosen what seem to me his two most enduring works; because of the need to consider a wide variety of works and different contexts, I have used O'Brien as the initial or sole focus for considering trauma; and because none of these courses is exclusively focused on trauma, I have found it necessary to provide four sorts of information as we consider this issue in O'Brien: clinical, rhetorical, biographical, and structural.

Through excerpts from Judith Herman's *Trauma and Recovery,* handouts in class, or lecture comments, students come to understand and distinguish among the three general categories of posttraumatic symptoms: hyperarousal (which includes paranoid anxieties and sleeplessness), intrusion (including nightmares, hallucinations, and flashbacks), and constriction (including lack of affect and speechlessness). Herman's book is particularly helpful when teaching *The Things They Carried*, since Herman quotes passages from it to illustrate the actual symptoms of post-traumatic stress disorder. (Interestingly, O'Brien is the author of one of the publisher's blurbs used to commend and advertise her book.) Because of its narrative and dramatic figuration, I have found Herman's landmark study more imaginatively useful than the American Psychiatric Association's official diagnostic criteria for post-traumatic stress disorder. However, these criteria might be useful to consider in relation to O'Brien's work—for illustration, for contrast between clinical paradigms and fictional truths, or to show how much the association deliberately leaves out of its diagnosis the ethical and political issues to which O'Brien's texts either directly or indirectly call attention.

A relatively extended focus in a junior honors course on trauma allows a consideration of Bao Ninh's *Sorrow of War* and Bobbie Ann Mason's *In Country* in relation to *The Things They Carried*, using post-traumatic stress disorder symptoms as at least starting points for comparison. O'Brien's works (and perhaps his own experience) are marked primarily by constriction, so the posttraumatic intrusions of the Vietnamese and American woman-centered novels provide valuable points of departure for discussion. In a sophomore literature course on war literature, awareness of traumatic symptoms provides targeting for students' reading of the World War I and Vietnam War poetry that precedes our reading of O'Brien as well as the works that follow: David Rabe's play *Sticks and*

Bones, Emily Mann's play *Still Life*, and *In Country*. Near the end of the course, an excerpt from Jonathan Shay's *Achilles in Vietnam* encourages students to reconsider our first reading in the course in relation to trauma and to see post-traumatic stress disorder and its representation as universal and timeless. Shay's clinical-literary treatment of Achilles's revenge on Hector allows us to examine berserking, the most deadly of hyperarousal symptoms, and to consider, under-stand, and question the breakdowns of Paul Berlin at the beginning of O'Brien's novel and Mark's abusive treatment of his wife in *Still Life*.

Kalí Tal's classic essay "Speaking the Language of Pain: Vietnam War Lit-erature in the Context of a Literature of Trauma" has been distributed to my sophomore students, critiqued by my graduate students, and either excerpted or summarized in the other courses. Besides arguing for the distinctive impor-tance of trauma literature written by combat veterans, Tal provides a valuable tripartite definition of the rhetorical conditions for such literature: the need to tell one's story, the impossibility or difficulty of telling it, and the need to have an audience willing to accept or acknowledge it. These conditions mirror the elements of trauma therapy as found in Herman and other clinically based writ-ers: being able to tell others one's own story of a self-shattering encounter with death is essential to personal recovery. All the issues raised by Tal are impor-tant for readers to consider, especially the difference between trauma narratives written by combat survivors and those by writers (like Bobbie Ann Mason) who are not representing their own experience in some way; the difficulty for trauma survivors to recover their experience in discourse that will be understood by the untraumatized; and the need to recognize the tropes of trauma through which survivor writers both conceal and reveal what is unspeakable. Tal's project in the essay, as well as in the later collection *Worlds of Hurt*, is to initiate a practice of reading and responding to trauma literature that is capable of recognizing, ac-cepting, and acting on its disfigurements.

I use Tal's emphasis on combat veteran writers' need to tell their stories as a way of introducing O'Brien's life and works, the incommunicability of trau-matic experiences as a way to discuss particular works and passages, and the importance of an audience as a means to distinguish O'Brien as a trauma sur-vivor from O'Brien as a writer. When asked to consider O'Brien's audience, students naturally identify themselves as readers of the work. Without such sup-port, O'Brien would never have continued writing about Vietnam, of course, but his literary career needs to be distinguished from whatever personal need such writing might provide him as a combat survivor. The distinction between trauma therapy and fictional representations of trauma is not always clear in Tal's discussion, but it is central to O'Brien's work, the product of a trauma sur-vivor who both conceals and reveals his experiences through literary figuration but for whom the fabricated story is more important personally and profession-ally than whatever happened to him in the war.

I use a brief chronology of O'Brien's life and works to introduce his identity as a trauma writer. The most important fact is his decision to go to Vietnam as a soldier against his better moral judgment. I usually summarize the details of "Escape," chapter 6 of *If I Die in a Combat Zone*, which describes O'Brien's failure to carry out his plan to desert from the army by traveling from Seattle to Vancouver in December 1968 while waiting to be sent to Vietnam. Even that account has been subject to revision and probable fictionalization (Did O'Brien actually intend to take a one- or two-day boat trip from Ireland to Sweden?), but at least *If I Die in a Combat Zone* explicitly purports to be autobiographical. The rewriting of his failure to escape in *Going After Cacciato* (the fantasy narrative) and *The Things They Carried* ("On the Rainy River") allows students to follow the distinctions between the author and his characters, nonfiction and fiction, and happening-truth and story-truth that are important to O'Brien's conception of literature. But the crucial importance of the decision to remain at Fort Lewis allows us to consider trauma as a moral or ethical wound as well as a physical or psychological injury and something that, for O'Brien—at least in the rewriting of his failure to disobey orders—preceded rather than followed combat. He throws up in Seattle, his namesake breaks down crying in the boat off the coast of Canada, and Paul Berlin suffers a full traumatic breakdown when Cacciato is about to be caught and later reflects bitterly on his cowardice. But these indirect symptoms of combat trauma, we come to realize, are effects of the moral disfigurement that is one of O'Brien's distinctive themes as a trauma writer—what Shay calls "the undoing of character" in his study of combat trauma in *The Iliad* and in the Vietnam War.

My chronology of O'Brien's works arranges the career in two columns, with Vietnam-sited works on the left (*If I Die in a Combat Zone*; *Going After Cacciato*; *The Things They Carried*) and non-Vietnam works on the right (*Northern Lights*; *The Nuclear Age*; *In the Lake of the Woods*; *Tomcat in Love*; *July, July*). This scheme is a residue of my earlier notion that O'Brien was trying to escape the war as a subject so that he would be recognized as a major American novelist, not simply as a Vietnam War writer. Although I begin by suggesting that there appears to be a complementary pull toward and away from the war from book to book until the writer seems to have finally exorcised the subject with the tragedy of *In the Lake of the Woods* and the comedy of *Tomcat in Love*, I end by correcting if not discrediting my apparatus altogether. The fictionalizing of the facts that lie behind *If I Die in a Combat Zone* has never left the war behind but has variously supplemented, extended, and rewritten O'Brien's experiences and his judgments on himself and his country as seen through the rewritten and revisited war and its consequences in America and for Americans. John Wade might be living physically in Minnesota, but the novel represents My Lai as his psychic terrain; Thomas Chippering is still obsessed with telling his war story, and the only willing auditors are his ghostly former comrades; *July, July* at least formally represents the war's effects on some American women on the home front, and O'Brien is most proud of its only Vietnam War–sited story ("July '69"). Conversely, the true fictional site of *Going After Cacciato* is the imagination of Paul Berlin, which attempts to take him away from the war; and *The Things*

They Carried presents a deliberately fabricated revision of the war that is also situated on the Rainy River, at readings of his work by a fictional version of the author, during a Fourth of July holiday in Minnesota, and while the figure Tim O'Brien is also remembering the life and death at age nine of his childhood sweetheart.

In sum, what I emphasize in briefly canvasing O'Brien's career is the persistence of the Vietnam War in this work of a lifetime, a phenomenon that uncannily resembles both the need of the traumatized survivor to tell his or her story and the inability to ever fully or satisfactorily convey it to an audience. Furthermore, representations of these self-conflicted conditions for trauma therapy (according to Herman) or trauma writing (according to Tal) may be found in all of O'Brien's fictional works after *If I Die in a Combat Zone*, ranging from Harvey Perry's inability to articulate anything about his missing eye to Thomas Chippering's self-absorbed logorrhea.

In dealing with *Going After Cacciato* and *The Things They Carried*, I emphasize the distinctive narrative structure of each in our reading of O'Brien as a trauma writer. I pass out a chapter-by-chapter outline of *Going After Cacciato*, partly because what is most difficult about the work for students is following the plot and the way it seems to switch bewilderingly from past to present and from the war to all those places between Vietnam and Paris. Students come to see that the chapters largely fall into three categories: "Observation Post" reflections by Paul Berlin, which take place in a fictional present; the fantasy pursuit of Cacciato to Paris, which imagines future possibilities; and scenes that have already occurred, the most important of which involve the earlier deaths of other members of Third Squad. Besides combining present, past, and future, the narrative is an attempt by Paul Berlin to recover from trauma both by remembering previous deaths and atrocities and by transcending them through an imagined escape from the war. The pursuit of Cacciato attempts to satisfy both duty (by capturing a deserter) and desire (by deserting). This literally impossible posttraumatic narrative mimics trauma therapy and is devised by Paul Berlin, the traumatized survivor, in the aptly titled "Observation Post" chapters. Students are led to see how Paul Berlin's narrative therapy mimics O'Brien's creation of a traumatic fiction, a creation in which his protagonist remains and can neither escape the war nor fully narrate or even understand his traumatization. Conversely, Paul Berlin's inability to reject the war even in imagination reflects O'Brien's actual failure to desert. The creation of the novel, therefore, and its acceptance and enjoyment by readers validate O'Brien's posttraumatic, postwar fiction and help to compensate for his actual war experiences.

Much of our discussion focuses on seeing how the novel is constructed as a narrative in a way that reflects both Paul Berlin's trauma and O'Brien's figuration of trauma. I encourage students to analyze the novel from numerous perspectives that reflect traumatic experience, including chapter-by-chapter fragmentation and interruption of the narrative (such as Paul Berlin's breaking off the apparent capture of Cacciato at the end of chapter 7 and preparations for repairing the narrative in the following "Observation Post" chapter); violations of fictional chronology (such as the description of Frenchie Tucker's corpse in chapter 9 before the moment of his being shot dead in chapter 14); chapter-by-chapter switches from present to past and from sites of unbearable experiences for Paul Berlin (such as the moments just before or just after the death of a comrade) to the continuing fantasy pursuit of Cacciato; and intrusions of terrible combat memories into the fantasy narrative (like the "flame-frisking" of Vietnamese hamlets that begins to infect Third Squad's search for Cacciato aboard the Delhi Express on "The Railroad to Paris" in chapter 21).

Most important among these traumatic plot ligatures are Paul Berlin's breakdowns at the end of the first chapter and near the beginning of the final chapter, which we discuss toward the end of our classes on the novel. Asking students why the title is the same for each ("Going After Cacciato") enables them to recognize the circular structure of the novel, which begins with a traumatic breakdown when Paul Berlin's wild firing either kills Cacciato or allows him to escape capture. The irresolvable conflict between duty and desire, what is legally necessary and what is morally satisfying, intrudes into and obliterates the fantasy narrative in the final chapter, at the end of which Paul Berlin returns to the primal scene of trauma after whatever has happened to Cacciato in "fact" has happened; he is left only with Lieutenant Corson's encouragement to imagine that the deserter might have reached Paris. The aftermath is the rest of the novel (chapters 2 through the first half of chapter 36) between the two breakdowns, a narrative in which Cacciato is both Third Squad's prey and their liberator and in which Paul Berlin imaginatively rewards Corson with both desertion and the affection of Sarkin Aung Wan while he chooses duty and obligation.

Paul Berlin's uncertainty about what happened to Cacciato results from his psychological, physical, and moral breakdown during the assault on Cacciato's hill. I encourage students to notice other examples of his emotional collapse or constriction in the face of traumatic circumstances as well as symptoms of emotional or moral revulsion, such as his fear "biles" and practice of being the last man in the column. Even the imaginative narrative Paul Berlin creates as compensation or redemption for his own turning away illustrates such constriction. Although he imaginatively and courageously recovers the details of all his former comrades' deaths — events that he has evidently repressed — each memory calls attention to his own fearful inertia. And he cannot describe the fate of Lieutenant Martin even in imagination, although Third Squad's being sentenced to a firing squad in Teheran for desertion is likely a product of guilt for killing their commanding officer as well as an acknowledgment of their true motivation for pursuing Cacciato.

Most readers may regard *The Things They Carried* (which I have taught more frequently) as a more polished work than *Going After Cacciato*. But I have found the earlier novel more interesting to teach, largely because of uncertainties among students about both the motivations for and the details of the plot and partly because of the many questions: Is Cacciato a "real" character or not? What actually did happen to him? Why do the soldiers meet Sarkin Aung Wan? Why do they fall into a Vietcong tunnel? These are questions that not even Paul Berlin can answer but that engage any reader of his trauma-saturated narrative. Seeing the novel as motivated by posttraumatic anxieties in Berlin (if not in O'Brien) may not answer the questions definitively, but it provides a useful way of considering them.

As with *Going After Cacciato*, I pass out an outline of chapters of *The Things They Carried* but add to it the dates of the original versions of pieces published as independent stories. I also identify the narrative point of view of each: third-person singular (omniscient), third person (direct narration), first-person plural (collective viewpoint), first-person singular. I ask students to group stories together and notice whether they are connected to another story. Grouping and then categorizing them is useful when we discuss genre (Is this a novel? a collection of short stories? a miscellany of fiction and nonfiction or other forms?) and in seeing how some of the later stories largely serve as postscripts to others ("Love," "Friends," "The Dentist," "Ambush," "Notes," "Good Form," "Field Trip," "Night Life") or suggest that what is narrated simply recounts an experience observed by or shared with several members of A Company ("Enemies," "Friends," "The Dentist," "Stockings," "Church").

These later pieces substantially extend the collection's emphasis on self-commentary, on the one hand, and, on the other, its effacing the distinction between actual experience and fictional representation. Students already aware of the factual circumstances of O'Brien's failure to "escape" the war readily appreciate how the apparent autobiographical confessions of "On the Rainy River" are a fabrication. From there, it is not difficult to have them separate the Tim O'Brien who appears in the first-person narratives from the writer of the entire book—although the knowledge that Tim's daughter, Kathleen, is also completely made up still comes as a surprise. When the author reveals in the final piece that Tim O'Brien first started making up stories after the death of his childhood sweetheart, I encourage students to see how the connection between traumatic experiences and the writing that they both generate and keep trying to recover functions as a final story and also as an apparent explanation for most of what has preceded it.

Whereas I emphasize constriction and trauma therapy in discussing Paul Berlin, I focus on repetition of the same scenes and actions and deliberate trauma writing in discussing *The Things They Carried*. The continual, quasi-intrusive references to Ted Lavender's death in the title story and its reappearance in the final story is only one of many examples of reimagining the same traumatic experience. (Others include the four versions of Curt Lemon's death in "How to Tell a True War Story," the bits and pieces and alternative versions of "The Man I Killed" at the end of "Spin" and in "Ambush" and "Good Form," and the constellation of stories and explanations that present and supplement the fates of Kiowa and Norman Bowker.) The collection is such a treasury of rewriting trauma that even ambiguous and paradoxical chapter titles ("The Things They

Carried," "How to Tell a True War Story," "Speaking of Courage," "The Lives of the Dead") are worth considering and discussing in class. Besides the fictional explanation of "How I became a (trauma) writer" in "The Lives of the Dead," students are directed to O'Brien's apparent explanation in "Good Form" of why he keeps writing about Vietnam: "I can look at things I never looked at. I can attach faces to grief and love and pity and God. I can be brave. I can make myself feel again" (180). Here, as throughout the collection, the distinction between actual experiences and fictions, or trauma therapy (here, overcoming constriction) and writing stories, is nearly obliterated, just as the enigmatic distinction between the author of *The Things They Carried* and the Tim O'Brien who is responding to his daughter's questions in "Good Form" seems to conceal as much as it reveals.

For me, "Speaking of Courage" is O'Brien's short-story masterpiece, and it opens up a rich variety of both literary and more specifically traumatic insights ranging from the shit field as synechdoche to O'Brien's revision of another prize-winning story ("Speaking of Courage," 1976) to the exfoliation of trauma from Paul Berlin (the original protagonist) to Norman Bowker and thence to Jimmy Cross and the unnamed soldier in "In the Field" to Tim O'Brien (in both "Notes" and "Field Trip"). The story is an ineffably powerful, moving study of constriction and suicide, its deadliest manifestation, and students come to see how the circular action, with "no place in particular to go" (137) for Norman Bowker except to drive around in his father's car, mimics the endless covering up of trauma and revises O'Brien's own aimless drives around his hometown's lake the summer before he went to Vietnam. Trauma, students come to recognize, not only survives and grows after combat is over but also can begin before its subject has been to the battlefield, as our study of "On the Rainy River" illustrates.

Viewing O'Brien as a trauma writer effects a mediation between literature and history and respects O'Brien's view of himself as writing for all audiences. Furthermore, because trauma and posttraumatic phenomena are not limited to war, male fortitude, or indeed the wounds of individuals, students can see that O'Brien is writing about a deeply disturbing human experience that cuts across gender lines, national boundaries, and time periods (even though "trauma" may be a clinical category and trope of post–World War I modernism).

O'Brien's use of repetition, fragmentation, nonchronological ordering, lack of closure, and lexical and other obsessions may help instructors and students recognize and appreciate the artistic skill that captivates us when reading O'Brien. Studying *Going After Cacciato, The Things They Carried*, or other works with reference to excerpts from Kalí Tal, Judith Herman, and other writers on trauma can provide a richer and more lasting transformation of readers' consciousness than whatever must (necessarily) be taught about Vietnam and O'Brien's experiences there.

Doing Gender and Going Native in "Sweetheart of the Song Tra Bong"

Elisabeth H. Piedmont-Marton

> What you have to do, Sanders said, is trust your own story. Get the hell out
> of the way and let it tell itself.   ("Sweetheart of the Song Tra Bong" 106)

Like many stories in *The Things They Carried*, "Sweetheart of the Song Tra
Bong" folds back on itself, at once asserting and challenging its own veracity,
telling a story and at the same time commenting on how to tell a story. Because
the stories are interrelated, "Sweetheart of the Song Tra Bong" invites readers to
read it against its companion stories. It is the central story of the book, and it's a
particularly rich one to teach, because it reaches beyond its own textual boundaries and refers to images and narratives of the Vietnam War in film, literature,
and popular imagination. Students respond powerfully to it, and their reading
can be deepened and complicated by encouraging them to unpack the layers of
narrative and metanarrative. This essay offers a close reading of "Sweetheart of
the Song Tra Bong," focusing on the theme of crossing over, or transgression,
and illuminates sites in the text that invite opportunities for students to engage
in complex, nuanced responses.

Technically a story within a story, "The Sweetheart of the Song Tra Bong"
is an account of what happens when Mark Fossie, a foot soldier — an ordinary
grunt — imports his girlfriend, Mary Anne Bell, from Cleveland Heights to
Vietnam. The story is related to Tim O'Brien the character by Rat Kiley, who
claims to have witnessed at least some of the events. (It's useful to call students'
attention to the differences among the three instantiations of Tim O'Brien at
work in the text: author, narrator, and character.) The point of the story is not,
as Rat's interlocutors and readers alike may suspect, the logistics of Fossie's daring feat of bringing Mary Anne and her pink sweater and white culottes to their
outpost. Instead, the narrative's power inheres in what happens to her once
she arrives in Vietnam and how her transformation from American suburban
schoolgirl to nascent guerrilla affects Mark, Rat, and the others in their sense of
who and where they are.

The story takes place near the village of Tra Bong, "in the mountains west of
Chu Lai" (90), in the early 1970s. O'Brien isn't specific about the date, but he
indicates that "in the early 1960s, the place had been set up as a Special Forces
outpost" and that "Rat Kiley [had] arrived nearly a decade later" (92). The
critic Benjamin Goluboff explains that this story, as well as others in O'Brien's
work, takes place in Quang Ngai Province, the tactical area of operations for
the United States Army's American Division in 1968 and 1969. A likely source
for O'Brien's Quang Ngai was the work of the journalist Jonathan Schell in the
New Yorker in 1967 and 1968, which later became a book, *The Military Half: An*

Account of the Destruction in Quang Ngai and Quang Tin. Chu Lai is located south of Danang, at the point where Vietnam narrows between the South China Sea and the wild Annamite Mountains to the west and the border with Laos. The medical post where Rat and Mark are stationed is "clearly indefensible" (91), but Rat claims that "he always felt a curious sense of safety there" because "[n]othing much ever happened" and "the war seemed to be somewhere far away" (92). In fact, according to the historian Marilyn Young, the war, at least as far as American forces were concerned, was changing course and winding down beginning in 1970. (Although there were still 334,000 American military personnel in Vietnam at the end of 1970, the number would drop to 23,000 by early 1973.) The year 1970 marked the beginning of the "Vietnamization" of the war, in which the United States decreased its participation in ground combat and handed over the responsibilities of defending border areas to the South Vietnamese Army.) During the first half of 1971, awareness of and resistance to the war in the United States was escalating; the Pentagon Papers were published in the *New York Times*, and the Winter Soldier Investigation, a protest organized by the Vietnam Veterans against the War, took place in Detroit. That year also brought a pause from the bombing of North Vietnam and a reduction of the United States forces to 156,800 by December.

The haunting story of what happens when Mark Fossie imports his Ohio girlfriend to Vietnam is arguably one of the most powerful and memorable American literary responses to the Vietnam War. Ultimately, it is a story about transgression, about the costs and consequences of crossing over boundaries and perimeters on whose impermeability a great deal depends. It is also a story that transgresses the normal boundaries of storytelling.

If students have read some or all of the stories in *The Things They Carried*, they will be familiar with O'Brien's metanarrative strategies and his deliberate blurring of the boundaries between truth and fiction. But even if "Sweetheart of the Song Tra Bong" is the only piece they read, it's worthwhile here to refer briefly to a passage in "How to Tell a True War Story." In that story, which functions as a kind of gloss for the book and a deliberately obtuse explanation of his technique, O'Brien deconstructs simple claims and offers instead a pluralistic and even contradictory model for evaluating the veracity of war stories. As Catherine Calloway explains:

> O'Brien draws the reader into the text, calling the reader's attention to the process of invention and challenging him to determine which, if any, of the stories are true. As a result, the stories become epistemological tools, multidimensional windows thorough which the war, the world, and the ways of telling a war story can be viewed from many different angles and visions. ("'How to Tell'" 249–50)

In a passage in "How to Tell a True War Story" that has particular resonance with "Sweetheart of the Song Tra Bong," O'Brien explains that "[f]or the common soldier, at least, war has the feel—the spiritual texture—of a great ghostly fog, thick and permanent" (82). Referring both to the war itself and to the acts of telling and reading war stories, O'Brien elaborates:

> There is no clarity. Everything swirls. The old rules are no longer binding, the old truths no longer true. Right spills over into wrong. Order blends into chaos, love into hate, ugliness into beauty, law into anarchy, civility into savagery. The vapors suck you in. You can't tell where you are, or why you're there, and the only certainty is overwhelming ambiguity.   (82)

For readers of "Sweetheart of the Song Tra Bong," the significance of this passage is its emphasis on the anxiety that surrounds fluidity and the breaching of boundaries thought to be fixed and impenetrable. At this point, it's useful to ask students to map the topography of the story and identify some of the boundaries and perimeters that O'Brien and his narrator describe and then to ask students to discuss or write about the metaphorical boundaries or the ways in which the story offers a critique of the idea of the boundary itself. Some of the boundaries they may find productive to discuss are those between the world and the war, the domestic and the military spheres, women and men, (Western) soldier and (Asian) enemy, and civilization and nature. Students will soon see that their mapping of boundaries won't hold, that O'Brien sets up expectations and then undermines them. The breach of perimeters, confusion of categories, and inversion of hierarchies cause tremendous anxiety among the men of O'Brien's company because their already tenuous and contingent position is revealed to be completely unanchored. Readers are in an analogous position: They don't know whom to believe or what to trust. The words in "How to Tell a True War Story" take on new meaning, as the sense of disorientation they describe becomes as intimately psychological as it is geographical: "You can't tell where you are, or why you're there" (82). Readers might also add, "You don't know who you are."

Students should be encouraged to push their analysis of the text and interrogate O'Brien's use of perimeter imagery. In what ways are these boundaries both literal methods of organizing the social world and metaphors for the metaphysical borders that are breached when Mary Anne Bell arrives in Vietnam? How do the boundaries get crossed and the positions inverted? Rat describes the outpost as being both "clearly indefensible" and "isolated and vulnerable" (91, 92). And yet, as he says, "he always felt a curious sense of safety there." As he goes on to describe the post in more detail, it appears that the sense of security is derived, at least in part, from its high level of organization: people stay where they are supposed to stay and do what they are expected to do. This is analogous to the highly structured and segmented nature of the military in general. Rat's duties are gory but predictable: casualties are flown in, have legs and feet amputated, then are flown back out. There's "[n]o humping at all. No officers, either" (91). And yet this organization, which appears natural and organic, is, in fact, highly artificial and unstable. The entire compound is surrounded by rolls of concertina wire and abutted on two sides by jungle, mountains, and gorges. At the outermost of the concentric circles are the Greenies (Green Berets, or Special Forces), with their own "hootch . . . fortified with sandbags and a metal fence" (92). It may appear that the Greenies are the defenders of the perimeter, but as the story unfolds, they are the boundary itself: porous, shifting, and illusory. They are liminal creatures, Rat suggests, whom it is best to avoid, as if whatever they have or know is contagious. Not only do they inhabit a space on the perimeter, they also instantiate a figurative perimeter, the last outpost of "civilized" behavior and values. All these boundaries and perimeters are threatened when Mark Fossie succeeds in flying Mary Anne Bell in from Cleveland Heights. What seems at first blush a story about a girl who comes to a remote part of Vietnam, takes up with a renegade band of Greenies, is last seen wearing a necklace of human tongues, and eventually disappears into the hills and the mists is, on closer reading, really a story about what happens to the men themselves—the men who witness, and are dislocated by, her transgression. As Alex Vernon argues, "Sweetheart of the Song Tra Bong" is "a story of the male imagination" in which Mary Anne is an "abstraction" among O'Brien's other fully drawn characters, on whom the men project their anxieties about the masculine enterprise of war making and about the women for whom they fight (*Soldiers* 249). Mark Fossie thought he could import Mary Anne into his world as if she were a care package or a personal USO tour. He regards her as an object, a prized possession, and his greatest fear is that she'll be unfaithful to him with one of the other Americans inside the concertina wire, that he will lose possession of her. This kind of infidelity would be a threat to his masculinity, and he does his best to prevent it. Neither he nor apparently any of the other witnesses anticipates that Mary Anne's actions are a threat to their very concept of masculinity. Insofar as American stories of the Vietnam War take up larger cultural narratives, the story of Mary Anne is about generalized anxiety regarding gender roles (both at the time the story is set, in the 1960s, and at the time of its publication). But the power of the story derives from more than its threat to gender roles. Because the concepts of masculine and feminine are integral to the entire chain of reasoning that justifies war, Mary Anne's dangerous transformation threatens to unravel the already strained fabric of rationalization that makes the men's missions in Vietnam appear worthwhile and purposeful. The taboo that's violated is the one that contains the feminine in the domestic sphere and the masculine in the martial sphere. In Vernon's words:

> Mary Anne paradoxically represents Vietnam and the enemy, and the United States and that social bond that sends men to suffer the horrors of war and thereby earns their hostility. As the fresh-faced sweetie and bride and mother-to-be, she clearly represents the culture and values men are willing to fight to preserve. (*Soldiers* 253)

As many military historians and war theorists (John Keegan and Elaine Scarry chief among them) have pointed out, men do not fight in wars for the sake of the larger geopolitical reasons that leaders offer for the war. Instead, they fight for more intimate and immediate reasons, such as loyalty to fellow soldiers, and for an entire constellations of reasons back home. Like ancient knights, men fight for women—and for what women represent. The qualities embodied in women are those most conspicuously absent from the experience of war: purity, goodness, cleanliness, civilization, pink culottes. Like Lieutenant Cross's beloved and remote Martha in the title story and the perpetually virginal child Linda in "The Lives of the Dead," Mary Anne is, from Mark Fossie's point of view, an object, a prized possession, a totem. Mary Anne's transformation not only challenges Mark Fossie's proprietary claim on her but, more important, exposes as a fiction or a lie the entire chain of reasons underpinning the idea "that men without women trip," to borrow Michael Herr's memorable phrase from *Dispatches* (226).   Misbehaviors

In the masculinist world of Mark Fossie and the others, Mary Anne's body, which has been the object of each man's gaze since she arrived, becomes the text on which her transgressions are inscribed. The pink sweater and culottes she wears when she arrives are an emblem of girlish American suburban innocence, and she looks to the men "like a cheerleader visiting the opposing team's locker room" when she visits the hamlet with Mark, Rat, and the other medics (96). Soon, however, her outward appearance begins to change, and to Mark "[h]er body seemed foreign somehow" (99). With her hair cut short and "wrapped . . . in a dark green bandanna," wearing "no cosmetics" and no jewelry, Mary Anne sheds her midwestern femininity, and she seems to move out of Mark's reach (98). Eventually, she moves so far beyond his tether that she stays out all night; she moves beyond the perimeter of war stories that would cloister her safely in Cleveland Heights. By the end of the story she has "moved through femininity and through masculinity to a place beyond gender" (Vernon, *Soldiers* 250).

Focused on her appearance and obsessed with her potential for sexual exploitation and his own cuckolding, Fossie concludes that Mary Anne has run off with one of the other men; or to put it more accurately, he thinks another man has taken her, since he views her as an object on which others act rather than an agent in her own right. Once Mark and Rat have searched the compound without finding her, Rat says, in a sentence that foreshadows the rest of the story, "Okay. . . . We got a problem" (101). The immediate problem—and the only one that Mark seems concerned about—is the mystery of Mary Anne's whereabouts. Why has she disappeared? The bigger and thornier problem is that though she's with the Greenies, it isn't for "sex or anything." She's been out all night "on fuckin' *ambush*" (102). When she walks back into the hootch she shares with Fossie, she's wearing "a bush hat and filthy green fatigues" (102). As Rat tells the story, Fossie hesitates, "as though he had trouble recognizing her" (102). Students should consider the significance of the conditional in this

sentence: he doesn't actually have trouble recognizing her—she's the only civilian American woman for miles around—but he is unable to see her without
her familiar outer attributes.) In fact, when Mary Anne and Mark appear in
the mess hall later that evening, it's her traditional suburban girlish appearance
that's been reconstituted, as if she could be brought back under Fossie's control
as long as he can keep her in "a white blouse, a navy blue skirt, [and] a pair of
plain black flats" (103)) But no matter what she wears, Mary Anne has already
moved beyond the perimeter, to shadowy places Rat and Mark haven't been
to, and she's undergone an inner transformation that no schoolgirl outfit can
disguise. In Vernon's words, "[S]he is either a body in front of them or a mystery
beyond them, either way teasing them in their desire to penetrate her" (*Soldiers*
250).

The truce that Mark Fossie achieves with Mary Anne is short-lived. After
a few weeks, during which she appeared "as if she had come up on the edge
of something, as if she were caught in that no-man's land between Cleveland
Heights and deep jungle," she disappears with the Greenies (105). Three weeks
later, Rat happens to be awake the night she and the ghostly column slip back
through the wire and into the Greenies' hootch. With Mary Anne inside the
hootch, Mark Fossie begins a vigil outside that dramatizes a version of the male
gaze in which the object is not only hidden from sight but has wrested the
power from the gazer. When he finally stumbles through the door of the hootch,
he finds himself in terra incognita, a shadowy hut filled with "a weird deep-
wilderness sound," a miasma of smoke, and a smell "like an animal's den, a mix
of blood and scorched hair and excrement and the sweet-sour odor of molder-
ing flesh—the stink of the kill" (109, 110). Fossie's first glimpse of Mary Anne
as she emerges from the shadows suggests for a moment that she's "the same
pretty young girl who had arrived a few weeks earlier" (110). But her clothing—a "pink sweater and a white blouse and a simple cotton skirt"—which had
in the past functioned as a sign of her reliably domesticated femininity, are now
appropriated into a new and strange semiotics that discards the expected strand
of pearls or girlish locket in favor of "a necklace of human tongues . . . one over-
lapping the next, the tips curled upward as if caught in a final shrill syllable" (110–
11). Mary Anne's appearance in the bizarre setting of the hootch, a chilling
retelling of the final spectacle of Kurtz in Joseph Conrad's *Heart of Darkness*,
certainly signifies her crossing over from Cleveland Heights to a Vietnam that
is beyond the bounds of even Fossie's experience. As if her physical attributes
weren't sufficient evidence of her transgression and transformation, her explanation, framed in the language of desire, proves to Fossie that she's escaped his
gaze and his possession. As Terry Martin and Margaret Stiner point out, Mark
Fossie, like Conrad's Intended, "desperately clings to the romanticized image
of his beloved" (99). Chiding him that "[y]ou're in a place where . . . you don't
belong," Mary Anne says, "Sometimes I want to *eat* this place. Vietnam. I want
to swallow the whole country—the dirt, the death—I just want to eat it and
have it there inside me" (111). Her assertion reorganizes the economy of desire

on which Fossie's masculine identity depends: the object of desire has become the agent of desire, and the landscape of fear has been transformed into one of empowerment. Mark, whose daring act set in motion Mary Anne's transformation, is reduced to a feminized passivity; he is rendered powerless and almost speechless and has to be physically supported by Rat Kiley.

Rat tells Mark, "She's already gone," suggesting not only that Mary Anne is lost to Mark but also that the version of American femininity and the social world it represents is lost forever in the jungles of Vietnam (112). But Rat, who has been the proprietor of the story since the beginning, offers a coda that suggests the possibility of a reaction to the final vision of Mary Anne different from Mark's paralysis and collapse. Conceding that the final chapter in the story is, in Mitchell Sanders's words, "speculation," Rat confesses that he "loved her." He loved her, he says, because "[t]he way she looked, Mary Anne made you think about all those girls back home, how clean and innocent they all are, how they'll never understand any of this, not in a billion years" (113). While this declaration suggests that Rat loved Mary Anne in her Cleveland Heights, culottes-wearing incarnation, his further explanation hints instead that it's the Mary Anne with the necklace of human tongues that he loves: "She was *there*. She was up to her eyeballs in it. After the war, man, I promise you, you won't find nobody like her" (114).

For Mark, the story of Mary Anne is a story of loss: of a world of innocence and purity that she represents, of masculine authority that licensed him to regard her as a possession, and of faith that the savagery of war exists only in the arena of war rather than in the human psyche. Rat's telling of the story suggests that Mary Anne's disappearance into the jungle is at least as much a story of liberation as it is one of loss. His final words turn mythic and wistful, as if Rat envies Mary Anne her escape. Despite his claim to love her, he expresses no desire to rescue or possess her. Rather, he seems to simply want to be her: "She had crossed to the other side. She was part of the land. She was wearing her culottes, her pink sweater, and a necklace of human tongues. She was dangerous. She was ready for the kill" (116).

As O'Brien does in much of his work, he thwarts readers' desires to tame the narrative, to find the moral of the story of Mary Anne and her disappearance into the jungles of Vietnam. "A true war story is never moral," he tells us in "How to Tell a True War Story" (68). "It does not instruct, nor encourage virtue, nor suggest models of proper human behavior, nor restrain men from doing the things men have always done" (68). Students should ask if O'Brien's warning in "How to Tell a True War Story" applies to their own readings: "[I]f you feel that some small bit of rectitude has been salvaged from the larger waste, then you have been made the victim of a very old and terrible lie" (68–69). Many students will be troubled by the difficulty of reading "Sweetheart of the Song Tra Bong" as a feminist text because Mary Anne is less a real person than an abstraction or a device and because her moral position at the end is highly ambiguous. Other students may want to explore how the narrative register of the story moves further and further away from Rat's "truth" to a fourth-hand account and is taken over by the unnamed narrator, who finally posits Mary Anne as a kind of mythic and allegorical creature:

> Late at night, when the Greenies were out on ambush, the whole rain forest seemed to stare in at them—a watched feeling—and a couple of times they almost saw her sliding through the shadows. Not quite, but almost. She had crossed to the other side.   (116)

Like Mary Anne herself, the story slides through the shadows of our under-standing, barely discernible, hauntingly familiar, yet strange, always eluding our interpretive grasp and continuing to seduce us into its dangerous enclosure.

what does Piedmont fail to account for - Martin

Critical Angles:
Reading Soldier-Author O'Brien
and *Going After Cacciato*

Tobey C. Herzog

"So you see," said Li Van Hgoc as he brought down the periscope and locked it with a silver key, "things may be viewed from many angles. From down below, or from inside out, you often discover entirely new understandings."
(*Going After Cacciato* 91)

Whether to flee or fight or seek an accommodation
(*Going After Cacciato* 80)

Everything that I am doing flows out of the life I have led. And the life I have led is a life of finding it hard to distinguish within myself and without about what's true and what's not.
(Herzog, "Tim O'Brien: An Interview" 97)

When teaching Tim O'Brien's writing, I begin the first class by citing the passages quoted above. The first, a North Vietnamese officer's epistemological advice to Paul Berlin's Third Squad about viewing reality, indirectly becomes helpful advice from author O'Brien to his readers about understanding some of his principal narrative strategies: fragmented structure, reiteration with variation, and multiple perspectives. The second quotation, the character Paul Berlin's existential dilemma, introduces an archetypal theme in war literature (whether to fight or flee) and a recurring activity in all of O'Brien's writings of characters adjudicating competing values. In the third quotation, O'Brien raises issues about the intersection of memory and imagination within his life and writings.

Collectively, these critical angles provide students with tools to link various O'Brien works to each other and to other war literature as well as to connect characters and incidents in a particular work. Furthermore, if students consider O'Brien's life, revealed through interviews or memoir, as constituting another text to be read, additional literary and life connections emerge. To illustrate these reading strategies, I want to examine in *Going After Cacciato* O'Brien's use of multiple narrative angles applied to a recurring moral choice in war. Specifically, I want to illustrate how I introduce students to the ways that O'Brien explores a flee-or-fight choice (one that occurred in his own life) from different perspectives, through memory and imagination, within and across texts. Such a teaching strategy enables students to learn more about literary analysis, the life of the soldier-author O'Brien and his approaches to writing fiction, and their own decision-making processes.

Readers familiar with several of O'Brien's eight books know that at the core of his writing is mystery: the maybes and what-ifs of events and the possibilities and whys of the human spirit and people's actions. O'Brien continually explores the hearts and minds of characters facing difficult choices in stressful situations—both on the battlefield and in everyday life. About these choices and the characters who make them, O'Brien doesn't arrive at definitive judgments. Instead, he lets ambiguity develop in the stories—specifically, in the structure, characters, and themes. As he notes, "Too many writers want to solve their own mysteries. That's what kills books. . . . What's interesting is what we don't know, which is why. These things are inaccessible" (Herzog, "Tim O'Brien: An Interview" 92).

One consequence of O'Brien's preoccupation with narrative mystery and ambiguity is his frequent revisiting of certain events and choices, both in a single book and in many books. Usually, he describes these situations from different perspectives and with added or subtracted details—a technique of repetition with variation suggested in Li Van Hgoc's observation about multiple perspectives and by the narrator in *In the Lake of the Woods*: "The angle shapes reality" (288). For example, in different contexts and for different reasons, variations of a scene of American soldiers shooting a water buffalo appear in *If I Die in a Combat Zone, Going After Cacciato*, and *The Things They Carried*. The death of Chip Merricks (a friend of the soldier O'Brien), described in *If I Die in a Combat Zone*, is revisited on multiple occasions in *The Things They Carried* through the recurring descriptions of Curt Lemon's death; in passing in the nonfiction essay "The Vietnam in Me"; and later in footnote 127 in *In the Lake of the Woods*. Also, in *In the Lake of the Woods*, as symbolized by the recurring mirror imagery, O'Brien presents various perspectives of his central character, John Wade, and his choices—everything from a psychiatrist's view to a neighbor's. Thus, across his works and within, through these different angles, the author O'Brien and his readers view recurring incidents and characters' choices anew—details, significance, truths, mysteries, and ambiguities. Such a revisiting of events and choices reflects O'Brien's own indecisions about the meanings of happenings, the outcomes of characters' choices, and even, perhaps, events and decisions in his own life. It also highlights the author's essential distinctions between happening-truth (facts) and story-truth (imagined events).

This narrative technique of repetition with variation leads to characters confronting similar competing values, acting on the results of this process, and living with the consequences. As O'Brien notes, "That is how novels work. They work on a series of choices. . . . Choices imply competing values. . . . Novels that matter to me are those that involve competing values" (Herzog, "Tim O'Brien: An Interview" 100). In choosing, a character might act decisively (e.g., John Wade covering up his involvement in the My Lai massacre) or indecisively (e.g., through the "sleepwalking feeling" of Paul Berlin's entry into the army [*Going After Cacciato* 227]). These decisions are often complicated by characters sacrificing one principle to satisfy another or committing to self or to others, to self at the expense of others, or to others at the expense of self. Thus O'Brien explores his characters and himself through this epistemological, moral, and thematic lens. He frequently returns to the same moral dilemma with its competing values, but he explores the resulting choices and their aftermath from different angles.

One significant recurring predicament facing O'Brien's characters is whether to flee or fight—either literally or figuratively. Such an option relates to the universal condition of life itself: to confront oneself, to choose virtuous actions, to fight an illness, to deny a father's wishes, to act out of public obligation rather than personal welfare, or to affirm or end one's life. In O'Brien's war writing, this quandary occurs metaphorically and literally on the battlefield—in, for example, a soldier's choice whether to explore a tunnel before blowing it up or a civilian's or a soldier's decision to participate in combat or to resist, flee, or establish a separate peace. O'Brien emphasizes that all good war literature is "about flight of some sort or another. If a book is about war, and it doesn't have the psychology of flight underneath it, it's not a very good book" (Herzog, "Tim O'Brien: An Interview" 104). Why do people choose to put their life in harm's way for their country? Why, in the midst of the battlefield horror and carnage, do soldiers continue to fight? Why do individuals opt for physical and spiritual exile in resisting their country's military draft? For O'Brien, such decisions to fight or to flee have inherent emotional tensions, moral weight, reader interest, potential life-or-death consequences, and avenues into a character's heart and mind.

As a result of exploring the psychology of battlefield flight, O'Brien finds himself in the company of many other authors writing about war across time and cultures. In *The Iliad*, Homer's brooding and petulant Achilles expresses his unwillingness to join his comrades in the battle for Troy ("Now it is I who do not care to fight" [*Illiad* (2004), 9.436]); Stephen Crane's Henry Fleming in *The Red Badge of Courage* displays both cowardice in fleeing the battlefield and courage in later choosing to fight; Ernest Hemingway's Frederic Henry in *A Farewell to Arms* declares his own separate peace: "You were out of it now. You had no more obligation" (232); and Can in Bao Ninh's *The Sorrow of War* deserts his North Vietnamese Army unit. All these characters manage competing values and pressures as best as they can. And such decisions, with their political, humanitarian, moral, and personal ramifications, become defining moments. As a character in O'Brien's novel *July, July* observes, "What we choose is what we are" (qtd. in Herzog, *Writing* 126). Consequently, for students, examining O'Brien's use of this recurring choice in the larger context of world literature leads to interesting comparisons of cultures, wars, characters, narrative strategies, definitions of courage and cowardice, and authors' creativity in infusing a recurring predicament with originality and meaningful insights.

But O'Brien's readers must consider one more work as they engage in an intertextual critique of the author's treatment of flee or fight: O'Brien's own life. Tim O'Brien is a very accessible contemporary writer. He willingly talks about his writing, and in direct and indirect ways he also shares details of his life—whether directly through his war autobiography, *If I Die in a Combat Zone*, and many interviews or obliquely through his fiction. Furthermore, he does not avoid, either in his public discourse or in his books, his own war-related flee-or-fight decisions. They were, perhaps, the most traumatic decisions of his life, and they continue to haunt him. In fact, the critic Mark Heberle persuasively details the significance of O'Brien's choice to fight, especially as it relates to his writing:

> O'Brien's works rewrite the same primal scenes and experiences, and the repetitions are so numerous and recurrent that the works have become an endless refiguration of trauma writing that constantly revises itself—or a symptom of trauma that is never healed.   (*Trauma Artist* xxiii)

For O'Brien, nothing has been more traumatic than his initial decision to enter the army in August 1968 and his subsequent choices to remain in the military. Consequently, I ask students to read one or more interviews in which he discusses his own flight decisions, ones made all the more difficult because the civilian-soldier O'Brien actively opposed the war in Vietnam: "In my case I committed an act of unpardonable cowardice and evil. I went to a war that I believed was wrong, and I actively participated in it. . . . And by being there I am guilty" (Herzog, "Tim O'Brien: An Interview" 89). I also present excerpts from *If I Die in a Combat Zone* directly commenting on the conclusion: "I was a coward" (68).

O'Brien's rewriting of his experience may be a form of catharsis (something he adamantly denies), a means of exploring alternative outcomes, a readily accessible emotional and narrative building block, a purely literary interest, or a combination of all these possibilities. Readers encounter reluctant civilians facing draft notices (the real Tim O'Brien in *If I Die in a Combat Zone*, the fictional Tim O'Brien in *The Things They Carried*, and William Cowling in *The Nuclear Age*); the veteran John Wade fleeing his involvement in the My Lai massacre (*In the Lake of the Woods*); and the draft resister Billy McMann fleeing to Canada while his girlfriend, Dorothy, elects not to go with him (*July, July*). However, in *Going After Cacciato*, O'Brien's award-winning first war novel, the soldier-author spends the most time exploring the flight theme through the lens of imagination.

In *Going After Cacciato*, characters' choices to flee or fight become much more than contrived opportunities for the civilian-soldier O'Brien's continued journey of personal reconsideration or convenient narrative occasions for the author O'Brien's probing of characters' hearts and minds. Rather, this recurring moral dilemma engenders the underlying structural and thematic threads woven throughout the seemingly disordered narrative fabric. Characters' choices and the consequences related to flight link past, present, and future time of the book and connect American soldiers with civilians as well as with North Vietnamese and Iranian soldiers. Such choices also stitch together the various plot strands from the real and imagined events within the novel. As a result, readers discover that the surface disorder of the novel's narrative time and plot masks an exquisitely crafted novel centered on Paul Berlin's dilemma of flight, heroism, or accommodation.

Paul Berlin, like the soldier Tim O'Brien, is a reluctant soldier, fearing war rather than opposing it. Berlin's sleepwalking default has led him to a tour in Vietnam and a position at the end of a column of thirty-nine marching soldiers. He fears the war and doubts his own courage yet daydreams about the possibility of securing a Silver Star for bravery—while also imagining leaving the war behind. Thus, at approximately the midpoint of his tour in Vietnam, while on night-guard duty, Paul Berlin spends six hours remembering and reimagining in random fashion the events and people of the previous five and half months. In particular, he imagines what Cacciato, a fellow soldier who months earlier went AWOL, might have done once he left Third Squad. At the core of Berlin's night of consideration and invention are two major issues—his real moments of battlefield fear and his ever-present flee-or-fight decision. O'Brien, drawing on personal experience, as well as other literary war stories, refashions this existential dilemma. The reluctant Berlin, with illusions of heroism, encounters a confusing war, enemy, people, and landscape. Also, the indecisive Berlin is led by events. As an additional complication, he is fighting in a controversial war, one that some of his peers at home have chosen to avoid, flee, or protest. Will he confront his competing claims of heroism and flight? Will indecision be transformed into action? How will he justify his choice?

As Berlin spends the night in a guard tower remembering and imagining, he becomes a novice author of a war story in which he seems preoccupied with other characters confronting flight decisions. This night of consideration and storytelling becomes a heuristic process that aids him with his own decision. Once more, typical of an O'Brien narrative, the repeated events and choices are significant. In addition to Berlin, eight others face the decision to flee, or as it is constantly referred to in the novel, to run.

Interestingly, what flight entails and what the characters are fleeing from or committing to vary from situation to situation. The first of this group is, of course, the enigmatic Cacciato, variously described by his fellow soldiers as "awful dumb" and a brave soldier. His farewell in the book's first chapter signals his going AWOL from Third Squad and becomes the catalyst for the rest of the novel. Cacciato's motivations, goals, and even degree of responsibility for his departure are never explained. Thus a few critics argue that Cacciato flees because he is traumatized by the fragging of Lieutenant Sidney Martin. But such a simple explanation opposes O'Brien's notions of the complexity of key flee-flight decisions and the author's emphasis on narrative mystery and ambiguity in his writing. Nevertheless, Cacciato's flight and its imagined consequences guide both Berlin and readers. The final flee-or-fight choice is Berlin's, described during the book's surreal version of the Paris peace talks. In between these two decisions, Berlin confronts, through memory and imagination, a host of other characters opting whether to flee or fight and then living with the consequences.

One early example involves the entire Third Squad. Members of the squad must decide, in Berlin's fantasy, whether to leave Vietnam and pursue Cacciato on the 8,600-mile journey to Paris. Is such an action part of their mission as soldiers (a decision to continue fighting), or is such a nonauthorized journey merely, as the Iranian secret police officer insists, "an alibi to cover cowardice" (231)? Other characters facing similar options populate numerous scenes in Berlin's imagined story. Harold Murphy early on elects not to accompany Third Squad on the rest of its mission: "Running off like this, it's plain desertion" (35). Soon after, Third Squad meets Major Hgoc, the North Vietnamese officer forced by his superiors to live in a tunnel because of his desire ten years earlier to flee his army: "I decided to resist. . . . I ran" (96). Next, in Tehran, Third Squad observes an Iranian soldier beheaded because he "had merely gone AWOL. For true deserters the punishment is not so kind" (201). Later, fearing capture by the Greek authorities, squad member Stink Harris abandons the unit by jumping overboard as the ship pulls into port. And in one of the final scenes, the leader of Third Squad, the aging, sick Lieutenant Corson, deserts his men in Paris (acting out of exhaustion rather than conscience) and flees with the Vietnamese refugee Sarkin Aung Wan: " [T]hey deserted like rats" (325). Of course, the civilian Aung Wan, along with her two aunts, earlier chose to flee Saigon and the war: "And now my aunts take me to become a refugee" (53).

Different circumstances, different motivations, but ultimately somewhat similar decisions to run—Paul Berlin has these many choices as models as he eventually, even in his imagination, must determine whether to flee or fight. Appropriately in Paris, the city of light, peace, and romance, where the real Paris peace conference dragged on for nearly five years, the soldier-storyteller Paul Berlin and the imaginary character Paul Berlin merge and must decide. Berlin opts to fight. He does so despite Sarkin Aung Wan's lengthy, persuasive argument to the contrary ("Give up this fruitless pursuit of Cacciato. . . . Live now the dream you have dreamed" [318]). In explaining his decision to continue the imaginary mission to capture Cacciato and in the real world to continue his tour of duty in Vietnam, Berlin cites obligations "to people, not to principle or politics or justice" and "the dread of abandoning all that I hold dear. I am afraid of running away. I am afraid of exile" (320). At this point in the novel, the soldier-author Tim O'Brien seems to merge with both Berlins as he revisits his own flight predicaments detailed in *If I Die in a Combat Zone*. Interestingly, the fictional Berlin's choice to fight is similar to the real O'Brien's ("Imagination, like reality, has its limits" [321]). Furthermore, Berlin's rationale for not fleeing and establishing a separate peace reminds readers of the soldier O'Brien's confessions of obligations and fear in explaining his stateside decision not to leave the military but to continue the mission: "I simply couldn't bring myself to flee.

Family, the home town, friends, history, tradition, fear, confusion, exile: I could not run" (*If I Die* 68). Such comments foreshadow the fictional Tim O'Brien's reasons for entering the military as detailed twelve years later in "On the Rainy River" in *The Things They Carried*.

All these literary and life connections related to flight lead to intriguing questions. For example, the real Tim O'Brien harshly judged his determination to fight as cowardly. Is Berlin likewise a coward for deciding to stay? Or is Berlin instead courageous for his willingness to endure the war, an accommodating type of courage that O'Brien labels in *If I Die in a Combat Zone* as "wise endurance" (137)? Is Berlin also courageous to confront, through imagination, his fears and the competing values of war and peace and to choose an action consistent with his obligations and sense of self? Complicating this debate is the author O'Brien's response to a question about whether the label of cowardice that he places on his own real-life decision not to flee the military should be applied to Paul Berlin. O'Brien answers, "No, good literature doesn't judge. . . . It is rather to watch a character deal . . . with the complications of life" (Herzog, "Tim O'Brien: An Interview" 104–05). These questions and complications instigate lively classroom discussions about this novel and O'Brien's other war writing.

Taking students on this flee-or-fight journey through other war texts, as well as within O'Brien's books and life, evolves into a complex mystery tour in its own right, complete with digressions, ambiguities, historical and cultural considerations, deconstructed gender identities, competing judgments of courage and cowardice, and many unanswered questions. Such a journey, however, is beneficial for students on many levels, including the literary and the personal. At the end of this trip, remaining questions and ongoing discussions, rather than definitive answers, become important teaching and learning aids. How do people choose? What is the psychology of decision making? Do we use memory and imagination as heuristic tools to recall similar incidents, explore possibilities, and arrive at decisions—a process at the core of O'Brien's decision making and that of his central characters? What can students learn from this procedure? Do free will and determinism affect individual choices? How do changing angles (different perspectives and different variables) alter judgments of similar decisions? How do individuals deal with the outcomes of their decisions? How do the flight adjudications of O'Brien's characters correspond to similar decisions by other characters in war literature? Does the author O'Brien inject a moral and psychological complexity into the decision making not found in other war stories? Why doesn't the soldier Paul Berlin choose differently from the soldier Tim O'Brien? Can biographical criticism offer a helpful critical angle for reading some literature? What emerges for students in this "angles-on-flight" approach to reading war literature in general and O'Brien's books in particular is their understanding that momentous decisions—especially those involving principles, moral issues, and life-and-death choices—are never simple. They are ambiguous and multilayered, involving emotions, principles, ego, the head, the heart, and other internal and external forces. Furthermore, after the fact, individuals and authors use memory and imagination to reexamine such decisions from different angles in a never-ending process of self-discovery and self-definition.

Identity in 10,000 Miles
of Nameless, Faceless Space:
A Postmodern Approach to
In the Lake of the Woods

Jennifer Peterson

> In any case, Kathy Wade is forever missing, and if you require solutions,
> you will have to look beyond these pages. Or read a different book.
>
> (*In the Lake of the Woods* 30)

Tim O'Brien's *In the Lake of the Woods* by turns engages, frustrates, captivates,
and stymies students, for it is a novel without end. Because of its lack of ending, it offers a rich excursion into the similarly engaging but frustrating experience of creating identity in the postmodern world. Hence, when I teach the
novel, I approach it as an introduction to postmodern literature, focusing on the
question, "How is identity—both individual (human) and collective (societal or
cultural)—conceptualized in *In the Lake of the Woods*?" As my students and
I work through the novel in class discussions, we examine several facets of the
novel that bear on identity creation. First, we explore how the narrative structure itself seems to defy identity—how is it a novel at all? What do we do with
a book that is not what we are expecting? What does its unconventionality mean
to us as readers who are in the process of trying to understand how a text—a
novel, specifically—makes meaning? Second, as we explore John Wade's character, we draw out the novel's use of symbols, such as mirrors and fog, which
demonstrate the difficulties of becoming a whole identity. Finally, we compare
the two main characters, John Wade and—strangely enough—the narrator, to
show a successful identity formation juxtaposed against a complete loss of self.
In the book's final pages, when students realize that the quest has not really
been about finding the missing Kathy Wade or even about finding the real John
Wade, there is inevitably a eureka moment as they discover how the narrator
and his narrative come together to create identity for the text, the narrator, and
the reader. It is not necessarily a comfortable moment. Nor are any of the three
identities necessarily a finished text—collectively, they are one whole, com-
posed of many seemingly nonfitting or ill-fitting parts.

To work with *In the Lake of the Woods* as a vehicle to explore the identity
problem in postmodern literature, I introduce key concepts from the theorists
Fredric Jameson and Linda Hutcheon before we begin the text. Much theoretical material addressing postmodernism is available, and as we move through the
book, I draw attention to other postmodern elements. But because of questions
of how narrated history constructs identity, Jameson and Hutcheon are our

theoretical foundation, even as they provide compelling and dueling perspectives on how, why, and whether history is narrated.[1]

Jameson's idea of postmodern narrative as pastiche, or blank parody, posits that any attempt to offer a history—a reconstruction of events—is not only impossible but meaningless. In "Cognitive Mapping," Jameson finds that the human subject is confronted with "radically discontinuous realities." Because of the difficulty of negotiating such terrain, he sees the "lived experience" as "fragmented and schizophrenic decentering and dispersion of [the subject]" (351). Accordingly, "postmodern hyperspace" has "finally succeeded in transcending the capacities of the individual human body to locate itself, to organize its immediate surroundings perceptually, and cognitively to map its position in a mappable external world" (Postmodernism 45). That lack of central context, he contends, results in cultural inability to feel deeply or to find any objective truth by which one can gauge the veracity of either personal experience or cultural history. Thus all narrative reconstruction is paradoxically valid and meaningless and, more important, devoid of wholeness, which is why postmodern culture is a dystopia filled with fragmentation. There are, though, ways of creating identity in the postmodern world and avoiding the threat of fragmentation to postmodern subjectivity. One way is through the use of a cognitive map. In short, one can no longer rely on the idea of an objective reality as a tool for identity formation; rather, one must evaluate experiences with people, places, and things, creating a map from the meaning one makes from the experiences. Jameson's point is that in the meeting of external and internal, one is able to create wholeness from the schizophrenia that results from the postmodern world's hyperspace.

Hutcheon arrives at wholeness differently. Arguing in A Poetics of Postmodernism that postmodernism is indeed parodic, she calls postmodernism's treatment of history "historiographic metafiction" (5) and explains that the postmodern "effects two simultaneous moves. It reinstalls historical contexts as significant and even determining, but in so doing, it problematizes the entire notion of historical knowledge." She agrees that at some point the "historical referent" (as Jameson terms it) disappears (89). However, she does not believe that what results is meaningless or blank parody. On the contrary, she finds that narratives of history question our linguistic, discursive systems and the way they construct culture and, in turn, individual identity (91–93). Hutcheon's concept of historiographic metafiction, then, allows for the idea that a whole identity can be created by exploring history and situating one's own story within the context of or against the histories of those with whom one has a connection, whether individual or cultural.

In the Lake of the Woods provides ample examples that paradoxically demonstrate and validate both scholars' arguments. After reading and discussing excerpts from Jameson and Hutcheon, we turn to the novel for illustration, referring to Jameson and Hutcheon as we work our way through the text.

First, I draw attention to the book's structure—one of the more challenging aspects for students used to the traditional narrative form. In itself, the structure underscores identity fragmentation, for it is without an expected linear progression. Rather, the structure of *In the Lake of the Woods* is circular, doubling back on itself repeatedly, never reaching any sort of climax at all. Discussions draw out chapter explorations, which move students from frustrated questions that range from why the book has weird footnotes to when the answer to the mystery will show up. The book is divided into chapters that I place in four categories based on their repeated titles and content: the "Evidence" chapters; "The Nature of" chapters; the "How," "What," or "Where" (journalist) chapters; and the "Hypothesis" chapters. There are roughly the same number of chapters in each category, which suggests that each piece of the investigation is equally important. In other words, the reconstructions of events that make up the journalist question chapters not only rely on evidence but also are paradoxically as important as the evidence on which they depend. Hence, the chapter types all work together to build the novel, providing a cognitive map within an extremely fragmented—or schizophrenic, to use Jameson's term—narrative. The narrative has a whole, if unexpected, identity, an identity that distinctly coheres by virtue of the interrelations among the chapters.

The identity of the narrative, however, is not static. The evidence changes, shifting to offer various hypotheses during the course of the novel. The "Hypothesis" chapters begin short and are spare of story elements and detail, growing throughout the narrative as more evidence factors into their formation; they become shorter again toward the end, the final three being approximately four pages each. This structure suggests that extant information creates reality; hence, an objective existence is impossible. Rather, perception—what one knows at any given narrative moment—defines identity. The narrative follows a basic pattern of small buildup of expectation through the use of a random combination of the three informational chapter types followed by a hypothesis, which is immediately negated by another buildup. The novel follows this pattern and ends with a "Hypothesis" chapter. Thus there is no final resolution, which means that reader anxiety is not dissipated, nor is expectation of a finale satisfied by the book's end. Indeed, it also means that while I can explain that there is identity to the narrative, there is no answer, which initially baffles students. Through the lack of traditional narrative structure, then, the novel forces the reader to locate meaning in some way and somewhere other than in the expected narrative form. Through the examination of narrative structure, we begin to explore how our expectations factor into our perceptions of identity. Students are fascinated by and skeptical about different constructions of creating a self, whether it is a text or a human being, and narrative form in *In the Lake of the Woods* begins this quest.

To address the unreliability of a traditionally conceptualized fixed identity, I also draw out the chapters that treat the idea of the essence, or inherent nature, of a thing. "The Nature of" chapters explore the nature of such things as loss, marriage, love, the beast (the Vietnam War—or is it?), politics, the spirit, the dark (the war—or is it?), and the angle (the setting of Angle Inlet—but more). By titling the chapters "The Nature of," O'Brien encourages readers to draw on anaphoric knowledge of the chapters' topics in order to question and explore what one believes to be the essence of things. And students have all sorts of set opinions—which they believe to be reliable—about politics, love, and so on, including our overarching theme, identity.

Readers enter the chapter that discusses the nature of marriage with pre-conceived notions of relationships between men and women, expecting the chapter to address primarily marriage. However, the chapter meanders through the maze of John Wade's father's death, his Vietnam War experience, and his relationship with Kathy. Their marriage is not recorded until the final page, and, indeed, the chapter focuses on the lack of honesty between the two char-acters—John's penchant for stalking and Kathy's for disappearing. Is this the nature of marriage? The novel suggests that rather than the fairy tale readers may imagine, marriage is the intersection of many parts of life, including those parts we would rather hide or ignore.

In the Lake of the Woods treats the other "Nature of" chapters similarly, turn-ing the abstractions back on themselves and revealing that the essences are empty and meaningless. The unusual "natures" of the chapters call to mind both Jameson's cognitive map and Hutcheon's historiographic metafiction and provide opportunities for discussion of both ideas. For example, how do the vignettes about John's or Kathy's life constitute a sort of cognitive map that constructs their identities? Or, how can the information offered be evaluated to show what cultural values are privileged or marginalized, thereby affirming certain actions or behaviors while negating others?

I find that the footnotes scattered throughout the novel provide an additional study of the nature of things, leading students to the end of the text, where the quest for identity is finally transferred fully to them as readers. The footnotes and the natures explored in them are yet another marker of how identity is constructed. The narrator draws repeated attention to concepts such as "hu-man nature," "human desire," and "soul" (101, 266), and he does so with less attention to his main character, John Wade, and more attention to himself and his conversant, the reader. That he does this indicates the importance of ex-ploring these deceptively familiar ideas as ideological constructs, for each time he refers to an "essence," he reveals its inconsistencies and the way in which culture utilizes its conceptualization as a tool of cultural organization and au-thority. His easy communication with the reader also suggests an awareness that the text itself contributes to the identity of the reader each and every time he or she interacts with it, because of the intimate conversation inherent to its structure. Hence, by the end of the book, the reader must confront his or her notion of the nature of endings, since the novel does not offer one. Further, since the novel questions the idea of an innate nature or essence, what is this text? The reader is forced to address the indeterminacy of the novel's identity as a novel. This is disconcerting, to say the least, and insofar as the traditional narrative form serves as a metaphor for human existence, one must then also admit the indeterminacy of human existence. And, of course, since the students are implicated in the narrative, they have become part of it, and their identities are inevitably changed—constructed—through and because of their interaction with it. All identity is relational, dependent on dynamic interactions.

Because the narrative presents itself as a mystery (What has become of Kathy Wade), I also emphasize the quest for discovery and the character trying to do the discovering. If the novel is a quest of sorts, there must be some sort of primary character on a journey, searching for something. In *In the Lake of the Woods*, that character is John Wade, who seems to be trying to piece together what has happened to his wife, Kathy. Students are quick to cast judgment in Wade's direction, though, so while we work with the indeterminate narrative structure, which never does tell them whether Wade is the good guy or the bad guy, we also focus on the development of his character, which is not as simple a task as it may seem. Wade's character—or that of Sorcerer or Javelin John or Lieutenant Governor or Jiggling John—is fragmented, shifting, and tenuous. At the beginning of the novel, he has suffered a landslide defeat in the Minnesota senate primary. The loss is devastating and poses a significant threat to Wade's self-definition. Wade claims that "it was more than a lost election." For him, it is "[h]is pride, his career, his honor and reputation, his belief in the future he had so grandly dreamed for himself" (5). Immediately notable is Wade's emphasis on himself and his own dreams. He is stilted and artificial, removed from both Kathy and external reality. His reality and identity are located inside his own head, but not in a way that suggests a soul or an essence of being.

Mirrors function as primary symbols of Wade's fragmented inward focus. He is obsessed with them; in fact, his mother notes in an early "Evidence" chapter that when he was a child, she often found him standing in front of a mirror, staring at himself. Furthermore, during his childhood Wade practiced magic in front of the mirror. The mirrors of Wade's adulthood direct his gaze continually inward, so that he processes reality only from the misleading, refracted images inside his head. Wade, a magician, has perfected this trick, not realizing that it obscures his ability to formulate identity and therefore to function in the external world. Hence, he becomes an imitation of himself that relies, paradoxically, on that image to reproduce his own identity. The mirrors actually hinder Wade from forming identity.

Steam, smoke, and fog similarly obscure external reality and the threat to image that external reality presents. Wade comments on the steamy air of Vietnam, air he identifies as "thin rosy sunlight" that is "wrong" because of its color, smell, and taste (104–05). However wrong it is, it has substance, which allows Wade to shape it according to the way he needs to remember his experience in Vietnam. Too, the smoke in Vietnam and its present manifestation in the Lake of the Woods' enshrouding fog further masks external reality, cocooning Wade inside the images he has created for himself, independent of external reality. In Vietnam there is also the steam, the white phosphorus that causes villages to disappear, the smoke of the fires that kill the people (and dead bodies) and burn the towns.

Wade relies on mirrors, fog, steam, and smoke, both in Vietnam and at Lake of the Woods to block the intrusive external world in moments of threat, such as his crushing defeat or the loss of Kathy. At the lake, during the important journalist chapters, the narrative carefully notes whether fog rolls in or is present, for fog marks moments when Wade cannot remember external events clearly. He can recall his thoughts and blurry impressions, but actual occurrences are hazy rather than definite. The fog that obscures his memory at the lake points to the steam that he equates with the jungles of Vietnam. To return to the peace of the steam, the fog, the total calm of the mirrors, Wade reproduces it by pouring the boiling water on the plants—and perhaps on Kathy. The external threat posed by his loss(es) must be overcome, and the only means whereby he can accomplish this is through total abjection of self, a feat he has always wanted to try. Indeed, while in Vietnam, Wade imagines himself "performing the ultimate vanishing act. A grand finale, a curtain closer" (76). Given that he views it as the grand finale, complete erasure of self is the ultimate honor and testament to skill.[2] He achieves this by forcing his internal mirror on his external, threatening reality—he joins the mirrors inside his head with the fog and mirrored surface of the lake, and the steam, or metaphorical, "home" of Vietnam he creates inside the cabin, a move that ultimately leads to his complete disappearance on the foggy, mirrored surface of Lake of the Woods. John Wade thus demonstrates the eventually inevitable demise of the internally focused, fragmented self.

Wade's character proves the need for Jameson's cognitive map. While constructing a cognitive map seems initially to be what Wade has done with his emphasis on interiority, it is not, for Jameson's map requires negotiation between interior and exterior spaces rather than Wade's dependence on the refracted or blurred images in his mind. One must focus outward on the social totality to glean information that one then turns inward and maps. Paradoxically, the narrator comments that Ruth Rasmussen has been trying to tell him that "[w]e find truth inside, or not at all" (295), which in the postmodern framework means that truth is the meaning one makes from sets of information—external information combined with interior maps of it. Thus truth cannot be refracted through metaphorical mirrors that trap it or obfuscated by fog and steam; it must be extractable so that the subject, reading it as a map, constructs and maintains a sense of wholeness. Wade, however, has been able to perceive external reality only according to the obfuscating mirrors inside his head. The narrative's exploration of all facets of Wade's life suggests that his inability to negotiate the postmodern world and gain some whole identity is caused by his focus on his schizophrenic self.

At this point, students begin to wonder whether Wade was ever really the main character in the book, for if Wade cannot construct a cognitive map, who in the text can? They are conditioned to expect if not a good guy, then at least a character who can be explained in some way and with whom they can somehow relate. Therefore, they search for a character to fulfill these expectations, and they find one. However, the character they find, while close at hand, is surprising. The main character — the identity whose existence is under construction — is not Wade but the narrator, who almost seems Wade's doppelgänger, juxtaposed as he is against Wade in his similarity of life situation as well as his admitted obsession with Wade's life. The narrator of *In the Lake of the Woods* posits Wade as his other, using his intersections with Wade's life as his cognitive map and questioning history to construct his own identity through his investigation of Wade, which is related to us as the novel. That it is an actual text that relates a history is not lost on students. What this attention to narrative structure and identity construction foregrounds, particularly with its focus on essence, perception versus objective reality, and "truth," is the text's exploration of how one narrates history, of the relation between historian and history, biographer and subject, and self and the self's story.

The novel is a dual reconstruction: it is both a fictional character's experience and a retelling of actual historical events, all pieced together through various footnotes, such as those from the Peers Commission, which in 1970 investigated what it called the My Lai Incident (136), and from fictional interviews with fictional characters such as Kathy's sister, Pat, or Wade's mother, Eleanor. That there is a blurred line between fact and fiction is underscored by the reconstructions offered by a narrator who admits to the reader that

> [e]ven much of what might appear to be fact in this narrative — action, word, thought — must ultimately be viewed as a diligent but still imaginative reconstruction of events. I have tried, of course, to be faithful to the evidence. Yet evidence is not truth. It is only evident.   (30)

In this statement the narrator calls the students' attention to a major proposition in postmodern thought (and in this text), which is that objective reality is no more and no less than one's active perception of an occurrence or event. Even as the narrator places his commentary in the footnotes that document his historical research — which readers consider reliable because they are footnotes, after all, and therefore scholarly and objective — he questions whether they mean anything, and if so, what that might be. Furthermore, he admits throughout the narrative that whatever meaning may be found is not fixed or final; instead, it is constantly changing, depending on experiences had, people met, places seen, thoughts encountered.

The evidence is, as the narrator says, simply that: what is present. For Jameson, this evidence holds meaning, perhaps simultaneous multiple meanings or no meaning at all, because meaning is inaccessible, thus requiring a cognitive map. For Hutcheon, the evidence similarly holds multiple meanings that are culturally constructed and implicate culture as much as they may (or may not) implicate Wade. Thus one might propose seven hypotheses for what happened to Kathy Wade or seven hundred or none. In the end, it is possible both to know and not to know, for the focus is less on knowing and more on trying to explain or at least understand how cultural and personal identity are organized through cultural and personal explorations of history. *In the Lake of the Woods* demonstrates through its dualities of fiction and nonfiction, and personal and cultural, that indeed one cannot exist without the other.

Ultimately, students find that the postmodern identity quest, both in this text and in their own lives, is unending and that identity is, paradoxically, knowable and unknowable. From the novel's structure and Wade's character, one learns that the very process of historicizing causes anxiety while driving one onward, because in constructing history one simultaneously constructs the self.[3] And the temptation to erase is present, but dangerously so, for erasure of places, things, and people leads inexorably to erasure of self, as Wade's character shows. Thus the narrator laments that he "cannot remember much, [he] cannot feel much. Maybe erasure is necessary" (298). But he clearly recognizes the danger of erasure, for his recording of events proves his commitment to cultural and personal discovery. The text's existence ensures that no erasure will occur. Also, he is saddened by the fact that the Vietnam War—his war, he claims—no longer belongs to him, and he muses that the novel may be a way of giving the war back to himself. And in giving himself the war, or his history, he builds identity though the re-creation.

But why does he create John Wade, a suspect, perhaps a murderer, a war criminal? Indeed, why the mixture of historical events and fictional characters? The postmodern narrative suggests that any history contains some of each and is, furthermore, simultaneously accessible and inaccessible. The same cultural authority that constructs Wade, Vietnam, the political system, marriage, love, childhood, and so on is the cultural authority that composes the narrator (and us); hence, his (and our) twin desires to forge ahead in discovery and to turn away. Wade's life experience, which constructs his identity, is ultimately an unsolvable mystery if one is looking for something knowable in the traditional sense of objectivity. So is each reader's, which is at least part of the reason the narrative that depicts it causes so much consternation among students who expect to be able to find an answer, a solution. Simply put, we want to either convict or acquit Wade. The novel's final questions ask us whether we can believe "[t]hat [Wade] was innocent of everything except his life[.] Could the truth be so simple? So terrible?" (303). But what do those questions really ask? Can one divorce the self from the life? Each student can easily substitute his or her name for Wade's, finding that, true to the indeterminacy of postmodern narrative and the difficulty of constructing postmodern identity, life—self—is a complex juxtaposition and the words *innocent*, *simple*, and *terrible* are concepts not so simple to explain or pin down. Ultimately, the text allows students to see that in life, in the space "between water and sky" (303), all human subjects are implicated by and complicit in their own existences; meaning and identity are both present and absent, possible and impossible, constructed and natural, knowable and unknowable, fixed only in the sense that they are always changing.

NOTES

[1] For further study of cultural and literary postmodernism, see Baudrillard; Harvey; Lyotard; Hutcheon; and Jameson (*Postmodernism*).

[2] Wade's desire to vanish completely certainly helps explain his obsession in Vietnam with the two snakes eating each other and his disappointment when one of the men in his company kills the snakes before Wade can see how the situation resolves itself. He is left to wonder what might have happened.

[3] T. S. Eliot's "Tradition and the Individual Talent" is an excellent essay for comparison here.

Diving into the Text beneath the Text: Gender and Revenge in *Tomcat in Love*

Catherine Calloway

Students frequently state that O'Brien's seventh book, *Tomcat in Love*, is one of their favorites, that it is, in fact, a course text they retain at the end of the semester and do not sell back to the campus bookstore. After the macabre humor of works such as *Going After Cacciato*, *The Things They Carried*, and *In the Lake of the Woods*, the lighthearted tone and comic nature of *Tomcat in Love* is a welcome change for readers.[1] Reviewers and critics have been quick to observe more than the comic distinction between *Tomcat in Love* and its predecessors, however. Especially noticeable is the presence of female characters in the text. Certainly, there has never been an absence of women in O'Brien's works—examples include Addie and Grace in *Northern Lights*; Bobbi, Melinda, and Sarah in *The Nuclear Age*; Sarkin Aung Wan in *Going After Cacciato*; Mary Anne Bell and the narrator's daughter in *The Things They Carried*; and Kathy Wade and her sister in *In the Lake of the Woods*. But scholars have looked on many of them as marginal figures who have been treated one dimensionally and essentially rendered silent. Some critics, in fact, have been incensed by O'Brien's relegating Sarkin Aung Wan to a figment of Paul Berlin's imagination and Mary Anne Bell to the shadows of the heart of darkness of the male-dominated Vietnam War. For this reason, it is insightful for instructors to consider the feminist dimensions of *Tomcat in Love* and to look at how and why O'Brien plays with the idea of gender in the novel.

As Patrick Smith notes, central to feminist criticism is how it "studies the ways in which women are portrayed in literature and how language is used to define them" (144). The notion of language is a good starting point for classroom discussions of *Tomcat in Love*. One of the most striking aspects of the novel is the obsessive attention paid by Thomas Chippering, the novel's protagonist, to diction. Instructors can ask students to think about why Chippering continually plays with language and, more specifically, why he uses such a variety of words and phrases to describe himself. Why, for example, does he term himself a "predator," a "deviant," a "cradle robber" (89), a "sick, dangerous, compulsive skirt chaser," a "sneak," and a "liar" (176)? What do such terms imply about how he treats women? Furthermore, why does O'Brien both create a character who appears to be such a self-centered tomcat and center the novel on that character's male point of view? Instructors may also ask students to consider why O'Brien makes Chippering a professor of linguistics and the holder of the University of Minnesota's Rolvaag Chair in Modern American Lexicology. Why is Chippering a man who speaks so knowingly of "linguistic contrivance" (15), of the potential of language to have "the power of an earthquake" (133), of the ways in which "our spirits [are] slashed by combinations of vowel and consonant" (18), of the power of words to cut like "linguistic butcher kni[ves]" (129)?

Once students have been alerted to the novel's interest in the power of language, instructors can have them contemplate the ways in which language is connected to other thematic concerns. By chapter 4, Chippering has extensively defined a word he considers significant, one that he uses so often in the novel that it takes on a thematic importance of unexaggerated dimensions: revenge. Chippering notes:

> The word comes to us from the Latin, *vindicare*, to vindicate, and in its most primitive etymology is without pejorative shading of any sort. To vindicate is to triumph over suspicion or accusation or presumed guilt, and for the ancients, such triumph did not exclude the ferocious punishment of false accusers. (Hence *vindicta*. Hence vengeance.)   (24)

The theme of revenge is well known in O'Brien's stories and novels. Examples include the revenge of the narrator of "The Ghost Soldiers" on Bobby Jorgenson, a medic, for his incompetence when he allows the narrator, who has been wounded in the buttocks, to develop gangrene; the revenge of Paul Berlin's platoon in *Going After Cacciato* on Lieutenant Sidney Martin for the deaths of Frenchie Tucker and Bernie Lynn, soldiers who died when Martin made them search tunnels; the revenge of Rat Kiley on the baby water buffalo in "How to Tell a True War Story" in retaliation for the death of Curt Lemon; and the revenge of Dorothy Stiers in *July, July* on her husband, Ron, for his emotional coldness to her after her surgery for breast cancer and the revenge of Billy McMann on Dorothy Stiers for marrying Ron instead of going to Canada with him during the Vietnam War.

In *Tomcat in Love* the issue of revenge is raised in the first chapter when Chippering asks, "If the opportunity arose, would revenge be an option? Against whom—a sick family, a jealous brother? Revenge how? Hammer and nails? A pithy sentence, a squeal of outrage" (18)? There is an allusion to spousal betrayal, but as it turns out, while Chippering is seeking revenge on his ex-wife, who has left him for another man, his revenge revolves around more than a betrayal of love. In a way, he feels that his whole life has been a series of betrayals. Not only has he been betrayed by his wife, but as a child, he was betrayed by his father, who brought him a turtle instead of the engine he had promised. Chippering has also been betrayed by Herbie Zylstra, his childhood friend, who implied that Chippering was involved in an act of arson at a church, who spied on Chippering and Lorna Sue throughout their courtship and marriage, and who now appears to take the side of the tycoon after Chippering and Lorna Sue's divorce. Acts of betrayal, Chippering believes, should end in acts of vengeance. As a result, the concept of revenge permeates the novel, making *Tomcat in Love* a litany of the many ways that people, including O'Brien the author, can and do take revenge on each other.

Chippering's quest is to exact vengeance on his ex-wife, Lorna Sue, who has divorced Chippering after twenty years of marriage to run off with a tycoon. At the beginning of the novel, Chippering is "sketching out a strategy of reprisal" and thinking of some of "the more intriguing methods [he could employ]—arson, food poisoning, transudative sailboats" (26). He decides instead to destroy Lorna Sue's new marriage, "[w]in her back. And then dump her like a truckload of used diapers" (54). Students enjoy contemplating Chippering's strategy of revenge, which includes planting "a pair of fluorescent purple panties and matching bra" (28) under the front seat of the tycoon's Mercedes and trying to trick the tycoon into thinking that Lorna Sue and her brother, Herbie, are having an incestuous relationship. Chippering also makes bombs, using gasoline and Mason jars, that he plans to set off on the Fourth of July to remind Lorna Sue, Herbie, and the tycoon that he is "a human being and not some game piece on the checkerboard of treachery" (284), even though he himself has instigated the game.

Revenge is also central to the novel's Vietnam War subplot, which reveals that Chippering has possessed a "lifelong propensity for exacting vengeance" (62). In Vietnam, Chippering is betrayed by six Special Forces soldiers, or Greenies, who disappear during the night while at a listening post, leaving him alone and lost in the jungle, where he wanders in circles for several days. He is betrayed as well by Thuy Ninh, a Vietnamese servant and Chippering's paramour, who, he realizes after numerous lovemaking sessions, is the lover of all the men in the Special Forces unit. In retaliation for the joint betrayal by Thuy Ninh and the Greenies, Chippering calls in firepower—napalm and high explosives—on his fellow soldiers' coordinates, quietly returns to his firebase, and types up a form that declares him a war hero and awards him a Silver Star for valor.

Through his vengeful acts, Chippering naturally invites and inspires counter-revenge from others, setting off a chain reaction. Lorna Sue, Herbie, and the tycoon, for instance, take revenge on Chippering in retaliation for the pranks he has pulled on them. They humiliate him by showing up in his classroom, writing obscenities on the chalkboard, and administering a public paddling of him in front of his students. The Special Forces soldiers not only take revenge on Chippering immediately after they are almost annihilated by the friendly fire, they also swear eternal revenge—to be taken on Chippering in postwar America, perhaps years later.

As students readily discover, even the minor characters in *Tomcat in Love* are obsessed with revenge. Carla, a saleswoman in the lingerie shop who educates Chippering on various means of enacting revenge, threatens revenge when he touches a tattoo of a rose on her breast after promising to only look at it. Toni, an honor student for whom Chippering is going to direct a thesis, threatens to charge him with sexual harassment after he quotes a line from Shakespeare ("come kiss me, sweet") and later promises to turn him in when he refuses *her* sexual advances once he has written the thesis for her. Megan, Toni's roommate, seeks revenge on Toni for her having dated some of Megan's boyfriends—she does so by complaining to university administrators that Chippering wrote Toni's honors thesis, which gets him fired. Even little Evelyn, a child Chippering disciplines with a swat on the backside at a daycare center where he teaches language skills to three- and four-year-olds, threatens revenge unless he lies next to her on the mat during rest period and auditions for the role of Captain 19 on a local television program.

Most students have no difficulty locating and understanding the preceding examples of revenge in *Tomcat in Love*. What instructors may have to point out is the underlying text of many of O'Brien's works. In *Going After Cacciato*, readers have to piece together the mysterious character of Cacciato and the fantastic journey to Paris in pursuit of him or the events that lead to the fragging of Lieutenant Sidney Martin, the one character whose death is mentioned but never detailed. In *In the Lake of the Woods*, readers must comb carefully through the "Evidence" chapters to find the details that John Wade has attempted to hide regarding his participation in the My Lai massacre or through the "Hypothesis" chapters to try to find proof that John Wade may have murdered his wife, Kathy, although the novel ends without resolution. If *Tomcat in Love* is like many of O'Brien's previous works, then there is a code that must be broken, a moral or a message that taunts and teases the reader, a puzzle that must be solved. What, then, is so important about the theme of revenge in this book, and how does it relate to subjects such as gender and language?

At first, students may think that the notion of a subtext relates to the Vietnam War subplot or to the footnotes and textual references that O'Brien uses to address a woman whose husband may have betrayed her—a subtext that begins in chapter 1 when the narrator suddenly stops and asks the reader a question: "Have you ever loved a man, then lost him, then learned he lives on Fiji with a new lover?" (4). It continues throughout the novel, sometimes in regular paragraphs, sometimes in the form of footnotes. According to Mark Heberle, the invoking of the reader is used by O'Brien "as a *female* counterpart to Chippering," a woman who is "traumatized by her husband's having abandoned her for a younger woman" (*Trauma Artist* 264), just as Chippering is traumatized by Lorna Sue's having betrayed him for the tycoon.

However, there is a subtext beneath the more obvious subtexts that O'Brien teases the clever reader to find. Instructors can ask students who they think is really seeking revenge. Is it only Thomas Chippering, the protagonist? Or is it perhaps also Tim O'Brien, the author? The novel contains considerable evidence that O'Brien intends his audience to be those who share the same profession as Chippering—academics—most specifically, feminist critics who O'Brien may feel have betrayed him by unjustly condemning him as a sexist writer and a woman basher.[2] By boldly playing with language and gender concepts and by incorporating a playful subtext, O'Brien subtly reveals what is perhaps an author's thirst for vengeance.

Upper-level English majors and graduate students are most likely to notice the novel's feminist subtext. Thomas Chipppering—perhaps a chip off the playful O'Brien block—speaks the language of sexism fluently. When asked to identify examples of sexist phrasing, students can quickly point out that Chippering, who obviously notices the "droll, well-sculpted" (24) young women in his classes, terms them and other women "choice little tidbit[s]" (187), "attentive, worshipful, ardent young lollipops" (11), "tempting Swedish apple[s]" (290), and "tart little lemon drop[s]" (32). Furthermore, the courses he teaches are recognizable as parodies of academia: "seminar[s] on the etymology of gender" (116), the "Methodologies of Misogyny" (205), or "the homographs of erotic slang" (24). Chippering entitles his favorite course "It's Your Thick Tongue" (87) and attends the Modern Language Association's annual convention, where he delivers a paper, "The Verbs of Erotica" (109).

At this point in a discussion of the novel, it is useful to assign Lorrie Smith's "'The Things Men Do': The Gendered Subtext in Tim O'Brien's *Esquire* Stories," an essay that argues that in *The Things They Carried* "the female reader, in particular, is rendered marginal and mute, faced with the choice . . . of either staying outside the story or reading against herself from a masculine point of view" (18–19), that the only views of gender and war that O'Brien includes are the conventional masculine ones.[3] Instructors may wish to have students examine Smith's earlier article, "Back against the Wall: Anti-feminist Backlash in Vietnam War Literature," and four precursor stories from *The Things They Carried* published in *Esquire* in the 1980s: "The Things They Carried," "Sweetheart of the Song Tra Bong," "How to Tell a True War Story," and "The Lives of the Dead." It is especially on these stories from *The Things They Carried* that Smith bases her argument, terming O'Brien's "polarity of gender" "antagonistic" and the stories "pernicious" (37, 38), and it is to this type of argument that O'Brien playfully directs his subtext in *Tomcat in Love*.

Particularly offensive to a feminist point of view is O'Brien's use of the word *cooze*. When Rat Kiley in "How to Tell a True War Story" writes a letter to Curt Lemon's sister after Curt's death and the sister does not write back, Kiley refers to her as a "dumb cooze" (68). The narrator stresses the significance of the word choice to the reader: "Listen to Rat Kiley. Cooze, he says. He does not say bitch. He certainly does not say woman, or girl. He says cooze" (69). According to Smith, the story "climaxes and hangs upon the resonance of [this] one drawn-out, dirty word" and becomes "the jumping-off point for a meditation on the amorality of war" ("Back" 122).

It is important for students to realize that if O'Brien is aware of this critical point of view, then his playful use of the word *cooze* in *Tomcat in Love* is deliberate.[4] He names Chippering's newfound woman friend Mrs. Robert Kooshof. It's a surname that seems harmless enough, but in public readings (such as the November 1999 reading at the University of Arkansas, Little Rock), he has pronounced the name "cooze-off." Thus Mrs. Kooshof's last name becomes a play on words that denounces the objections of feminist scholars to O'Brien's having Rat Kiley call Curt Lemon's sister a "dumb cooze." O'Brien also has Chippering get into trouble for referring to the university president's wife as a "dumb cooze" at a black-tie event. The remark costs him the annual teaching award. "And over what?" he laments. "Two consonants, three vowels. What if the *z* and the *c* had been transposed? Would I have been blackballed for describing President Pillsbury's wife as a 'dumb zooce'?" (113).

O'Brien even has Chippering mention that Chippering's paramour is under the mistaken impression that he is writing an article for *Critique*, an actual academic journal that has published articles on O'Brien's work, including Smith's essay on his arguably misogynist view of the war. Feminist academics are playfully alluded to throughout *Tomcat in Love*. Chippering notes that an assistant professor in the gender studies department at his university, "a blackguard feminist who for years had [him] locked in her sights" (217), dislikes him. After he is publicly humiliated by Lorna Sue, Herbie, and the tycoon, he thinks, "I can hear the feminist flies buzzing at my buttocks, those jackbooted squads of Amazon storm troopers denouncing my indefatigable masculinity," and envisions "thousands of ill-mannered, cement-headed, shrill-voiced, holier-than-thou guardians of ovarian rectitude, each squealing with delight at [his] public humiliation" (213). He jokes about finding a job teaching gender studies after he is fired from the university, but instead he finds work teaching linguistics to toddlers, stating, "I did not descend to teaching gender studies" (239).

Interestingly, the women Chippering courts frequently outsmart him. For example, when Peg and Patty, two women whom Chippering meets at a bar, begin to tie him up, he thinks that they are merely "two youthful pussycats" (145) who are playing a kinky game of bondage, so he offers no resistance. When he realizes that the "bondage antics [have] gone a step too far" and that Peg and Patty really view him as a "pig," he asks them, "What did I *do*?" (148, 149). Peggy laughs and says:

> It's not what you did, man, it's who you are. Your whole sleazy personality. How you talk, how you walk. How you put the scam on every poor woman who walked through here tonight. Us included. Talk about an ogler. . . . You *don't* look [women] in the eye. You look them in the tits.   (149)

Even Mrs. Kooshof is no pushover. While she has succumbed to Chippering's charms, she is also not adverse to pointing out his immature behavior and threatening to kick him out. The middle-aged Chippering is frequently told not to act like "an eighteen-year-old" (19), perhaps another allusion to a criticism by Lorrie Smith, who condemns O'Brien for making eighteen-year-olds into vicious killers; and in response to her assertion that O'Brien presents the women in his *Esquire* stories as "dangerous" ("Things" 23), O'Brien has Chippering gleefully sing that he himself is "dangerous." In fact, he is more than dangerous; "I am," he states, "hazardous. I can kill with words, or otherwise" (27).

In contrast to *The Things They Carried*, *Tomcat in Love* does not contain the homosocial bonding that some critics have found present in O'Brien's work.[5] There are no other men with whom Chippering can bond and exert power over women or reinforce male values—he makes as many enemies of men as he does of women. As Patrick Smith points out, the novel centers on the solipsism of Chippering, who has "little regard for the thoughts and feelings of others" (137). He not only renders women mute, but as Jane Smiley notes in a review of the novel, he silences all the other characters as well, egocentrically focusing on his own voice at the expense of others (11).

Instructors may ask students if this silencing of the other characters, many of them women, condemns *Tomcat in Love* and O'Brien to more reproach by feminist critics. Feminists would argue, of course, that Chippering's use of only Mrs. Kooshof's surname renders her invisible, and Patrick Smith, who provides an alternate feminist reading in his critical study, notes that Chippering's refusal to call Mrs. Kooshof by her first name "relegates her to the same list as the women, many of them anonymous, detailed in his love ledger" (138). But as Heberle points out, Chippering's "misadventures with variously foul-mouthed, previously abused, sexually provocative, and/or shrewdly manipulative predatory females reverse the normal myths of male control and conquest" (*Trauma Artist* 291). The ending of the novel is especially significant, as it is there that Chippering succumbs to Mrs. Kooshof; begins calling her Donna instead of by only her last name, even though "the word *Donna* remains unwieldy on [his] tongue" (340); heeds her advice that revenge is silly; and relocates to the tropics with her, where she sells pots and he braids hair. In the novel's final paragraphs, Chippering also empathizes with the "you" whose husband "is in Fiji, with another woman," encouraging her to "[t]ake heart" (342) and blessing her—proof, Heberle believes, that Chippering is able to "sympathetically imagin[e] the suffering of a female Other who is not simply an object for ogling or adoration" (288). Instructors thus have even more fodder for classroom debate. Students can be asked to consider whether O'Brien is in danger of creating another misogynist text. Is the end of the novel too late for Chippering to acknowledge Donna Kooshof? Or is O'Brien showing us that people do indeed have the potential for change?

It is obvious that O'Brien delights in creating a battle of the sexes in which the women ultimately win out. By teaching *Tomcat in Love*, instructors can show students how an entire novel can be created as a response to a criticism of the author's previous work. O'Brien's focus on the concept of performance provides a final narrative clue to the novel's gendered subtext. Throughout the novel, Chippering calls attention to the fact that people, himself included, frequently perform. For example, it is easy for him to "summon . . . the evidence of tears" (76) at a moment's notice when trying to elicit sympathy or to portray himself as the victim of Toni and Megan's "flamboyant performance" (218) when they accuse him of sexual harassment in President Pillsbury's office. "In one way or another," Chippering declares, "virtually every human utterance represents a performance of sorts, and I, too, have been known to lay on the flourishes. I enjoy the decorative adjective, the animating adverb. I use words, in other words, as a fireman uses water" (81–82). Thus, while "performance" may refer to a variety of situations, such as Chippering's "youthful [sexual] performance" (105) with Lorna Sue or Mrs. Kooshof's feeble promises not to trust Chippering, which he deems only "a performance" (82), or his teaching Thuy Ninh to waltz—"we could have been actors in some silver-screen musical" (160)—the concept of performance also reflects the very idea that O'Brien is trying to get across to his audience. What writers do, O'Brien suggests, is create narrative performances, and their characters—whether they are young soldiers or lusty wordsmiths—are creations who perform for an audience of readers and who do not necessarily represent the ideas or opinions of their authors. "We live," states Chippering, "in a world increasingly populated by know-it-alls and backbiters and conclusion-jumpers and ignorant moral watchdogs" (89). And readers who ignore narrative performance and thus judge too quickly, O'Brien seems to be saying, fall into this category.

NOTES

[1] That is not to say that *Tomcat in Love* does not contain some of the more serious subject matter of O'Brien's earlier works. The novel's background includes the trauma of the Vietnam War, and characters cope with such issues as divorce, betrayal, self-mutilation, mental illness, and the desperate things that individuals do in an effort to hold on to love.

[2] In a 1994 interview with Brian McNerney, O'Brien acknowledged that he found the antifeminist charges by female academics hurtful ("Responsibly Inventing History" 15).

[3] In addition, instructors may wish to assign Susan Farrell's "Tim O'Brien and Gender: A Defense of *The Things They Carried*," which counters Smith's feminist views.

[4] As Mark Heberle points out, "*Tomcat in Love* seems an ironic response to such criticism. Chippering is both victim and epitome of the minicontestations and follies of academic life, which are broadly burlesqued in the novel" (*Trauma Artist* 304).

[5] For example, Lorrie Smith notes that "*The Things They Carried* preserves a very traditional gender dichotomy, insistently representing abject femininity to reinforce dominant masculinity and to preserve the writing of war stories as a masculine privilege. Specifically, O'Brien uses female figures to mediate the process in homosocial bonding" ("Things" 19). She uses Eve Kosofsky Sedgwick's theory from *Between Men: English Literature and Male Homosocial Desire* to explain "how O'Brien's representations of 'contemptible' femininity strengthen male bonds and deflect the contemporaneous assaults of an emasculating lost war, the woman's movement, and feminist theory" (19). If one reads the five *Esquire* stories in order, Smith argues, they "make up an increasingly misogynist narrative of masculine homosocial behavior under fire" (20). In "The Things They Carried," for instance, "imagination = women = distraction = danger = death. The story's dramatic resolution turns on recovering masculine power by suppressing femininity in both female and male characters. Survival itself depends on excluding women from the masculine bond" (24).

What High School Students Carry
to and from *The Things They Carried*

Kathleen M. Puhr

When I began teaching Honors American Literature at suburban Clayton High School in Saint Louis in 1985, I wanted students to have the opportunity to read a novel set in Vietnam. Few of the students' parents had served in the military; many had enjoyed college deferments or connections that allowed them to protest the war or ignore it altogether. I'm sure I wanted to provoke something in my students—mild interest, outrage, maybe a little guilt—and I knew that to touch them deeply I needed to introduce them to Tim O'Brien. In the mid-1980s the only O'Brien Vietnam War novel was *Going After Cacciato*. (Years later it remains a rich text for high school students, structurally interesting and narratively complex, allowing them to grapple with the frustration and delight of magic realism and the war's pathos and absurdity.) Then 1991 brought the paperback edition of *The Things They Carried*.

The Things They Carried is one of O'Brien's three personal favorites, along with *In the Lake of the Woods* and *July, July* (Puhr). It turns "Once upon a time" on its head, transforming specific narratives into universal tales. The tales that make up *The Things They Carried* speak to experiences that all of us know: fear, disappointment, courage, forgiveness, death. We may not have been to war, but we know what it means to be in love, to bear guilt, to tremble in fear, to carry physical or emotional burdens, to act courageously, to desire revenge, to offer forgiveness, to atone. O'Brien's fiction—and nowhere more than in this work—relies on one essential premise: the more we tell a story, the better we tell it, because the less the facts matter. What does matter is the truth. In *The Things*

They Carried—in the luminous "How to Tell a True War Story"—the narrator moves from absolutes to ambiguities: from "A true war story is never moral" to "if there's a moral at all," culminating in "a true war story is never about war. It's about sunlight" (68, 77, 85).

For O'Brien the art of storytelling involves tracing and retracing experiences, elevating them to the universal. We appreciate these observations from "The Lives of the Dead":

> The thing about a story is that you dream it as you tell it, hoping that others might then dream along with you, and in this way memory and imagination and language combine to make spirits in the head. There is the illusion of aliveness. (230)

> That's what a story does. The bodies are animated. You make the dead talk. (231–32)

> [T]his too is true: stories can save us. (225)

> [A]nd when I take a high leap into the dark and come down thirty years later, I realize it is as Tim trying to save Timmy's life with a story. (246)

The last word of *The Things They Carried* is "story." Stories save our lives, too.

Like *Going After Cacciato* and *In the Lake of the Woods*, *The Things They Carried* walks the line between what happened and what could have happened. The oft-quoted distinction that O'Brien's narrator draws between story-truth and happening-truth is a good thematic starting point for high school students. In "Good Form," the narrator writes, "I want you to feel what I felt. I want you to know why story-truth is truer sometimes than happening-truth" (179). He adds:

> What stories can do, I guess, is make things present.
> I can look at things I never looked at. I can attach faces to grief and love and pity and God. I can be brave. I can make myself feel again. (180)

Like all of us, high school students can appreciate that the more one tells a story, the truer the story becomes—a function, paradoxically, of both repetition and revision.

Students study O'Brien's work within the context of English II (10th grade English), which features an exploration of nonfiction narrative (*Black Boy*, by Richard Wright; *Night*, by Elie Wiesel; *I Know Why the Caged Bird Sings*, by Maya Angelou), the Bible as literature, *Othello*, essays in several modes, propaganda (George Orwell's *1984* being central to this unit), and various other teacher-chosen works. To begin study of *The Things They Carried*, teachers ask students to generate questions about the Vietnam War. Although many students have studied the war in history classes, they remain tentative and confused about what it meant at the time and especially about what it means to us today. Teachers sometimes show movies to help establish context; among the favorites are *Dear America: Letters Home from the Vietnam War*, *Platoon*, and *Apocalypse Now*. Students have seen footage from the Gulf War and the Iraq war, but their visual sense of the Vietnam War is virtually nonexistent, and seeing these movies helps them gather images. Teachers also show excerpts from the PBS series *Vietnam: A Television History*. Guest speakers—veterans of the war—share their stories with students, and often students are asked to interview someone from the Vietnam War era (not necessarily a combat veteran) to gain a sense of the person's real-life experiences. All these sources help contextualize the war for these fifteen- and sixteen-year-olds.

A logical strategy for starting a discussion about O'Brien's novel is to examine the design of the cover, particularly by comparing the cover of the hardback edition with those of the subsequent paperback editions. We note the progression from the plain black cover with the bold red and white letters of the hardback edition to the somewhat cluttered, and green, cover of the paperback edition published in 1991 to the cover of the 1998 edition with its depiction in black, white, and gray of soldiers, in silhouette, walking on a dike. Asking students to assess the covers and their intended audiences helps attune students to the connection between packaging and sales and rhetorically to the relations among subject, audience, and purpose. A broader discussion about the covers of mass-market paperbacks compared with those of trade books in the literature section of bookstores can follow. Students recognize that what transpires socially, politically, and economically has great bearing on the cover design.

Discussions of the title come next. One teacher at Clayton High School asks students to itemize what they are carrying in their backpacks, listing the items and estimating their weight. The students write an initial piece in response to the question, "What do you carry?" Sometimes, they're invited to model the writing style of the title story of *The Things They Carried*. Through these two activities, students are encouraged to recognize how the book explores the connections between concrete and abstract, tangible and intangible. One further activity, connected primarily with "On the Rainy River," is having students research the option of declaring oneself a conscientious objector. They write a letter requesting this status and exchange the letters anonymously in the classroom. The letters are assessed on their content and especially on their tone. Students are also invited to assume the persona of a soldier and write a letter home from the war.

Another teacher invites students to explore *The Things They Carried* in terms of the rules about storytelling that the narrator presents throughout the book. Students are asked to select a story and determine how it embodies one or more of them. For example, in "Sweetheart of the Song Tra Bong," one rule, or observation, is that when Rat Kiley tells a story, he makes the truth "burn so hot that you would feel exactly what he felt" (89). In "On the Rainy River," the rule is that O'Brien wants the reader to feel what it felt like to be in a canoe, just in sight of the Canadian shore, trying to decide whether to swim for the border. Students thus analyze not only the content of the stories but also the craft of storytelling as the narrator has presented it.

A thematic approach to the text is reflected in the assignment that another teacher gives. Students in small groups explore a particular theme in one or more of the stories and prepare four resources: a visual that summarizes the story, a handout containing quotations from the story that illustrate the theme, an audiovisual aid illustrating the theme in another Vietnam-related source, and questions for a brief class discussion of the audiovisual source. The themes and their related stories are Truth and Lies—"How to Tell a True War Story"; Surrealism—"Sweetheart of the Song Tra Bong"; Alienation—"The Man I Killed," "Ambush," and "Field Trip"; Nothingness—"Speaking of Courage" and "Notes"; and Fear and Trembling Anxiety—"The Ghost Soldiers." Students are given several days in class to prepare their presentations, and then each day several groups of students present their work.

In addition to what *The Things They Carried* teaches about the war and about numerous universal themes, it provides students with the opportunity to encounter what may be their first postmodern novel. A little literary theory goes a long way with high school sophomores, so teachers don't belabor the theoretical. They do, however, need to explain that postmodernism embraces uncertainty and ambiguity and delights in self-referentiality, narrative tricks, and other hallmarks of metafiction. Multiple tellings of the same event and the merging of author, narrator, and character befuddle and challenge readers of this text. But what is the purpose of education if not to challenge conventions and assumptions?

One of my own assignments is designed to establish the theme of multiple perspectives and multiple truths. I do this by assigning to individual students or to a small group of students one story from a set of four stories. Thus four or five students read only one of the following: "Speaking of Courage," "Notes," "In the Field," and "Field Trip." O'Brien's narrator in "Notes" links these stories:

> You start sometimes with an incident that truly happened, like the night in the shit field, and you carry it forward by inventing incidents that did not in fact occur but that nonetheless help to clarify and explain.   (158)

First, the students discuss their assigned story in their small group. Then, in a jigsaw format, one student from each story group joins with students who have read each of the other three stories. Every student then explains what happened in his or her story. Having read only one version of the events, students are understandably puzzled about what actually did happen; they are aware that they have only a piece of the "truth."

Student discussions within the context of this activity illustrate a central concern of all of O'Brien's work: the intersecting, sometimes colliding, perspectives from which we see the world. These different perspectives can both enlighten and disturb us. O'Brien creates mosaics, doling out pieces in seemingly random order, sometimes not giving us the piece that we really need in order to see the big picture. This can be frustrating to high school students, who tend to prefer neat and unambiguous narrative lines, but O'Brien — like William Faulkner, Toni Morrison, Gabriel García Márquez, and other celebrated writers — embodies in his work the fragmentary nature of our lives and the limited understanding that we bring to them. Even if students learn almost nothing else from O'Brien's text, they realize that the question "What happened?" never offers easy answers.

Over the course of the reading and discussion, students develop clear favorites among the stories. Inviting students to pick their favorites and to present their rationale for choosing them is another engaging activity. Debates can and should ensue. Students invariably name the title story as well as "On the Rainy River" and "Sweetheart of the Song Tra Bong." Regarding "Sweetheart of the Song Tra Bong," O'Brien has said in several contexts that it is the only "true" story in the text, but he may not have been telling the truth as we conventionally understand it. "Speaking of Courage" is worth noting because O'Brien told the interviewer Brian McNerney that he thinks it is the finest story he has written (McNerney, "Speaking"). I must state here that I would be misrepresenting reality — if not truth — if I did not say that although students appreciate the complexity of the author-narrator distinction, deep down they still want to know what actually happened and how much of the real Tim O'Brien and his experiences in Vietnam appear in the text. O'Brien has said that every high school class with whom he speaks wants an answer to these questions (O'Brien, Left Bank).

Ultimately, through their study of *The Things They Carried*, students recognize themes related to courage, responsibility, and communication. They come to see "Field Trip" as a response to the opening story, offering a symbolic and ironic resurrection as the narrator pushes something into the muck and takes something else — himself — out. The narrator rids himself of things he has carried, including Kiowa's moccasins ("old hunting hatchet" in the original hardcover edition [211]) and his own clothes. "In a way, maybe, I'd gone under with Kiowa, and now after two decades I'd finally worked my way out" (187). As students tease out the connections among the stories, they begin to appreciate the larger philosophical and stylistic concerns in O'Brien's text — namely, the interplay of surface and depth and our limited angle on any experience. They discern that the less we hold on to, the more we can grasp. Letting go of the expectations of novels and especially of war stories, being willing to hear the truth rather than just the facts, downplaying mere details, and holding on to the unbearable lightness of the story and extracting the simple theme are keys to appreciating this book. In the title story, the men imagine a bird carrying them away:

They were flying. The weights fell off; there was nothing to bear. . . . [I]t was flight, a kind of fleeing, a kind of falling, falling higher and higher, spinning off the edge of the earth and beyond the sun and through the vast, silent vacuum where there were no burdens and where everything weighed exactly nothing.   (22–23)

In our best work, we help our students to soar too.

Teaching Hemingway and O'Brien in an Inner-City High School

Reita Gorman

Teaching the American novel to inner-city students in public schools in Memphis, Tennessee, comes with challenges. Many of my students prefer watching the movie to reading the book. However, students' interest can be piqued when the stories relate to conflicts they face in their everyday lives. I pair novels and short stories to help reinforce critical thinking and reading skills as well as the moral lessons learned by fictional characters. Students read William Faulkner's *As I Lay Dying* and Louise Erdrich's *Tracks* to establish how multiple narration effects the reader's understanding of a novel's characters and the author's purpose. Students understand how stories change depending on the speaker's perspective, and for the first time they begin to realize that a character's narration can be unreliable. Truman Capote's *Breakfast at Tiffany's* and F. Scott Fitzgerald's *The Great Gatsby* are paired to help students understand why Holly Golightly and Jay Gatsby are driven to reinvent themselves. Through these short novels, students begin to see how unrealistic the idea of permanently escaping one's past really is. Ernest Hemingway's *A Farewell to Arms* and Tim O'Brien's *The Things They Carried* connect the ideas of internal and external conflicts that are more pertinent to students than ancient wars. (As difficult as it may be for educators to remember, students come to the readings with the notion that any event that occurred before their personal memory is ancient history and that ancient history and its stories have no relevance to their modern lives.) Since both Hemingway and O'Brien address the American ideas of the hero and the coward, my discussions of the texts focus on the realities and ramifications of these cultural icons and the application of these realities to my students' lives in the twenty-first century.

Textbook publishers widely anthologize Hemingway's "In Another Country," the short story precursor to *A Farewell to Arms*, and O'Brien's "Ambush" from *The Things They Carried*.[1] I use these short stories to introduce the novels. The psychological conflicts Hemingway and O'Brien present in their antiheroes are part and parcel of every inner-city student's internal dialogue. Hemingway's story is set in a Milan hospital after the narrator's injury. The doctor asks the character, "What did you like best to do before the war? Did you practice a sport?" The narrator responds, "Yes, football" (169). Since sports are a central aspect of most of my students' hopes and dreams, I begin the discussion by asking whether the doctor's diagnosis is realistic: Will this man with a knee injury be able to "play football again like a champion" (169)? The football players in the class know immediately that the doctor's statement is a lie meant to instill hope in his patient. They also recognize that the patient has to know the doctor is lying. We then discuss the psychological conflicts a former athlete might encounter when faced with the reality that his life will never be the same after an injury. We also consider how an injury will affect his masculine self-concept. The male students soundly agree that "real men" play contact sports, and they understand only too well the type of psychological conflicts that Hemingway raises.

The class then turns to the short story "Ambush" from *The Things They Carried*. In it the narrator answers his nine-year-old daughter's question whether he had ever killed anyone in the war. He lies to her, then writes the story he will tell her if she asks him again when she has grown up. First, I ask if the daughter, Kathleen, knows that her father has lied to her. Students think not. I then ask why parents lie to their children and what psychological effect parental lies have on children. Most agree that the lies are in the best interest of the child, although they may erode trust between the parent and the child if the parent tells lies in situations where the child needs to know the correct answer.

Once the issue of parental trust is introduced, we can begin the meat of the discussion, which is the psychological effect that killing another human being has on this former soldier. O'Brien first justifies the character's actions: "I was afraid of him . . . and killed him" (131). We then discuss how fear of others who are not like us often leads to regrettable actions, and we examine Kiowa's response to the kill: "that [O'Brien] was a soldier and this was a war" and that "if things were reversed," the other man would have killed him (133, 134). Students see this as a valid argument, given that it is perfectly acceptable to kill people in war. The discussion then swings to "anybody who is willing to kill you first," a subject that students can readily address. One student wrote in her journal that she had been expelled in the ninth grade because she brought a "blade" to school. This was because another girl liked her boyfriend and had told her friends that she was going to "take out" the girl so she could have the boyfriend for herself. The girl with the knife was "ready to defend" herself but got caught. The other girl didn't.

Another student wrote that his father was in prison for killing a man who had started a fight in a bar. The father cut the man's throat with a beer bottle and got a sentence of ten to twelve years for manslaughter. The student wrote that his father was not sorry he killed the man. He had to "do it or die."

From such comments, it is apparent that these students know the psychological conflicts that Hemingway's and O'Brien's characters face: life after injury and life after killing. Some students are planning, with the prewar zeal of Hemingway's Frederic Henry, on pursuing military careers following graduation. Others wonder about the legitimacy of the United States' involvement in Iraq and Afghanistan and the war's intimate intrusion into family members' lives. Still others are actively involved in organized and culturally related gang activity, where their personal worth and reputation are integrally tied to acts of violence and life-threatening conflicts. Inner-city students comprehend every aspect of the character Tim O'Brien's statement "I would kill and maybe die—because I was embarrassed not to" (59).

Both Hemingway and O'Brien place their fictional characters in settings where personal worth and reputation are tied to acts of violence and life-threatening conflicts, and both characters make the choice to join the conflict. Henry joins the Italian army (the United States had not yet entered the war) to experience the masculine heroic ideal of soldiering, even though it is in the relative safety of the ambulance corps. The character Tim O'Brien chooses between becoming a coward by draft dodging or a hero by draft-board coercion. In each case external pressure to please self as well as community leads the character to a life-threatening, life-altering situation.

The discussion of acts of heroism and cowardice associated with social mores begins before the reading of the short stories and continues through the reading of both novels. The discussion focuses on the perceptions that students bring to the readings. True to O'Brien's analogies to 1950s movie heroes, students spontaneously list characteristics of movie and television characters, sports icons, and recording artists. They recognize a few historically heroic figures like Martin Luther King, Jr., and Nelson Mandela. However, they know myriad cowards—fictionally, nonfictionally, and personally. I ask them to make lists of the characteristics of the hero and the coward as defined by our culture. They declare that cowards are "fools" who are "afraid" to act unselfishly to help or "save" others. (Interestingly, their definitions of cowards and heroes never approach the concept of someone willing to stand against the crowd.) After sharing the lists in groups, students decide on the qualities that constitute working definitions of each word. This dialogue is then followed by a series of free writings and, ultimately, persuasive essays about the clear characteristics of the hero and the coward in modern culture.

The students keep dialectic journals as they read. They divide each page into two columns and write key passages on the left side and reflective responses on the right. I propose questions for them to reflect on as they read the books. These are not one-time questions; students must be constantly aware of how the author deals with certain issues throughout the work. A key question is how the author presents the ideas of heroism and cowardice. The essays and journals become the visual diagram that allows the student (and the teacher) to determine how convincing Hemingway and O'Brien make their antihero arguments. The journals force the students to articulate their beliefs and consider how they themselves might respond in similar circumstances. Their initial writings allow the teacher to determine whether they can comfortably question their cultural belief system concerning societal expectations and, more important, whether they are making personal, real-life connections with the lessons and dilemmas presented in the books.

Class discussions target crucial passages in the texts. The situations in which Hemingway and O'Brien place their characters are more familiar than students initially recognize. Hemingway's Frederic Henry drinks himself to sleep; he also drinks to eradicate the pain in his leg and to socialize. His actions reflect the culture of the early twentieth century when the consumption of alcohol and tobacco was ubiquitous. O'Brien's Ted Lavender smokes dope to cope; his actions reflect the culture of American society in the last half of the twentieth century, when the wording of the DuPont advertisement became the ironic countercultural norm: "Better living through chemistry." Both Henry and Lavender openly engage in self-destructive behavior. Friends and casual acquaintances either encourage or enable each man to continue to destroy his body or his mind. After Henry is wounded, Rinaldi visits him in the field hospital. When Rinaldi leaves, Henry is "quite drunk" (77). In the American hospital in Milan, the porter smuggles in wine concealed in a newspaper. Henry's nurse, Miss Gage, hides his vermouth bottles from the head nurse, Miss Van Campen, who understands the damage that alcohol is causing to his liver, but his surgeon, Dr. Valentini, drinks with him, and Catherine Barkley pours the drinks. During his recovery, Henry wanders the streets of Milan drinking alone or with others. When his condition worsens to jaundice and Van Campen discovers "loads" of empty bottles in Henry's armoire, she alone accuses him of "self-inflicted jaundice" in an effort to "escape the front" (143–44). Only Van Campen reports Henry's self-destructive behavior. Henry and Gage understand her actions to be the result of her not liking him and being "mean" (145). In the face of disciplinary actions, Gage claims, "I'll swear you've never taken a drink. Everybody will swear you've never taken a drink" (145). Students understand this kind of loyalty, and they initially argue strongly that Henry's friends are behaving correctly. Most disagree with Van Campen's prognosis of alcoholism as an excuse to escape the reality of the front (144). However, some, who recognize the classic characteristics of alcoholism, make insightful journal entries—but they remain silent in class discussions on the subject.

While only a few of my students recognize the patterns of both alcoholics and enablers, almost all recognize Lavender, O'Brien's pill-popping character, and the need to deal with the death of friends. They quickly justify Lavender's addiction as ordinary, acceptable behavior. When I ask, "Why? Because he was involved in a brutal war?," their answers indicate that taking pills or smoking marijuana are acceptable ways to "ease on back" (231). Students also recognize the necessary stoicism in Mitchell Sanders's response to Lavender's death as a survival skill they too have acquired. Most, if not all, of my students have been personally touched by the death of a friend their own age or younger. One student wrote that he and others talked to their friends after they had died, just the way Sanders did. In his journal he wrote dialogue between himself and a dead friend opposite Mitchell Sanders's "Stay cool now. . . . Just ease on back, then. Don't need no pills. . . . [T]his once in a lifetime mind-trip" (231).

Students recognize some of the characters' actions as prideful, adolescent lapses in judgment. They see the actions of Henry's lieutenant-colonel when stopped by Italian guards during their retreat as an example of letting pride get in the way of good sense. Yet when the man chooses to be executed facedown in the mud rather than answer "stupid" questions, they acknowledge that they have made similar mistakes with parents and teachers. When I challenge them on the difference between getting in trouble and being shot in the back of the head, I always have one student who comments, "You don't know my mamma," and the class laughs in agreement. When Kiowa dies in a "shit field" because of a quick glance at a picture of Jimmy Cross's girlfriend, students recognize the momentary lapses in judgment that he and Jimmy Cross make. The characters briefly forget where they are and the danger they are in. Students relate this incident to times when they made a childish decision because they were trying to be nice to a friend. Several students wrote about taking a parent's car in the middle of the night (with no driver's license) to joyride or pick up a friend who had run away from home. One student wrote about hiding his runaway girlfriend in his attic for over a week, until the police found her and he and his whole family ended up in trouble.

However, the most clearly understood and hotly debated topics are the ones that center on Frederic Henry's responsibility for Catherine Barkley's death in *A Farewell to Arms* and Mark Fossie's culpability in Mary Anne Bell's deadly inculcation in "Sweetheart of the Song Tra Bong." Students enter the classroom full of opinions about the fact that Henry unintentionally impregnates a young woman with no prior thought of marrying her. When we read *The Things They Carried*, students are equally animated about how Mark Fossie unknowingly propels his high school girlfriend into "the shadows" of the thrill of the kill (116). These are topics that echo in their own lives. Virtually all my students know someone who got pregnant by a man who, in their words, only wanted sex. They also know someone who was brought into gang activity and whose personality became unrecognizable to his or her friends and family.

Many of my students have children at home. In my last school, there were never fewer than twenty students pregnant at one time. Teen pregnancy, for some students, is a badge of honor. That Frederic Henry and Catherine Barkley talk about marrying but never do is an issue only for those students (definitely not the majority—but extremely vocal nonetheless) who see the pitfalls of children raising children. The arguments on this topic are long and loud. The vocal minority see Catherine as a fool from the beginning. They find her too eager to please. They see Henry using her for sex, and they never believe, even when Henry repeatedly swears it is true, that he loves her. I have taught this book for several years, and I have never had a student who believed that Henry loved Catherine.

The topic of Mary Anne Bell brings out another side of inner-city culture that rarely is part of a classroom discussion. Inner-city schools have been inundated and infiltrated by gangs. Students, male and female, become gang members in middle school, and by the time they reach my classroom they all know volumes about gang activity, recruitment, and status. Colors are only one part of the formula. The pink sweater that Mary Anne wears takes on a different meaning within the gang culture. There is one "organized sorority," which is definitely not school-related, whose members dress in pink to show their affiliation. Students are reluctant to discuss gang activity openly, except in general terms. But they open up about how girls they know have crossed over into Mary Anne. Their comments are supported by the secrecy of the girls' activities. When O'Brien writes about "the Greenies" (and later, by association, Mary Anne), who were "far from social" and "secretive and suspicious" and "would sometimes vanish for days at a time, or even weeks, then . . . magically reappear" (92), students write about the similarities between these characters and gang queens. Students either do not know what these girls do during these mysterious absences or are unwilling to talk about it. One observation is certain: they fear these young women. They write about the look in their eyes, and it is apparently the same look Mary Anne has when she reappears wearing a necklace consisiting of human tongues. O'Brien writes, "In part it was her eyes: utterly flat and indifferent. There was no emotion in her stare, no sense of the person behind it" (110). Students clearly understand the look, and they know what the person who wears it is capable of doing and the pleasure such actions bring her.

One incident borders on the absurd, and students strongly relate to it: Frederic Henry's war injury and the incidents leading up to it. In the midst of random shelling and gunfire, Henry risks his life to retrieve food, and he and his companions are either critically wounded or killed while eating macaroni and cheese. Students initially wonder why Henry would go looking for food when his life is in danger. However, after some reflection, they begin to identify with his state of mind. "He's hungry!" someone will exclaim. The discussion turns toward the danger Henry faces, but the answers begin to echo: "They're hungry." Maslow's hierarchy remains intact with their resolve and Henry's actions: food before shelter.

Students find an equally absurd scene in *The Things They Carried*. O'Brien has just described in graphic detail Rat Kiley's savage attack on the baby water buffalo and the explicit particulars of recovering Lemon's body fragments after "the booby-trapped 105 round blew him into a tree" (83). My students are stunned by Kiley's destructive reaction to the loss of his friend. They are shocked by the difference a single step can make when two "kids" are playing catch. They even think the fact that Lemon and Sanders are tossing smoke grenades is reasonable for "kids fighting in a war." However, they balk at the absurdity of "Dave Jensen singing 'Lemon Tree' as [the soldiers] threw down the parts" (83). One student wrote that he could understand the mutilation of the baby buffalo, as horrible as it was—when a best friend dies, some people want to hurt someone or something. But the "singing and playing around" not only seemed implausible but angered him. Clearly, the student missed O'Brien's point in having the character sing; however, the student's comment also indicated that he profoundly understood the characters' actions.

Inner-city students understand only too well the scenarios depicted by Hemingway and O'Brien. The absurd actions and seemingly harmless personal choices made by the characters are actions and choices the students, or their friends, have experienced. They can appreciate O'Brien's character's decalaration: "I survived, but it's not a happy ending" (61). Students begin to see relevancies in reading about characters who lived and fought through two wars long before their births. They see the constancy of human nature that transgresses through time. The foreign countries and the named wars become irrelevant as we read and discuss the novels; the students' battlefields may not be in the mountains of Italy or the jungles of Vietnam, but the students understand life-threatening situations. They know Ted Lavenders, Lieutenant Henrys, Mary Anne Bells, Kiowas, Catherine Barkleys, and Timmys. They have a better understanding of human nature—their own and others'. They have transposed characters' absurdity and naïveté to parallel their own actions and thinking. They have discussed the effects of casual sex, drug use, and alcoholism. They become thinking, reflective readers, and some even begin to like to read. We cry together when we read "The Lives of the Dead," the last chapter of O'Brien's book, and we sit in stunned silence when Hemingway's Frederic Henry walks away from the hospital in the rain after the death of Catherine Barkley. But most important, students leave the novels with a life lesson that, because of their reading, they may not have to learn from experience. Students learn that O'Brien's and Hemingway's characters present the critical concept that joining can be an act of cowardice and the outcomes associated with accepted social mores are often an unhappy ending.

NOTE

[1] For a discussion of O'Brien's *The Things They Carried* as a short-story cycle, see James Nagel's chapter "The Nightmare as Resonance: Tim O'Brien's *The Things They Carried*" in his *The Contemporary American Short-Story Cycle: The Ethnic Resonance of Genre*. Since Nagel covers this topic so thoroughly, no effort will be made to duplicate it here.

The Things They Carried
and the First-Year College Experience

Eric G. Waggoner

In fall 2003 West Virginia Wesleyan College selected *The Things They Carried* as the standard text for its freshman seminar program. Like many institutions that assign common readings for freshman seminar, West Virginia Wesleyan College does so largely on the basis of a book's relevance to current events and controversies. *The Things They Carried* was chosen as a result of the war in Iraq, begun on March 19 of that year, in which some of our students and several of our students' friends and family members were serving.

West Virginia Wesleyan College offers two freshman seminar courses: a traditional one-hour Intro to College and a pilot four-hour Research Writing, which is open to students who have placed into Composition II. In addition to providing the standard Intro to College materials, the four-hour sections are multidisciplinary research writing courses in which students study a particular topic and write a series of research essays. Current and past topics include the 1960s in America, family communications, the Holocaust, human conflict, computers and technology. Students who opt to take the four-hour class can use it to meet both their freshman seminar and their Composition II requirements. *The Things They Carried* is the standard text for both the one-hour and four-hour models, and our experience teaching O'Brien's metafictional meditation on the Vietnam War in this variety of contexts suggests that it is an ideal text for a freshman seminar program.

The Things They Carried is a challenging book for incoming students, one that encourages them to examine their ethical values and assumptions in deep, personal ways. Though it is written in a fairly straightforward narrative style, its conceptual and rhetorical structure is complex and demanding. O'Brien depicts violent events graphically but clinically and without the moral contexts and heroic tropes common to conventional war narratives. The narrator's refusal to provide a clear ethical judgment or dramatic resolution in several of the book's more disturbing vignettes leaves many students feeling dissatisfied and confused, unsure of how they should respond.

Perhaps most significant, the discrepancies between the book's dramatic action and the verifiable facts of O'Brien's own life constitute a conceptual hurdle for first-year students. Readers familiar with the free interplay of fact and fiction in *The Things They Carried* sometimes forget how disorienting that element can be to students coming to the book for the first time. Students often report feeling cheated or betrayed when the O'Brien narrator-character admits to having falsified certain details in the text or when their independent research reveals inconsistencies between book and biography. This quality can be especially infuriating to students with a personal or family history of military service. In one memorable class session, a student whose father, uncles, and brothers were all Vietnam or Gulf War veterans actually threw her copy of the book across the room after she learned of the high degree of fictional embellishment in this work of fiction.

Why assign first-year students a work that seems so thoroughly resistant to historical verification, particularly when it discusses the effects of national and individual war trauma in such unsettlingly confessional and personal terms? And why do so during a year in which many students are coming to terms with the importance of rigorous research and authorial integrity in academic writing for the first time? In our experience, *The Things They Carried* is an ideal choice for freshman readers primarily because its rhetorical positioning in the gray zone between cultural certainties—bravery and cowardice, individual autonomy and the duties of community, past and present, even truth and fiction—is a useful point of departure for discussing the paradoxical combination of freedom and constraint that characterizes college life.

Several factors contribute to this usefulness. As I point out to my seminar classes, the students' demographic makeup is, at least on the surface, not unlike that of the platoon of grunts in O'Brien's book. The students are young—most of them are in their late teens; they have been removed from home and sent to an unfamiliar location for a predetermined period of time, with the expectation that they will perform appropriately under stressful conditions; and they have been thrust arbitrarily into the company of roughly twenty strangers from various cultural and geographic backgrounds. And in a somewhat less superficial way, they are responsible for their own survival; many of them are operating without parental monitoring and restriction for the first extended time in their lives, and the behavioral decisions they make can levy high personal, financial, and even physical costs.

In a comparative study of *If I Die in a Combat Zone* and *The Things They Carried*, Marilyn Wesley contrasts the literary realism of the former, a straightforward memoir, with the metafictional style of the latter. She links her observations to the rhetorical obsession with the "truth" of war stories in *The Things They Carried*. Arguing that the generic structure of the book allows O'Brien to explode heroic conventions and that the more traditional narrative of *If I Die in a Combat Zone* is largely circumscribed by them, Wesley suggests that

> it is only through the unflinching willingness to evade the consoling simplicity built in to [sic] the formulaic war narrative process that genuine responsibility can be attempted. (13)

Steven Kaplan likewise asserts that O'Brien's metafictional approach to the interaction between memory and history derives from a general human urge toward self-conceptualization, a process that demands that we continually revise our objective sense of our own identity:

> We constantly make new attempts to conceptualize our lives and uncover our true identities because looking at who we might be is as close as we can come to discovering who we actually are. ("*Undying*" 47–48)

In a similar way, the formulaic narrative of college success we tend to impress on freshmen—that the student who goes to classes, takes careful notes, avoids risky behaviors, and manages time well will succeed—is, as first-year students quickly discover, hardly a complete representation of their actual college experience, which is often unpredictable and chaotic, filled with frustrations such as arguments with roommates, financial crises, grade anxiety, rushed mealtimes, scheduling conflicts, and romantic dramas. The "genuine responsibility" they must develop in college is the result of a constant mediation between these two compelling but somewhat conflicting narratives: one ideal and orderly, the other experienced and chaotic—like the military and combat.

In addition to this broad thematic applicability, the range of subjects and concerns in *The Things They Carried* renders it adaptable even for the diversity of approaches in our four-hour course model. In the section on the Holocaust, the book's blending of fiction and nonfiction is emphasized in discussions of Holocaust historiography, and the question of bias in personal narratives is situated in broad historical contexts. In the class on human conflict, the class which presupposes "struggle and dissatisfaction as basic human conditions," the book is used to highlight "how such individual conditions, both biological and emotional, extend to and possibly even cause outer conflicts between people, races, and countries." Students in the class on computers and technology research the standards of military technology in the Vietnam War and subsequent wars, much of which O'Brien identifies by name in the titular chapter, and they discuss how our apprehension and understanding of our place in the world is often mediated by technology. As several commentators have pointed out, an updated list of the things soldiers carry would need to include virtual media and communications devices such as laptops, cell phones, and mobile music file storage systems in addition to static media like letters and photographs. The class on family communications focuses on the dynamics of communication between the "situational" family of soldiers in O'Brien's platoon and the biological family he elsewhere references, particularly the narrator's concern with how much, and in what detail, he should tell his daughter about his war experiences.

The four-hour seminar course I teach on the 1960s in America allows for a deep reading of *The Things They Carried*. To highlight the split between idealized rhetoric and actual experience, our first discussion centers on the difference between "macronarratives," or comprehensive summaries of historical events, and "micronarratives," or individual accounts of personal experiences within the context of those historical events. Proceeding from the assumption that the book cannot be understood outside its sociohistorical context, before we read it I assign a group project in which four or five students together conduct historical research and draft a quick study guide to the Vietnam War. Each study guide includes four major components:

> a descriptive time line of major events leading up and related to the war, beginning with the ousting of French colonial forces and ending with the removal of United States troops and the defeat of the ARVN in 1975

a list of major United States and international historical figures, with a brief (one- or two-sentence) description of their significance to the history of the Vietnam War

a short section that lists a few of the major contemporary and current sources of controversy surrounding the Vietnam War (e.g., the draft, the perceived lack of a coherent war strategy, and differing interpretations of which side "won"), with a short discussion of each

a short section that tracks the increasing cost of the Vietnam War to the United States as measured in money, resources, and human lives over the nearly twenty-year history of direct American involvement

Using the strongest elements from each group's resulting document, I compile and provide to the class a Vietnam Study Guide, which we keep handy as we read O'Brien's book.

One difference between those two types of narratives, as students are quick to recognize, is signaled by their more visceral response to violence when depicted in *The Things They Carried* as opposed to statistical representations of violence in historical documents. The official total of United States casualties in Vietnam, just over 58,000, is an upsetting figure to consider. But O'Brien famously claims in the chapter "How to Tell a True War Story" that one of the standards for recognizing "truth" in war narratives is that the story makes us believe with the *stomach*, not the head, and so after my students finish reading *The Things They Carried*, I ask which scenes or stories of violence affected them most deeply. Throughout the book five human deaths—Curt Lemon, by land mine; Ted Lavender, by sniper fire while returning from urinating; Kiowa, by drowning in an excrement-saturated "latrine field"; an unnamed Vietcong fighter, by O'Brien's grenade; and Norman Bowker, by suicide after he returns from the war—receive extensive and detailed narrative treatment. But the two moments my students regularly find most distressing are the mean-spirited Azar's strapping of a claymore mine to a puppy and detonating it (an event narrated in a single sentence) and Bob "Rat" Kiley's methodical execution of a baby water buffalo, shooting it to death piece by piece after the killing of his friend Lavender.

When reminded of the detailed appearance of human mortality in the book, my students counter that O'Brien frequently, though not invariably, depicts human death with an ironic distance that borders on absurdist comedy—for example, the platoon singing the trite folk song "Lemon Tree" as they pick pieces of Curt's blasted body out of high branches or Kiowa's pithy observation that Lavender was "[z]apped while zipping" (17). Even the stories of the Vietcong soldier and Norman Bowker, which are in no degree ironic or absurdist, are presented in meditative, oddly beautiful language that partially numbs the horror:

His jaw was in his throat, his upper lip and teeth were gone, his one eye was shut, his other eye was a star-shaped hole, his eyebrows were thin and arched like a woman's. . . .   (124)

[Bowker] walked down to the beach, and waded into the lake without undressing. The water felt warm against his skin. He put his head under. He opened his lips, very slightly, for the taste, then he stood up and folded his arms and watched the fireworks.   (154)

By contrast, the killing of the puppy and the buffalo constitute moments of unironic viciousness whose impact is sharpened, not blunted, by the characters' apparent cynicism. When castigated for killing the puppy, Azar protests, "What's everybody so upset about? . . . Christ, I'm just a *boy*" (37). Kiley offers the cornered buffalo canned peaches before shrugging and opening fire. The mitigating reasons given for these actions—Azar's youth and Kiley's grief—are invariably rejected by my students, who concede that these young men are caught up in extreme circumstances but are not willing to excuse them on that basis. As one student with military (though not combat) experience observed in a journal entry:

> Azar and Rat Kiley take out their frustrations on the nearest living thing that is not a U.S. soldier. In war there is acceptable and unacceptable violence, and these scenes are examples of unacceptable violence because the violent behavior is not motivated by self-defense or military necessity. They are simply killing for killing's sake.[1]

This notion of acceptable versus unacceptable responses to stress is mentioned every time I discuss these scenes with first-year college students. It is an observation applicable to virtually all the internal and external conflicts in *The Things They Carried* (particularly those in "On the Rainy River," which presents the narrator's torturous struggle between reporting for induction and crossing into Canada), and it is useful in moving class discussion beyond questions of factuality into considerations of reader responses to the decisions characters make, keeping in mind what O'Brien says about the value of story-truth—that in addition to making us believe in our guts, stories can save and preserve us. Connecting the events in *The Things They Carried* with first-year students' new and bewildering experiences requires students to consider the narratives of their own lives and the various ways they might script them during and beyond college.

Whenever a student raises that distinction, I ask the class to consider the differences between acceptable and unacceptable responses to difficult or stressful circumstances in their college lives: What is an acceptable way of attempting to resolve a conflict between roommates? What is an unacceptable way of responding to receiving consistently low grades in a particular class? What makes such responses appropriate or inappropriate? Do appropriate responses represent an attempt to impose order on their often disorderly lives, and can we also recognize inappropriate responses by their tendency to foster or exacerbate chaos?

In considering these questions, students always begin by speaking about successful college behaviors in stock phrases and general terms gleaned from their workshops with high school and college counselors. But if prompted, they gradually relate their own stories—some funny, some sad, some upsetting—of life in the dorms and in the campus commons. As they relate their and other people's "true war stories" of the first weeks of college, they begin to see that Azar's and Kiley's actions are not simply behaviorally inappropriate, which is the element of the stories that provokes their immediate response. The actions are also conceptually inappropriate, because they represent an attempt to respond to high stress by engaging in chaotic and aggressive behavior, a tactic that invariably results in injury and destruction. Because one of the main conceptual challenges faced by first-year students is how to maintain control and predictability over a multitude of commitments and responsibilities, the concern with order, chaos, and the difficulty of making appropriate choices in ambiguous circumstances makes *The Things They Carried* an especially useful text for first-year readers.

In a more sustained way, the notion of multiple selves emerging under stressful conditions is a principal element of "Sweetheart of the Song Tra Bong," the chapter to which my students usually respond most strongly. The story of Mary Anne Bell's transformation from a "tall, big-boned blonde" with "long white legs and blue eyes and a complexion like strawberry ice cream" (93) to an enigmatic oracle with "jungle green" eyes (106) and a necklace made of dried human tongues, told second- and third-hand by Rat Kiley to the men of Alpha Company, neatly addresses many of the critical themes of the book, such as the cultural linkage of masculinity with violence, the psychological effects of military training, and the largely ineffable nature of personal trauma. The chapter has been frequently criticized, most notably by Lorrie Smith in a widely quoted 1994 essay, as an essentially reactionary and misogynistic tale that only seems to deconstruct hierarchal gender binaries while it actually reinforces them:

> In the end, social order is restored and male homosocial bonds are reestablished. . . . Through storytelling, the men close ranks and banish the woman beyond the periphery of civilization.   ("'Things'" 36)

Smith's assessment raises valuable questions about "Sweetheart of the Song Tra Bong," but my students frequently cite Mary Anne's speech to her boyfriend, Mark Fossie, as the pivotal moment in the chapter precisely because it is the only place in *The Things They Carried* where any character (including the narrator) attempts to articulate the constitutional transformation effected by the Vietnam experience in subjectively descriptive terms. In other words, it is arguably the only place in the book where one character speaks to another *about* Vietnam from a desire to be understood:

> When I'm out there at night [on ambush patrol], I feel close to my own body, I can feel my blood moving, my skin and my fingernails, everything, it's like I'm full of electricity and I'm glowing in the dark—I'm on fire

almost — I'm burning away into nothing — but it doesn't matter because I
know exactly who I am. You can't feel like that anywhere else.   (111)

What Smith reads as Mary Anne's circumscription within the boundaries of
male narrative, my students tend to read as the inability of the narrative to con-
fine her, citing the soldiers' criticisms of Kiley when he attempts to finish the
story without a satisfying conclusion, summed up in Mitchell Sanders's protest:
"This elaborate story, you can't say, Hey, by the way, I don't know the *ending*. I
mean, you got certain obligations" (113). As one student pointed out in a class
discussion, the geography of Vietnam is consistently represented in *The Things
They Carried* as the most inscrutable element of the war, the one element of
the soldiers' surroundings that they cannot subdue through intellectualization
or physical violence. (Several cite the chapters "The Field" and "The Ghost Soldiers" as textual evidence.) It is into the geography that Mary Anne disappears
at the end of the chapter, her very body dissolving into the landscape.

When discussing "Sweetheart of the Song Tra Bong," students often posit
that the progressive and multiple selves that Mary Anne exhibits during her
time in Vietnam would likely never have emerged without the stimulus provided by the war. They seem to agree with O'Brien that though the catalyst is
external, her slow change is a matter of genuine metamorphosis, not simply
external reaction. As Rat Kiley puts it, "This Mary Anne wasn't no virgin but at
least she was real" (106). Of course, one effect of O'Brien's making Mary Anne
the central character in a tale about war trauma is that it attempts to defamiliarize the archetypal rhetoric of male war experience. But the deeper significance
of "Sweetheart of the Song Tra Bong" has to do with Mary Anne's conceptual
response to unfamiliar and ambiguous moral and ethical circumstances. As one
student wrote:

> Mary Anne buys into the Vietnam War as a testing ground for courage and
> violence, which is the same thing the men do. But she disappears into the
> landscape because she completely accepts the story that war is mainly a
> personal test. She accepts it so completely that she finally embodies it.

Her disappearance is one example of personal absorption within the larger narrative of war, a dissolving of individuality that recurs throughout the book in the
form of casualties, suicides, and post-traumatic stress disorder. The narrator,
who places his faith in the power of stories to preserve, rescues himself from
such absorption by writing his way out of disappearing and into a reasonably
coherent selfhood.

Each year since our initial selection of *The Things They Carried* as our standard freshman seminar book, West Virginia Wesleyan College's theater faculty
and students have sponsored a reading drawn from it, using text from "How to
Tell a True War Story" and "Sweetheart of the Song Tra Bong." Approximately
twenty first-year students participate, and the event is open to the campus and

attended by the entire incoming class. Female students read the "Mary Anne" sections, both individually and in unison, resulting in an external sign of an internal truth suggested by the book: that we choose among multiple responses to high stress and that the multiple selves we thereby embody are largely determined by the choices we make. And yet none of those selves are determinative; we have the option to revisit and revise our choices as we work to become who we want to be.

The student-performed reading provides an additional sense of community for the incoming class, an important aim of any freshman seminar course, and it allows students to engage with the book in ways that move beyond a traditional classroom context, a goal of any meaningful academic inquiry. In literal and figurative terms, our incoming class "carries" O'Brien's book with them throughout the semester, and our experience has demonstrated that *The Things They Carried* can encourage first-year students not only to reflect on war and human conflict but also to begin envisioning their own lives as a changing, and changeable, text—a concept that can help them start to internalize the responsibilities of authorship in both academic and personal contexts.

NOTE

[1] Unless otherwise attributed, all direct quotes in this essay are taken from discussions with my colleagues and students at West Virginia Wesleyan College, 2003–05, whom I thank for their assistance in preparing this manuscript.

Writing across the Disciplines
with *The Things They Carried*

Brenda M. Boyle

"Everything's an argument," claim Andrea Lunsford and her colleague, John Ruszkiewicz, in the title of their composition handbook. "Thus an argument can be any text—whether written, spoken, or visual—that expresses a point of view" (4). It is difficult to convince early college students that arguments can be so all-encompassing, are not exclusively combative or negative, and are not just a matter of opinion. It is also difficult to make college students realize they are responsible for producing arguments in their own writing. In my experience, few students new to college understand their responsibility to be producers of arguments rather than synthesizers and importers of objective, uncontestable information delivered by those whom they consider the *real* experts: published writers. This mistaken belief in who is an expert, who has the responsibility to make arguments, is perhaps the biggest hurdle for early college writers to overcome.

Using *The Things They Carried*, Tim O'Brien's "composite novel," in a writing class that emphasizes a writing-across-the-disciplines approach helps students deal with this obstacle (O'Gorman). One reason the novel works is that students like it. I have used it in a variety of literature and composition classes, from those focusing specifically on Vietnam War texts to those concerned with American war literature in general to first- and second-level composition courses. Almost all students—men and women alike—appreciate the book. But while I can count on students' enjoying the reading, I can also count on their not knowing much about the Vietnam War except for a handful of myths: that veterans of the war have universally been abused and spat on; that veterans of the war are a depressed lot, subject to sudden and irrational fears because of flashbacks; that most American citizens always were opposed to American involvement in Vietnam; and that despite all the above, war is still an appropriate venue for boys to be transformed into men. Belief in these myths is compounded by students' fear of argument.

The Things They Carried offers ways to get around both of these issues. The content of the stories puts the lie to, or at least challenges, many of the myths; the form of storytelling challenges the idea that a single set of coherent and nonconflicting truths about the war can be fashioned; and O'Brien's distinct interweaving of multiple Tim O'Briens—the author, the narrator, and the character—disrupts the students' assumption that only certain people have the authority to speak on particular subjects while it also forces the students to pay attention to which Tim O'Brien is telling the story. Given that students are attracted to the text, I don't have to struggle to get them to read and pay attention to it. Their attention may be attributable to the fact that, though many if not most of the texts we read for the class are literary, the writing assignments, intended to reflect writing expectations across the disciplines, are not literary analyses.[1] In short, students are willing to learn about this text because it does not (apparently) tax them and its many facets intrigue them.

A crucial element in getting students to feel responsible for argument is having them understand their and the text's rhetorical situatedness. That is, students need to know that as writers they are at least an equal third in the triangular relation among themselves, the text they are creating, and their audience. When they assume responsibility for their own arguments, they learn that good writing depends on the purpose of the text and the needs of their readers — and thus on having a flexible response to purpose and needs as they work to persuade their readers to believe them.

The five-paragraph essay is, in my experience, almost universally taught in high school as *the* model of exemplary writing. Most students arrive at college wedded to its template: an introductory paragraph, concluding with a thesis statement articulating three points; discussion of the three points in three body paragraphs ordered according to the thesis; and a conclusion that reiterates the three points discussed. Certainly, learning the five-paragraph-essay form is beneficial; it acts as a useful organizational tool, since an essay *should* have an introduction, a body, and a conclusion, and the form can be an effective template for hurried exam essays. What is a problem is students' religious adherence to the model, as it limits, if not eliminates, their ability to construct arguments that reveal their rhetorical situatedness. As Keith Hjortshoj argues in *The Transition to College Writing*, "Use of the five-paragraph formula make[s an] essay seem an empty formality rather than a thoughtful response to [a] question" (39). The abject self-consciousness of the narrator Tim O'Brien models for students the critical awareness that helps them move away from dependence on the five-paragraph form.

One way I get around its rigidity is to have students compose weekly informal works. Informal writing is not news to teachers of composition; we agree it is crucial to have students write frequently and informally so they can work out their ideas and see development in their thinking and writing. However, instead of having students write in journals that I might collect and respond to only periodically, I have them post to a weekly online discussion board. The students must write at least 250 words and respond to the current reading assignment. The venue also makes it possible for them to respond to one another's postings. Though I read and respond to these postings in writing, I do not participate in the online conversation. Unlike the private journal that only I see, this electronic informal writing is public, and students engage in casual conversation about the course's ideas. There they can voice their half-formed ideas and receive responses from their classmates without the pressures that formal writing or even classroom presence exert. In fact, in later formal essays I require that the students cite their classmates from this electronic source to ensure they are paying attention to one another as well as learning how to incorporate others' voices into their texts. Without the restrictions of the five-paragraph-essay form, students see just how complicated, elaborate, and authentic their writing can be.

A conversation that always arises about *The Things They Carried* is how to untangle the multiple Tim O'Briens. The distinction between author and character often is a difficult one for students to make in any text, especially fiction with a first-person narrator, and O'Brien complicates the difficulty. At the same time that the author works to gain the confidence of the reader in his first-person writer-narrator, the writer-narrator defies that trust by introducing a character of the same name. Thus the author O'Brien's work exemplifies for students the rhetorical awareness they should adopt, especially in the writer-narrator's first-person self-consciousness as a writer.

While the novel abounds with examples of the narrator O'Brien's reflexivity, the examples I use to model the writer-narrator's attentiveness to his rhetorical situation are the stories "The Man I Killed" and "Good Form." In the first, the narrator Tim O'Brien tells the story of a young Vietnamese man he killed. It opens with a catalog of the physical injuries to the Vietnamese man, and though there are two "maybe"s in the initial description—"a scholar, maybe" (124) and "He had been born, maybe, in 1946" (125)—the reader can overlook them, the possibilities about this young man, in favor of the certain things we know from the catalog. We know the young man was killed, and we know that the narrator O'Brien confesses to the killing. However, several stories later the narrator disavows his confession. "I did not kill him," he claims in "Good Form":

> But I was present, you see, and my presence was guilt enough. I remember his face, which was not a pretty face, because his jaw was in his throat, and I remember feeling the burden of responsibility and grief. I blamed myself. And rightly so, because I was present.
> But listen. Even *that* story is made up.
> I want you to feel what I felt. I want you to know why story-truth is truer sometimes than happening-truth. (179)

That a narrator would confess in his writing to an untruth startles students. Simultaneously, they wonder at the writer-narrator's concern for his audience. The stories demonstrate the writer-narrator's attention to his relationship with his readers as he constructs a truth that will evoke the appropriate emotional response from them, even though the "truth" is not what actually happened. Thus, instead of being understood as a complete and utter prevarication, the story of the Vietnamese man's death encourages young writers to manipulate language for persuasive effect. This manipulation, of course, is what students understand negatively as "rhetoric," that public obscenity in which only (rotten) politicians, (capitalist-hating) Communists, and (ham-fisted) tyrants engage. But it is the writer-narrator's admission about his manipulation that makes students not just forgive this move but actually admire it. They learn two lessons at this point: that a writer may manipulate language to serve his or her purpose and that one may be explicit about one's rhetorical moves. For students who often have been forbidden from using the first-person pronoun, the ability to use "I" can be liberating. For those who prefer not to use "I" but do want to be self-reflexive in their writing and discuss their rhetorical moves and concerns, O'Brien also provides a model. Primarily, however, students learn from these two stories and from O'Brien's distinction between story-truth and happening-truth that while academic writing must in some way be substantiated, it does not have to be definitive and absolute in its quest for a single "truth." This frees them to think critically and to develop truths, or arguments, in their own writing.

But before student writers can learn how to construct academic arguments, they must recognize argument. An early assignment I give them is to summarize a story in *The Things They Carried*, usually one of the longer ones, like "On the Rainy River," "Sweetheart of the Song Tra Bong," or "The Lives of the Dead." Few of my students have declared a major, and few of them have any expectation of being an English major, so part of my objective in this assignment is to persuade students from many disciplines to see that fiction is not simply entertainment but also argument. Each of the three longer stories includes multiple arguments—about concepts such as courage, masculinity, femininity, truth, and the purposes of storytelling. Before we discuss the stories, the students are asked to write the one-page summary. The assignment asks them to interpret a main point (i.e., the argument) of the story and its supporting evidence. The assignment implicitly presumes there is no single, correct interpretation of the story. When shared in class, these summaries reveal how multiple arguments can be gleaned from a single text, as different students invariably reach different conclusions for each of the stories.

One student might conclude that the argument of "On the Rainy River" involves the definition of courage. The writer-narrator writes, "I would go to the war—I would kill and maybe die—because I was embarrassed not to" and "I survived [the war], but it's not a happy ending. I was a coward. I went to the war" (59, 61). Another student, however, might focus on the relation between the Tim O'Brien character and the old man who hosts him at the end-of-the-season fishing camp, admiring the old man's willingness to allow the young man to make his own decision and reading that willingness as quintessentially American. Similarly, a student summarizing "Sweetheart of the Song Tra Bong" might see the story of Mary Anne Bell as a cautionary tale: that anyone, even the most innocent and "pure" American, could find the war enrapturing, that any one of us, even a woman, might be seduced by it. So argues Rat Kiley, the original narrator of the story, which is then retold by the writer-narrator:

> What happened to her, Rat said, was what happened to all of them.
> You come over clean and you get dirty and then afterward it's never the

same. A question of degree. Some make it intact, some don't make it
at all.   (114)

Another student might conclude that Mary Anne's case was not what "happened
to all of them," since Mary Anne does what none of the men did, not even
the weird, secretive Green Berets with whom she'd been going out on am-
bushes. Mary Anne disappeared into the bush, to the astonishment of all the
men. Thus a student might argue that a woman won't behave like "all of them"
but instead exceed the exploits of men in Vietnam, looking hysterical next to the
men's calm.

The value of this exercise is that students learn that fiction can be other than
entertainment and that it can yield multiple "truths." The exercise also teaches
them their place in the rhetorical triangle of writer-audience-text. They learn that
O'Brien the author had to gain their confidence as readers, and though his text
may have challenged their received notions of bravery, masculinity, and truth,
his gaining their trust makes them willing to entertain his ideas. Thus student
writers learn to consider their own audiences, to ponder how best to gain the
confidences of their own readers in order to challenge generally accepted
ideas.

Finally, using *The Things They Carried* in a writing-across-the-disciplines
classroom suggests to students the kinds of questions that can lead to effective
research projects. Because few of them understand the historical, political, and
military background of the war, most of their research questions fall under these
headings. Furthermore, because I am teaching students more about writing
than about Vietnam War fiction, I encourage students—the vast majority of
whom will major in disciplines like political science, sociology, communication,
and chemistry—to find a research topic that interests them, one that compels
them to do the research. This approach to the uses of fiction works because I
teach my students that fiction is a cultural artifact and, as such, can tell us about
the sensibilities of a period. (Just as O'Brien makes a place for both story-truth
and happening-truth, I see fiction as alternative history; *The Things They Carried* can tell us as much about the era in which it was published as it does about
the Vietnam War.)

If while reading and discussing, students express an interest in a particular
issue in *The Things They Carried*, I suggest that the issue may be appropriate as
a research topic. Otherwise, I meet individually with students to help them discover what topics in our class readings have interested them. The research project takes several weeks. From the beginning of the project, I impress on them
the difference between a research topic and an essay's eventual argument—the
argument being their ultimate goal. Once they decide on their topic, I have
them develop research questions that help them refine their research and develop an argument. After the students have developed the questions that aid
them in finding sources, I ask them to compose an annotated biography of ten

sources. The annotation process forces them to understand different writers' arguments and evaluate their usefulness.

By this point, students will have done enough research and thinking to formulate a paper proposal. In that part of the assignment I ask them to write on one page the problems or questions that led them to their research, to itemize the primary and secondary sources on which they will rely, and to propose an argument. Finally, after having learned how to select a topic, develop research questions, find and discriminate among sources, and construct a preliminary argument, students are ready to write their final paper.

I have seen research prompted by *The Things They Carried* on subjects as diverse as women in war and postmodern modes of storytelling. Students may be interested (especially now, a time of war) in researching the Vietnam War era's Selective Service after reading "On The Rainy River," or they may want to explore the involvement of Native Americans in the Vietnam War after reading "In the Field." "Sweetheart of the Song Tra Bong" can prompt research into the status of the women's liberation movement, both at the time of the war and at the time of the book's publication, the 1990s. "Speaking of Courage" can motivate an investigation into post-traumatic stress disorder. Students who want to engage in more conventional literary research and analysis are free to do so and will sometimes read other O'Brien works, especially his memoir, *If I Die in a Combat Zone,* and *Going After Cacciato,* to study the tropes, themes, language patterns, images, and narrative techniques he employs.

The Things They Carried is an emotionally and intellectually provocative work of fiction that resonates for students who are now living through more American wars. It is a book that demonstrates writing that is committed, nonformulaic, argumentative, challenging, and self-reflexive. In teaching methods of effective academic writing, I do not ask students to write fiction, as O'Brien does. What I do ask of them is that they accept the responsibility—and freedom!—of producing argument about ideas that fascinate them.

NOTE

[1] In a system of quarters, I would also teach two other Vietnam War novels, books like Bobbie Ann Mason's *In Country,* Larry Heinemann's *Paco's Story,* or Robert Olen Butler's *A Good Scent from a Strange Mountain.* In the longer, semester, system, I might add two other novels, books like John Williams's *Captain Blackman,* Bao Ninh's *The Sorrow of War,* or Joe Haldeman's *The Forever War.* Alternatively, I might add a couple of Vietnam memoirs, texts like Tobias Wolff's *In Pharaoh's Army: Memories of the Lost War,* selections from Keith Walker's *A Piece of My Heart,* or David Harris's *Our War: What We Did in Vietnam and What It Did to Us.*

How to Write a True Essay:
The Things They Carried
in the Composition Classroom

David Magill

In the first class period dealing with Tim O'Brien, I ask my students to write an in-class essay titled "The Things I Carry as a Writer." I ask only that they mimic O'Brien's style; otherwise, I give them free rein. They have just read the story "The Things They Carried," and they scribble their sentences onto the page. Many students use O'Brien's subjects as metaphors for their own process: pens as weapons, paper as territory to be conquered, words as enemy soldiers. The students approach writing as if going into battle. They throw their knapsacks onto their backs and march off to the assignment. They hunker down in the trenches of the computer lab, fire a few words into cyberspace, and then surrender their paper to me. Given their attitude, *The Things They Carried* is a wonderful choice for them. After a semester at war, they identify with the soldier-narrator and enjoy reading about him. In those twenty-two tales, however, lie lessons on composition that students need, from uses of discourse to lessons on style and the process of revision. By looking at O'Brien's writing, students can learn about their own processes and their own thoughts, eventually producing better writing.

The Things They Carried works well in a composition classroom because it is not simply imaginative literature; it deals with a historical event. Hayden White defines a historical work as "[a] verbal structure in the form of a narrative prose discourse that purports to be a model, or icon, of past structures and processes in the interest of explaining what they were by representing them" ("Question" 2). O'Brien uses a discourse that tries to explain past structures and processes, to "attempt a dialogue with the dead reconstructed from 'texualized' remainders" (Dillon 121). His book works as a historical icon, yet it blurs the distinction by mingling fact and fiction. As Linda Hutcheon notes:

> What the postmodern writing of both history and literature has taught us is that both history and fiction are discourses, that both constitute systems of signification by which we make sense of the past. . . . In other words, the meaning and shape are not *in the events* but *in the systems* which make those past "events" into present historical "facts." (89)

O'Brien tries to make sense of the past through writing, even while he "questions[s] whether we can ever know that past other than through its textualized remains" (Hutcheon 20). He uses language to find the answers, and he uses various forms of writing to "force language to reach beyond the meanings that precede and prepare it" (Kartiganer 73). Martin Naparstek points out that

The Things They Carried "resists easy characterization: it is part novel, part collection of stories, part essays, part journalism; it is, more significantly, all at the same time" (1). Precisely because it combines so many different types of writing, the book allows us to examine choices that writers make. O'Brien shows my students that writing is as much about form as it is about content, that the ways in which writers present their ideas matter as much as the ideas themselves.

I teach O'Brien's work within a larger discussion of writing as the conscious manipulation of modes of discourse, focusing specifically on reflecting, reporting, explaining, and arguing. O'Brien provides specific examples of all four types of discourse in the novel, often using more than one in the same story. By connecting them, he creates meaning through form. The various discourses, juxtaposed against one another, suggest the limitations of a fixed form in trying to define "truth." This juxtaposition "has the effect of drawing attention to the impossibility of producing an absolutist history, whether personal or public" (Thieme 44). O'Brien moves between the factual and the fictive, never demarcating the boundary. He slides between discourses, forcing us to follow the narrative, taking us on a textual journey toward illumination. But we never completely reach it. O'Brien notes:

> As a species, I believe, we are beguiled by uncertainty. It is both a gift and a burden. We crave knowledge, yes, but we also crave its absence, for the absence alone makes possible the joy of discovery.
>
> ("Magic Show" 180–81)

O'Brien will not give us the "truth"; instead, he tells us the story of a war where "the only certainty is overwhelming ambiguity" (82). At the end of "Notes," he writes:

> Norman Bowker was in no way responsible for what happened to Kiowa. Norman did not experience a failure of nerve that night. He did not freeze up or lose the Silver Star for valor. That part of the story is my own.
>
> (161)

O'Brien's statement, instead of allowing us to reach the truth, pushes us further away. The statement could mean that the story is fictional, or it could mean that the failure of nerve that killed Kiowa was O'Brien's own. His refusal to state the truth—his constant faith in uncertainty—is something from which students can learn. They need his ambiguity. Directness is not a quality lacking in my students; they know the answer, and they want to state it and move to the next assignment. O'Brien shows them that a full-frontal assault can leave them dead. For example, one student started a rough draft with the following statement: "Abortion is completely wrong." But as Nancy Sommers notes, "These either/or ways of seeing exclude life and real revision by pushing us to safe positions, to what is known" (29). After we discussed one of O'Brien's ambiguous spots, I asked the student to write the thesis as O'Brien might have. She returned with a new opening: "Abortion is a subject where people clash in a struggle with no clear answer." Her final draft was much stronger because she was willing to enter the dialogue and not simply espouse one side uncritically. O'Brien's text is often a lesson in negotiation; students can emulate this trait, gaining authority through ethos and making their writing better.

O'Brien uses the four types of discourse listed above throughout his work. My students spend the semester writing essays that tackle each mode, and they tend to compartmentalize writing into the "either/or distinctions" that Nancy Sommers delineates. But O'Brien works against that tendency because he juxtaposes different discourses in the search for meaning. For example, in "The Things They Carried," he starts with an explanation:

> First Lieutenant Jimmy Cross carried letters from a girl named Martha, a junior at Mount Sebastian College in New Jersey. They were not love letters, but Lieutenant Cross was hoping, so he kept them folded in plastic at the bottom of his rucksack. . . . He would imagine romantic camping trips into the White Mountains in New Hampshire. He would sometimes taste the envelope flaps, knowing her tongue had been there.   (1)

O'Brien explains to his reader the situation of Jimmy Cross. He does not simply report what he does; instead, he explains his thoughts and motivations. Then he shifts to another discourse, reporting:

> The things they carried were largely determined by necessity. Among the necessities or near-necessities were P-38 can openers, pocket knives, heat tabs, wristwatches, dog tags, mosquito repellent, chewing gum, candy, cigarettes, salt tablets, packets of Kool-Aid, lighters, matches, sewing kits, Military Payment Certificates, C rations, and two or three canteens of water. Together, these items weighed between 15 and 20 pounds, depending upon a man's habits or rate of metabolism.   (2)

In this detailed list of the physical items carried by each soldier, O'Brien uses an "academic tone that at times makes the narrative sound like a government report" (S. Kaplan, "Undying" 45). The cataloging continues throughout the story, allowing O'Brien to connect the physical weight and the emotional burden.

The third section returns to Jimmy Cross and to explaining:

> To carry something was to hump it, as when Lieutenant Jimmy Cross humped his love for Martha up the hills and through the swamps. In its intransitive form, to hump meant to walk, or to march, but it implied burdens far beyond the intransitive.   (3–4)

O'Brien here moves back to explanation, away from mere reporting of the facts. This movement between discourses forces the reader to analyze their connection, comparing the relative burdens of the things they carried physically and emotionally.

O'Brien continues to use this juxtaposition throughout other individual stories and in the book as a whole. For instance, "Speaking of Courage" is a reflective story and O'Brien follows it with "Notes," an explanatory discourse that not only sheds light on its predecessor but also explains "much about the process of writing" (Calloway, "'How to Tell'" 251). When I reach these two stories, I spend time reiterating the idea of revision in the light of a veteran author's work. "Speaking of Courage" originally appeared in the *Massachusetts Review*; as O'Brien tells us, its final form is much different. Kiowa's death in the shit field returns. Paul Berlin is gone. Norman Bowker takes the driver's seat for the ride around the lake. But is it rightfully his? We spend a class period examining the differences between the stories, between an earlier draft and a later draft. Why does O'Brien make his changes? Are his changes for the better? Is he forthright in "Notes," or does he have other motives? Calloway's look at the *Esquire* stories proves helpful in this case: "truth" is again subverted.

Along with the lesson on process comes another tidbit: writing is work. O'Brien himself notes, "Anybody who's done it knows that just making a simple sentence is work" (Naparsteck 11). My students prefer to see writing as a "magic show," full of conjurations that they cannot perform because they do not know the secret. They believe the magic of writing is in the putting of the words on the page, not in the creation of reality out of language, "the apparatus—the magic dust—by which a writer performs his miracles." They see words as monsters that will devour them rather than as "explicit incantations that invite us into and guide us through the universe of the imagination" (O'Brien, "Magic Show" 177). In other words, my students believe that the person using the apparatus is magical, not the apparatus itself. But I want them to realize what Paul Berlin does: "It could be done. That was the crazy thing about it—for all the difficulties, for all the hard times and stupidity and errors, for all that, it could truly be done" (*Going After Cacciato* 48). Hearing O'Brien discuss his revisions enables the students to see that all writers "pay attention to craft" ("Magic Show" 176). In addition to "Speaking of Courage" and "Notes," I often bring in other O'Brien magazine stories to compare with the finished product of the book. As Calloway writes, "Such differences in versions draw the reader into the text, leading him to question the ambiguous nature of reality" ("Pluralities" 214). They also allow the student to consider the idea of "product" in writing. "When is a piece of writing finished?" is a question I pose at the beginning of the semester. O'Brien provides a concrete example of the answer: never.

"That's what stories are for. Stories are for joining the past to the future"—so says O'Brien at the end of "Spin" (38). I tell my students, "*Essays* are for joining the past to the future." I want them to see the power of language, how it shapes our perceptions. I direct them to particular sentences in "The Things They Carried": "They used a hard vocabulary to contain the terrible softness. *Greased* they'd say. *Offed, lit up, zapped while zipping.* It wasn't cruelty, just stage presence. They were actors" (20). This particular passage allows us to discuss the power of language to change our views of a particular subject. In "Politics and the English Language," George Orwell says, "In our time, political speech and writing are largely the defense of the indefensible" (39). While Orwell focuses on the negative uses of language, O'Brien is interested in just the opposite. For him, language can help us speak the unspeakable. A hard vocabulary, the narrator tells us, allows the soldiers to handle the death of a comrade and continue; it offers a buffer against a reality too brutal to face head-on. O'Brien returns to this theme in the last story, "The Lives of the Dead":

> By our language, which was both hard and wistful, we transformed the bodies into piles of waste. Thus, when someone got killed, as Curt Lemon did, his body was not really a body, but rather one small bit of waste in the midst of a much wider wastage. I learned that words make a difference. It's easier to cope with a kicked bucket than a corpse.   (238)

Language makes it "easier to cope." "Stories can save us." These lessons are the ones I try to teach in my composition class.

Another sentence stands out: "They were actors" (20). O'Brien himself is an actor in his book, a character telling stories in such a way that the reader never really knows the truth about the experiences of the author Tim O'Brien as opposed to the narrator-character Tim O'Brien. He "makes visible the ways in which we use language to construct, confer, and consume identity" (Tremonte 54). Even the book's inscriptions shed no light as to the historical veracity of O'Brien's stories. When he seems most truthful in his stories, he backs away with comments that force the reader to doubt him. Writers create personae to tell their stories; budding writers must learn this skill by controlling voice and tone, by learning to make choices of viewpoint and discourse. My students read *The Things They Carried* to watch a professional writer at work, then forage out on their own, looking for ghosts to bring to life, as Tim O'Brien brings Linda back to life in the last story.

The Things They Carried is full of individual lessons on writing as well. "Sweetheart of the Song Tra Bong" is a wonderful lesson on how to write an essay. The story moves between the actual events of Rat Kiley's experience and the telling of the narrative to Mitchell Sanders and Tim O'Brien. After detailing the disappearance of Mary Anne Bell, the story shifts to the present. Rat asks where Mary Anne went, and Sanders's answer is illuminating:

> "The Greenies," Sanders said.
> "Yeah?"

> Sanders smiled. "No other option. That stuff about the Special Forces—how they used the place as a base of operations, how they'd glide in and out—all that had to be there for a *reason*. That's how stories work, man."   (101–02)

Immediately, my students and I discuss how to choose which items stay in an essay. A problem my students have is an inability to distinguish between necessity and superfluity. They throw their ideas out in a jumble, assuming they will all sort themselves out. We spend time discussing what *necessity* means, looking at sample student essays for practice; then they revise, looking to make their essays work.

The next interruption provides more fodder for the discussion of writing. According to the narrator:

> Whenever he told the story, Rat had a tendency to stop now and then, interrupting the flow, inserting little clarifications or bits of analysis and personal opinion. It was a bad habit, Mitchell Sanders said, because all that matters is the raw material, the stuff itself, and you can't clutter it up with your own half-baked commentary. That just breaks the spell. It destroys the magic. What you have to do, Sanders said, is trust your own story. Get the hell out of the way and let it tell itself.   (106)

Using O'Brien's story and various types of music, I teach a lesson on tone, first using classical opera and the band Nirvana as musical examples, then analyzing sample paragraphs using Sanders's definition of tone: "The *sound*. You need to get a consistent sound, like slow or fast, funny or sad" (107). I ask my students to remove the sentences that break up the sound. We go back to Rat's story, identifying the "half-baked commentary" that interrupts the magic show. Throughout this discussion, we are constantly defining tone in precise terms. The students go home to focus on their own drafts with a clearer view of what tone does in a piece of writing.

Another lesson comes at the end of "Sweetheart of the Song Tra Bong." Kiley and Sanders discuss the idea of a conclusion after Rat stops his story seemingly without an ending:

> "You can't do that."
> "Do what?"
> "Jesus Christ, it's against the *rules*," Sanders said. "Against human *nature*. This elaborate story, you can't say, Hey, by the way, I don't know the *ending*. I mean, you got certain obligations."   (112–13)

My students and I spend time discussing the idea of the conclusion and its "obligations." They feel Sanders's frustration when Kiley seems to end the story unsatisfactorily; I use this instance to demonstrate how their writing can be similarly inhibited. We discuss the nature and form of the conclusion, and I send them off to rewrite a conclusion for their paper using their newfound knowledge.

Ultimately, as O'Brien notes, "[W]riting is essentially an act of faith. Faith in the heuristic power of the imagination . . . [f]aith that language will continue to serve us from day to day" ("Magic Show" 179). My students have no faith; it is my job to show them the way. My mission is to convert them, to show them the power of the word. The problem is that they have trouble believing. O'Brien continues:

> And just as faith seems essential to me as a writer, and maybe to all of us, it seems also true that crises of faith are common to the vocation of the storyteller: writer's block, lapses of confidence, the terror of aesthetic subjectivity as the final arbiter of excellence.   ("Magic Show" 179)

Although he is discussing fiction writing, O'Brien strikes at the root of my students' writing problems as well, for many of them fear the inability to express themselves. O'Brien's struggles both as a man and as a writer allow students to see that they are not the only ones who are language-deficient, that even the best writers struggle with a language that controls and constructs them as they construct it.

As I stated earlier, *The Things They Carried* utilizes four types of discourse. By the end of our first week on the novel, students have identified the modes of reflecting, reporting, and explaining. They ask, "Where's the argument?" We then turn to "How to Tell a True War Story," a tale that O'Brien describes as "part essay and part fiction, but in a way it's neither" (Naparsteck 9). Although its title suggests an explanatory mode, the story moves from an explanation of facts to an argument about the nature of truth. It starts, "This is true" (67), but O'Brien interrogates truth in the rest of the story. "[I]n a true war story," he writes, "nothing is ever absolutely true" (82). He recounts a graphic story about the slaughter of a water buffalo, saying, "[H]ere's what actually happened" (78). At the end, however, he confesses, "Beginning to end . . . it's all made up" (85). He casts doubt on his own verisimilitude. He tells conflicting grenade stories, showing us "a true story that never happened" (84). As he says, however, "A true war story, if truly told, makes the stomach believe" (78). So too for a true essay. I want my students to feel the artistry of an essay such as Langston Hughes's "Salvation," where the end grabs you by the neck. I want them to strive for that effect. By questioning the difference between story-truth and happening-truth, my students can make a breakthrough, even if only for a brief moment. Alan France notes that "[t]hose who theorize and practice instruction in writing are becoming increasingly aware that they are engaged in the discursive reproduction of one 'truth-regime' or another" (607). O'Brien's book works well to undermine that regime because it consistently refuses to allow the reader any chance to find the "truth." Ultimately, O'Brien's argument about a true war story and my argument about a true essay are the same: they make the stomach believe. No other criterion is necessary.

When we reach the end of the book, I ask the students to look back and think about what argument the text makes as a whole. The twenty-two stories that make up the novel use the same characters and often the same events; I ask my students to consider what this says about the book. After a few timid generalizations about "the horror of war," they start to tackle the questions of truth we have discussed before. Some students connect the various writing strategies we have discussed with O'Brien's own craft. Every class, however, comes back to the last line of the book:

> I'm skimming across the surface of my own history, moving fast, riding the melt beneath the blades, doing loops and spins, and when I take a high leap into the dark and come down thirty years later, I realize it is as Tim trying to save Timmy's life with a story.   (246)

This quotation, and indeed the whole book, addresses the question, "Why do we write?" O'Brien tells us, "But this too is true: stories can save us" (225); my goal is to show my students this "truth" and hope that they accept it for themselves. O'Brien's book is about writing and life, truth and fact, memory and imagination, and the dialectic between the terms. His book is a survival guide for the composition student, full of lessons on art, on life, and sometimes on the convergence of the two.

Questioning Language:
The Things They Carried
in an Upper-Level Literature Class

Janis E. Haswell

In my senior-level English capstone course, I have sought ways to maximize learning opportunities centered on *The Things They Carried*. The key, I have found, is in the groundwork established by initial class readings and activities. The readings focus on major trauma events of the twentieth century: World War I, the Depression, World War II, the Holocaust, and the Vietnam War. We begin the course with three basic questions: What are the limits of language in expressing and communicating these events? What genre is more effective to use, oral (as in first-person testimony) or written (as in memoirs, poetry, and fiction)? How effectively do the writer's experience and abilities match up with the reader's expectations and desires?

Such questions allow students to draw on what they have learned from previous coursework: literary stylistics, historical periods, genres, narrative theory. In addition, at the end of the semester, simplified views about why and how we write are undone. *The Things They Carried* marks the endpoint of students' readings but not their reflections, as they apply issues we examined through the semester to a current event or research project of their choice.

Laying the Groundwork

The basic theme of the course is that "all telling modifies what is being told" (Langer, *Versions* xii). To frame this theme, we read the preface to *Holocaust Testimonies: The Ruins of Memory*, in which Lawrence Langer argues that oral testimony (as opposed to written memoir or fictionalized account) more accurately captures the trauma event in its raw, unguarded reality. In doing so, oral testimony widens the divide between survivor and nonsurvivor, since the trauma victim works to remember and recount the event rather than establish a bridge between himself or herself and the interviewer.[1] If readers value effective communication, written accounts will be more desirable. But if we seek the "truth" of an event, then oral accounts will provide a better path, even if it's one that fewer readers will be able to follow.

As a counter to Langer's view, we read Walter Ong's essay "Writing Is a Technology That Restructures Thought." Here Ong argues that written texts allow more sophisticated mental activities (like deep-level analysis, precision through revision, and abstract reasoning) than oral language does. In addition, the writer is constantly aware of his or her rhetorical responsibilities and so consciously bridges the gulf between writer and reader. Taken together, the Langer-Ong arguments prompt students to recognize (perhaps for the first time) that meaning is dependent on form. "All telling modifies what is being told."

While students see the value of the deep psychological exploration, complex symbolic development, ironic perspective, and parallel plots and subplots possible in written texts, they often prefer more simply structured testimonies. Certainly they find compelling Jan Karski's account of his missions for the Polish underground and also his journeys to London and Washington to convey the desperate pleas for help from Jewish ghetto and concentration-camp inmates. But because his *Story of a Secret State* reads like a polished novel, students are unable to ignore a sense of Karski as author, mediating and shaping events. Far more powerful for students are excerpts from *With the Old Breed: At Peleliu and Okinawa*, which E. B. Sledge began on the battlefield with notes hidden in his Bible. Students find Sledge's account more realistic because it places them more immediately in the events. In the same way, they are touched by Ronald Glasser's short story "I Don't Want to Go Home Alone" about the death of a burn patient in a base hospital in Japan during the Vietnam War (256–88). But more riveting is an account in Al Santoli's collection of testimonies, *Everything We Had*, where Mike Beaman describes his missions as a member of a Navy Seal covert team, penetrating enemy territory at night, kidnapping a suspected Vietcong sympathizer, then dissolving into the jungle (203–19).[2]

In an effort to gain access to and an understanding of trauma events, students privilege nonfiction over fiction: the closer to reality, the more effective the text, they assume.[3] In the early weeks of the course, reality is equated with what is completely factual, accurate, and true. And the facts of an event are better understood by eyewitnesses, who thereby make the account authentic. Authenticity renders a text reliable (because of the author's identity and experience) and unmediated (because of the raw, unpolished realism of the account). Realism, reliability, authenticity, proximity—these attributes render a text trustworthy and its language effective, or so students believe as they begin the course.

The problem with such equations (nonfiction = reality = authenticity) becomes more apparent as we proceed through the readings. The texts of Karski and Sledge are both nonfiction; they are both "factual" and written by eyewitnesses. While Sledge's book sounds like an oral account, its origins were written, like Karski's. A further complication emerges when we read *Maus II*, Art Speigelman's attempt to document his father's concentration-camp experiences during World War II while relying on his father's failing memory. This is followed by Dan Bar-On's interview with a physician who worked at Auschwitz and who still denies personal responsibility. Assumptions about eyewitnesses are tested, affirmed, and retested as students interrogate the texts through their reading journals, share ideas in class, and articulate their evolving reflections about language and genre in a formal paper at the end of each unit.[4] Here is one student's, Laura's, assessment of the issues raised in the course[5] before our reading of *The Things They Carried*:

The more removed you are from an experience, the less authentic something becomes. . . . [But] I think authenticity is determined not only by whether it's factual, reliable, or believable, but by the person reading. The reader must take into account the facts stated, how far or close the writer was to the event, whether or not it was censored or edited, and what genre the writing falls into.

Laura's idea of authenticity being in the writer's experience and accuracy—but also (secondarily) determined by the reader—marks a major breakthrough in the student's assessment of the complexity of language. Authenticity may be commanded by the writer-witness, but it is also conferred by the judgment of the reader. The issues of genre remain simplified, however, insofar as she is still thinking in terms of nonfiction as the receptacle or conveyer of authentic texts. *The Things They Carried* had a dramatic impact on her perspective.

Reading The Things They Carried

Does language allow experience, memory, and history to be shared? How does it do this? While it may seem that O'Brien challenges the efficacy of language—by deconstructing genre conventions, making and then rescinding claims of veracity, all the while toying with readers' expectations—in fact, *The Things They Carried* challenges simplified boundaries between fiction and nonfiction and, by doing so, modifies our simplistic assumptions about the purpose of fiction. By exploring the techniques I list below, students ultimately reassess their notions about authenticity and become convinced that fiction can equal if not surpass nonfiction in allowing writers to communicate experiences to the reader.

Imitating the Conventions of Memoir   Students reading *The Things They Carried* quickly recognize that O'Brien deliberately problematizes the demarcation between author and narrator. The narrator identifies himself by name (Tim O'Brien), age (forty-three in 1991), and occupation (writer). Because his stories appear rooted in the author's real-life experiences, it comes as no surprise that the book is dedicated to the members of Alpha Company—that is, the characters in the stories. Yet in "Field Trip" the narrator's ten-year-old daughter accompanies him back to Vietnam—a daughter who does not exist in the author's life. The narrator ultimately confesses that aside from his age and veteran status, "[a]lmost everything else is invented" (179). How do students respond to such rhetorical moves? One student, Kathy, had acted in a play called *A Piece of My Heart*, based on Keith Walker's collection of stories told by women who served in Vietnam during the war. She helped her fellow students understand the importance of accurate representation in art by saying, "When O'Brien was writing about all the various things people carry, and how much those things weigh, I really felt like he was speaking a language that I knew; he was getting the details right." Kathy helped us realize that details of a story can be accurate even when they are fabricated, just as her play was authentic even though it was staged—or because it was staged.

Multiple Versions of Events   The narrator offers multiple versions of various episodes (e.g., the deaths of Ted Lavender, Curt Lemon, Kiowa, and a nameless Vietcong). These versions are often contradictory, each one being presented as true but later renounced as false. The narrator corrects his "mistakes," then adds, "Even *that* story is made up" (179). Rather than being guilty of falsifying events, he ultimately insists that there is a distinction between story-truth and happening-truth. Truth is not mimetic; it is felt in the gut. Students can be frustrated, feel yanked around, by a voice full of contradictions. But on reflection, such variation makes sense. Listen to the comments from Eunice, another student, about Kiowa's death: "Everyone witnessed it from a different vantage and emotional point. . . . The different versions suggest that the company was very tight. . . . The stories show the grieving process of the soldiers/friends." Even though all the stories are different, the students can accept them as story-truth and recognize that they complement one another.

Claims of Verisimilitude   As we follow O'Brien's tales, we realize that yes, we'd "feel cheated if it never happened" (83), if the story isn't grounded in reality. But that is our mistake for expecting "[a]bsolute occurrence" between story and fact (83). Not all the tales of O'Brien's narrator are happening-truth. But they are story-truth. *The Things They Carried* is not a report of the war but a "rehappening" shaped by memory and imagination, placing storytelling or writing itself on a par with the war as the subject of the collection. If students enter into the spirit of the book, they might well find the outlandish "The Sweetheart of Song Tra Bong" one of the most psychologically realistic stories of the collection. Kathy, a student and a veteran of the Canadian army, reacts to it this way:

> I wasn't exactly the girl in the pink sweater and white culottes, but I was pretty close, and the military took me in and I learned to shoot well and move silently in the woods and be a good soldier. Those parts of the story I lived myself, so I know that can happen. As for getting sucked into the crazy "greenie" mentality, wearing a necklace of human tongues, well, if men can get that way, why not women?

Sequence of Chapterlike Stories   The bulk of the chapters in *The Things They Carried* were originally published independently as stand-alone short stories.[6] Choreographing them in a sequence creates (as in the modern poetic sequence) "disparate and often powerfully opposed tonalities and energies" (Rosenthal and Gall 3). Of course, O'Brien puts a new spin on the modernist convention of sequence, folding in the hyper self-consciousness that is characteristic of postmodern prose. The result is a reading process that, for students, becomes recursive. We normally expect that the later stories cannot be understood without knowing the stories that precede them. In this case, the full implications of the opening story, "The Things They Carried," are not grasped apart from the second story, "Love," or the closing story, "The Lives of the Dead."[7] In sum, O'Brien the author doesn't wish to inform us with happening-truth. Rather, he wishes us to understand through story-truth. Students (rightly) realize that authenticity is beginning to fall out of the mix, to be replaced by another value that O'Brien himself embraces: the power of the imagination.

View of War and War Stories We also consider the various narrative intrusions, such as the often-quoted passage "A true war story is never moral" (68). In this example, all the pieties about heroism, about moral cause and venerable tradition, are cast in derisive doubt. Rob, another student, understands this passage in the following way:

> If you want truth, you must be obscene, absolutely and uncompromisngly so, says O'Brien. Obscenity is the truth of war. He also comments that "any battle or bombing raid or artillery barrage has the aesthetic purity of absolute moral indifference—a powerful, implacable beauty" (81). This is similar to James Dickey's poem "The Firebombing," where he comments on the beauty of the moon and water and the blue fire down below him.

As Rob makes sense of what *The Things They Carried* asserts about war, he realizes that the subject of war's immorality and obscenity is only part of O'Brien's message. O'Brien doesn't just write about the war; he writes about writing about the war—which is quite another enterprise. O'Brien as author makes his readers remember we are in a book, not a psyche. Insofar as he makes us aware of the beauty of stories, he is writing a love story. "That's funny on some level," Rob notes.

> The song "Lemon Tree" is a love song, or at least it's about love. This is a subtle . . . what . . . allusion? I would say a well-placed thematic element of unity in the book, a foreshadowing of the revelation in the final story.

Metaconsciousness and Metafiction O'Brien's collection combines the metaconsciousness of an intrusive narrator with temporal and structural fragmentation to create a metaconceptualization of narrative itself. Story is "a form," "not a game"—so the narrator notes (179). As many of the students come to appreciate, narrative is not only a means of representing but also a means of understanding. The great distance between the narrated event in *They Things They*

Carried (the Vietnam War) and the later narrating event (beginning in 1976, when O'Brien published "Speaking of Courage," and extending into 1990) is that O'Brien has, in the act of forming his experience and memories into stories, realized their healing power. His stated purpose as the narrator Tim is to save prewar Timmy with a story.

The Seductive Power of Story

The moral continuum between Tim and Timmy, more than any other, speaks to students and helps them grasp how their expectations about authenticity in trauma literature reflects simplistic assumptions about language. O'Brien hasn't attempted to write the history of the Vietnam War or even recount his experience of it. As author, O'Brien seeks to realign himself morally with his own innocent boyhood, saving Timmy by placing him in a story.

O'Brien's notion of story-truth helped Laura reassess her definition of authenticity. She hadn't given enough credit to the power of the imagination:

> For most of the way through *The Things They Carried*, I was right there with O'Brien. When I found out he was making a lot of it up, I was thrown for a loop, and yes, a little angry. I questioned his credibility, his honor, *his* authenticity. Then I realized when I realized the events weren't real, they did not lose their impact. O'Brien forced me to analyze my concepts of truth, genre, and story, all of which relate to authenticity. By provoking this reconsideration, O'Brien forces the reader to question not only what's authentic in writing but also what's authentic in life.

In effect, Laura redraws the line between fiction and nonfiction by interrogating her own demand for authenticity in texts. Like others, she hungers for facts (the happening-truth) about the Vietnam War—an event sadly neglected and sanitized in our educational system.[8] But facts alone cannot inspire understanding, which springs from an author's attempt to "tell" and a reader's embrace of the resulting language that modifies the event. O'Brien's story-truth speaks to students; they feel it in their gut: they recognize it as human and valid, offered by an author willing to refashion experience through fiction (as Langer reminds us) to connect with readers.

Why do I teach war literature in an English capstone course? As Samuel Hynes notes, the telling of these stories "gives disordered experience order and therefore meaning. . . . [I]n the telling [the teller] finds the man he was and the war he fought, and how he was changed, and why" (284). That is, experience and language marry. That marriage does not simply reflect the facts of an event in a kind of dumb show but rather generates meaning, and that meaning prompts teller (and reader) to contemplate identity. As is often the case, the courage of my students continues to make teaching *The Things They Carried* more successful than I initially imagined it could be. While we would like to privilege experience and knowledge, what becomes deeply personal and therefore fecund with possibility is memory and imagination. These are the two pillars on which *The Things They Carried* rests; through them, students' lives are affected and their understanding of language deepened. The result is that students can apply these lessons to the oral accounts, written testimonies, poetry, fiction, and even media coverage of current traumatic events that engulf their lives.

NOTES

[1] According to Langer, written texts (whether memoirs or fiction) allow the victim to render the experience "tell-able" through the use of familiar genres, tropes, and so on. Too often the survivor falls into the trap of incorporating moral formulas that "rapidly disintegrate into meaningless fragments of rhetorical consolation" (*Holocaust Testimonies* xi). In her study of narrative patterns in written survivor accounts, Andrea Reiter is surprised by how abnormal experiences so easily lend themselves to conventional genres. She concludes, "It is astonishing how unoriginal the choice of these usually is" (170).

[2] Students' reaction is complicated by the fact that evidence suggests this testimony is fabricated.

[3] To simplify this section on the structure of the course, I omit our discussions of poetry, which is neither fish nor fowl in a fiction-nonfiction dichotomy. We weigh Theodor Adorno's assertion that to write a poem after Auschwitz is barbaric (qtd. in Schiff xx). We also discuss the different tones of poetry written about World Wars I, II, and Vietnam.

[4] Two other assigned readings complicate the idea of the eyewitness by examining the reliability of participants and observers. In *The Great War and Modern Memory*, Paul Fussell argues that memoirs are as much fiction as fact, an observation evident from the near unintelligibility of personal diaries (even to their authors who reread them after the event) versus the readability of published memoirs. Accounts by "objective" observers such as journalists can also be suspect. Phillip Knightly's essay "The Last War, 1914–1918" suggests that military and war journalists can strike diabolic bargains to bend the truth for the sake of winning and sustaining public support. In *Wartime*, Fussell argues that journalists and historians will not cover the truth about war because the American public insists on being spoon-fed Disneyfied gruel.

[5] In this essay I am reporting student comments from across four different semesters, 2001–05. I believe it is important to include comments from students to show the real (not just theoretical) instructional potential of *The Things They Carried*.

[6] Comparisons between the original version and the form of the story included in *The Things They Carried* reveal that the "I-narrator," whose presence unifies the chapters, came into existence only as O'Brien revised and assembled each tale for the collection. See Haswell.

[7] In English courses that take a more traditional approach to literature, comparing O'Brien's sequence of stories with Susan O'Neill's *Don't Mean Nothing* and Robert Olen Butler's *A Good Scent from a Strange Mountain* would prove a fruitful study.

[8] See James Loewen's chapter about the Vietnam War, "Down the Memory Hole," in *Lies My Teacher Told Me*.

NOTES ON CONTRIBUTORS

Milton J. Bates is the author of *The Wars We Took to Vietnam: Cultural Conflict and Storytelling* and *Wallace Stevens: A Mythology of Self*. He teaches at Marquette University.

Brenda M. Boyle is the director of the writing center and assistant professor of English at Denison University, where she teaches twentieth-century United States narratives and academic writing. She is the author of *Masculinity in Vietnam War Narratives: A Critical Study of Fiction, Films, and Nonfiction Writings*.

Russell Morton Brown is coeditor of *An Anthology of Canadian Literature in English* (now in its fourth edition). In addition to his essays on various Canadian writers, he has written on Canadian-American literary relations.

Catherine Calloway is professor of English at Arkansas State University. She is a regular contributor to *American Literary Scholarship: An Annual* and has published widely on Vietnam War literature, especially on the work of O'Brien, and in such forums as *Critique: Studies in Contemporary Fiction, Tampa Review, Bulletin of Bibliography*, and essay collections.

Doug Davis is associate professor of English at Gordon College, in Georgia, where he teaches American literature and creative writing. He is the author of essays on the relations of literature and film to American defense policy and is completing a book manuscript, "Strategic Fictions: War Stories of the Nuclear Ages."

Jen Dunnaway is a PhD candidate in American literature at Cornell University. She has written articles on the literature of the Vietnam War; her published work can be found in *Arizona Quarterly* and *Soldier Talk: The Vietnam War in Oral Narrative*.

Benjamin Goluboff teaches English at Lake Forest College, where he offers a course on the literature of the Vietnam War. His work has appeared in *Northwestern Review, New England Quarterly, American Studies*, and elsewhere.

Reita Gorman has taught for twenty years at Arkansas State University and Belhaven University and also in inner-city schools in Memphis and in a rural school district. She is dean of general education at Ozarks Technical Community College.

Jeremy Green teaches in the English department of the University of Colorado, Boulder. He is the author of *Late Postmodernism: American Fiction at the Millennium*.

Janis E. Haswell is professor of English at Texas A&M University, Corpus Christi. She has published books on W. B. Yeats and Paul Scott. Her most recent book is *Authoring: An Essay on Potentiality and Singularity for the English Profession*, written with Richard Haswell. She has also published articles on Tim O'Brien, Robert Olen Butler, and teaching trauma literature.

Mark Heberle is professor and chair of English at the University of Hawai'i at Mānoa, Honolulu. He is the author of *A Trauma Artist: Tim O'Brien and the Fiction of Vietnam* and the editor of *Thirty Years After: New Essays on Vietnam War Literature, Film, and Art*.

Tobey C. Herzog is professor of English at Wabash College, where he has taught nineteenth-century British literature, business and technical writing, and American literature about the Vietnam experience. He is the author of *Vietnam War Stories: Innocence Lost*; *Tim O'Brien*; and *Writing Vietnam, Writing Life: Caputo, Heinemann, O'Brien, Butler*. He is a Vietnam veteran.

Christopher Kocela is associate professor of English at Georgia State University. His essays have appeared in *Postmodern Culture, LIT, Genders*, and the *Journal of Popular Film and Television*. He is the author of *Fetishism and Its Discontents in Post-1960 American Fiction*.

David Magill is assistant professor of English at Longwood University. He has published articles on race and gender identities in American modernism and popular culture.

Derek C. Maus is associate professor of English at the State University of New York, Potsdam, where he teaches courses on contemporary American and world literature. He has coedited a collection of scholarly essays on Walter Mosley and has a forthcoming book on Russian and American satirical fiction during the cold war.

Zivah Perel is associate professor at Queensborough Community College, City University of New York. She is working on a project about Persian Gulf War narratives and the news media.

Jennifer Peterson is assistant professor of English at Morningside College. She has published essays on the cultural myths of the nineteenth-century American cowboy and the medieval English knight. Her research and teaching interests include twentieth-century adolescent fiction, twentieth-century American literature, and the nineteenth-century British novel.

Elisabeth H. Piedmont-Marton is associate professor of English at Southwestern University, where she directs the writing center and teaches and writes about war and American literature and modern American poetry.

Kathleen M. Puhr taught at Clayton High School in Saint Louis from 1982 to 2004 and now teaches AP English at Central Visual and Performing Arts High School. She has published articles in *English Journal, Modern Fiction Studies, Twentieth-Century Literature*, and *North Dakota Quarterly* and in an anthology about Vietnam War literature, *Search and Clear*.

Edward J. Rielly is professor of English at Saint Joseph's College of Maine and editor of the MLA volume *Approaches to Teaching Swift's Gulliver's Travels*. He has published ten collections of his poetry, biographies of F. Scott Fitzgerald and Sitting Bull, a study of the popular culture of the 1960s, and books on baseball and American society.

Alex Vernon is associate professor of English at Hendrix College. He is the author of *Soldiers Once and Still: Ernest Hemingway, James Salter, and Tim O'Brien*; *On Tarzan*; *Most Succinctly Bred*; and *The Eyes of Orion: Five Tank Lieutenants in the Persian Gulf War*. He is the editor of *Arms and the Self: War, the Military, and Autobiographical Writing*.

Eric G. Waggoner is associate professor of American literature and cultural studies at West Virginia Wesleyan College. His critical work has appeared in the *Hemingway Review*, *a/b: The Journal of Auto/Biographical Studies*, and elsewhere.

SURVEY PARTICIPANTS

Jon Adams, *Western Michigan University*
Virginia Agnew, *University of Florida*
Thomas Austenfeld, *North Georgia College and State University*
Jessica Baldanzi, *Indiana University*
Milton J. Bates, *Marquette University*
Mashey Bernstein, *University of California, Santa Barbara*
Brenda M. Boyle, *Denison University*
Will Brannon, *Cameron University*
Patricia Brooke, *Fontbonne University*
Russell Morton Brown, *University of Toronto, Scarborough*
Nancy L. Chick, *University of Wisconsin, Barron County*
Christine Peters Cucciarre, *Bowling Green State University*
Doug Davis, *Georgia Institute of Technology*
Glenn Dayley, *United States Air Force Academy*
Mark Decker, *University of Wisconsin, Stout*
Peter Dempsey, *University of Sunderland*
James J. Donahue, *University of Connecticut*
Jen Dunnaway, *Cornell University*
Stacy Erickson, *University of Iowa*
Charlotte Fairlie, *Wilmington College*
Petra Feld, *Johann Wolfgang Goethe University*
Joseph P. Fisher, *George Washington University*
Benjamin Goluboff, *Lake Forest College*
Jeremy Green, *University of Colorado, Boulder*
Janis E. Haswell, *Texas A&M University, Corpus Christi*
Tobey C. Herzog, *Wabash College*
Jen Hill, *University of Nevada, Reno*
Lisa Hinrichsen, *Boston University*
Dale Jacobs, *University of Windsor*
Michael F. Kaffer, *Spring Hill College*
Elizabeth Kimball, *Temple University, Philadelphia*
Katherine Kinney, *University of California, Riverside*
Christopher Kocela, *Georgia State University*
John Lennon, *Lehigh University*
Joe Letter, *Louisiana State University*
Derek C. Maus, *State University of New York, Potsdam*
Jennifer Moskowitz, *University of South Dakota*
Nicholas L. Nownes, *Barry University*
Zivah Perel, *Queensborough Community College, City University of New York*
Elisabeth H. Piedmont-Marton, *Southwestern University*
Kathleen M. Puhr, *Clayton High School* (Saint Louis)
Edward J. Rielly, *Saint Joseph's College, ME*
Cathy J. Schlund-Vials, *University of Massachusetts, Amherst*

Adam Sol, *Wilfrid Laurier University*
Susan Soroka, *Northeastern University*
Margaret Stiner, *Baldwin-Wallace College*
Gavin Sturges, *Souhegan High School* (Amherst, NH)
Nicholas J. Valenti, *Northern Illinois University*
Eric G. Waggoner, *West Virginia Wesleyan College*
Holly Welker, *Penn State University, Erie-Behrend*
Lynn Wharton, *King Alfred's College*
Jeanna Fuston White, *University of Texas, Arlington*

WORKS CITED

The Vietnamese and Vietnamese American authors whose works are listed here have been alphabetized according to family name. If the author is known in the traditional sequence of family name–middle name–given name, then this sequence is maintained and no comma is used in the Works Cited listing (e.g., *Nguyen Thi Dinh* in the text, *Nguyen Thi Dinh* in Works Cited). If, however, the author is known in the Westernized style of given name first, family name last, then the name has been inverted and a comma added (e.g., *Kien Nguyen* in the text; *Nguyen, Kien* in Works Cited). This style is also followed in the index to this book.

Interviews with Tim O'Brien are listed under the name of the interviewer.

Print, Electronic, and Miscellaneous Sources

Achebe, Chinua. *"Girls at War" and Other Stories*. New York: Anchor, 1991. Print.

Acker, Kathy. *Great Expectations*. New York: Grove, 1994. Print.

Acton, Carol. "Diverting the Gaze: The Unseen Text in Women's War Writing." *College Literature* 31.2 (2004): 53–79. Print.

Adair, Gilbert. *Hollywood's Vietnam: From* The Green Berets *to* Full Metal Jacket. London: Heinemann, 1989. Print.

Addington, Larry H. *America's War in Vietnam: A Short Narrative History*. Bloomington: Indiana UP, 2000. Print.

Allison, Dorothy. *Two or Three Things I Know for Sure*. New York: Dutton, 1995. Print.

Alter, Nora M. *Vietnam Protest Theatre: The Television War on Stage*. Bloomington: Indiana UP, 1996. Print.

American Experience: Vietnam Online. Public Broadcasting Service, 2009. Web. 4 Sept. 2009.

Anderegg, Michael, ed. *Inventing Vietnam: The Vietnam War in Film and Television*. Philadelphia: Temple UP, 1991. Print.

Anderson, Benedict. *Imagined Communities: Reflections on the Origin and Spread of Nationalism*. Rev. ed. London: Verso, 1991. Print.

Anderson, David L. *The Columbia Guide to the Vietnam War*. New York: Columbia UP, 2002. Print.

Anderson, David L., and John Ernst. *The War That Never Ends: New Perspectives on the Vietnam War*. Lexington: UP of Kentucky, 2007. Print.

Anderson, Donald, ed. *Aftermath: An Anthology of Post-Vietnam Fiction*. New York: Henry Holt, 1995. Print.

Anderson, Maxwell, and Laurence Stallings. *What Price Glory? Three American Plays*. New York: Harcourt, 1926. 57–89. Print.

Anderson, Sherwood. *Winesburg, Ohio*. 1919. New York: Penguin, 1960. Print.

Anderson, Terry. *The Movement and the Sixties: Protest in America from Greensboro to Wounded Knee*. New York: Oxford UP, 1995. Print.

Andresen, Lee. *Battle Notes: Music of the Vietnam War*. 2nd ed. Superior: Savage, 2003. Print.

Angelou, Maya. *I Know Why the Caged Bird Sings*. New York: Random, 1970. Print.

Anisfeld, Nancy, ed. *Vietnam Anthology: American War Literature*. Bowling Green: Bowling Green State U Popular P, 1987. Print.

Apple, R. W., Jr. "Done: A Short Persuasive Lesson in Warfare." *New York Times* 3 Mar. 1991: 4.1. *New York Times*. Web. 17 June 2009.

Appy, Christian G. *Patriots: The War Remembered from All Sides*. New York: Viking, 2003. Print.

———. *Working-Class War: American Combat Soldiers and Vietnam*. Chapel Hill: U of North Carolina P, 1993. Print.

Asquith, Herbert. "The Volunteer." *A Treasury of War Poetry: British and American Poems of the World War, 1914–1917*. Ed. George Herbert Clarke. Boston: Houghton, 1917. 153. Print.

Atkins, Stephen E. *Writing the War: My Ten Months in the Jungles, Streets, and Paddies of South Vietnam, 1968*. Jefferson: McFarland, 2010. Print.

Atwood, Margaret. "Death by Landscape." *Harper's* Aug. 1990: 49–57. Print.

———. "Happy Endings." *Good Bones and Simple Murders*. 1983. New York: Doubleday, 1994. 50–56. Print.

———. *Surfacing*. New York: Anchor, 1972. Print.

Auster, Albert, and Leonard Quart. *How the War Was Remembered: Hollywood and Vietnam*. New York: Praeger, 1988. Print.

Bahnsen, John C. *American Warrior: A Combat Memoir of Vietnam*. With Wess Roberts. New York: Citadel, 2007. Print.

Bailey, Beth. "Sexual Revolutions." Farber, *The Sixties* 235–62.

Baker, Mark. *Nam: The Vietnam War in the Words of the Men and Women Who Fought There*. New York: Quill, 1981. Print.

Bakhtin, Mikhail M. "Forms of Time and of the Chronotope in the Novel: Notes toward a Historical Poetics." 1937–38. *The Dialogic Imagination*. Ed. Michael Holquist. Trans. Caryl Emerson and Holquist. Austin: U of Texas P, 1981. 84–254. Print.

Balaban, John, trans. *Ca Dao Viet Nam: Vietnamese Folk Poetry*. Port Townsend: Copper Canyon, 2003. Print.

———. *Remembering Heaven's Face: A Story of Rescue in Wartime Vietnam*. New York: Simon, 1991. Print.

———. "Story." *The Best American Poetry, 1999*. Ed. Robert Bly. New York: Scribner's, 1999. 35–36. Print.

Bao Ninh. *The Sorrow of War: A Novel of North Vietnam*. 1991. Trans. Phan Thanh Hao. New York: Riverhead, 1993. Print.

Barker, Pat. *Regeneration*. New York: Plume, 1991. Print.

Bar-On, Dan. "The Physician from Auschwitz and His Son." *Legacy of Silence: Encounters with Children of the Third Reich*. Cambridge: Harvard UP, 1989. 14–41. Print.

Barritz, Loren. *Backfire: A History of How American Culture Led Us into Vietnam and Made Us Fight the Way We Did*. New York: Harper, 1985. Print.

Barth, John. "The Literature of Exhaustion." *Atlantic Monthly* Aug. 1967: 29–34. Print.

———. "The Literature of Replenishment." *Atlantic Monthly* Jan. 1980: 65–71. Print.

———. *Lost in the Funhouse*. 1963. New York: Anchor, 1988. Print.

Bartimas, Tad, et al. *War Torn: Stories of War from the Women Reporters Who Covered Vietnam*. Introd. Gloria Emerson. New York: Random, 2002. Print.

Bates, Milton J. "Men, Women, and Vietnam." Gilman and Smith 27–63.

———. "Tim O'Brien's Myth of Courage." *Modern Fiction Studies* 33.2 (1987): 263–79. Print.

———. *The Wars We Took to Vietnam: Cultural Conflict and Storytelling*. Berkeley: U of California P, 1996. Print.

Bates, Ralph. "Brunete Ballad." *"Sirocco" and Other Stories*. New York: Random, 1939. 244–52. Print.

Baudrillard, Jean. *Simulacra and Simulations*. Trans. Sheila Faria Glaser. Ann Arbor: U of Michigan P, 1994. Print.

Beidler, Philip D. *American Literature and the Experience in Vietnam*. Athens: U of Georgia P, 1982. Print.

———. "Calley's Ghost." *Virginia Quarterly Review* 79.1 (2003): 30–50. Rpt. in Beidler, *Late Thoughts* 153–73.

———. *Late Thoughts on an Old War: The Legacy of Vietnam*. Athens: U of Georgia P, 1991. Print.

———. "Re-writing America: Literature as Cultural Revision in the New Vietnam Fiction." Gilman and Smith 3–9.

———. *Re-writing America: Vietnam Authors in Their Generation*. Athens: U of Georgia P, 1991. Print.

———. "Thirty Years After: The Archaeologies." Heberle, *Thirty Years After* 10–27.

Belsey, Catherine. *Critical Practice*. London: Methuen, 1980. Print.

———. *Poststructuralism: A Very Short Introduction*. New York: Oxford UP, 2002. Print.

Berrigan, Daniel. *The Trial of the Catonsville Nine*. New York: Fordham UP, 2004. Print.

Bettelheim, Bruno. "Returning to Dachau." *"Freud's Vienna" and Other Essays*. New York: Knopf, 1990. 230–42. Print.

Bibby, Michael. *Hearts and Minds: Bodies, Poetry, and Resistance in the Vietnam Era*. New Brunswick: Rutgers UP, 1996. Print.

———. "The Post-Vietnam Condition." Bibby, *The Vietnam War and Postmodernity*. 143–71.

———, ed. *The Vietnam War and Postmodernity*. Amherst: U of Massachusetts P, 1999. Print.

Bierce, Ambrose. "An Occurrence at Owl Creek Bridge." *Great American Short Stories*. Ed. Paul Negri. Mineola: Dover, 2002. 171–78. Print.

———. *Tales of Soldiers and Civilians*. 1891. Ed. Donald T. Blume. Kent: Kent State UP, 2004. Print.

Bilton, Michael, and Kevin Sim. *Four Hours in My Lai*. New York: Penguin, 1992. Print.

Bishop, Elizabeth. "In the Waiting Room." *The Complete Poems: 1927–1979*. New York: Farrar, 1983. 159–61. Print.

Bloom, Alexander, and Wini Brienes, eds. *"Takin' It to the Streets": A Sixties Reader*. New York: Oxford UP, 2003. Print.

Bodemer, Margaret B. Rev. of *Ao Dai: My War, My Country, My Vietnam*, by Xuan Phuong and Danièle Mazingarbe. *Explorations in Southeast Asian Studies* 6.1 (2006): 45–47. Print.

Bolt, Ernest, and Amanda Garrett. *People's War and Tran Van Tra*. U of Richmond, 1999. Web. 10 Sept. 2009.

Bonn, Maria S. "Can Stories Save Us? Tim O'Brien and the Efficacy of the Text." *Critique: Studies in Contemporary Fiction* 36.1 (1994): 2–15. Print.

Borton, Lady. *After Sorrow: An American among the Vietnamese*. New York: Viking, 1995. Print.

———. "A Boom, a Billow." Van Devanter and Furey 13.

———. "Row upon Endless Row." Van Devanter and Furey 53.

———. *Sensing the Enemy: An American Woman among the Boat People of Vietnam*. Garden City: Doubleday, 1984. Print.

———. "Walking Class." Van Devanter and Furey 25.

Bosmajian, Haig A. *Freedom Not to Speak*. New York: New York UP, 1999. Print.

Bowen, Kevin, and Nguyen Ba Chung, eds. and trans. *Six Vietnamese Poets*. Willimantic: Curbstone, 2002. Print.

Bowen, Kevin, and Bruce Weigl, eds. *Writing between the Lines: An Anthology on War and Its Social Consequences*. Amherst: U of Massachusetts P, 1997. Print.

Bowen, Kevin, Bruce Weigl, and Nguyen Ba Chung, eds. *Mountain River: Vietnamese Poetry from the Wars, 1948–1993*. Amherst: U of Massachusetts P, 1998. Print.

Bowie, Thomas G. "Reconciling Vietnam: Tim O'Brien's Narrative Journey." *The United States and Viet Nam from War to Peace*. Ed. Robert M. Slabey. Jefferson: McFarland, 1996. 184–97. Print.

Bowman, John S., ed. *The Vietnam War: An Almanac*. New York: World Almanac, 1985. Print.

Boyer, Paul. *By the Bomb's Early Light: American Thought and Culture at the Dawn of the Atomic Age*. Chapel Hill: U of North Carolina P, 1994. Print.

Boyle, Brenda M. *Masculinity in Vietnam War Narratives: A Critical Study of Fiction, Films, and Nonfiction Writings*. Jefferson: McFarland, 2009. Print.

Bradley, Mark Philip. *Imagining Vietnam and America: The Making of Postcolonial Vietnam, 1919–1950*. Chapel Hill: U of North Carolina P, 2000. Print.

Brand, Dionne. *A Map of the Door of No Return: Notes to Belonging*. Mississauga: Random, 2001. Print.

Brands, H. W. *The Devil We Knew: Americans and the Cold War*. New York: Oxford UP, 1993. Print.

Brigham, Robert K. *ARVN: Life and Death in the South Vietnamese Army*. Lawrence: UP of Kansas, 2006. Print.

Brokaw, Tom. *The Greatest Generation*. New York: Random, 1998. Print.

Brown, Harry. *A Walk in the Sun*. 1944. Lincoln: U of Nebraska P, 1998. Print.

Brown, Russell [Morton]. "The Road Home." *Context North America: Canadian/U.S. Literary Relations*. Ed. Camille R. La Bossière. Ottawa: U of Ottawa P, 1994. 23–48. Print.

Brown, T. Louise. *War and Aftermath in Vietnam*. London: Routledge, 1991. Print.

Brownmiller, Susan. *Against Our Will: Men, Women, and Rape*. 1975. New York: Ballantine, 1993. Print.

Broyles, William, Jr. "Vietnam: How the War Became the Movie." *Smart* 11 (1990): 81–96. Print.

———. "Why Men Love War." *Esquire* Nov. 1984: 55–65. Print.

Brune, Lester H., and Richard Dean Burns. *America and the Indochina Wars, 1945–1990: A Bibliographical Guide*. Claremont: Regina, 1992. Print.

Bui Diem. *In the Jaws of History*. Bloomington: Indiana UP, 1999. Print.

Bui Tin. *Following Ho Chi Minh: The Memoirs of a North Vietnamese Colonel*. Honolulu: U of Hawai'i P, 1995. Print.

———. *From Enemy to Friend: A North Vietnamese Perspective on the War*. Trans. Nguyen N. Bich. Annapolis: Naval Inst. P., 2002. Print.

Burke, Carol. *Camp All-American, Hanoi Jane, and the High-and-Tight: Gender, Folklore, and Changing Military Culture*. Boston: Beacon, 2004. Print.

Burns, John Horne. *The Gallery*. 1947. New York: New York Review Books, 2004. Print.

Burrows, Larry. *Vietnam*. Introd. David Halberstam. New York: Knopf, 2002. Print.

Butler, Deborah A. *American Women Writers on Vietnam: Unheard Voices—A Selected Annotated Bibliography*. New York: Garland, 1990. Print.

Butler, Robert Olen. *A Good Scent from a Strange Mountain*. 1992. Expanded ed. New York: Penguin, 2001. Print.

Buzzell, Colby. *My War: Killing Time in Iraq*. New York: Berkley, 2005. Print.

Calloway, Catherine. "American Literature and Film of the Vietnam War: Classroom Strategies and Critical Sources." Gilbert, *Vietnam War* 139–59.

———. "History Has a Way of Dissolving: A Conversation with Tim O'Brien." *Tampa Review* 20 (2000): 25–35. Print.

———. "'How to Tell a True War Story': Metafiction in *The Things They Carried*." *Critique: Studies in Contemporary Fiction* 36.4 (1995): 249–57. Print.

———. "Pluralities of Vision: *Going After Cacciato* and Tim O'Brien's Short Fiction." Gilman and Smith 213–24.

———. "Tim O'Brien: A Checklist." *Bulletin of Bibliography* 48.1 (1991): 6–11. Print.

———. "Tim O'Brien (1946–): A Primary and Secondary Bibliography." *Bulletin of Bibliography* 50.3 (1993): 223–29. Print.

Campbell, Christopher D. "Conversation across a Century: The War Stories of Ambrose Bierce and Tim O'Brien." *War, Literature, and the Arts: An International Journal of the Humanities* 10.2 (1998): 267–88. Print.

Cantelon, Philip L., Richard G. Hewlett, and Robert C. Williams, eds. *The American Atom: A Documentary History of Nuclear Policies from the Discovery of Fission to the Present.* 2nd ed. Philadelphia: U of Pennsylvania P, 1991. Print.

Cao, Lan. *Monkey Bridge.* New York: Viking, 1997. Print.

Capps, Walter H., ed. *The Vietnam Reader.* London: Routledge, 1991. Print.

Caputo, Philip. "In the Forest of the Laughing Elephant." *Exiles: Three Short Novels.* New York: Knopf, 1997. 255–353. Print.

———. *A Rumor of War.* 1977. New York: Henry Holt, 1996. Print.

———. *10,000 Days of Thunder: A History of the Vietnam War.* New York: Simon, 2005. Print.

Carpenter, Lucas. "'It Don't Mean Nothin': Vietnam War Fiction and Postmodernism." *College Literature* 30.2 (2003): 30–50. Print.

———. "Vietnam War." *Encyclopedia of American War Literature.* Ed. Philip K. Jason and Mark A. Graves. Westport: Greenwood, 2001. 348–52. Print.

Carroll, Andrew, ed. *Operation Homecoming: Iraq, Afghanistan, and the Home Front, in the Words of U.S. Troops and Their Families.* New York: Random, 2006. Print.

Carton, Evan. "Vietnam and the Limits of Masculinity." *American Literary History* 3.2 (1991): 294–318. Print.

Caruth, Cathy. *Trauma: Explorations in Memory.* Baltimore: Johns Hopkins UP, 1995. Print.

———. *Unclaimed Experience: Trauma, Narrative, and History.* Baltimore: Johns Hopkins UP, 1996. Print.

Casey, Michael. *Obscenities.* New Haven: Yale UP, 1972. Print.

Celan, Paul. "Todesfuge." *Selected Poems and Prose of Paul Celan.* Trans. John Felstiner. New York: Norton, 2000. 30–33. Print.

Chanoff, David, and Doan Van Toai. *"Vietnam": A Portrait of Its People at War.* 1986. New York: Tauris, 2001. Print.

Chatman, Seymour Benjamin. *Story and Discourse: Narrative Structure in Fiction and Film.* Ithaca: Cornell UP, 1978. Print.

Chattarji, Subarno. *Memories of a Lost War: American Poetic Responses to the Vietnam War.* New York: Oxford UP, 2001. Print.

Cheever, John. "The Swimmer." *The Stories of John Cheever.* New York: Vintage, 2000. 603–12. Print.

Chen, Tina. "'Unraveling the Deeper Meaning': Exile and the Embodied Poetics of Displacement in Tim O'Brien's *The Things They Carried.*" *Contemporary Literature* 39.1 (1998): 77–98. Print.

Choy, Wayson. *Paper Shadows: A Chinatown Childhood.* New York: Penguin, 1999. Print.

Christopher, Renny. *The Viet Nam War / The American War: Images and Representations in Euro-American and Vietnamese Exile Narratives.* Amherst: U of Massachusetts P, 1995. Print.

Clark, Gregory R. *Words of the Vietnam War: The Slang, Jargon, Abbreviations, Acronyms, Nomenclature, Nicknames, Pseudonyms, Slogans, Specs, Euphemisms, Double-Talk, Chants, and Names and Places of the Era of United States Involvement in Vietnam*. Jefferson: McFarland, 1990. Print.

Clodfelter, Mark. *The Limits of Air Power: The American Bombing of North Vietnam*. New York: Free, 1989. Print.

Clymer, Kenton J., ed. *The Vietnam War: Its History, Literature and Music*. El Paso: Texas Western P, 1998. Print.

Cmiel, Kenneth. "The Politics of Civility." Farber, *The Sixties* 263–90.

Cold War Museum. Cold War Museum, 2008. Web. 13 Oct. 2009.

Conelrad. Conelrad, 2007. Web. 13 Oct. 2009.

Connerton, Paul. *How Societies Remember*. Cambridge: Cambridge UP, 1989. Print.

Conrad, Joseph. *Heart of Darkness*. 1899. New York: Penguin, 1999. Print.

Cooper, John Milton, Jr. "Over There." *New York Times Book Review* 24 June 2001: 15. Print.

Coover, Robert. "The Babysitter." *Pricksongs and Descants*. New York: Grove, 1969. 206–39. Print.

Couser, G. Thomas. "*Going After Cacciato*: The Romance and the Real War." *Journal of Narrative Technique* 13.1 (1983): 1–10. Print.

Crane, Stephen. "The Little Regiment." Crane, *Stephen Crane* 647.

———. *The Red Badge of Courage*. 1895. New York: Simon, 2005. Print.

———. *Stephen Crane: Prose and Poetry*. New York: Lib. of Amer., 1984. Print.

———. "The Veteran." Crane, *Stephen Crane* 666.

———. "War Is Kind." Crane, *Stephen Crane* 1325–45.

Crawford, John. *The Last True Story I'll Ever Tell*. New York: Riverhead, 2006. Print.

Culler, Jonathan. "Story and Discourse in the Analysis of Narrative." *The Pursuit of Signs: Semiotics, Literature, Deconstruction*. Ithaca: Cornell UP, 1981. 169–87. Print.

Cummings, E. E. *The Enormous Room*. New York: Barnes, 2006. Print.

D'Agata, John. "Joan Didion's Formal Experiment of Confusion." *The Believer* Oct. 2003: 5–14. Print.

Dang Thuy Tram. *Last Night I Dreamed of Peace*. New York: Harmony, 2007. Print.

De Groot, Gerard J. *A Noble Cause? America and the Vietnam War*. New York: Longman, 1999. Print.

DeLillo, Don. *Libra*. New York: Viking, 1988. Print.

———. "Videotape." *Antaeus* 75-76 (1994): 55–59. Print.

———. *White Noise*. New York: Penguin, 1985. Print.

Dell, Diana J. "*A Saigon Party*" and Other Vietnam War Short Stories*. Bloomington: iUniverse, 2000. Print.

Del Vecchio, John. *The Thirteenth Valley*. New York: Bantam, 1982. Print.

Devine, Jeremy M. *Vietnam at 24 Frames a Second: A Critical and Thematic Analysis of Over 400 Films about the Vietnam War*. Austin: U of Texas P, 1999. Print.

Dickerson, James. *North to Canada: Men and Women against the Vietnam War*. Westport: Praeger, 1999. Print.

Dickinson, Emily. "Because I could not stop for Death." Dickinson, *Complete Poems* 712.

———. *The Complete Poems of Emily Dickinson*. Ed. Thomas H. Johnson. Boston: Little, 1960. Print.

———. "I heard a Fly buzz when I died." Dickinson, *Complete Poems* 465.

Didion, Joan. *Democracy*. New York: Simon, 1984. Print.

Dillon, George L. *Contending Rhetorics: Writing in Academic Disciplines*. Bloomington: Indiana UP, 1981. Print.

Dinh, Linh. *Fake House: Stories*. New York: Seven Stories, 2000. Print.

———. *Night, Again: Contemporary Fiction from Vietnam*. 1996. New York: Seven Stories, 2006. Print.

Dittmar, Linda, and Gene Michaud, eds. *From Hanoi to Hollywood: The Vietnam War in American Film*. New Brunswick: Rugers UP, 1990. Print.

Doctorow, E. L. "The Writer in the Family." *Lives of the Poets*. New York: Random, 1984. 3–17. Print.

Donovan, Christopher. *Postmodern Counternarratives: Irony and Audience in the Narratives of Paul Auster, Don DeLillo, Charles Johnson, and Tim O'Brien*. New York: Routledge, 2005. Print.

Dos Passos, John. *Three Soldiers*. New York: Random, 2002. Print.

Doyle, Edward, and Stephen Weiss, eds. *Collision of Cultures: The Americans in Vietnam, 1954–1973*. Boston: Boston, 1985. Print.

Dulles, John Foster. "The Evolution of Foreign Policy." *Department of State Bulletin* 25 Jan. 1954: 107–10. Print.

Dunnaway, Jen. "Approaching a Truer Form of Truth: The Appropriation of the Oral Narrative Form in Vietnam War Literature." *Soldier Talk: The Vietnam War in Oral Narrative*. Ed. Paul Budra and Michael Zeitlin. Bloomington: Indiana UP, 2004. 26–51. Print.

Duong, Uyen Nicole. *Daughters of the River Huong*. Vienna: RavensYard, 2005. Print.

Duong, Van Nguyen. *Tragedy of the Vietnam War: A South Vietnamese Officer's Analysis*. Jefferson: McFarland, 2008. Print.

Duong Thi Thoa. "Changing My Life: How I Came to the Vietnamese Revolution." Trans. Mark Sidel. *Signs* 23.4 (1998): 1017–30. Print.

Duong Thu Huong. *Memories of a Pure Spring*. Trans. Nina McPherson and Phan Huy Duong. New York: Penguin, 2001. Print.

———. *No Man's Land: A Novel*. Trans. Nina McPherson and Phan Huy Duong. New York: Hyperion, 2006. Print.

———. *Novel without a Name*. Trans. Phan Huy Duong and Nina McPherson. New York: Penguin, 1995. Print.

Durand, Maurice M., and Nguyen Tran Huan. *An Introduction to Vietnamese Literature*. Trans. D. M. Hawke. New York: Columbia UP, 1985. Print.

Duras, Marguerite. *The Lover*. New York: Pantheon, 1985. Print.

———. *The Sea Wall*. 1950. Trans. Herma Briffault. 3rd ed. New York: Farrar, 1985. Print.

Durham, Weldon B. "Gone to Flowers: Theatre and Drama of the Vietnam War." Gilman and Smith 332–62.

Early, Emmett. *The War Veteran in Film*. Jefferson: McFarland, 2003. Print.

Eastlake, William. *The Bamboo Bed*. 1969. Champaign: Dalkey Archive, 2001. Print.

Eberwein, Robert T., ed. *The War Film*. Piscataway: Rutgers UP, 2005. Print.

Eggers, Dave. *A Heartbreaking Work of Staggering Genius*. New York: Simon, 2000. Print.

Ehrhart, W. D., ed. *Carrying the Darkness: The Poetry of the Vietnam War*. Lubbock: Texas Tech UP, 1985. Print.

———. *Unaccustomed Mercy: Soldier-Poets of the Vietnam War*. Lubbock: Texas Tech UP, 1989. Print.

Einstein, Albert. "Albert Einstein to Franklin D. Roosevelt, August 2, 1939." Cantelon, Hewlett, and Williams 9–11.

Eliot, T. S. "Tradition and the Individual Talent." *Selected Prose of T. S. Eliot*. Ed. Frank Kermode. New York: Harcourt, 1975. 37–44. Print.

Elliott, Duong Van Mai. *The Sacred Willow: Four Generations in the Life of a Vietnamese Family*. New York: Oxford UP, 1999. Print.

Elwood-Akers, Virginia. *Women War Correspondents in the Vietnam War, 1961–1975*. Metuchen: Scarecrow, 1988. Print.

Emerson, Gloria. *Winners and Losers: Battles, Retreats, Gains, Losses, and Ruins from the Vietnam War*. 1976. New York: Penguin, 1986. Print.

Encyclopedia of American Studies. Amer. Studies Assn., Johns Hopkins UP, 2009. Web. 4 Sept. 2009.

———. Ed. George T. Kurian et al. 4 vols. New York: Grolier, 2001. Print.

Eng, Robert Y. *East and Southeast Asia: An Annotated Directory of Internet Resources*. Eng, 2006. Web. 4 Sept. 2009.

Enloe, Cynthia. *Does Khaki Become You? The Militarization of Women's Lives*. Rev. ed. Kitchener: Rivers Oram–Pandora, 1988. Print.

Erdrich, Louise. *Tracks*. New York: Perennial, 1988. Print.

Erlich, Victor. *Russian Formalism: History-Doctrine*. 3rd ed. New Haven: Yale UP, 1965. Print.

Esper, George, and the Associated Press. *The Eyewitness History of the Vietnam War, 1961–1975*. New York: Random, 1983. Print.

Evans, Martin, and Ken Lunn, eds. *War and Memory in the Twentieth Century*. London: Borg, 1997. Print.

Evans, Sara M. *Tidal Wave: How Women Changed America at Century's End*. New York: Simon, 2004. Print.

Faas, Horst, and Tim Page, eds. *Requiem: By the Photographers Who Died in Vietnam and Indochina*. New York: Random, 1997. Print.

Fahs, Alice. *The Imagined Civil War: Popular Literature of the North and South, 1861–1865*. Chapel Hill: U of North Carolina P, 2001. Print.

Fall, Bernard B. *Street without Joy: The French Debacle in Indochina*. 1961. Mechanicsburg: Stackpole, 1994. Print.

———. *The Two Viet-Nams: A Political and Military Analysis*. Rev. ed. New York: Praeger, 1971. Print.

———. *Viet-Nam Witness, 1953–66*. New York: Praeger, 1966. Print.

Fallows, James. "What Did You Do in the Class War, Daddy?" *Washington Monthly* Oct. 1975: 5–20. Print.

Farber, David R. *The Age of Great Dreams: America in the 1960s*. New York: Farrar, 1994. Print.

———, ed. *The Sixties: From Memory to History*. Chapel Hill: U of North Carolina P, 1994. Print.

Farrell, Susan. "Tim O'Brien and Gender: A Defense of *The Things They Carried*." *CEA Critic: An Official Journal of the College English Association* 66.1 (2003): 1–21. Print.

Farrington, Tim. *Lizzie's War*. New York: Harper, 2005. Print.

Faulkner, William. *Go Down, Moses*. 1942. New York: Vintage, 1970. Print.

Faulks, Sebastian, ed. *The Vintage Book of War Stories*. London: Random, 2005. Print.

Feltskog, E. N. Introduction. *The Oregon Trail*. By Francis Parkman. Madison: U of Wisconsin P, 1969. 11a–75a. Print.

Fenn, Jeffrey W. *Levitating the Pentagon: Evolutions in the American Theatre of the Vietnam War Era*. Newark: U of Delaware P, 1992. Print.

Fenton, James, ed. *The Fall of Saigon*. Spec. issue of *Granta* 15 (1985): 1–288. Rpt. in *The Granta Book of Reportage*. Introd. Ian Jack. London: Granta, 2006. 27–104. Print.

Fiedler, Leslie. *Love and Death in the American Novel*. 1966. Rev. ed. New York: Anchor, 1992. Print.

Filkins, Dexter. "A Skeptical Vietnam Voice Still Echoes in the Fog of Iraq." *New York Times*. New York Times, 25 Apr. 2007. Web. 18 June 2009.

Fischer, Jeffrey. "Killing at Close Range: A Study in Intertextuality." *English Journal* 95.3 (2006): 27–31. Print.

Fitzgerald, Frances. *Fire in the Lake: The Vietnamese and the Americans in Vietnam*. 1972. Boston: Little, 2002. Print.

Flax, Jane. "Postmodernism and Gender Relations in Feminist Theory." *Signs* 12.4 (1987): 621–43. Rpt. in *Feminism/Postmodernism*. Ed. Linda J. Nicholson. New York: Routledge, 1990. 39–62. Print.

Foertsch, Jacqueline. "Not Bombshells but Basketcases: Gendered Illness in Nuclear Texts." *Studies in the Novel* 31.4 (1999): 471–88. Print.

Forché, Carolyn. "The Colonel." *The Country between Us*. New York: Harper, 1981. 16. Print.

Ford, Daniel. *The Warbird's Forum*. Ford, 2009. Web. 4 Sept. 2009.

Ford, Nancy Gentile. "The My Lai Massacre: Crossing the Line in Vietnam." *Issues of War and Peace*. Westport: Greenwood, 2002. 263–86. Print.

Foucault, Michel. *The Archaeology of Knowledge and the Discourse on Language*. New York: Pantheon, 1972. Print.

France, Alan W. "Assigning Places: The Function of Introductory Composition as a Cultural Discourse." *College English* 55.6 (1993): 593–609. Print.

Frank, Pat. *Alas, Babylon*. Cutchogue: Buccaneer, 1990. Print.

Franklin, H. Bruce. "From Realism to Virtual Reality: Images of America's Wars." *The Norton Reader*. Ed. Linda H. Peterson and John C. Brereton. New York: Norton, 2008. Print.

———. "Kicking the Denial Syndrome: Tim O'Brien's *In the Lake of the Woods*." *Novel History: Historians and Novelists Confront America's Past (and Each Other)*. Ed. Mark C. Carnes. New York: Simon, 2001. 332–43. Print.

———. *M.I.A., or, Mythmaking in America*. New Brunswick: Rutgers UP, 1993. Print.

———. *Vietnam and Other American Fantasies*. Amherst: U of Massachusetts P, 2000. Print.

———. "The Vietnam War as American Science Fiction and Fantasy." *Science-Fiction Studies* 17.1 (1990): 34–59. Print.

———, ed. *The Vietnam War in American Stories, Songs, and Poems*. New York: Bedford–St. Martin's, 1995. Print.

Freedman, Dan, and Jacqueline Rhoads. *Nurses in Vietnam: The Forgotten Veterans*. Austin: Texas Monthly, 1987. Print.

Freedman, Lawrence. *The Evolution of Nuclear Strategy*. 2nd ed. New York: St. Martin's, 1989. Print.

Freeman, James M. *Hearts of Sorrow: Vietnamese-American Lives*. Palo Alto: Stanford UP, 1989. Print.

Freud, Sigmund. *Beyond the Pleasure Principle*. 1961. Trans. James Strachey. New York: Barnes, 2006. Print.

Friedl, Vicki L., comp. *Women in the United States Military, 1901–1995: A Research Guide and Annotated Bibliography*. Westport: Greenwood, 1996. Print.

Fromm, Erich. *The Essential Fromm: Life between Having and Being*. Ed. Rainier Funk. New York: Continuum, 1958. Print.

———. *The Sane Society*. 1955. New York: Henry Holt, 1990. Print.

Fulbright, J. William. *The Vietnam Hearings*. New York: Vantage, 1966. Print.

Fuller, Margaret. "Leila." *The Essential Margaret Fuller*. Ed. Jeffrey Steele. New Brunswick: Rutgers UP, 1992. 53–58. Print.

Fusco, Coco. *A Field Guide for Female Interrogators*. New York: Seven Stories, 2008. Print.

Fussell, Paul. *The Great War and Modern Memory*. New York: Oxford UP, 1985. Print.

———. "My War: How I Got Irony in the Infantry." *The Boy Scout Handbook and Other Observations*. New York: Oxford UP, 1985. Print.

———, ed. *The Norton Book of Modern War*. New York: Norton, 1990. Print.

———. "Thank God for the Atom Bomb." *"Thank God for the Atom Bomb" and Other Essays*. New York: Ballantine, 1990. Print.

———. *Wartime: Understanding and Behavior in the Second World War*. New York: Oxford UP, 1989. Print.

García Márquez, Gabriel. "The Handsomest Drowned Man in the World." *Collected Stories*. Trans. Gregory Rabassa and J. S. Bernstein. New York: Harper-Perennial, 1984. 247–54. Print.

Gellhorn, Martha. *The Face of War*. 1936. New York: Atlantic Monthly, 1988. Print.

———. *The Point of No Return*. Lincoln: U of Nebraska P, 1995. Print.

Genette, Gérard. *Narrative Discourse: An Essay in Method*. Trans. Jane E. Lewin. Ithaca: Cornell UP, 1981. 169–87. Print.

Gettleman, Marvin E., Jane M. Franklin, Marilyn Young, and H. Bruce Franklin, eds. *Vietnam and America: A Documented History*. 2nd rev. ed. New York: Grove, 1995. Print.

Geyh, Paula, Fred G. Leebron, and Andrew Levy. *Postmodern American Fiction: A Norton Anthology*. New York: Norton, 1998. Print.

Gibson, William. *Pattern Recognition*. New York: Putnam, 2003. Print.

Gilbert, Marc Jason, ed. *The Vietnam War: Teaching Approaches and Resources*. New York: Greenwood, 1991. Print.

———, ed. *Why the North Won the Vietnam War*. New York: Palgrave, 2002. Print.

Gilman, Charlotte Perkins. *"Herland," "The Yellow Wall-paper," and Selected Writings*. New York: Penguin, 1999. Print.

Gilman, Owen W., Jr. *Vietnam and the Southern Imagination*. Jackson: UP of Mississippi, 1992. Print.

Gilman, Owen W., Jr., and Lorrie Smith, eds. *America Rediscovered: Critical Essays on Literature and Film of the Vietnam War*. New York: Garland, 1990. Print.

Gilmore, Barry, and Alexander Kaplan. *Tim O'Brien in the Classroom: "This Too Is True: Stories Can Save Us."* Urbana: NCTE, 2007. Print.

Gilmore, Donald L., and D. M. Giangreco. *Eyewitness Vietnam: Firsthand Accounts from Operation Rolling Thunder to the Fall of Saigon*. Fwd. Lester W. Grau. New York: Sterling, 2006. Print.

Ginsberg, Allen. "A Supermarket in California." *Allen Ginsberg: Collected Poems, 1947–1980*. New York: Harper, 1988. 136. Print.

Glasser, Ronald J. "I Don't Want to Go Home Alone." *365 Days*. New York: Braziller, 1971. 256–88. Print.

Goldensohn, Lorrie, ed. *American War Poetry: An Anthology*. New York: Columbia UP, 2006. Print.

———. *Dismantling Glory: Twentieth-Century Soldier Poetry*. New York: Columbia UP, 2004. Print.

———. "Men and Women and Women." Goldensohn, *Dismantling* 297–328.

Goldstein, Donald M., Katherine V. Dillon, and J. Michael Wegner. *The Vietnam War: The Story and Photographs*. Dulles: Potomac, 1997. Print.

Goluboff, Benjamin. "Tim O'Brien's Quang Ngai." *ANQ: A Quarterly Journal of Short Articles, Notes, and Reviews* 17.2 (2004): 53–58. Print.

Goodman, Paul. *Growing Up Absurd: Problems of Youth in the Organized Society*. New York: Vintage, 1960. Print.

Gotera, Vince. *Radical Visions: Poetry by Vietnam Veterans*. Athens: U of Georgia P, 1994. Print.

Graham, Jorie. *Overlord: Poems*. New York: Harper, 2005. Print.

Graves, Robert. "Recalling War." 1938. *Collected Poems*. New York: Penguin, 2003. 358. Print.

Grealy, Lucy. *Autobiography of a Face*. Boston: Houghton, 1994. Print.

Green, Eric. *Civil Defense Museum*. Civil Defense Museum, 2009. Web. 13 Oct. 2009.

Greene, Graham. The Quiet American: *Text and Criticism*. 1955. Ed. John Clark Pratt. New York: Penguin, 1996. Print.

Grey, Anthony. *Saigon*. New York: Bantam, 1983. Print.

Griffin, William L., and John Marciano. *Teaching the Vietnam War: A Critical Examination of School Texts and an Interpretive Comparative History Utilizing the Pentagon Papers and Other Documents*. Lanham: Rowman, 1979. Print.

Griffiths, Philip Jones. *Agent Orange: "Collateral Damage" in Viet Nam*. London: Trolley, 2004. Print.

———. *Viet Nam at Peace*. Fwd. John Pilger. London: Trolley, 2005. Print.

———. *Vietnam Inc.* Rev. ed. London: Phaidon, 2006. Print.

Habich, John. "The Battlegrounds Are Personal in Tim O'Brien's Latest Novel." *Star Tribune* [Minneapolis] 27 Oct. 2002: 1F. Print.

Haeberle, Ron. Photographs. *Life* 5 Dec. 1969. Print.

———. Photographs. *Plain Dealer* [Cleveland] 20 Nov. 1969. Print.

Ha Jin. *Ocean of Words: Army Stories*. New York: Random, 1998. Print.

———. *War Trash*. New York: Knopf, 2005. Print.

Haldeman, Joe. *The Forever War*. 1974. New York: St. Martin's, 1997. Print.

———. *1968*. New York: Avon, 1995. Print.

———. *War Stories*. San Francisco: Night Shade, 2005. Print.

Hall, Mitchell K. *The Vietnam War*. 2nd ed. New York: Longman, 2007. Print.

Hamill, Sam, ed. *Poets against the War*. New York: Thunder's Mouth–Nation, 2003. Print.

Hammel, Eric M. *Khe Sanh: Siege in the Clouds—An Oral History*. Pacifica: Pacifica Military Hist., 2007. Print.

Hardy, Thomas. "The Man He Killed." *Selected Poems*. New York: Penguin, 1998. 63. Print.

Harper, Michael S. "Debridement." *Songs in Michaeltree: New and Collected Poems*. Urbana: U of Illinois P, 2000. 83–98. Print.

Harper, Phillip Brian. *Framing the Margins: The Social Logic of Postmodern Culture*. New York: Oxford UP, 1994. Print.

Harris, David. *Our War: What We Did in Vietnam and What It Did to Us*. New York: Random, 1996. Print.

Harrison, Jim. *A Good Day to Die*. New York: Dell, 1973. Print.

Harvey, David. *The Condition of Postmodernity: An Enquiry into the Origins of Cultural Change*. Cambridge: Blackwell, 1989. Print.

Hasford, Gustav. *The Short-Timers*. New York: Bantam, 1979. Print.

Haswell, Janis E. "The Craft of the Short Story in Retelling the Viet Nam War: Tim O'Brien's *The Things They Carried*." *South Carolina Review* 37.1 (2004): 94–109. Print.

Hayslip, Le Ly. *Child of War, Woman of Peace*. With James Hayslip. New York: Anchor, 1993. Print.

———. *When Heaven and Earth Changed Places: A Vietnamese Woman's Journey from War to Peace*. With Jay Wurts. New York: Plume, 1989. Print.

Heat-Moon, William Least. [William Trogdon]. *Blue Highways: A Journey into America*. Boston: Little, 1982. Print.

Heberle, Mark A. "Darkness in the East: The Vietnam Novels of Takeshi Kaiko." Jason, *Fourteen Landing Zones* 189–99.

———, ed. *Thirty Years After: New Essays on Vietnam War Literature, Film, and Art*. Newcastle upon Tyne: Cambridge Scholars, 2009. Print.

———. *A Trauma Artist: Tim O'Brien and the Fiction of Vietnam*. Iowa City: U of Iowa P, 2001. Print.

Heinemann, Larry. *Black Virgin Mountain: A Return to Vietnam*. New York: Doubleday, 2005. Print.

———. *Close Quarters*. New York: Fawcett, 1977. Print.

———. *Paco's Story*. 1986. New York: Penguin, 1989. Print.

Heller, Joseph. *Catch-22*. New York: Dell, 1955. Print.

Hellman, John. *American Myth and the Legacy of Vietnam*. New York: Columbia UP, 1986. Print.

Hemingway, Ernest. *A Farewell to Arms*. 1929. New York: Simon, 1995. Print.

———. *For Whom the Bell Tolls*. New York: Simon, 1995. Print.

———. "In Another Country." Hemingway. *The Nick Adams Stories*. 168–74.

———. *In Our Time*. New York: Simon, 1996. Print.

———, ed. *Men at War*. New York: Random, 1992. Print.

———. "A Natural History of the Dead." *The Short Stories*. New York: Scribner's, 1955. 440–49. Print.

———. *The Nick Adams Stories*. New York: Scribner's, 1972. Print.

———. *The Sun Also Rises*. New York: Simon, 1995. Print.

Hendin, Herbert, and Ann Polllinger Haas. *Wounds of War: The Psychological Aftermath of Combat in Vietnam*. New York: Basic, 1984. Print.

Henriksen, Margot. *Dr. Strangelove's America: Society and Culture in the Atomic Age*. Berkeley: U of California P, 1997. Print.

Herman, Judith. *Trauma and Recovery: The Aftermath of Violence—from Domestic Abuse to Political Terror*. Rev. ed. New York: Basic, 1997. Print.

Herr, Michael. *Dispatches*. New York: Avon, 1977. Print.

Herring, George C. *America's Longest War: The United States and Vietnam, 1950–1975*. 4th ed. New York: McGraw, 2001. Print.

Herzog, Tobey C. "*Going After Cacciato*: The Soldier-Author-Character Seeking Control." *Critique: Studies in Contemporary Fiction* 24.2 (1983): 88–96. Print.

———. "John Wayne in a Modern Heart of Darkness: The American Soldier in Vietnam." *Search and Clear: Critical Responses to Selected Literature and Films on the Vietnam War*. Ed. William J. Searle. Bowling Green: Bowling Green State U Popular P, 1988. 16–25. Print.

———. *Tim O'Brien*. New York: Twayne, 1997. Print.

———. "Tim O'Brien: An Interview." *South Carolina Review* 31.1 (1998): 78–109. Print.

———. "Tim O'Brien's 'True Lies'(?)" *Modern Fiction Studies* 46.4 (2000): 893–916. Print.

———. *Vietnam War Stories: Innocence Lost*. London: Routledge, 1992. Print.

———. "Writing about Vietnam: A Heavy Heart of Darkness Trip." *College English* 41.6 (1980): 680–95. Print.

———. *Writing Vietnam, Writing Life: Caputo, Heinemann, O'Brien, Butler*. Iowa City: U of Iowa P, 2008. Print.

Hicks, Patrick. "A Conversation with Tim O'Brien." *Indiana Review* 27.2 (2005): 85–95. Print.

Hillstrom, Kevin, and Laurie Collier Hillstrom. *The Vietnam Experience: A Concise Encyclopedia of American Literature, Songs, and Films*. Westport: Greenwood, 1998. Print.

Hixson, Walter L., ed. *The United States and the Vietnam War: Significant Scholarly Articles*. New York: Garland, 2000. Print.

Hjortshoj, Keith. *The Transition to College Writing*. New York: Bedford–St. Martin's, 2001. Print.

Ho Anh Thai. *Behind the Red Mist*. Willimantic: Curbstone, 1998. Print.

Hoban, Russell. *Riddley Walker*. New York: Summit, 1980. Print.

Hofman, Bettina. "On the Battlefield and Home Front: American Women Writing Their Lives on the Vietnam War." Vernon, *Arms and the Self* 202–17.

Holm, Jeanne. *Women in the Military: An Unfinished Revolution*. 1982. Rev. ed. New York: Random, 1992. Print.

Holsinger, M. Paul, ed. *War and American Popular Culture: A Historical Encyclopedia*. Westport: Greenwood, 1999. Print.

Homer. *Iliad*. Trans. Robert Fitzgerald. New York: Anchor, 1985. Print.

———. *Iliad*. Trans. Robert Fitzgerald. New York: Farrar, 2004. Print.

Horner, Carl S. "Challenging the Law of Courage and Heroic Identification in Tim O'Brien's *If I Die in a Combat Zone* and *The Things They Carried*." *War, Literature, and the Arts: An International Journal of the Humanities* 11.1 (1999): 256–67. Print.

Ho Xuan Huong. *Spring Essence*. Ed. and trans. John Balaban. Port Townsend: Copper Canyon P, 2000. Print.

Hoy, Pat C., II. "The Beauty and Destructiveness of War: A Literary Portrait of the Vietnam Conflict." *A Concise Companion to Postwar American Literature and Culture*. Ed. Josephine G. Hendin. Malden: Blackwell, 2004. 168–86. Print.

———. Rev. of *In the Lake of the Woods*, by Tim O'Brien. *The World and I* May 1995: 296. Print.

Hudson, Gabe. *Dear Mr. President*. New York: Knopf, 2003. Print.

Huebner, Andrew. *We Pierce*. New York: Simon, 2004. Print.

Hughes, James P. *Fear and Courage in Tim O'Brien's* If I Die in a Combat Zone, Going After Cacciato, *and* The Things They Carried. Wright-Patterson Air Force Base: Storming Media, 1998. Print.

Hughes, Langston. "Salvation." *The Big Sea: An Autobiography*. New York: Hill, 1993. 18–20. Print.

Hunt, Michael H., ed. *A Vietnam War Reader: A Documentary History from American and Vietnamese Perspectives*. Chapel Hill: U of North Carolina P, 2010. Print.

Huo, T. C. *Land of Smiles*. New York: Plume, 2000. Print.

———. *A Thousand Wings*. New York: Dutton, 1998. Print.

Hutcheon, Linda. *A Poetics of Postmodernism: History, Theory, Fiction*. New York: Routledge, 1988. Print.

Huynh, Jade Ngoc Quang. *South Wind Changing*. Saint Paul: Graywolf, 1994. Print.

Huynh Sanh Thong, ed. and trans. *An Anthology of Vietnamese Poems: From the Eleventh through the Twentieth Centuries*. New Haven: Yale UP, 1996. Print.

Hynes, Samuel. *The Soldiers' Tale: Bearing Witness to Modern War*. London: Pimlico, 1998. Print.

"Interview with Tim O'Brien." *Readers Read*. Readers Read, 2006. Web. 7 May 2007.

Isaacs, Arnold R. *Vietnam Shadows: The War, Its Ghosts, and Its Legacy*. Baltimore: Johns Hopkins UP, 1997. Print.

James, David E. "The Vietnam War and American Music." Rowe and Berg 226–54.

Jameson, Fredric. "Cognitive Mapping." *Marxism and the Interpretation of Culture*. Ed. Cary Nelson and Lawrence Grossberg. Urbana: U of Illinois P, 1988. 347–57. Print.

———. *The Political Unconscious: Narrative as a Socially Symbolic Act*. Ithaca: Cornell UP, 1982. Print.

———. *Postmodernism; or, The Cultural Logic of Late Capitalism*. Durham: Duke UP, 1997. Print.

Jamieson, Neil L. *Understanding Vietnam*. Berkeley: U of California P, 1995. Print.

Jarraway, David R. "'Excremental Assault' in Tim O'Brien: Trauma and Recovery in Vietnam War Literature." *Modern Fiction Studies* 44.3 (1998): 695–711. Print.

Jarrell, Randall. "The Death of the Ball Turret Gunner." *The Norton Anthology of American Literature*. Ed. Nina Baym et al. 7th ed. Vol. E. New York: Norton, 2007. 2268. Print.

Jarvis, Brian. "Skating on a Shit Field: Tim O'Brien and the Topography of Trauma." *American Fiction of the 1990s: Reflections of History and Culture*. Ed. Jay Prosser. New York: Routledge, 2008. 134–47. Print.

Jason, Philip K. *Acts and Shadows: The Vietnam War in American Literary Culture*. Lanham: Rowman, 2000. Print.

———, ed. *Fourteen Landing Zones: Approaches to Vietnam War Literature*. Iowa City: U of Iowa P, 1991. Print.

———. *The Vietnam War in Literature: An Annotated Bibliography of Criticism*. Pasadena: Salem, 1992. Print.

Jeffords, Susan. *The Remasculinization of America: Gender and the Vietnam War*. Bloomington: Indiana UP, 1989. Print.

Jewett, Sarah Orne. *The Country of the Pointed Firs and Other Stories*. New York: Mod. Lib., 2000. Print.

Johannessen, Larry R. *Illumination Rounds: Teaching the Literature of the Vietnam War*. Urbana: NCTE, 1992. Print.

Johnson, Denis. *Fiskadoro*. New York: Vintage, 1985. Print.

———. *Jesus' Son: Stories*. 1992. New York: Picador, 2009. Print.

———. *Tree of Smoke*. New York: Farrar, 2007. Print.

Jones, Chris. "The Things That Carried Him." *Esquire* May 2008: 102–17. Print.

Jones, James. *The Thin Red Line*. 1962. New York: Dell, 1998. Print.

———. *Viet Journal*. New York: Dell, 1974. Print.

Joseph, William A. *Vietnam War Internet Links*. Dept. of Political Science, Wellesley Coll., n.d. Web. 4 Sept. 2009.

Joyce, James. *Dubliners*. New York: Penguin, 1967. Print.

Juncker, Clara. "Not a Story to Pass On? Tim O'Brien's Vietnam." *Transnational America: Contours of Modern US Culture*. Ed. Russell Duncan and Juncker. Copenhagen: Museum Tusculanum, 2004. 111–24. Print.

Kaiko, Takeshi. *Darkness in Summer*. Trans. Cecilia Segawa Seigle. New York: Knopf, 1973. Print.

———. *Into the Black Sun: Vietnam, 1964–1965*. Trans. Cecilia Segawa Seigle. Tokyo: Kodansha, 1980. Print.

Kaplan, Fred. *The Wizards of Armageddon*. New York: Simon, 1983. Print.

Kaplan, Steven. "An Interview with Tim O'Brien." *Missouri Review* 14.3 (1991): 95–108. Print.

———. *Understanding Tim O'Brien*. Columbia: U of South Carolina P, 1995. Print.

———. "The Undying Uncertainty of the Narrator in Tim O'Brien's *The Things They Carried*." *Critique: Studies in Contemporary Fiction* 35.1 (1993): 43–52. Print.

Karlin, Wayne. *War Movies: Journeys to Viet Nam—Scenes and Out-takes*. Willimantic: Curbstone, 2005. Print.

Karlin, Wayne, and Ho Anh Thai, eds. *Love after War: Contemporary Fiction from Viet Nam*. Willimantic: Curbstone, 2003. Print.

Karlin, Wayne, Le Minh Khue, and Truong Vu, eds. *The Other Side of Heaven: Postwar Fiction by Vietnamese and American Writers*. Willimantic: Curbstone, 1995. Print.

Karlin, Wayne, Larry Rottmann, and Basil T. Pacquet, eds. *Free Fire Zones: Short Stories by Vietnam Veterans*. New York: McGraw, 1973. Print.

Karnow, Stanley. "*Tiger Force* Not for the Squeamish." *Washington Post* 21 May 2006: BW06. Rpt. in *Arkansas Democrat Gazette* 4 June 2006: 4H. Print.

———. *Vietnam, A History*. New York: Viking, 1983. Print.

Karr, Mary. *The Liar's Club: A Memoir*. 10th anniversary ed. New York: Penguin, 2005. Print.

Karski, Jan. *Story of a Secret State*. Boston: Houghton, 1944. Print.

Kartiganer, Donald M. "Now I Can Write: Faulkner's Novel of Invention." *New Essays on* The Sound and the Fury. Ed. Noel Polk. Cambridge: Cambridge UP, 1993. 71–97. Print.

Kaufmann, Michael. "The Solace of Bad Form: Tim O'Brien's Postmodernist Revisions of Vietnam in 'Speaking of Courage.'" *Critique: Studies in Contemporary Fiction* 46.4 (2005): 333–43. Print.

Keegan, John. *The Book of War*. New York: Viking, 1999. Print.

Kellner, Hans. *Language and Historical Representation: Getting the Story Crooked*. Madison: U of Wisconsin P, 1989. Print.

Kelsey, Ann L., and Anthony O. Edmonds, eds. *Resources for Teaching the Vietnam War: An Annotated Guide*. Pittsburgh: Center for Social Studies Educ., 1996. Print.

Kennan, George. "The Sources of Soviet Conduct." *Foreign Affairs* 25.4 (1947): 566–82. Print.

Kerouac, Jack. *On the Road*. New York: Penguin, 1957. Print.

Khadra, Yasmina. *The Sirens of Baghdad*. Trans. John Cullen. New York: Talese-Doubleday, 2007. Print.

Kincaid, Jamaica. "Girl." *New Yorker* 26 June 1978: 29. Print.

King, Martin Luther, Jr. "Letter from a Birmingham Jail." *Why We Can't Wait*. 1964. New York: Signet, 2000. 64–84. Print.

Kingston, Maxine Hong. "No Name Woman." *The Woman Warrior: Memoirs of a Girlhood among Ghosts*. New York: Knopf, 1977. 1–16. Print.

———, ed. *Veterans of War, Veterans of Peace*. Kihei: Koa, 2006. Print.

Kinney, Katherine. *Friendly Fire: American Images of the Vietnam War*. New York: Oxford UP, 2000. Print.

Klein, Naomi. "Bring Najaf to New York." *Nation* 14 Sept. 2004: 22. Print.

Klepfisz, Irena. "Bashert." *Jewish American Literature: A Norton Anthology*. Ed. Jules Chametzky et al. New York: Norton, 2000. 1082–83. Print.

Klinkowitz, Jerome. "Writing under Fire: Postmodern Fiction and the Vietnam War." *Postmodern Fiction: A Bio-bibliographical Guide*. Ed. Larry McCaffrey. New York: Greenwood, 1986. 79–92. Print.

Knightly, Phillip. "The Last War, 1914–1918." *The First Casualty*. New York: Harcourt, 1995. 80–112. Print.

Komunyakaa, Yusef. *Dien Cai Dau*. Middletown: Wesleyan UP, 1988. Print.

Kroes, Rob. *If You've Seen One, You've Seen the Mall: Europeans and American Mass Culture*. Champaign: U of Illinois P, 1996. Print.

Kroll, Barry M. *Teaching Hearts and Minds: College Students Reflect on the Vietnam War in Literature*. Carbondale: Southern Illinois UP, 1992. Print.

Kumin, Maxine. "Woodchucks." *Selected Poems, 1960–1999*. New York: Norton, 1998. 80. Print.

Kutler, Stanley I. *Encyclopedia of the Vietnam War*. New York: Scribner's, 1996. Print.

LaCapra, Dominick. *Writing History, Writing Trauma*. Baltimore: Johns Hopkins UP, 2001. Print.

Lam, Andrew. *Perfume Dreams: Reflections on the Vietnamese Diaspora*. Berkeley: Heyday, 2005. Print.

Langer, Lawrence L. *Holocaust Testimonies: The Ruins of Memory*. New Haven: Yale UP, 1991. Print.

———. *Versions of Survival: The Holocaust and the Human Spirit*. Albany: State U of New York P, 1982. Print.

Lappeé, Anthony, writer. *Shooting War*. Illus. Dan Goldman. New York: Grand Central, 2007. Print.

Laub, Dori. "Bearing Witness or the Vicissitudes of Listening." *Testimony: Crises of Witnessing in Literature, Psychoanalysis and History*. Ed. Shoshana Felman and Laub. London: Taylor, 1991. 57–74. Print.

Laurence, John. *The Cat from Hue: A Vietnam War Story*. New York: Public Affairs, 2002. Print.

Lawson, Jacqueline E. "'She's a Pretty Woman . . . for a Gook': The Misogyny of the Vietnam War." Jason, *Fourteen Landing Zones* 15–37.

Lazzarini, Tony. *Highest Traditions: Memories of War*. Greenbrae: Voyager, 2003. Print.

Le, Nam. *The Boat*. New York: Knopf, 2008. Print.

Lederer, William J., and Eugene Burdick. *The Ugly American*. 1958. New York: Norton, 1999. Print.

Leepson, Marc, and Helen Hannaford, eds. *Webster's New World Dictionary of the Vietnam War*. New York: Macmillan, 1999. Print.

Lehman, Daniel W. "Reading Outside In: Over the Edge of Genre in the Case of Private O'Brien." *Matters of Fact: Reading Nonfiction over the Edge*. Columbus: Ohio State UP, 1997. 164–93. Print.

Leimbach, Marti. *The Man from Saigon*. New York: Doubleday, 2009. Print.

Le Luu. *A Time Far Past: A Novel of Viet Nam*. Trans. Ngo Vinh Hai, Nguyen Ba Chung, Kevin Bowen, and David Hunt. Amherst: U of Massachusetts P, 1997. Print.

Lembcke, Jerry. *The Spitting Image: Myth, Memory, and the Legacy of Vietnam*. New York: New York UP, 1998. Print.

Le Minh Khue. *The Stars, the Earth, the River*. Trans. Bac Hoai Tran and Dana Sachs. Willimantic: Curbstone, 1997. Print.

Leroy, Catherine, ed. *Under Fire: Great Photographers and Writers in Vietnam*. New York: Random, 2005. Print.

Le Thi Diem Thuy. *The Gangster We Are All Looking For*. New York: Anchor, 2003. Print.

Levi, Primo. *Survival in Auschwitz*. New York: Simon, 1995. Print.

Levi, Primo, Marco Belpoliti, and Robert Gordon, eds. *Voices of Memory: Interviews, 1961–1987*. New York: New, 2001. Print.

Lewis, Lloyd B. *The Tainted War: Culture and Identity in Vietnam War Narratives*. Westport: Greenwood, 1985. Print.

Lewis, Sinclair. *Free Air*. New York: Grosset, 1919. Print.

Lewy, Guenter. *America in Vietnam*. New York: Oxford, 1978. Print.

Leys, Ruth. *Trauma: A Genealogy*. Chicago: U of Chicago P, 2000. Print.

Li, Xiaobing. *Voices from the Vietnam War: Stories from American, Asian, and Russian Veterans*. Lexington: UP of Kentucky, 2010. Print.

Lim, Shirley Geok-lin, and Cheng Lok Chua, eds. *Tilting the Continent: Southeast Asian American Writing*. Moorhead: New Rivers, 2000. Print.

Lind, Michael. *Vietnam: The Necessary War: A Reinterpretation of America's Most Disastrous Military Conflict*. New York: Simon, 2002. Print.

Linney, Romulus. "*Going After Cacciato* from the Novel by Tim O'Brien." *Kenyon Review* 27.2 (2005): 21–64. Print.

Liparulo, Steven P. "'Incense and Ashes': The Postmodern Work of Refutation in Three Vietnam War Novels." *War, Literature, and the Arts: An International Journal of the Humanities* 15.1-2 (2003): 71–94. Print.

Lockhart, Bruce M., and William J. Duiker. *Historical Dictionary of Vietnam.* 3rd ed. Lanham: Scarecrow, 2006. Print.

Loeb, Jeffrey. "The African American Autobiography of the Vietnam War." Vernon, *Arms* 218–35.

Loewen, James W. "Down the Memory Hole." *Lies My Teacher Told Me: Everything Your American History Textbook Got Wrong.* New York: Touchstone, 1995. 238–53. Print.

Lomperis, Timothy, and John Clark Pratt. *"Reading the Wind": The Literature of the Vietnam War.* Durham: Duke UP, 1987. Print.

Louvre, Alf, and Jeffrey Walsh, eds. *Tell Me Lies about Vietnam: Cultural Battles for the Meaning of the War.* Berkshire: Open UP, 1989. Print.

Lucas, Brad. "Traumatic Narrative, Narrative Genre, and the Exigencies of Memory." *Utah Foreign Language Review* 9.1 (1999): 30–38. Print.

Lunsford, Andrea A., and John J. Ruszkiewicz. *Everything's an Argument: With Readings.* 3rd ed. New York: Bedford–St. Martin's, 2004. Print.

Lyotard, Jean-François. *The Postmodern Condition: A Report on Knowledge.* Trans. Brian Massuini and Geoff Bennington. Minneapolis: U of Minnesota P, 1984. Print.

Mabry, Donald J. *Historical Text Archive.* Mabry, 2009. Web. 4 Sept. 2009.

Maclear, Michael. *The Ten Thousand Day War: Vietnam, 1945–1975.* New York: St. Martin's, 1981. Print.

Macpherson, Malcolm Cook. *Hocus Potus.* Hoboken: Melville, 2007. Print.

MacPherson, Myra. *Long Time Passing: Vietnam and the Haunted Generation.* 1984. New York: Doubleday, 2001. Print.

Mahedy, William P. *Out of the Night: The Spiritual Journey of Vietnam Vets.* New York: Random, 1988. Print.

Mahony, Phillip. *From Both Sides Now: The Poetry of the Vietnam War and Its Aftermath.* New York: Scribner's, 1998. Print.

Mailer, Norman. *Armies of the Night: History as a Novel, the Novel as History.* New York: Signet, 1968. Print.

———. *The Naked and the Dead.* 5th anniversary ed. New York: Picador, 1998. Print.

———. *Why Are We in Vietnam? A Novel.* New York: Putnam, 1967. Print.

Mann, Emily. *Still Life. Testimonies: Four Plays.* New York: Theatre Communications Group, 1997. 31–132. Print.

Maraniss, David. *They Marched into Sunlight.* New York: Simon, 2003. Print.

Marlantes, Karl. *Matterhorn: A Novel of the Vietnam War.* New York: Atlantic Monthly, 2010. Print.

Marshall, Kathryn. *In the Combat Zone: Vivid Personal Recollections of the Vietnam War from the Women Who Served There.* New York: Penguin, 1988. Print.

Martin, Andrew. *Receptions of War: Vietnam in American Culture.* Norman: U of Oklahoma P, 1993. Print.

Martin, Terry J., and Margaret Stiner. "'Sweetheart of the Song Tra Bong': Tim O'Brien's (Feminist?) *Heart of Darkness*." *Short Story* 9.2 (1998): 94–104. Print.

Mascaro, Tom. "The Uncounted Enemy: A Vietnam Deception." *The Museum of Broadcast Communications*. Museum of Broadcast Communications, n.d. Web. 18 Aug. 2008.

Mason, Bobbie Ann. *In Country*. New York: Harper, 1985. Print.

Mason, Robert C. *Chickenhawk*. New York: Penguin, 1983. Print.

Matelski, Marilyn J., and Nancy Lynch Street, eds. *War and Film in America: Historical and Critical Essays*. Jefferson: McFarland, 2003. Print.

Maus, Derek, ed. *Postmodernism*. San Diego: Greenhaven, 2001. Print.

May, Ernest R., ed. *American Cold War Strategy: Interpreting NSC 68*. New York: Bedford–St. Martin's, 1993. Print.

McBride, James. *Miracle at St. Anna*. New York: Penguin, 2002. Print.

McCaffery, Larry. "Interview with Tim O'Brien." *Chicago Review* 33.2 (1982): 129–49. Print.

McCarthy, Cormac. *Blood Meridian; or, The Evening Redness in the West*. New York: Vintage, 1985. Print.

McCarthy, Mary. *Vietnam*. New York: Harcourt, 1967. Print.

McCay, Mary A. "The Autobiography of Guilt: Tim O'Brien and Vietnam." *Writing Lives: American Biography and Autobiography*. Ed. Hans Bak and Hans Krabbendam. Amsterdam: VU UP, 1998. 115–21. Print.

McClatchy, J. D., ed. *Poets of the Civil War*. New York: Lib. of Amer., 2005. Print.

McDonald, Walter. *After the Noise of Saigon*. Amherst: U of Massachusetts P, 1988. Print.

McDonough, Christopher Michael. "'Afraid to Admit We Are Not Achilles': Facing Hector's Dilemma in Tim O'Brien's *The Things They Carried*." *Classical and Modern Literature: A Quarterly* 20.3 (2000): 23–32. Print.

McHale, Brian. *Constructing Postmodernism*. Oxford: Taylor, 1993. Print.

———. *Postmodernist Fiction*. New York: Methuen, 1987. Print.

McKelvey, Tara, ed. *One of the Guys: Women as Aggressors and Torturers*. Emeryville: Seal, 2007. Print.

McMahon, Robert J., and Thomas Paterson, eds. *Major Problems in the History of the Vietnam War*. 4th ed. Boston: Houghton, 2007. Print.

McNamara, Robert S., and Brian VanDeMark. *In Retrospect: The Tragedy and Lessons of Vietnam*. New York: Knopf, 1996. Print.

McNay, John. Rev. of *A Noble Cause? America and the Vietnam War*, by Gerard J. DeGroot. *H-War*. H-War, Dec. 2000. Web. 1 Aug. 2008.

McNerney, Brian C. "Responsibly Inventing History: An Interview with Tim O'Brien." *War, Literature, and the Arts: An International Journal of the Humanities* 6.2 (1994): 1–26. Print.

———. "Speaking of 'Speaking of Courage.'" Joint annual meeting of the Popular Culture Assn. and Amer. Culture Assn. Las Vegas, Mar. 1996. Address.

McPhee, John. *The Curve of Binding Energy*. New York: Noonday, 1973. Print.

Meek, James. *We Are Now Beginning Our Descent*. Edinburgh: Canongate, 2008. Print.

Melley, Timothy. "Postmodern Amnesia: Trauma and Forgetting in Tim O'Brien's *In the Lake of the Woods*." *Contemporary Literature* 44.1 (2003): 106–31. Print.

Melling, Philip H. *Vietnam in American Literature*. Boston: Twayne, 1990. Print.

Menand, Louis. "Nanook and Me: 'Farenheit 9/11' and the Documentary Tradition." *New Yorker* 9 Aug. 2004: 90+. Print.

Mersmann, James F. *Out of the Vietnam Vortex: A Study of Poets and Poetry against the War*. Lawrence: UP of Kansas, 1974. Print.

Middleton, Drew. "Vietcong Charge Drowning of 1,200." *New York Times* 20 Nov. 1969: A1. Print.

Mikhail, Dunya. *The War Works Hard*. Manchester: Carcanet, 2006. Print.

Miller, Arthur. *The Crucible*. 1952. New York: Penguin, 1982. Print.

Miller, Walter M. *A Canticle for Leibowitz*. 1969. New York: Harper, 2006. Print.

Millet, Allan R., ed. *A Short History of the Vietnam War*. Bloomington: Indiana UP, 1978. Print.

Misra, Kalidas. "The American War Novel from World War II to Vietnam." *Indian Journal of American Studies* 14.2 (1984): 73–80. Print.

Moddelmog, Debra A. "The Unifying Consciousness of a Divided Conscience: Nick Adams as Author of *In Our Time*." *American Literature* 60.4 (1988): 591–610. Print.

Moïse, Edwin E. *A Historical Dictionary of the Vietnam War*. Lanham: Scarecrow, 2001. Print.

———. *Vietnam War Bibliography*. Moïse, 2009. Web. 4 Sept. 2009.

Moore, Harold G., and Joseph L. Galloway. *We Were Soldiers Once . . . and Young: Ia Drang—The Battle That Changed the War in Vietnam*. New York: Random, 1992. Print.

Morris, Wright. *The Territory Ahead*. 1958. New York: Atheneum, 1963. Print.

Morrison, Toni. *Beloved*. 1987. New York: Vintage, 2004. Print.

———. "Memory, Creation, and Writing." *Thought* 59 (1984): 385–90. Print.

———. *Paradise*. New York: Plume, 1997. Print.

———. "Recitatif." *The Norton Anthology of American Literature*. Ed. Nina Bayam et al. Abr. 5th ed. New York: Norton, 1999. 2419–33. Print.

———. *Sula*. 1973. New York: Vintage, 2004. Print.

———. "Unspeakable Things Unspoken: The Afro-American Presence in American Literature." *Michigan Quarterly Review* 28.1 (1989): 1–34. Print.

Moyar, Mark. *Triumph Forsaken: The Vietnam War, 1954–1965*. New York: Cambridge UP, 2006. Print.

Myers, Thomas. "Tim O'Brien (1 October 1946–)." *American Novelists since World War II*. 4th series. *Dictionary of Literary Biography*. Vol. 152. Ed. James R. Giles and Wanda H. Giles. Detroit: Gale, 1995. 140–57. Print.

———. *Walking Point: American Narratives of Vietnam*. New York: Oxford UP, 1988. Print.

Nagel, James. *The Contemporary American Short-Story Cycle: The Ethnic Resonance of Genre*. Baton Rouge: Louisiana State UP, 2001. Print.

Naparsteck, Martin. "An Interview with Tim O'Brien." *Contemporary Literature* 32.1 (1991): 1–11. Print.

"The National Security Strategy of the United States, September 2002." *White House.* White House, 17 Sept. 2002. Web. 5 June 2006.

"The National Security Strategy of the United States, March 2006." *White House.* White House, 16 Mar. 2006. Web. 5 June 2006.

Naylor, Gloria. *The Women of Brewster Place.* New York: Penguin, 1982. Print.

Neilson, Jim. *Warring Fictions: American Literary Culture and the Vietnam War Narrative.* Jackson: UP of Mississippi, 1998. Print.

Newman, John, David A. Willson, David J. DeRose, Stephen P. Hidalgo, and Nancy J. Kendall. *Vietnam War Literature: An Annotated Bibliography of Imaginative Works about Americans Fighting in Vietnam.* 3rd ed. Lanham: Scarecrow, 1996. Print.

Nguyen, Kien. *Le colonial.* Boston: Little, 2004. Print.

———. *The Tapestries.* Boston: Back Bay, 2003. Print.

———. *The Unwanted: A Memoir of Childhood.* Boston: Little, 2002. Print.

Nguyen, Nathalie Huynh Chau. *Vietnamese Voices: Gender and Cultural Identity in the Vietnamese Francophone Novel.* DeKalb: Center for Southeast Asian Studies, 2003. Print.

Nguyen, Thanh T., and Bruce Weigl, eds. and trans. *Poems from Captured Documents: A Bilingual Edition.* Amherst: U of Massachusetts P, 1994. Print.

Nguyen, Van Huy, and Laurel Kendall. *Vietnam: Journeys of Body, Mind, and Spirit.* Berkeley: U of California P, 2003. Print.

Nguyen Du. *The Tale of Kieu: A Bilingual Edition.* 1813. Trans. Huynh Sanh Thong. New Haven: Yale UP, 1983. Print.

Nguyen Thi Dinh. *No Other Road to Take.* Ithaca: Cornell UP, 1976. Print.

Nhat Linh. "The Dream of Tu Lam." *Viet Nam Literature Project.* Viet Nam Lit. Project, 2005. Web. 22 June 2009.

———. "Going to France." *Viet Nam Literature Project.* Viet Nam Lit. Project, 2005. Web. 22 June 2009.

Nora, Pierra. "Between Memory and History: *Les Lieux de Memoire.*" *Representations* 26 (1989): 7–24. Print.

Norindr, Panivong. *Phantasmatic Indochina: French Colonial Ideology in Architecture, Film, and Literature.* Durham: Duke UP, 1996. Print.

Norman, Elizabeth. *Women at War: The Story of Fifty Military Nurses Who Served in Vietnam.* Philadelphia: U of Pennsylvania P, 1990. Print.

Novak, Marian Faye. *Lonely Girls with Burning Eyes.* Boston: Little, 1991. Print.

Nunez, Sigrid. *For Rouenna.* New York: Picador, 2001. Print.

Oates, Joyce Carol. "The Turn of the Screw." *Where Are You Going? Where Have You Been? Selected Early Stories.* New York: Ontario Review, 1993. 302–20. Print.

O'Brien, Tim. "All Quiet on the Western Front." *TV Guide* 10 Nov. 1979: 19–20. Print.

———. "Ambush." *Boston* Apr. 1993: 62+. Print.

———. "The Best of Times." *Life: America's Weekend Magazine* 16 June 2006: 18–19. Print.

———. "Class of '68." *Esquire* Mar. 1968: 160. Print.

———. "Claudia Mae's Wedding Day." *Redbook* Oct. 1973: 103+. Print.

———. "The Crumbling of Sand Castles." *Washington Post* 18 Nov. 1973: C1+. Print.

———. "Darkness on the Edge of Town." *Feature* Jan. 1979: 42+. Print.

———. *En el lago de los bosques*. Barcelona: Anagrama, 1999. Print.

———. *Enemies/Friends*. Arizona: Synaesthesia, 2001. Print.

———. "Faith." *New Yorker* 12 Feb. 1996: 62–67. Print.

———. "The Ghost Soldiers." *Esquire* Mar. 1981: 90–100. Print.

———. *Going After Cacciato*. New York: Broadway, 1978. Print.

———. "Half Gone." *New Yorker* 8 July 2002: 66–71. Print.

———. Hendrix Col., AR. 6 Nov. 2003. Lecture.

———. *Honto no senso no hanashi o shiyo*. Tokyo: Bungei Shunju, 1990. Print.

———. "How to Tell a True War Story." *Esquire* Oct. 1987: 208–15. Print.

———. "How Unhappy They Were." *Esquire* Oct. 1994: 136–38. Print.

———. *If I Die in a Combat Zone, Box Me Up and Ship Me Home*. 1973. New York: Broadway, 1999. Print.

———. "In the Field." *Gentlemen's Quarterly* Dec. 1989: 217+. Print.

———. *In the Lake of the Woods*. 1994. New York: Penguin, 1995. Print.

———. Ithaca Coll., NY. 8 Sept. 2005. Lecture.

———. *July, July*. New York: Penguin, 2002. Print.

———. "July '69." *Esquire* July 2000: 102–09. Print.

———. "Keeping Watch by Night." *Redbook* Dec. 1976: 65–67. Print.

———. "Keynote Address: Thirty Years After." Heberle, *Thirty Years* 3–9. Print.

———. Left Bank Books, St. Louis. 26 Oct. 2003. Lecture.

———. "A Letter to My Son." *Life: America's Weekend Magazine* 15 Oct. 2004: 14–15. Print.

———. "Little People." *Esquire* Oct. 2001: 98+. Print.

———. "The Lives of the Dead." *Esquire* Jan. 1989: 134+. Print.

———. "Loon Point." *Esquire* Jan. 1993: 90–94. Print.

———. "The Magic Show." *Writers on Writing*. Ed. Robert Pack and Jay Parini. Hanover: UP of New England, 1991. 175–83. Print.

———. "The Man I Killed." *The Perimeter of Light: Short Fiction and Other Writing about the Vietnam War*. Ed. Vivian Vie Balfour. Minneapolis: New Rivers, 1992. 33–37. Print.

———. "A Man of Melancholy Disposition." *Ploughshares* 2.2 (1974): 46–60. Print.

———. "Medals! Medals! Everyone's Got Medals." *Los Angeles Times* 18 Mar. 1973, sec. 6: 1+. Print.

———. "My Kind of Town: Fenced In." *Smithsonian* Nov. 2009: 14+. Print.

———. "The Mystery of My Lai." *Facing My Lai: Moving beyond the Massacre*. Ed. David L. Anderson. Lawrence: UP of Kansas, 1998. 171–78. Print.

———. "Nogales." *New Yorker* 8 Mar. 1999: 68–73. Print.

———. *Northern Lights*. New York: Broadway, 1999. Print.

———. *Northern Lights*. New York: Delacorte, 1975. Print.

———. *The Nuclear Age*. 1985. New York: Penguin, 1996. Print.

———. *The Nuclear Age*. Portland: Press-22, 1981. Print.

———. "On the Rainy River." *Playboy* Jan. 1990: 97+. Print.

———. "The People We Marry." *Atlantic Monthly* Jan. 1992: 90+. Print.

———. "Prisoners of Peace." *Penthouse* Mar. 1974: 44+. Print.

———. "Revolt on the Turnpike." *Penthouse* Sept. 1974: 62+. Print.

———. "Speaking of Courage." *Massachusetts Review* 17.2 (1976): 243–53. Print.

———. *Speaking of Courage*. Santa Barbara: Neville, 1980. Print.

———. "Step Lightly." *Playboy* July 1970: 138–39. Print.

———. "The Streak." *New Yorker* 28 Sept. 1998: 88–91. Print.

———. *Supsok ui hosu*. Soul-si: Hanttut, 1996. Print.

———. "Sweetheart of the Song Tra Bong." *Esquire* July 1989: 94+. Print.

———. "Telling Tails." *The Atlantic.com*. Atlantic Monthly Group, Aug. 2009. Web. 14 Aug. 2009.

———. "The Things They Carried." *Esquire* Aug. 1986: 76–81. Print.

———. *The Things They Carried*. 1990. Boston: Mariner Books, 2009. Print.

———. *The Things They Carried*. Boston: Houghton, 1990. Print.

———. *Tomcat in Love*. New York: Broadway, 1998. Print.

———. "Too Skinny." *New Yorker* 10 Sept. 2001: 92+. Print.

———. University of Arkansas, Little Rock. 22 Nov. 1999. Lecture.

———. "The Vietnam in Me." *New York Times Magazine* 2 Oct. 1994: 48–57. Print.

———. "The Vietnam Veteran: The GI Bill—Less than Enough." *Penthouse* Nov. 1974: 76+. Print.

———. "The Violent Vet." *Esquire* Dec. 1979: 96+. Print.

———. "We've Adjusted Too Well." *The Wounded Generation: America after Vietnam*. Ed. A. D. Horne. Englewood Cliffs: Prentice, 1981: 205–07. Print.

———. "What Went Wrong." *Esquire* Aug. 2002: 124–28. Print.

———. "The Whole Story." *Novel History: Historians and Novelists Confront America's Past (and Each Other)*. Ed. Mark C. Carnes. New York: Simon, 2001. 344–45. Print.

———. "Winnipeg." *New Yorker* 14 Aug. 2000: 72–77. Print.

———. "Writing Vietnam: Tim O'Brien, President's Lecture." Ed. Alice Lovejoy. *Scholarly Technology Group*. Brown U, 21 Apr. 1999. Web. 2 July 2008.

———. "The Youth Vote." *New Republic* 19-26 Aug. 1972: 12–15. Print.

O'Brien, Tim, and David Burnett. "A Letter from Home." *Under Fire: Great Photographers and Writers in Vietnam*. Ed. Catherine Leroy. New York: Random, 2005. 124–25. Print.

O'Gorman, Farrell. "*The Things They Carried* as Composite Novel." *War, Literature, and the Arts: An International Journal of the Humanities* 10.2 (1998): 289–309. Print.

Olson, James S., ed. *Dictionary of the Vietnam War*. New York: Greenwood, 1988. Print.

Olson, James S., and Randy W. Roberts. *Where the Domino Fell: America and Vietnam, 1945–2004*. 4th ed. Boston: Wiley, 2004. Print.

O'Nan, S., ed. *The Vietnam Reader: The Definitive Collection of American Fiction and Nonfiction on the War*. New York: Anchor, 1998. Print.

O'Neill, Susan. *Don't Mean Nothing: Short Stories of Vietnam*. New York: Ballantine, 2001. Print.

Ong, Walter. "Writing Is a Technology That Restructures Thought." *Literacy: A Critical Sourcebook*. Ed. Ellen Cushman et al. New York: Bedford–St. Martin's, 2001. 19–31. Print.

Orlean, Susan. "Riding High." *New Yorker* 15-22 Feb. 2010: 64–69. Print.

Orwell, George. "Politics and the English Language." *"Shooting an Elephant" and Other Essays*. New York: Harcourt, 1946. Rpt. in *The Dialogue of Learning: Reading, Writing, and Reflecting*. Ed. Dennis Young and Will Helms. New York: McGraw, 1993. 34–42. Print.

Owen, Wilfred. "Dulce et Decorum Est." *Wilfred Owen's Collected Poems*. Ed. Edmund Blunden. London: Chatto, 1963. 66. Print.

Page, Tim. *Another Vietnam: Pictures of the War from the Other Side*. Ed. Doug Niven and Chris Riley. Washington: Natl. Geographic Soc., 2002. Print.

Palaima, Thomas G. "Courage and Prowess Afoot in Homer and the Vietnam of Tim O'Brien." *Classical and Modern Literature: A Quarterly* 20.3 (2000): 1–22. Print.

Paley, Grace. "A Conversation with My Father." *The Collected Stories*. New York: Farrar, 1994. 232–37. Print.

Palmer, Bruce, Jr. *The 25-Year War: America's Military Role in Vietnam*. 1984. Lexington: UP of Kentucky, 2002. Print.

Park, Jinim. *Narratives of the Vietnam War by Korean and American Writers*. New York: Lang, 2007. Print.

Parkman, Francis. *The Oregon Trail*. 1849. New York: Penguin, 1985. Print.

———. *The Oregon Trail*. 1892. Ed. E. N. Feltskog. Madison: U of Wisconsin P, 1969. Print.

Parks, David. *GI Diary*. Washington: Howard UP, 1968. Print.

Pasternak, Donna. "Keeping the Dead Alive: Revising the Past in Tim O'Brien's War Stories." *Irish Journal of American Studies* 7 (1998): 41–54. Print.

Peake, Louis A. *The United States in the Vietnam War, 1954–1975: A Selected Annotated Bibliography of English-Language Sources*. 2nd ed. New York: Routledge, 2008. Print.

Perone, James E. *Songs of the Vietnam Conflict*. Westport: Greenwood, 2001. Print.

Pettus, Ashley. *Between Sacrifice and Desire: National Identity and the Governing of Femininity in Vietnam*. New York: Routledge, 2003. Print.

Pfarrer, Donald. *The Fearless Man*. New York: Random, 2004. Print.

———. *Neverlight*. New York: Laurel, 1982. Print.

Pham, Andrew X. *Catfish and Mandala: A Two-Wheeled Voyage through the Landscape and Memory of Vietnam*. New York: Farrar, 1999. Print.

———. *The Eaves of Heaven: A Life in Three Wars*. New York: Three Rivers, 2008. Print.

Pham, Quang X. *A Sense of Duty: My Father, My American Journey*. New York: Ballantine, 2005. Print.

Piedmont-Marton, Elisabeth. "Writing against the Vietnam War in Two Gulf War Memoirs: Anthony Swofford's *Jarhead* and Joel Turnipseed's *Baghdad Express*." Vernon, *Arms* 257–72.

Pirsig, Robert M. *Zen and the Art of Motorcycle Maintenance*. 1974. New York: Bantam, 1975. Print.

Piwinski, David J. "My Lai, Flies, and Beezlebub in Tim O'Brien's *In the Lake of the Woods*." *War, Literature, and the Arts: An International Journal of the Humanities* 12.2 (2000): 196–202. Print.

Plath, Sylvia. "Daddy." *Ariel*. New York: Harper-Perrenial, 1965. 56–59. Print.

Porter, Katherine Anne. "Pale Horse, Pale Rider." *Pale Horse, Pale Rider: Three Short Novels*. New York: Harcourt, 1939. 179–264. Print.

Powell, Mary Reynolds. *A World of Hurt: Between Innocence and Arrogance in Vietnam*. Austin: Greenleaf, 2000. Print.

Prados, John. *The Hidden History of the Vietnam War*. 1995. Chicago: Dee, 1998. Print.

Pratt, John Clark. "Tim O'Brien's Reimagination of Reality: An Exercise in Metafiction." *War, Literature, and the Arts: An International Journal of the Humanities* 8.2 (1996): 115–31. Print.

———, comp. *Vietnam Voices: Perspectives on the War Years, 1941–1975*. 1984. Athens: U of Georgia P, 1999. Print.

———. "Yossarian's Legacy: *Catch-22* and the Vietnam War." Jason, *Fourteen Landing Zones* 88–110.

Pratt, Ray. " 'There Must Be Some Way Outta Here!': The Vietnam War in American Popular Music." Clymer 168–89.

Preparing Makes Sense. Get Ready Now. US Dept. of Homeland Security, 5 June 2006. Web. 22 June 2009.

Puhr, Kathleen M. Tim O'Brien. Personal interview. 26 Oct. 2003.

Pynchon, Thomas. *The Crying of Lot 49*. 1966. New York: Harper-Perennial, 2006. Print.

———. *Gravity's Rainbow*. 1973. New York: Penguin, 1995. Print.

———. "The Secret Integration." *Slow Learner: Early Stories*. Boston: Little, 1984. 139–93. Print.

Rabe, David. *The Basic Training of Pavlo Hummel* [and] *Sticks and Bones*. New York: Grove, 1993. Print. Vol. 1 of *The Vietnam Plays*.

———. *Streamers* and *The Orphan*. New York: Grove, 1994. Print. Vol. 2 of *The Vietnam Plays*.

Ransom, John L. *Andersonville Diary, Escape, and List of the Dead, with Name, Company, Regiment, Date of Death and Number of Grave in Cemetery*. 1881 Salem: Higginson, 1998. Print.

Reagan, Ronald. "Peace: Restoring the Margin of Safety." VFW Convention, Chicago. 18 Aug. 1980. Address.

Reed, Ishmael. *Yellow Back Radio Broke-Down*. 1969. Champaign: Dalkey, 2000. Print.

Reiter, Andrea. *Narrating the Holocaust*. New York: Continuum, 2000. Print.

Remarque, Erich Maria. *All Quiet on the Western Front*. 1929. Trans. A. W. Wheen. New York: Ballantine, 1958. Print.

Reporting Vietnam. New York: Lib. of Amer., 1998. Print.

Reston, James A., Jr., ed. *Coming to Terms: American Plays and the Vietnam War*. New York: Theatre Communications, 1985. Print.

Richey, Frances. *The Warrior*. New York: Viking, 2008. Print.

Ringnalda, Donald. "Doing It Wrong Is Getting It Right: America's Vietnam War Drama." Jason, *Fourteen Landing Zones* 67–87.

———. "Fighting and Writing: America's Vietnam War Literature." *Journal of American Studies* 22.1 (1988): 25–42. Print.

———. *Fighting and Writing the Vietnam War*. Jackson: UP of Mississippi, 1994. Print.

Riverbend. *Baghdad Burning: Girl Blog from Iraq*. Fwd. Ahdaf Soueif. Introd. James Ridgeway. New York: Feminist, 2005. Print.

Robinson, Daniel. "Getting It Right: The Short Fiction of Tim O'Brien." *Critique: Studies in Contemporary Fiction* 40.3 (1999): 257–64. Print.

Rosenthal, M. L., and Sally M. Gall. *The Modern Poetic Sequence: The Genius of Modern Poetry*. London: Oxford UP, 1983. Print.

Rosso, Stefano. "Labyrinths and Tunnels, from the Jungle to Sewage." *America Today: Highways and Labyrinths*. Ed. Gigliola Nocera. Siracusa: Grafia, 2003. 133–40. Print.

Roszak, Theodore. "Technocracy's Children." *The Making of a Counter Culture: Reflections on the Technocratic Society and Its Youthful Opposition*. New York: Anchor, 1969. 1–41. Print.

Rotter, Andrew J., ed. *Light at the End of the Tunnel: A Vietnam War Anthology*. Rev. ed. Wilmington: Scholarly Resources, 1999. Print.

Rottman, Larry, Jan Barry, and Basil T. Pasquet, eds. *Winning Hearts and Minds: War Poems by Vietnam Veterans*. New York: McGraw, 1972. Print.

Rowe, John Carlos. "Postmodernist Studies." *Redrawing the Boundaries: The Transformation of English and American Literary Studies*. Ed. Stephen Greenblatt and Giles Gunn. New York: MLA, 1992. 179–208. Print.

Rowe, John Carlos, and Rick Berg, eds. *The Vietnam War and American Culture*. New York: Columbia UP, 1991. Print.

Rowlandson, Mary White. *The Sovereignty and Goodness of God by Mary Rowlandson with Related Documents*. Ed. Neil Salisbury. New York: Bedford, 1997. Print.

Rutledge, Paul James. *The Vietnamese Experience in America*. Bloomington: Indiana UP, 1992. Print.

Ryan, Maureen. *The Other Side of Grief: The Home Front and the Aftermath in American Narratives of the Vietnam War*. Amherst: U of Massachusetts P, 2008. Print.

Salka, Agnieszka. "Re-visioning the Democratic Imagination: Tim O'Brien's Vietnam Fiction." *Polish-American Literary Confrontations*. Ed. Joanna Durczak and Jerzy Durczak. Lublin: Maria Curie-Sklodowska UP, 1995. 113–29. Print.

Sallah, Michael, and Mitch Weiss. *Tiger Force: A True Story of Men and War*. Boston: Little, 2006. Print.

Salter, James. *Burning the Days: Recollection*. New York: Random, 1997. Print.

———. *The Hunters*. Rev. ed. Washington: Counterpoint, 1997. Print.

San Jose Mercury News, De Tran, Andrew Lam, and Hai Dai Nguyen. *Once upon a Dream . . . : The Vietnamese-American Experience*. Kansas City: Andrews, 1995. Print.

Santoli, Al, ed. *Everything We Had: An Oral History of the Vietnam War by Thirty-Three American Soldiers Who Fought It*. New York: Random, 1981. Print.

Sassoon, Siegfried. "Repression of War Experience." 1947. *Selected Poems: 1908–1956*. London: Faber, 1971. 89–90. Print.

Sawyer, Scott. "In the Name of Love: An Interview with Tim O'Brien." *Mars Hill Review* 4 (1996): 117–26. Print.

Saywell, Shelley. *Women in War: First-Hand Accounts from World War II to El Salvador*. New York: Penguin, 1985. Print.

Scarry, Elaine. *The Body in Pain: The Making and Unmaking of the World*. New York: Oxford UP, 1987. Print.

Schacter, Daniel L. *Searching for Memory: The Brain, the Mind, and the Past*. Basic, 1996. Print.

Schaeffer, Susan Fromberg. *Buffalo Afternoon*. New York: Knopf, 1989. Print.

Schell, Jonathan. *The Military Half: An Account of the Destruction in Quang Ngai and Quang Tin*. New York: Knopf, 1968. Print.

Schiff, Hilda, ed. *Holocaust Poetry*. New York: St. Martin's, 1995. Print.

Schramer, James. "Magical Realism in Tim O'Brien's Vietnam War Fiction." *Revista Canaria de Estudios Ingleses* 39 (1999): 135–46. Print.

Schroeder, Eric James. "The Past and the Possible: Tim O'Brien's Dialectic of Memory and Imagination." Searle, *Search and Clear* 116–34.

———. "Two Interviews: Talks with Tim O'Brien and Robert Stone." *Modern Fiction Studies* 30.1 (1984): 125–64. Print.

———. *Vietnam, We've All Been There: Interviews with American Writers*. Westport: Praeger, 1992. Print.

Schuller, Constance. "The Things They Carried into Middle Age." *Ottawa Citizen* 27 Oct. 2002: C10. Print.

Schulzinger, Robert D. *A Time for War: The United States and Vietnam, 1941–1975*. New York: Oxford UP, 1997. Print.

Schumock, Jim. "Interview: Tim O'Brien." *Glimmer Train* 16 (1995): 87–102. Rpt. in *Story, Story, Story: Conversations with American Authors*. Ed. Schumock. Mill Creek: Black Heron, 1998. Print.

Schweninger, Lee. "Ecofeminism, Nuclearism, and O'Brien's *The Nuclear Age*." *The Nightmare Considered: Critical Essays on Nuclear War Literature*. Ed. Nancy Anisfield. Bowling Green: Bowling Green State U Popular P, 1991. 151–85. Print.

Scott, Joan W. "The Evidence of Experience." *Critical Inquiry* 17.4 (1991): 773–97. Print.

Searle, William J. "Dissident Voices: The NVA Experience in Novels by Vietnamese." *War, Literature, and the Arts: An International Journal of the Humanities* 10.2 (1998): 224–38. Print.

————, ed. *Search and Clear: Critical Responses to Selected Literature and Films of the Vietnam War*. Bowling Green: Bowling Green State U Popular P, 1988. Print.

Sedaris, David. *Naked*. Boston: Little, 1997. Print.

Sedgwick, Eve Kosofsky. *Between Men: English Literature and Male Homosocial Desire*. New York: Columbia UP, 1985. Print.

Shaheen. Jack G. *Guilty: Hollywood's Verdict on Arabs after 9/11*. Northampton: Olive Branch, 2008. Print.

Shapiro, Harvey, ed. *Poets of World War II*. New York: Lib. of Amer., 2002. Print.

Shaw, Irwin. *The Young Lions*. Fwd. James Salter. Chicago: U of Chicago P, 2000. Print.

Shay, Jonathan. *Achilles in Vietnam: Combat Trauma and the Undoing of Character*. 1994. New York: Scribner's, 1995. Print.

Sheehan, Neil. *A Bright Shining Lie: John Paul Vann and America in Vietnam*. New York: Random, 1988. Print.

Shephard, Ben. *A War of Nerves: Soldiers and Psychiatrists in the Twentieth Century*. Cambridge: Harvard UP, 2003. Print.

Shim, Kyung Seok. "The Journey of Dream: Tim O'Brien's Metaphysical Exploration in *Going After Cacciato*." *Journal of English Language and Literature* 44.4 (1998): 831–48. Print.

Shklovsky, Viktor. "Art as Technique." 1917. *Literary Theory: An Anthology*. Ed. Julie Rivkin and Michael Ryan. Oxford: Blackwell, 1998. 17–23. Print.

Shostak, Debra, and Daniel Bourne. "*Artful Dodge* Interviews Tim O'Brien." *Artful Dodge* 22-23 (1991): 74–90. Print.

Silko, Leslie Marmon. *Ceremony*. New York: Penguin, 1986. Print.

————. *Storyteller*. New York: Arcade, 1981. Print.

Singleton, Carl. *Vietnam Studies: An Annotated Bibliography*. Lanham: Scarecrow, 1997. Print.

Slabey, Robert M. "*Going After Cacciato*: Tim O'Brien's 'Separate Peace.'" Gilman and Smith 205–12.

————. *The United States and Viet Nam from War to Peace*. Jefferson: McFarland, 1996. Print.

Slater, Lauren. *Lying: A Metaphorical Memoir*. New York: Penguin, 2001. Print.

Sledge, E. B. *With the Old Breed: At Peleliu and Okinawa*. New York: Oxford UP, 1990. Print.

Slotkin, Richard. *Gunfighter Nation: The Myth of the Frontier in Twentieth-Century America*. Norman: U of Oklahoma P, 1998. Print.

Smiley, Jane. "Catting Around." *New York Times Book Review* 20 Sept. 1998: 11–12. Print.

Smiley, Pamela. "The Role of the Ideal (Female) Reader in Tim O'Brien's *The Things They Carried*: Why Should Real Women Play?" *Massachusetts Review* 43.4 (2003): 602–13. Print.

Smith, Helen Zenna. *Not So Quiet: Stepdaughters of War*. 1930. New York: Feminist, 1989. Print.

Smith, J. A. *Voices from the Wall: Anthology of Short Stories from the Vietnam War*. Bloomington: Author, 2006. Print.

Smith, Lorrie. "Back against the Wall: Anti-feminist Backlash in Vietnam War Literature." *Vietnam Generation* 1.3-4 (1989): 115–26. Print.

———. "Resistance and Revision in Poetry by Vietnam War Veterans." Jason, *Fourteen Landing Zones* 49–66.

———. "'The Things Men Do': The Gendered Subtext in Tim O'Brien's *Esquire* Stories." *Critique: Studies in Contemporary Fiction* 36.1 (1994): 16–40. Print.

Smith, Patrick A. *Tim O'Brien: A Critical Companion*. Westport: Greenwood, 2005. Print.

Smith, Roger. "Tim O'Brien." *Notable American Novelists*. Ed. Carl Rollyson. Rev. ed. Vol. 2. Pasadena: Salem, 2008. 1001–06. Print.

Soli, Tatjana. *The Lotus Eaters*. New York: St. Martin's, 2010. Print.

Solzhenitsyn, Alexander. *One Day in the Life of Ivan Denisovich*. Trans. H. T. Willetts. 1963. New York: Penguin, 2000. Print.

Sommers, Nancy. "Between the Drafts." *College Composition and Communication* 43.1 (1992): 23–31. Print.

Sontag, Susan. *Trip to Hanoi*. New York: Farrar, 1968. Print.

Spanos, William V. *American Exceptionalism in the Age of Globalization: The Specter of Vietnam*. Albany: State U of New York P, 2008. Print.

Spiegelman, Art. *Maus II*. New York: Pantheon, 1991. Print.

Standiford, Les, ed. and comp. *The Putt at the End of the World*. New York: Warner, 2000. Print.

Steel, Danielle. *Message from Nam*. New York: Dell, 1990. Print.

Steinbeck, John. *The Grapes of Wrath*. 1939. New York: Penguin, 1986. Print.

Steiner, Peter. *Russian Formalism: A Metapoetics*. Ithaca: Cornell UP, 1984. Print.

Steinman, Ron. *The Soldiers' Story: Vietnam in Their Own Words*. New York: Barnes, 1999. Print.

Stockdale, Jim, and Sybil Stockdale. *In Love and War*. 1984. Rev. ed. Annapolis: Naval Inst. P, 1990. Print.

Stocks, Claire. "Acts of Cultural Identification: Tim O'Brien's *July, July*." *European Journal of American Culture* 25.3 (2006): 173–88. Print.

Stoffey, Robert E. *Fighting to Leave: The Final Years of America's War in Vietnam, 1972–1973*. Minneapolis: Zenith, 2008. Print.

Stone, Robert. *Dog Soldiers*. New York: Mariner, 1997. Print.

Strom, Dao. *The Gentle Order of Girls and Boys*. Berkeley: Counterpoint, 2006. Print.

———. *Grass Roof, Tin Roof*. Boston: Houghton, 2003. Print.

Sturken, Marita. *Tangled Memories: The Vietnam War, the AIDS Epidemic, and the Politics of Remembering*. Berkeley: U of California P, 1997. Print.

Suid, Lawrence H. *Guts and Glory: The Making of the American Military Image in Film*. Rev. ed. Lexington: UP of Kentucky, 2002. Print.

Suskind, Ron. "Without a Doubt: Faith, Certainty, and the Presidency of George W. Bush." *New York Times Magazine* 17 Oct. 2004: 44–51+. Print.

Swofford, Anthony. *Jarhead*. New York: Pocket, 2003. Print.

Taft-Kaufman, Jill. "How to Tell a True War Story: The Dramaturgy and Staging of Narrative Theatre." *Theatre Topics* 10.1 (2000): 17–38. Print.

Tai, Hue-Tam Ho. *The Country of Memory: Remaking the Past in Late Socialist Vietnam.* Berkeley: U of California P, 2001. Print.

Tal, Kalí. "The Mind at War: Images of Women in Vietnam Novels by Combat Veterans." *Contemporary Literature* 31.1 (1990): 76–96. Print.

———. "Speaking the Language of Pain: Vietnam War Literature in the Context of a Literature of Trauma." Jason, *Fourteen Landing Zones* 217–50.

———. "When History Talks Back: Using Combat Narratives and Vietnam Veteran Speakers to Teach the Vietnam War." *Kalí Tal.* Tal, n.d. Web. 22 June 2009.

———. *Worlds of Hurt: Reading the Literatures of Trauma.* Cambridge: Cambridge UP, 1996. Print.

Tambakis, Anthony. "Tim O'Brien: An Interview." *Five Points: A Journal of Literature and Art* 4.1 (1999): 94–114. Print.

Tan, Amy. *The Joy Luck Club.* New York: Penguin, 2006. Print.

Tarkington, Edward. "Things People Do for Love: A Conversation with Tim O'Brien." *Southwest Review* 22 (2003): 136–41. Print.

Tatum, James. *The Mourner's Song: War and Remembrance from the Iliad to Vietnam.* Chicago: U of Chicago P, 2003. Print.

Taylor, Clyde. "Black Consciousness in the Vietnam Years." *Black Scholar* 5.2 (1973): 2–8. Print.

Taylor, Mark. "Tim O'Brien's War." *Centennial Review* 39.2 (1995): 213–30. Print.

———. *The Vietnam War in History, Literature, and Film.* Tuscaloosa: U of Alabama P, 2003. Print.

Taylor, Sandra C. *Vietnamese Women at War: Fighting for Ho Chi Minh and the Revolution.* Lawrence: UP of Kansas, 1999. Print.

Taylor, Telford. *Nuremberg and Vietnam: An American Tragedy.* Chicago: Quadrangle, 1970. Print.

Tegmark, Mats Erik. *In the Shoes of a Soldier: Communication in Tim O'Brien's Vietnam Narratives.* Uppsala: Uppsala, 1998. Print.

Terry, Wallace, ed. *Bloods: An Oral History of the Vietnam War by Black Veterans.* New York: Random, 1984. Print.

Thieme, John A. "'Historical Relations': Modes of Discourse in Michael Ondaajte's *Running in the Family.*" *Narrative Strategies in Canadian Literature: Feminism and Postcolonialism.* Ed. Coral Ann Howells and Lynette Hunter. Philadelphia: Open UP, 1991. 40–48. Print.

Thompson, Hunter. *Fear and Loathing in Las Vegas: A Savage Journey to the Heart of the American Dream.* New York: Random, 1971. Print.

Thoreau, Henry. *Walden* and *Civil Disobedience.* New York: Barnes, 2005. Print.

Timmerman, John H. "Tim O'Brien and the Art of the True War Story: 'Night March' and 'Speaking of Courage.'" *Twentieth Century Literature: A Scholarly and Critical Journal* 46.1 (2000): 100–14. Print.

"Tim O'Brien." *American Writers of the Vietnam War*. Ed. Ronald Baughman. *Dictionary of Literary Biography Documentary Series: An Illustrated Chronicle*. Vol. 9. Detroit: Gale, 1991. 137–214. Print.

Todorov, Tzvetan. *The Fantastic: A Structural Approach to a Literary Genre*. Trans. Richard Howard. Ithaca: Cornell UP, 1970. Print.

Tran, Barbara, Monique T. D. Truong, and Luu Truong Khoi, eds. *Watermark: Vietnamese American Poetry and Prose*. Philadelphia: Temple UP, 1998. Print.

Tran, Nhung Tuyet, and Anthony Reid, eds. *Viet Nam: Borderless Histories*. Madison: U of Wisconsin P, 2006. Print.

Tran, Truong. *Dust and Conscience*. Berkeley: Apogee, 2002. Print.

———. *Placing the Accents*. Berkeley: Apogee, 1999. Print.

Tran Tu Binh. *Red Earth: A Vietnamese Memoir of Life on a Colonial Rubber Plantation*. Athens: Center for Southeast Asian Studies, Ohio U Center for Intl. Studies, 1985. Print.

Tran Van Dinh. *Blue Dragon, White Tiger: A Tet Story*. Philadelphia: TriAm, 1983. Print.

Tremonte, Colleen M. "Gravedigging: Excavating Cultural Myths." *Left Margins: Cultural Studies and Composition Pedagogy*. Ed. Karen Fitts and Alan W. France. Albany: State U of New York P, 1995. 53–68. Print.

Tritle, Lawrence A. *From Melos to My Lai: War and Survival*. New York: Routledge, 2000. Print.

Trudeau, G. B. *Doonesbury.com's The Sandbox: Dispatches from Troops in Iraq and Afghanistan*. Kansas City: Andrews, 2007. Print.

Trumbo, Dalton. Introduction. *Johnny Got His Gun*. New York: Bantam, 1970. Print.

———. *Johnny Got His Gun*. 1939. New York: Citadel, 2007. Print.

Truong, Monique T. D. *The Book of Salt*. Boston: Houghton, 2003. Print.

Truong Nhu Tang. *A Vietcong Memoir: An Inside Account of the Vietnam War and Its Aftermath*. New York: Vintage, 1985. Print.

Tuchman, Barbara W. *The March of Folly: From Troy to Vietnam*. New York: Random, 1984. Print.

Tucker, Spencer C., ed. *Encyclopedia of the Vietnam War: A Political, Social, and Military History*. 3 vols. New York: Oxford UP, 1998. Print.

———. *Vietnam*. Lexington: UP of Kentucky, 1999. Print.

Turner, Brian. *Here, Bullet*. Farmington: James, 2005. Print.

Turner, Fred. *Echoes of Combat: The Vietnam War in American Memory*. New York: Doubleday Religious, 1996. Print.

Turner, Karen Gottschang. *Even the Women Must Fight: Memories of War from North Vietnam*. New York: Wiley, 1998. Print.

Turnipseed, Joel. *Baghdad Express: A Gulf War Memoir*. New York: Penguin, 2003. Print.

Twain, Mark [Samuel Clemens]. *Adventures of Huckleberry Finn*. 1885. New York: Norton, 1985. Print.

Tyson, Lois. *Critical Theory Today: A User-Friendly Guide*. London: Taylor, 1999. Print.

United States. Cong. Senate. *Report of the Select Committee of POW/MIA Affairs.* 103rd Cong., 1st sess. Washington: GPO, 1993. *Library of Congress.* Web. 20 Aug. 2008.

Updike, John. *Too Far to Go: The Maples Stories.* New York: Fawcett, 1978. Print.

Updike, John, and Katrina Kenison, eds. *The Best American Short Stories of the Century.* Expanded ed. Boston: Houghton, 2000. Print.

Ut, Nick. Photograph. Associated Press, 8 June 1972. Print.

Van Devanter, Lynda. *Home before Morning: The Story of an Army Nurse in Vietnam.* 1983. Amherst: U of Massachusetts P, 2001. Print.

Van Devanter, Lynda, and Joan Furey, eds. *Visions of War, Dreams of Peace: Writings of Women in the Vietnam War.* New York: Warner, 1991. Print.

Vannatta, Dennis. "Theme and Structure in Tim O'Brien's *Going After Cacciato.*" *Modern Fiction Studies* 28.2 (1982): 242–46. Print.

Vernon, Alex, ed. *Arms and the Self: War, the Military, and Autobiographical Writing.* Kent: Kent State UP, 2005. Print.

———. "Fiction from the First Gulf War." *EnterText* 6.2 (2006–07): n. pag. Web. 29 June 2009.

———. *Most Succinctly Bred.* Kent: Kent State UP, 2006. Print.

———. "Salvation, Storytelling, and Pilgrimage in *The Things They Carried.*" *Mosaic: A Journal for the Interdisciplinary Study of Literature* 36.4 (2003): 171–88. Print.

———. *Soldiers Once and Still: Ernest Hemingway, James Salter, and Tim O'Brien.* Iowa City: U of Iowa P, 2004. Print.

———. "Submission and Resistance to the Self as Soldier: Tim O'Brien's Vietnam War Memoir." *A/B: Auto/Biography Studies* 17.2 (2002): 161–79. Print.

Vernon, Alex, with Neal Creighton, Jr., Greg Downey, Rob Holmes, and Dave Trybula. *The Eyes of Orion: Five Tank Lieutenants in the Persian Gulf War.* Kent: Kent State UP 1999. Print.

Veterans History Project. Amer. Folklife Center, Lib. of Cong., 2009. Web. 4 Sept. 2009.

Vickroy, Laurie. *Trauma and Survival in Contemporary Fiction.* Charlottesville: U of Virginia P, 2002. Print.

Vidimos, Robin. "O'Brien Shows Life, Like War, Can Be a Battle." *Denver Post* 6 Oct. 2002: EE01. Print.

Vietnam Center and Archive. Office of Intl. Affairs, Texas Tech U, 2009. Web. 26 Aug. 2009.

Viet Nam Literature Project. Viet Nam Lit. Project, 2005. Web. 10 Sept. 2009.

Vietnam Studies Group. Assn. for Asian Studies, n.d. Web. 4 Sept. 2009.

Volkmer, Jon. "Telling the 'Truth' about Vietnam: Episteme and Narrative Structure in *The Green Berets* and *The Things They Carried.*" *War, Literature and the Arts: An International Journal of the Humanities* 11.1 (1999): 240–55. Print.

Vonnegut, Kurt. *Bluebeard.* New York: Delta, 1998. Print.

———. *Cat's Cradle.* New York: Dell, 1998. Print.

———. *Slaughterhouse-Five; or, The Children's Crusade*. 1969. New York: Delacorte, 1994. Print.

Vu Trong Phung. *Dumb Luck*. 1936. Trans. Peter Zinoman and Nguyen Nguyet Cam. Ann Arbor: U of Michigan P, 2002. Print.

Walker, Alice. "Everyday Use." *In Love and Trouble: Stories of Black Women*. New York: Harcourt, 2003. 47–59. Print.

Walker, Keith, ed. *A Piece of My Heart: The Stories of Twenty-Six American Women Who Served in Vietnam*. Novato: Presidio, 1985. Print.

Wallace, David Foster. "Lyndon." *Girl with Curious Hair*. New York: Norton, 1989. 75–118. Print.

Walsh, Jeffrey, and James Aulich, eds. *Vietnam Images: War and Representation*. New York: St. Martin's, 1989. Print.

Warren, James A. *Portrait of a Tragedy: America and the Vietnam War*. New York: Harper, 1990. Print.

Webb, James. *Fields of Fire*. New York: Bantam, 1978. Print.

Weigl, Bruce. *Song of Napalm*. New York: Atlantic Monthly, 1988. Print.

Werner, Jayne S., and Luu Doan Huynh. *The Vietnam War: Vietnamese and American Perspectives*. Armonk: Sharpe, 1993. Print.

Wesley, Marilyn. "Truth and Fiction in Tim O'Brien's *If I Die in a Combat Zone* and *The Things They Carried*." *College Literature* 29.2 (2002): 1–18. Print.

West, Nathanael. *Miss Lonelyhearts* and *The Day of the Locust*. 1933. New York: New Directions, 1962. Print.

West, Philip, Steven I. Levine, and Jackie Hiltz, eds. *America's Wars in Asia: A Cultural Approach to History and Memory*. Armonk: Sharpe, 1998. Print.

Wharton, Edith. *One of Ours*. 1922. Lincoln: U of Nebraska P, 2006. Print.

Wharton, Lynn. "Hand, Head, and Artifice: The Fictive World of Tim O'Brien." *Interdisciplinary Literary Studies: A Journal of Criticism and Theory* 3.1 (2001): 131–35. Print.

———. "Journeying from Life to Literature: An Interview with American Novelist Tim O'Brien." *Interdisciplinary Literary Studies: A Journal of Criticism and Theory* 1.2 (2000): 229–47. Print.

———. "Tim O'Brien and American National Identity: A Vietnam Veteran's Imagined Self in *The Things They Carried*." *49th Parallel: An Interdisciplinary Journal of North American Studies* 5 (2000): 1–8. Web. 29 June 2009.

White, Hayden. "The Question of Narrative in Contemporary Historical Theory." *History and Theory* 23.1 (1984): 1–33. Print.

———. "Storytelling: Historical and Ideological." *Centuries' Ends, Narrative Means*. Ed. Robert Newman. Stanford: Stanford UP, 1996. 58–78. Print.

Whitfield, Stephen. *The Culture of the Cold War*. 1991. 2nd ed. Baltimore: Johns Hopkins UP, 1996. Print.

Whyte, William H., Jr. *The Organization Man*. New York: Doubleday-Anchor, 1956. Print.

Wideman, John Edgar. *Philadelphia Fire*. New York: Vintage, 1991. Print.

Wiedemann, Barbara. "American War Novels: Strategies for Survival." *War and Peace: Perspectives in the Nuclear Age*. Ed. Ulrich Goebel and Otto Nelson. Lubbock: Texas Tech UP, 1988. 137–44. Print.

Wiesel, Elie. *Night*. Trans. Marion Wiesel. New York: Hill, 2006. Print.

Wiest, Andy. *Essential Histories: The Vietnam War, 1956–1975*. Oxford: Osprey, 2002. Print.

Williams, John A. *Captain Blackman*. 1972. Minneapolis: Coffee House, 2000. Print.

Williams, Kayla. *Love My Rifle More than You: Young and Female in the U.S. Army*. With Michael E. Staub. New York: Norton, 2005. Print.

Williams, Tennessee. *The Glass Menagerie*. 1945. New York: New Directions, 1999. Print.

Wilson, James C. *Vietnam in Prose and Film*. Jefferson: McFarland, 1982. Print.

Winston, Jane Bradley, and Leakthina Chau-Pech Ollier, eds. *Of Vietnam: Identities in Dialogue*. New York: Palgrave, 2001. Print.

Wolfe, Tom. *The Electric Kool-Aid Acid Test*. New York: Farrar, 1968. Print.

Wolff, Tobias. *The Barracks Thief and Other Selected Stories*. New York: Harper, 1990. Print.

———. "Casualty." *The Night in Question: Stories*. New York: Vintage, 1997. 14–32. Print.

———. *In Pharaoh's Army: Memories of the Lost War*. New York: Random, 1994. Print.

———. "The Other Miller." *The Night in Question: Stories*. New York: Vintage, 1997. 86–101. Print.

———. "Soldier's Joy." *Our Story Begins: New and Selected Stories*. New York: Knopf, 2008. 54–72. Print.

———. "Wingfield." *In the Garden of the North American Martyrs: Stories*. 1976. New York: Ecco, 1981. 117–22. Print.

Woods, Shelton. *Vietnam: An Illustrated History*. New York: Hippocrene, 2002. Print.

Wright, C. D. *Rising, Falling, Hovering*. Port Townsend: Copper Canyon, 2008. Print.

Wright, Evan. *Generation Kill: Devil Dogs, Iceman, Captain America, and the New Face of American War*. 2004. New York: Penguin, 2008. Print.

———. "The Killer Elite." *Rolling Stone*. Rolling Stone, 26 June 2003. Web. 29 June 2009.

———. "The Killer Elite, Part Two: From Hell to Baghdad." *Rolling Stone*. Rolling Stone, 10 July 2003. Web. 29 June 2009.

———. "The Killer Elite, Part Three: The Battle for Baghdad." *Rolling Stone*. Rolling Stone, 24 July 2003. Web. 29 June 2009.

Wright, Richard. *Black Boy*. New York: HarperPerennial, 1998. Print.

Wright, Stephen. *The Amalgamation Polka*. New York: Knopf, 2006. Print.

———. *Going Native*. 1994. New York: Dell, 1995. Print.

———. *Meditations in Green*. New York: Scribner's, 1983. Print.

Xuan Phuong, and Danièle Mazingarbe. *Ao Dai: My War, My Country, My Vietnam*. Great Neck: Emquad Intl., 2004. Print.

Yamamoto, Hisaye. "Seventeen Syllables." *"Seventeen Syllables" and Other Stories*. New Brunswick: Rutgers UP, 2001. 8–19. Print.

Young, Marilyn B. *The Vietnam Wars, 1945–1990.* New York: Harper, 1991. Print.

Young, Marilyn B., and Robert Buzzanco, eds. *A Companion to the Vietnam War.* Malden: Blackwell, 2002. Print.

Young, Marilyn B., John J. Fitzgerald, and A. Tom Grunfeld. *The Vietnam War: A History in Documents.* New York: Oxford UP, 2002. Print.

Young, William. "Missing in Action: Vietnam and Sadism in Tim O'Brien's *In the Lake of the Woods.*" *Midwest Quarterly: A Journal of Contemporary Thought* 47.2 (2006): 131–43. Print.

Zimmerman, Dwight Jon, and Wayne Vansant. *The Vietnam War: A Graphic History.* New York: Hill, 2009. Print.

Zinman, Toby Silverman. "Search and Destroy: The Drama of the Vietnam War." *Theatre Journal* 42.1 (1990): 5–26. Print.

Zinn, Howard. *A People's History of the United States: 1492–Present.* 1980. New York: Harper, 2005. Print.

Žižek, Slavoj. *The Sublime Object of Ideology.* New York: Verso, 1997. Print.

———. *Tarrying with the Negative: Kant, Hegel, and the Critique of Ideology.* Durham: Duke UP, 1993. Print.

Films, Television, Radio, and Sound Recordings

All Quiet on the Western Front. Dir. Lewis Milestone. Universal, 1930. Film.

American Experience: Daughter from Danang. Dir. Gail Dolgin. PBS, 2002. Television.

American Experience: Two Days in October. Dir. Robert Kenner. PBS, 2005. Television.

The Anderson Platoon. Dir. Pierre Schoendoerffer. Films, 1967. Film.

Apocalypse Now: The Complete Dossier. Dir. Francis Ford Coppola. Paramount, 2006. Film.

Appalachian State University. Convocation 2002, with Tim O'Brien. Appalachian State University, 2002. Videorecording.

———. *Tim O'Brien: Book Reading.* Introd. Leon Lewis. Appalachian State University Visiting Writers Series, 2002. Videorecording.

———. *Tim O'Brien: Panel Discussion.* Tim O'Brien with Thomas A. McGowan, Kristina K. Groover, and Michael L. Krenn. Appalachian State University, 2002. Videorecording.

———. *Tim O'Brien: Q & A.* Appalachian State University, 2002. Videorecording.

———. *A Veteran's Thoughts on the Implications of War, Featuring Tim O'Brien.* Appalachian State University: Office of Public Affairs, 2002. Videorecording.

Atomic Platters: Cold War Music from the Golden Age of Homeland Security. Prod. Bill Geerhart and Ken Sitz. Bear Family Records, 2005. CD.

Baghdad ER. Dir. Jon Alpert and Matthew O'Neill. HBO, 2006. Film.

Band of Brothers. Prod. Tom Hanks and Steven Spielberg. HBO, 2001. Film.

The Beautiful Country. Dir. Hans Petter Moland. Sony Pictures, 2005. Film.

The Best Years of Our Lives. Dir. William Wyler. MGM, 1946. Film.

Born on the Fourth of July. Dir. Oliver Stone. Universal, 1989. Film.

Brothers. Dir. Jim Sheridan. Lionsgate, 2010. Film.

Brothers at War. Dir. Jake Rademacher. Summit Entertainment, 2010. Film.

Buffalo Boy. Dir. Minh Nguyen-Vo. First Run, 2004. Film.

Casualties of War. Dir. Brian de Palma. Sony Pictures, 1989. Film.

China Beach. Dir. Rod Holcomb. ABC. 1988–91. Television.

Colossus: The Forbin Project. Dir. Joseph Sargent. Universal, 1970. Film.

Combat Diary: The Marines of Lima Company. Dir. Michael Epstein. Arts and Entertainment Home Video, 2006. DVD.

Coming Home. Dir. Hal Ashby. MGM, 1978. Film.

Conan, Neil. "*The Things They Carried* 20 Years On." Natl. Public Radio. 24 Mar. 2010. Radio.

Control Room. Dir. Jehane Noujaim. Lions Gate, 2003. Film.

Country Joe McDonald. "I-Feel-Like-I'm-Fixin'-to-Die Rag." *Vietnam Experience*. CD.

Creedence Clearwater Revival. "Fortunate Son." *Chronicle, vol. 1: The 20 Greatest Hits*. Fantasy, 1990. CD.

Crosby, Stills, Nash, and Young. "Ohio." *4 Way Street*. Atlantic/Wea, 1971. CD.

Cyclo. Dir. Anh Hung Tran. New Yorker Video, 2004. Film.

Dat Kho: Land of Sorrows. Dir. Ha Thuc Can. CreateSpace, 2007. Film.

Dear America: Letters Home from Vietnam. Dir. Bill Couturié. HBO Films, 1987. Television.

The Deer Hunter. Dir. Michael Cimino. Universal, 1978. Film.

The Dirty Dozen. Dir. Robert Aldrich. MGM, 1967. Film.

The Dreams of Sparrows. Dir. Hayder Mousa Daffar. Go Kart, 2004. Film.

Dr. Strangelove; or, How I Learned to Stop Worrying and Love the Bomb. Dir. Stanley Kubrick. Columbia, 1964. Film.

Duck and Cover. Dir. Anthony Rizzo. Archer, 1951. Film.

84 Charlie MoPic. Dir. Patrick Sheane Duncan. Mopic–Sundance Inst., 1989. Film.

Fahrenheit 9/11. Dir. Michael Moore. Weinstein, 2004. Film.

Fail-Safe. Dir. Sidney Lumet. Columbia, 1964. Film.

First Kill. Dir. Coco Schrijber. Icarus, 2001. Film.

The Fog of War: Eleven Lessons from the Life of Robert S. McNamara. Dir. Errol Morris. Sony Pictures, 2004. Film.

Forrest Gump. Dir. Robert Zemeckis. Paramount, 1994. Film.

Full Metal Jacket. Dir. Stanley Kubrick. Warner Brothers, 1987. Film.

Gallipoli. Dir. Peter Weir. Paramount, 1981. Film.

Generation Kill. HBO, 2008. Television.

Good Morning, Vietnam. Dir. Barry Levinson. Touchstone-Disney, 1987. Film.

Go Tell the Spartans. Dir. Ted Post. Spartan-MarVista, 1978. Film.

The Graduate. Dir. Mike Nichols. United Artists, 1967. Film.

The Green Berets. Dir. Ray Kellogg. Warner Brothers, 1968. Film.

Green Zone. Dir. Paul Greenglass. Universal, 2010. Film.

The Ground Truth. Dir. Patricia Foulkrod. Universal, 2006. Film.

Gunner Palace. Dir. Michael Tucker and Petra Eppeplein. Palm Pictures, 2004. Film.

Hamburger Hill. Dir. John Irvin. Lion's Gate, 1987. Film.

Hearts and Minds. Dir. Peter Davis. Warner Brothers–Columbia, 1974. Film.

Heaven and Earth. Dir. Oliver Stone. Warner Brothers, 1993. Film.

Henry V. Dir. Kenneth Branagh. MGM, 1989. Film.

The Hurt Locker. Dir. Kathryn Bigelow. 2008. Summit Entertainment, 2010. Film.

Indochine. Dir. Regis Wargnier. Sony Pictures, 1992. Film.

In the Lake of the Woods. Dir. Carl Schenkel. RHI, 1996. Film.

In the Valley of Ellah. Dir. Paul Haggis. Blackfriar Bridge, 2007. Film.

In the Year of the Pig. Dir. Emile de Antonio. Cinetree–New Yorker, 1969. Film.

Jacob's Ladder. Dir. Adrian Lyne. Tri-Star, 1990. Film.

Jarhead. Dir. Sam Mendes. Universal, 2005. Film.

Johnny Got His Gun. Dir. Dalton Trumbo. Cinemation, 1971. Film.

The Killing Fields. Dir. Roland Joffe. Warner Brothers, 1984. Film.

The Kingdom. Dir. Peter Berg. Universal, 2007. Film.

Let There Be Light. Dir. John Huston. United States Army, 1945. Film.

Lioness. Dir. Meg McLagan and Daria Sommers. Room 11, 2007. Film.

Lions for Lambs. Dir. Robert Redford. United Artists, 2007. Film.

Little Birds. Dir. Watai Takeharu. Yasuoka, 2005. Film.

Little Dieter Needs to Fly. Dir. Werner Herzog. Starz–Anchor Bay, 1998. Film.

The Long Haired Warriors. Dir. Mel Halbach. Under-Arm, 1998. Film.

The Lover. Dir. Jean-Jacques Annand. MGM, 1992. Film.

The Manchurian Candidate. Dir. John Frankenheimer. MGM, 1962. Film.

The Messenger. Dir. Oren Morerman. Oscilloscope, 2010. Film.

My Journey Home. Dir. Renee Tajima-Pena and Lourdes Portillo. WETA, 2004. Film.

No End in Sight. Dir. Charles Ferguson. Red Envelope, 2007. Film.

Occupation: Dreamland. Dir. Ian Olds and Garrett Scott. GreenHouse, 2005. Film.

Off to War: From Rural Arkansas to Iraq. Dir. Brent Renaud and Craig Renaud. Kino, 2005. Film.

Over There. Dir. Chris Gerolmo and Mikael Solomon. 20th Century Fox, 2005. Film.

Platoon. Dir. Oliver Stone. MGM, 1986. Film.

The Quiet American. Dir. Joseph L. Mankiewicz. MGM, 1958. Film.

The Quiet American. Dir. Phillip Noyce. Miramax, 2002. Film.

A Reading by Tim O'Brien. Radford University: Telecommunications Bureau, 1992. Videotape.

Redacted. Dir. Brian De Palma. Film Farm, 2007. Film.

Regret to Inform. Dir. Barbara Sonneborn. Docurma, 1998. Film.

Rendition. Dir. Gavin Hood. New Line, 2007. Film.

Reporting America at War. Dir. Stephen Ives. PBS, 2003. Television.

Restrepo. Dir. Sebastian Junger and Tim Hetherington. National Geographic, 2010. Film.

Return with Honor. Dir. Terry Sanders and Freida Lee Mock. PBS, 1998. Television.

Rosica, Karen. "Interview with Tim O'Brien—From Life to Fiction." Natl. Public Radio. 29 Oct. 1998. Radio.

A Rumor of War. Dir. Richard T. Heffron. Fries, 1980. Film.

Rushmore. Dir. Wes Anderson. Touchstone, 1998. Film.

Sadler, Barry. "The Ballad of the Green Berets." *Ballads of the Green Berets*. Collectors Choice 1998. CD.

Saigon, U.S.A. Dir. Lindsey Jang and Robert C. Winn. KOCE-TV, 2003. Film.

Sands of Iwa Jima. Dir. Allen Dwan. Republic, 1949. Film.

Saving Private Ryan. Dir. Steven Spielberg. DreamWorks, 1998. Film.

The Scent of Green Papaya. Dir. Anh Hung Tran. Columbia-Tristar, 1993. Film.

Schindler's List. Dir. Steven Spielberg. Universal, 1993. Film.

Seeger, Pete. "Waist Deep in the Big Muddy." *Waist Deep in the Big Muddy and Other Love Songs*. Sony, 1967. CD.

Le 17ème Parallèle (The 17th Parallel). Dir. Joris Ivens and Marceline Loridan. France: CAPI Films, Argos Films, 1968. Film.

Sherman's March: A Mediation to the Possibility of Romantic Love in the South during an Era of Nuclear Weapons Proliferation. Dir. Ross McElwee. First Run, 1986. Film.

Shoah. Dir. Claude Lanzmann. New York Video, 1985. Film.

Siegel, Robert, and Jacki Lyden. *All Things Considered*. Natl. Public Radio. 3 Oct. 2002. Radio.

The Situation. Dir. Philip Haas. New Video, 2006. Film.

A Soldier's Sweetheart. Dir. William S. Gilmore. Paramount; Showtime, 1998. Film.

Springsteen, Bruce. "Born in the U.S.A." *Born in the U.S.A.* Columbia, 1984. CD.

Standard Operating Procedure. Dir. Errol Morris. Sony Pictures, 2008. Film.

Stop-Loss. Dir. Kimberly Peirce. Paramount, 2008. Film.

Target You. Ragan, 1953. Film.

Taxi Driver. Dir. Martin Scorsese. Sony Pictures, 1976. Film.

Taxi to the Dark Side. Dir. Alex Gibney. Jigsaw, 2007. Film.

10000 Maniacs. "The Big Parade." *Blind Man's Zoo*. Electra/Wea, 1989. CD.

They Marched into Sunlight. Dir. Paul Greengrass. Universal, 2003. Film.

Three Kings. Dir. David O. Russell. Warner Brothers, 1999. Film.

Three Seasons. Dir. Tony Bui. Gai Phong, 1999. Film.

Tim O'Brien. Brockport Writers Forum: State U College of NY at Brockport, 1998. Videorecording.

Tour of Duty: The Complete Series. Dir. Stephen Caffrey and Reynaldo Villalobos. Sony Pictures, 2005. Television.

The Vertical Ray of the Sun. Dir. Tran Anh Hung. Sony Pictures, 2000. Film.

Vietnam: An American Journey. Dir. Robert Richter. Richter, 1979. Film.

Vietnam: A Television History. Dir. Matthew Collins III and Rocky Collins. PBS, 1983. Television.

Vietnam's Unseen War—Pictures from the Other Side. Dir. Nicolas Noxon and Robert Guenette. National Geographic, 2002. Film.

Vietnam: The Ten Thousand Day War. Dir. Karil Daniels. Image Entertainment, 1980. Television.

The Visitor. Dir. Thomas McCarthy. Groundswell Productions, 2007. Film.

A Walk in the Sun. Dir. Lewis Milestone. 20th Century Fox, 1945. Film.

The War at Home. Dir. Barry Alexander Brown. First Run Features, 1979. Film.

Wargames. Dir. John Badham. MGM, 1983. Film.

The War Lover. Dir. Philip Leacock. Columbia, 1962. Film.

The War Tapes. Dir. Deborah Scranton. SenArt Films, 2006. Film.

The Weather Underground. Dir. Sam Green and Bill Siegel. The Free History Project, 2002. Film.

We Were Soldiers. Dir. Randall Wallace. Paramount, 2002. Film.

When I Came Home. Dir. Dan Lohaus. Lohaus Films, 2006. Film.

Why We Fight. Dir. Eugene Jarecki. Sony Pictures Classics, 2005. Film.

Winter Soldier. Dir. Winterfilm Collective. Third World Newsreel, 1972; Milliarium Zero, 2006. Film.

INDEX OF NAMES

Modern Language Association of America

Approaches to Teaching World Literature

Eliot's Middlemarch. Ed. Kathleen Blake. 1990.

Eliot's Poetry and Plays. Ed. Jewel Spears Brooker. 1988.

Shorter Elizabethan Poetry. Ed. Patrick Cheney and Anne Lake Prescott. 2000.

Ellison's Invisible Man. Ed. Susan Resneck Parr and Pancho Savery. 1989.

English Renaissance Drama. Ed. Karen Bamford and Alexander Leggatt. 2002.

Works of Louise Erdrich. Ed. Gregg Sarris, Connie A. Jacobs, and
    James R. Giles. 2004.

Dramas of Euripides. Ed. Robin Mitchell-Boyask. 2002.

Faulkner's The Sound and the Fury. Ed. Stephen Hahn and Arthur F. Kinney. 1996.

Fitzgerald's The Great Gatsby. Ed. Jackson R. Bryer and Nancy P. VanArsdale. 2009.

Flaubert's Madame Bovary. Ed. Laurence M. Porter and Eugene F. Gray. 1995.

García Márquez's One Hundred Years of Solitude. Ed. María Elena de Valdés and
    Mario J. Valdés. 1990.

Gilman's "The Yellow Wall-Paper" and Herland. Ed. Denise D. Knight and
    Cynthia J. Davis. 2003.

Goethe's Faust. Ed. Douglas J. McMillan. 1987.

Gothic Fiction: The British and American Traditions. Ed. Diane Long Hoeveler
    and Tamar Heller. 2003.

Grass's The Tin Drum. Ed. Monika Shafi. 2008.

Hebrew Bible as Literature in Translation. Ed. Barry N. Olshen and
    Yael S. Feldman. 1989.

Homer's Iliad *and* Odyssey. Ed. Kostas Myrsiades. 1987.

Hurston's Their Eyes Were Watching God *and Other Works.* Ed. John Lowe. 2009.

Ibsen's A Doll House. Ed. Yvonne Shafer. 1985.

Henry James's Daisy Miller *and* The Turn of the Screw. Ed. Kimberly C. Reed and
    Peter G. Beidler. 2005.

Works of Samuel Johnson. Ed. David R. Anderson and Gwin J. Kolb. 1993.

Joyce's Ulysses. Ed. Kathleen McCormick and Erwin R. Steinberg. 1993.

Works of Sor Juana Inés de la Cruz. Ed. Emilie L. Bergmann and Stacey Schlau. 2007.

Kafka's Short Fiction. Ed. Richard T. Gray. 1995.

Keats's Poetry. Ed. Walter H. Evert and Jack W. Rhodes. 1991.

Kingston's The Woman Warrior. Ed. Shirley Geok-lin Lim. 1991.

Lafayette's The Princess of Clèves. Ed. Faith E. Beasley and
    Katharine Ann Jensen. 1998.

Works of D. H. Lawrence. Ed. M. Elizabeth Sargent and Garry Watson. 2001.

Lazarillo de Tormes *and the Picaresque Tradition.* Ed. Anne J. Cruz. 2009.

Lessing's The Golden Notebook. Ed. Carey Kaplan and Ellen Cronan Rose. 1989.

Mann's Death in Venice *and Other Short Fiction.* Ed. Jeffrey B. Berlin. 1992.

Marguerite de Navarre's Heptameron. Ed. Colette H. Winn. 2007.

Medieval English Drama. Ed. Richard K. Emmerson. 1990.

Melville's Moby-Dick. Ed. Martin Bickman. 1985.

Metaphysical Poets. Ed. Sidney Gottlieb. 1990.

Miller's Death of a Salesman. Ed. Matthew C. Roudané. 1995.

Milton's Paradise Lost. Ed. Galbraith M. Crump. 1986.

Milton's Shorter Poetry and Prose. Ed. Peter C. Herman. 2007.

Molière's Tartuffe *and Other Plays.* Ed. James F. Gaines and
    Michael S. Koppisch. 1995.

Momaday's The Way to Rainy Mountain. Ed. Kenneth M. Roemer. 1988.

Montaigne's Essays. Ed. Patrick Henry. 1994.

Novels of Toni Morrison. Ed. Nellie Y. McKay and Kathryn Earle. 1997.

Murasaki Shikibu's The Tale of Genji. Ed. Edward Kamens. 1993.

Nabokov's Lolita. Ed. Zoran Kuzmanovich and Galya Diment. 2008.

Works of Tim O'Brien. Ed. Alex Vernon and Catherine Calloway. 2010.

Works of Ovid and the Ovidian Tradition. Ed. Barbara Weiden Boyd and
    Cora Fox. 2010.

Poe's Prose and Poetry. Ed. Jeffrey Andrew Weinstock and Tony Magistrale. 2008.

Pope's Poetry. Ed. Wallace Jackson and R. Paul Yoder. 1993.

Proust's Fiction and Criticism. Ed. Elyane Dezon-Jones and
    Inge Crosman Wimmers. 2003.

Puig's Kiss of the Spider Woman. Ed. Daniel Balderston and Francine Masiello. 2007.

Pynchon's The Crying of Lot 49 *and Other Works.* Ed. Thomas H. Schaub. 2008.

Novels of Samuel Richardson. Ed. Lisa Zunshine and Jocelyn Harris. 2006.

Rousseau's Confessions *and* Reveries of the Solitary Walker. Ed. John C. O'Neal
    and Ourida Mostefai. 2003.

Scott's Waverley Novels. Ed. Evan Gottlieb and Ian Duncan. 2009.

Shakespeare's Hamlet. Ed. Bernice W. Kliman. 2001.

Shakespeare's King Lear. Ed. Robert H. Ray. 1986.

Shakespeare's Othello. Ed. Peter Erickson and Maurice Hunt. 2005.

Shakespeare's Romeo and Juliet. Ed. Maurice Hunt. 2000.

Shakespeare's The Tempest *and Other Late Romances.* Ed. Maurice Hunt. 1992.

Shelley's Frankenstein. Ed. Stephen C. Behrendt. 1990.

Shelley's Poetry. Ed. Spencer Hall. 1990.

Sir Gawain and the Green Knight. Ed. Miriam Youngerman Miller and
    Jane Chance. 1986.

Song of Roland. Ed. William W. Kibler and Leslie Zarker Morgan. 2006.

Spenser's Faerie Queene. Ed. David Lee Miller and Alexander Dunlop. 1994.

Stendhal's The Red and the Black. Ed. Dean de la Motte and Stirling Haig. 1999.

Sterne's Tristram Shandy. Ed. Melvyn New. 1989.

Stowe's Uncle Tom's Cabin. Ed. Elizabeth Ammons and Susan Belasco. 2000.

Swift's Gulliver's Travels. Ed. Edward J. Rielly. 1988.

Teresa of Ávila and the Spanish Mystics. Ed. Alison Weber. 2009.

Thoreau's Walden *and Other Works.* Ed. Richard J. Schneider. 1996.

Tolstoy's Anna Karenina. Ed. Liza Knapp and Amy Mandelker. 2003.

Vergil's Aeneid. Ed. William S. Anderson and Lorina N. Quartarone. 2002.

Voltaire's Candide. Ed. Renée Waldinger. 1987.

Whitman's Leaves of Grass. Ed. Donald D. Kummings. 1990.

Wiesel's Night. Ed. Alan Rosen. 2007.
Works of Oscar Wilde. Ed. Philip E. Smith II. 2008.
Woolf's Mrs. Dalloway. Ed. Eileen Barrett and Ruth O. Saxton. 2009.
Woolf's To the Lighthouse. Ed. Beth Rigel Daugherty and Mary Beth Pringle. 2001.
Wordsworth's Poetry. Ed. Spencer Hall, with Jonathan Ramsey. 1986.
Wright's Native Son. Ed. James A. Miller. 1997.